"Browning, an octogenarian, a professor of the humanities, and a decades-long social activist, struggles for the soul of America. He sees a nation spellbound by violence, immediate gratification, and capitalism that breeds sick individuals and is unable to face up to climate change and other unprecedented problems of our age. Being the primary threat to world order through its militarism, economic imperialism and patterns of consumption, it deprives people, within and outside of the United States, of their land, resources, ways of life, and prospects. Browning recounts his life-long journey of deciphering this spell and discovering antidotes. Caught between anger and hope he refuses to recognize existing social structures as realistically necessary. While recognizing that alternatives such as Christian socialism may be viewed as Utopian, he views adherence to the status quo to be more fantastic and dangerous by far. Browning's critiques are insightful, but more impressive are the ways he constructively offers the wisdom of the great thinkers of his time, such as Thomas Berry, Martha Nussbaum, E. Maynard Adams, Pope Francis, David Korten, Robert Bellow, Paul Tillich, Richard Rorty, and others, as well as his own thought, to recovery of the soul of a nation. This book will be particularly meaningful to progressive Christians and Jews who seek to understand the social relevance and imperatives of their traditions in a secular age."

—**Herman F. Greene**, President, Center for Ecozoic Societies

"A passionate concern for the spiritual health of America infuses Browning's work. This bold and provocative cultural critique grows out of a lifetime of commitment to politics, ideas, and social justice."

—**Richard Todd**, Author

Struggling for the Soul of Our Country

Struggling for the
Soul of Our Country

ESSAYS

Preston M. Browning Jr.

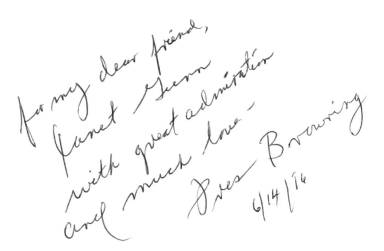

For my dear friend,
Janet Green
with great admiration
and much love—
Pres Browning
6/14/16

WIPF & STOCK · Eugene, Oregon

STRUGGLING FOR THE SOUL OF OUR COUNTRY

Wipf & Stock
An Imprint of Wipf and Stock Publishers
199 W. 8th Ave., Suite 3
Eugene, OR 97401

www.wipfandstock.com

PAPERBACK ISBN: 978-1-4982-0994-6
HARDCOVER ISBN: 978-1-4982-0996-0
EBOOK ISBN: 978-1-4982-0995-3

Manufactured in the U.S.A.

Original sin consists in the turning from God to other gods, more specifically in the attempt to make a god out of oneself. But the demonic of capitalism, at the deepest level, consists in its drive to become God and king of this world. "Usury lives securely and rages, as if he were God and lord in all lands." [Martin] Luther sees the final coming to power in this world of Satan in the coming to power of capitalism. The structure of the entire kingdom of Satan is essentially capitalistic: we are the Devil's property. Hence Luther's deepest sentence on capitalism is the statement that "money is the word of the Devil, through which he creates all things, the way God created through the true word."

—NORMAN O. BROWN, *LIFE AGAINST DEATH*

The worship of the ancient golden calf has returned in a new and ruthless guise in the idolatry of money and the dictatorship of an impersonal economy lacking a truly human purpose. The worldwide crisis affecting finance and the economy lays bare their imbalances and, above all, their lack of real concern for human beings.

Today everything comes under the laws of competition and the survival of the fittest, where the powerful feed upon the powerless. As a consequence, masses of people find themselves excluded and marginalized: without work, without possibilities, without any means of escape.

While the earnings of a minority are growing exponentially, so too is the gap separating the majority from the prosperity enjoyed by those happy few. This imbalance is the result of ideologies, which defend the absolute autonomy of the marketplace and financial speculation. . . . A new tyranny is thus born. . . . The thirst for power and possessions knows no limits. In this system, which tends to devour everything which stands in the way of increased profits, whatever is fragile, like the environment, is defenseless before the interests of a deified market, which become the only rule.

—POPE FRANCIS, *APOSTOLIC EXHORTATION 2013*

For Hazel, Ben, Grace, Sam, and Dakota

and

Janet Brof

CONTENTS

ACKNOWLEDGMENTS

ONE OF THE PLEASURES that writing a book such as this affords its author is the opportunity to thank sundry friends and acquaintances for help rendered along the way. Since in this case the way has been lengthy and at times circuitous, a good number of kind souls have made contributions, sometimes with nothing more than encouragement, always an indispensable feature of the whole. Several have read one or more of the chapters, often offering suggestions for improvement. I begin with them: John Wood, Nancy Cirillo, Frank Reynolds, June Nash, Nancy Tilly, Janet Gunn, Lou Ratté, Margaret Bullitt-Jonas, Chris Jerome, Robert Jonas, Mariel Kinsey, the Reverend Cara Hochhalter, Mary Snow, Richard Prée, the Reverend Dr. Jennifer Walters, Giles Gunn, Margaret Randolph. Don Faulkner, Arlyn Miller, the Reverend Addison Hall, Patricia Lee Lewis, Trish Crapo, Mary McAvoy, Claire Miraglia, Johan and Donna Stohl, Margaret Bullitt-Jonas, Daniela Gioseffi, Laura D. Bellmay, the Rev. Eliot Moss, and Catherine Clarke. Thank you, all.

Maynard Kaufman, a friend of many years standing, read early versions of most of these pieces and responded with gentle, insightful criticism. My former student Matthew Baker played a major role in a revision of chapter 6 and for years has been a source of enthusiastic encouragement, as have been Boman Desai and Rita Gőndőcs, also former students. I want to thank also Hetty Startup, who for months relieved me of chores related to the running of Wellspring House, thereby freeing time for writing. Claire Miraglia gave generously from her store of kindness and nursing skills during my wife Ann's final years and again and again helped restore my flagging spirit. My debt to her is beyond calculation. I am deeply grateful to Judie Isabella for keeping the dust kittens and cobwebs at bay.

My friend and neighbor Dick Todd rescued me with a hasty revision of notes for a lecture on Christian socialism. He also warned me about a propensity evidenced in some of my essays to adopt the tone of the prophet Jeremiah. I thank him for his kind assistance in both instances.

Another friend, Eben Tilly, provided invaluable help by sending me the *National Geographic* articles concerning the havoc climate change will cause Miami and other Florida locales, as well as the DVD "Chasing Ice" and articles from major newspapers about the inadequacy of the response to global warming made by the United States and other governments. My indebtedness to him is substantial. Nancy Tilly, a friend of many decades, has given warm endorsement of my work, for which I am deeply grateful.

John Ratté, a dear friend whose interest in and support of my writing have for years provided sustenance and challenge, has earned my gratitude again and again. I have trusted his judgments implicitly and welcomed his guidance when reflecting on various issues, particularly matters related to Christian belief and ethics. My debt to John is huge.

My debt to the members of a reading group of which I was a part—Mary Snow, Lou Ratté, John Ratté, and Richard Prée—is incalculable. We discussed books by Sallie McFague, Martha Nussbaum, Thomas Berry, and Marilynne Robinson, among many others, and engaged again and again in friendly debate—one of life's great pleasures. This was also a grand educational experience. A warm "thank you" to all!

I wish to thank the Reverend Kate Stevens and the First Congregational Church of Ashfield for allowing the use of the church "building" for a weekend forum on Christian Socialism and also for a symposium on global warming. She and members of that congregation were heavily involved in planning both events, as were members of St. John's Episcopal Church. The Reverend Gordon Dean, when vicar of St. John's, warmly supported that symposium and assisted in securing financial support from the Diocese of Western Massachusetts. A friend in need, for sure.

Special thanks are due to Herman Greene, director of the Center for Ecozoic Studies in Chapel Hill, North Carolina, who has spent many years spreading the word concerning the brilliance and the importance of the thought of Father Thomas Berry. Had Herman not encouraged me to write an essay about Father Berry's work, which appeared in 2003 in the *Ecozoic Reader*, of which Herman is editor, it is quite possible that it would not have occurred to me to continue writing essays, sometimes on subjects only tangentially related to my formal academic training.

I also want to take this opportunity to thank the members of the "Standing Tree Affinity Group" which was formed in the months immediately before the US invasion of Iraq. With steady will, keen minds, and gentle hearts, this gang of a dozen or so has committed many hours to projects in pursuit of a more just, peaceful and sustainable national and global community. As the world and our country have lurched toward what at times has seemed a great unraveling, and as I have struggled in my writing to deal with that threat, my involvement with this group has provided me with inspiration and support way beyond what I expected when I joined Pam Walker, Sherrill Hogan, John Hoffman, Susie and Les Patlove, Kate Stevens, Ellen Kaufmann, Liz Kelner, Randy Kehler, Betsy Corner, Rita Hindin, Carl Doerner, Suzanne Carlson, Phyllis Loomis, Miriam Kelner, Charlie King, Mariel Kinsey, and Karen Brandow on a blustery winter's evening in 2002. "Thank you" doesn't begin to cover the debt.

Many of the more than one thousand former residents at Wellspring House, the retreat for writers and artists that I operate in western Massachusetts, have listened as I've read portions of one or another of these essays. The discussions that followed those readings have contributed welcome suggestions for revisions. I am deeply indebted to these talented and dedicated writers for encouragement and inspiration. It is impossible, of course, to thank more than a tiny fraction of the total for listening and then offering suggestions for strengthening an argument or clarifying a claim. One of these, Tehila Lieberman, was generous with her time and critical skills when working over a very early version of the introduction.

Another former resident, Maya Liebermann, took on the task of wrestling a mass of paragraphs and pages into the essay that became chapter 5. I'm indebted to her skills as an editor and to her persistence. I also want to acknowledge the assistance of Len Krimerman, who provided information regarding co-ops in the United States, as well as teaching for democracy, and Colleen Geraghty for enthusiastic support of my writing and for information regarding the violence that American women experience at the hands of angry males. Jocelyn Cullity and Prakash Younger, wife and husband, have spent many weeks, off and on, at Wellspring House, always adding to the liveliness of conversation, the wisdom of moral judgment, and the warmth of friendship. I am deeply indebted to both.

I am mightily beholden to Greg Bates, an editor of extraordinary tact and skill, who shepherded this manuscript through its early stages. With an eye for shaping a sometimes tangled collection of ideas and insights into a coherent whole, Greg contributed greatly to my conviction that a publishable book was gradually emerging from our collaboration. My debt to him is substantial. Greg, of course, bears no responsibility for flaws and lapses readers may detect in these essays.

Nor does Christian DiVitorrio, a.k.a. Ryan O'Connor, my talented assistant manager at Wellspring House, who proved no less capable as editor when he took over after Greg moved to other projects. I do not exaggerate when I say that without Christian's steady prodding, keen literary sensibilities, and never wavering confidence in this project's worth, *Struggling for the Soul of Our Country* would never have been completed. A thousand thanks, Christian!

I wish also to thank my children—Katie Browning, Sarah Browning, Rachel Browning, and Preston Browning III—for their continuing love and confidence that "Dad" had it in him to complete this project that began more than ten years ago. As I've watched each of them pursue demanding careers and not flinch when the going got tough, I've taken inspiration from their examples. They brighten my life.

My brother, Charlie Browning, has for more than eighty-five years watched me struggle and falter and complain and sometimes give up and then start over and fail again and start once more—but his love and support have never wavered. I am blessed to have had such a life companion. "Thank you" doesn't begin to cover the debt.

A latecomer to my circle of friends and supporters is Janet Brof, a person of extraordinary intelligence and talent. A poet, translator, editor, teacher, and all-around accomplished individual, Janet has filled a void in my life. Her support for my work came at a critical moment in the completion of this manuscript, and for her belief in me and in the value of this book I am at pains to find words adequate to express my gratitude.

Five grandchildren—Hazel, Ben, Grace, Sam, and Dakota—are seldom far from my waking dreams. Or from my waking nightmares. They, I'm confident, will face with courage and creativity the overheated and partially dying planet I and my generation are leaving them. Possibly something they read in this book will strengthen their determination to struggle for Earth's health and long life as a home fit for human beings. *Struggling for the Soul of Our Country* is my gift to them.

IN MEMORIAM

Ann Hutt Browning, Cornelia Cabell Stephenson, Gertrude Stephenson Browning, Annie Stephenson, Harry Stephenson, Anne Browning Ripley, Preston M. Browning Sr., Marjorie Hutt, James E. Miller Jr., Alvin Pitcher, Fred Stern, Ben McKulik, John Brentlinger, the Right Reverend David Lewis, Norman Gritz, David Gritz, Peter Homans, Nathan A. Scott Jr., Leonard Dick, Raleigh Taylor, Ruth Lea Davies.

INTRODUCTION

I WANT TO BEGIN by introducing myself. I am a Southerner, an octogenarian, a socialist and, with reservations, a Christian. Now a question, one that some who glance at the title of this book may be asking themselves: Does America have a soul? If it does, what does it mean to struggle for it? The essays gathered here represent my answer developed over decades of reading, reflection, and writing. It's a struggle undertaken by one whose childhood was coterminous with the Great Depression. I was born in Virginia in 1929 and raised in a Christian family. My life's effort to contribute to the soul of our country springs from and is shaped by that background and the times in which I have lived.

I invite you to join me on a psychological and spiritual journey and to look through my eyes, not just at what I as an individual have lived through but at the history of the times, to better understand the soul of the country that you, too, may be struggling with.

As a child growing up in the rural South of the thirties, I saw more than my fair share of deep poverty. And, as an Episcopalian, I heard on many a Sunday morning the words of Isaiah, Amos, Jeremiah and the other Hebrew prophets, as well as those of Jesus. They all excoriated the wealthy of their day for oppressing the poor and ignoring the suffering of the neglected and dispossessed in their midst.

I was also blessed to have a mother who spent much of her time as a kind of unlicensed and unpaid social worker, visiting some of the most destitute citizens of our county, bringing to these wretched folk food, clothing, and sometimes a little cash but most importantly, a reminder that they were not forgotten. If the word were not so abused in this culture and not used so promiscuously, I'd say she even brought them *love*. Thus it happened that I saw at a very tender age—and I literally *saw*, for my mother often took me

1

with her on her rounds of mercy—Christian faith in action. It would be no exaggeration to say that I never recovered.

At a fairly early age I developed a distinct distaste for money-grubbing and an inchoate suspicion of capitalist ideologues, though it would be several decades before I was able to clearly articulate my deep repugnance and later yet before I realized that, although I had read little of Marx since my college days and had never attended a gathering of socialists, I was, in all but name, a socialist. Hence the motif that appears in one way or another in many of these pieces—an unqualified antipathy toward contemporary multinational capitalism and the American empire that supports it—follows quite naturally from the impressions and experiences of my childhood.

Clearly, my animus toward the kind of heartless destruction of individuals, communities, and habitats that the practices of contemporary "free market" economics frequently result in was closely connected to my religious upbringing. And while it is true that I am no longer a traditionalist in religious belief, I like to think that I am guided in my thinking and my actions by the teachings of the Hebrew prophets and Jesus.

When writing *Struggling for the Soul of Our Country*, the reader I wrote for was the educated layperson. Over the years I have, of course, been influenced by numerous scholars. More recently, the two writers whose work has had the greatest impact on my own writing are Pope Francis and Naomi Klein.

A word about the title. Adrienne Rich defined a patriot as someone who "wrestles for the soul of her country."[1] There was a time, not long ago, when almost everyone was sure that both individuals and nations possessed a soul. In the fifties, an African American maid in Montgomery, Alabama, who walked to work for weeks during the bus boycott in that city, surely did not fuss about the reality of *her* soul. When, in her grand vernacular English, she declared, "My feets is tired but my soul is rested," she and everyone for whom or to whom she spoke knew just what she meant. Although we may not be able to define the word, I suspect that most people still believe they possess a soul.

But what exactly constitutes the soul of a country? In the preface to her collection of essays, *When I Was a Child I Read Books*, Marilynne Robinson sketches out an argument supporting the notion that the soul of America is tightly bound up with our country's ongoing progress toward a truly democratic society. Taking Whitman's conception of the universal significance of this process as a point of departure, she says, "By Whitman's lights, this process of discovery, with all its setbacks, is a metaphysically brilliant passage

---

1. Rich, *Atlas of the Difficult World*, 23.

in human history." And Whitman, the Quaker, appreciated its religious grounding "because it honors and liberates the sacred human person."[2]

In *Leaves of Grass*, Whitman celebrated the human soul: "All religion, all solid things, arts, governments, all that was or is . . . falls into niches and corners / before the procession of souls along / the grand roads of the universe." As Robinson emphasizes, this imputing to human beings a cosmic significance is foundational for Whitman's belief that only such respect and reverence for others and oneself can lead to the realization of the democratic ideal. America's soul, in short, emerges out of the ongoing creative process as individuals strive to bring forth a truly democratic commonwealth.

But I still had questions. Finally I decided to settle for the notion that the soul of a country is not unlike the soul of an individual—a complex mixture of beliefs, passions, conflicting desires, hopes, fears and contradictions. My discussion in chapter 3, "Why I Am a Christian Socialist," of Martha Nussbaum's *Political Emotions: Why Love Matters for Justice* should shed more light on this question.

As Nussbaum's extraordinary work affirms, hints of America's soul are found in the Declaration of Independence and the Constitution and in many famous speeches. These include Lincoln's Gettysburg Address, some of the speeches of Franklin D. Roosevelt, such as his State of the Union in 1944, and speeches by Dr. Martin Luther King Jr. It is also found in the poetry of Walt Whitman and the songs of Woody Guthrie, especially "This Land Is Your Land, This Land Is My Land." In *Political Emotions*, Nussbaum writes about how art, music, memorials, for instance the Vietnam Memorial, patriotic songs and other emblems and symbols embodying feelings of love and pride and belonging can serve to strengthen a nation's cohesion and harmony.

But how can all of these and dozens of other expressions of love and hope for one's country be reduced to a single defining statement regarding America's soul? Obviously, they cannot.

At least I once thought so. Until, that is, I read the essay by the philosopher Richard Rorty "American National Pride: Whitman and Dewey," from *Achieving Our Country*. Writing about the similarities found in the thought of Walt Whitman and John Dewey, Rorty claims that both wanted "the utopian America to replace God as the unconditional object of desire. They wanted the struggle for social justice to be the country's animating principle, the nation's soul."[3]

2. Robinson, *When I Was a Child*, xii.

3. Rorty, *Achieving Our Country*, 18.

The notion of America's struggle for social justice as an expression of its soul is something I've tried frequently to address in these essays. But the idea of America replacing God as the ultimate object of desire I consider idolatry, and idolatry almost always leads to ruin.

I believe, in fact, that it was just this tendency of nineteenth-century Americans to approach the deification of the country that led to the idea of American exceptionalism, an article of political faith that has been described as the nation's "original sin." That inclination to embrace the country's indisputable virtues as absolute proof of its superiority to all other nations was almost certainly the major factor in the unwavering self-righteousness explored over half a century ago by William Appleman Williams in *The Tragedy of American Diplomacy* (1959).

No judgment regarding the state of the nation's soul can be considered sound that does not take into account an American propensity to studiously disregard the opinions of other peoples respecting our country's actions and, in fact, to regard any opposition to official US decisions as outright hostility. A perfect example was the openly expressed contempt for "old Europe," for refusing to join the United States in its disastrous attack on Iraq in 2003. President Bush's secretary of defense Donald Rumsfeld's snide comments as he rebuked especially France and Germany quite naturally provoked a heated response from our European allies.[4] Our original sin seems today as robust as ever.

A concomitant sin is our national ignorance of history and inclination to live always in the present moment, with what amounts to an almost unmovable disdain for the lessons of the past; this inclination represents a childish innocence that can be maddeningly annoying in an adult and exceedingly dangerous in a nation.

In chapter 8, I return to Rorty and to Whitman, arguing that the America I learned to love as a child was, like many childhood images, a chimera. In early adulthood, especially during the Vietnam War era, I came to know the dark underside of America's history. And like many of my generation and even more so the generation just behind me, I suffered immense anguish, experiencing more than mere disillusionment. I felt betrayed. The soul of the country was, I came to believe, irredeemably corrupt, with many of its citizens willing to be deceived by their government and unwilling or unable to respond with horror to the atrocities the United States was visiting upon the people of Vietnam, Laos, and Cambodia. A poem I wrote in the early seventies expresses the angst I felt as I tried to reconcile two seemingly irreconcilable feelings.

4. Shanker, "Rumsfeld Rebukes U.N."

LOVE IT AND LEAVE IT

Somewhere between Tonkin Gulf and My Lai
you began to leave it. You want, it's true,
to love it. Impossible! Each day new
treachery blights the flower. Should you cry?
Brave men don't cry. Your hand fumbles a door.
Sad retreat, while your heart shouts,
"They lie! They lie!"

They also entertain. So with a sigh
you try to accept: Her beauty's that of a whore.
How hard to let go, refuse, say goodbye.
Where love once lived,
the new lodger's name is "Hate"?
Where love once lived, rough grief is now the mate
That taunts the writhing love that will not die.

Deceit! Deceit! Most choose to believe it.
You can't. You try, and cry, but cannot leave it.

The struggle over the soul of our country inevitably creates a struggle
within our own souls. The feelings expressed in that poem were reinforced
later when I visited Nicaragua, twice during the contra war period in the
1980s. I knew before I arrived in Managua in '84 that much of what was
being told to the American public about the Sandinistas and the contras
was pure despicable rubbish. Far from being "the moral equivalent of the
Founding Fathers," as President Ronald Reagan declared, the contras were
terrorists. And they were adept at using the tools and tactics of terrorists—
rape, murder, destruction of health clinics and any other evidence of the
Sandinistas' determination to rescue the impoverished masses of the country from disease, illiteracy, and landlessness.

I returned four years later and saw the effects of this gringo determination to destroy a revolution based on truly humane values—a society wracked
by sky-high inflation, scarcity of everything from toilet paper to cooking oil
(the US embargo insured that result), and starving children. I was almost consumed by rage. It didn't help to know that my taxes were being expended to
bring such suffering upon a people who had recently lost many thousands of
their youth in a bloody struggle to overthrow a vicious dictatorship that had
enjoyed US support for decades. Thus my cynicism about the protestations of
US leaders regarding their fervent support for liberty and self-determination
and their outrageous lies about the genocide going on in Guatemala and El
Salvador—all with US support—only intensified.

My response was to attend many demonstrations, to get myself arrested a couple of times, and to write a play set at Reagan's State Department. My protagonist, Peter Cabell, ranted about the crimes his government was guilty of, just as I had done, and achieved some relief only with the help of his wife's close friend, a Jungian analyst. What Peter came to understand was that his idealization of the country's founders, especially Thomas Jefferson, and by extension the country itself, amounted to unquestioning worship and that such worship cannot help but result in a feeling of betrayal simply because of the inevitable fallibility of human choices.

Creating *Struggling for the Soul of Our Country* has been both painful and liberating. I have probed that soul and have repeatedly found our country's soul to be far from well. I do what I can toward its healing. It is little, I know, but it's love more than duty that has prompted the probing.

Most of the essays gathered in this volume deal with a single subject—the land that has supported me for more than eight decades. More precisely, they deal with the health of the soul of this aggregation of regions, states, cities, towns, and inhabitants we call the United States of America. I come at this topic from a number of perspectives—political, economic, cultural, religious—but at bottom my analysis rests on four assumptions: (1) that the many pathologies that undermine the psychological and spiritual health of America, including our addiction to violence of all sorts, are closely associated with the brutal, unrelenting quest for wealth that US capitalism epitomizes; (2) that an economic system that destroys lives, families, communities, and the Earth, as does contemporary multinational capitalism, is neither sustainable nor worthy of the support of those who suffer its abuses; (3) that America is a sick society breeding sick individuals and that only a radical revolution of mind and heart is likely to prevent future catastrophe; (4) that as a society we face several major crises, the most immediately threatening of which is global warming, with which we are unprepared and seemingly unwilling to deal, at least with the seriousness such a threat requires.

As my thinking about these subjects evolved following the publication of "American Global Hegemony vs. the Quest for a New Humanity" in 2003, the growth of America as a global empire soon emerged as a major theme in these reflections, though oftentimes not highlighted but always there, one might say as low-intensity background "noise." A theme that inevitably demanded attention was how those things that appear to drive all empires—the lust for wealth and power—had for so many generations existed in relative harmony with the liberal, democratic values America has long proclaimed to be its own.

My fascination with and concern about the state of the soul of our country long predated my beginning to write essays on that subject soon after moving to Massachusetts from Chicago in 1999. I had taught American literature for decades at a public university in Chicago; I had spent many hours protesting the Vietnam War; I had also taken part in activities supporting the Civil Rights movement, including joining followers of Dr. Martin Luther King Jr. in Selma, Alabama, in March 1965; I had gone to jail for actions opposing Reagan Administration policies in Central America; I had served as a Fulbright scholar in a socialist country, Yugoslavia, in the late seventies; I had worked in the early eighties at a small NGO in Washington, DC, writing and speaking about world hunger. And I had read a good deal about the origins of US involvement in Vietnam and about America's history of military interventions and occupations in the Western Hemisphere.

In addition, I had twice taught at the Episcopal seminary in Virginia a brief course on the ecological crisis paired with feminist theology and Third World poverty coupled with liberation theology. I was, in other words, primed to reflect on and write about some of the issues that might occur to any reasonably well-informed and concerned citizen, the chief of which gradually became this question: why a nation which professed such avid dedication to liberty and self-determination had so often acted like a "dominator nation," again and again since the early twentieth century sending its troops to impose America's will upon other nations, usually weak and virtually defenseless ones, near and far?

The notion of America as a "closet empire" emerged early in this inquiry, that is, an empire which could not only not acknowledge to the world that it was driven by those impulses that motivate all empires but could not even admit it to itself, though the language of empire is found everywhere in the writings of the country's founders. Before long it came to me that America, a nation that has done much good in the world and has often acted in the interests of other peoples—the Marshall Plan comes to mind immediately—has also been guilty of enormous wrongs leading to the deaths of millions, mostly civilians, among the dark-skinned peoples of the Earth, and thus was perhaps *the* quintessential schizophrenic nation of the modern era.

Several historians writing about America as empire, including William Appleman Williams, Howard Zinn and Andrew Bacevich, have been of help in clarifying my understanding of the trajectory of those audacious thirteen colonies rebelling against the world's most powerful empire, then morphing into an awesomely powerful global empire themselves. But it was an Englishman, Bernard Porter, teaching American history at a US university, who probably taught me most about this subject. Before reading his *Empire and Superempire: Britain, America and the World,* I was surely aware of how thoughts of empire haunted the imaginations of the founders of the new nation. But it was only after examining Porter's carefully researched and persuasively argued volume that I fully understood just how committed Jefferson, Madison, Adams, et al. were to the notion of this upstart confederation of former colonies becoming a world power to rival the British Empire. One of Porter's summary passages is worthy of extensive quotation:

> Few of the original American revolutionaries were against imperialism in principle; they were just against *Britain's* imperial rule over *them.* One of the grievances they had against that . . . was that it prevented the westward expansion that London was chary of. Once Britain was shaken off, the colonists were free to pursue their own imperial designs. America, wrote one enthusiastic Bostonian in 1789, would probably become in time the largest empire that ever existed, covering first the entire North American continent, then the Caribbean islands, and then—who knew? John Quincy Adams predicted her dominating South as well as North America ultimately. George Washington thought that, however insignificant the thirteen states seemed then, there would come a time "when this country will have some weight in the scale of Empires." Many early leading Americans saw their nation as a fundamentally *expansionist* power, right from the beginning; with their expansion not necessarily stopping at the borders of Canada or Mexico, or at the shores of the Pacific. For many of them . . . "expansion" was as important and as American as "liberty."[5]

In two of these essays, "American Pathologies and the Response of Faith" and "America's Forgotten Wars," I have briefly explored our country's record of imperialist intervention and domination. In the first of these I quote Chalmers Johnson, from his book *The Sorrows of Empire: Militarism, Secrecy and the End of the Republic,* who declares his conviction that once the United States assumed "the role that included the permanent military domination of the world," we were headed down a path that spelled awesome danger for our position in the family of nations. We were, he wrote, "on our own—feared, hated, corrupt and corrupting, maintaining 'order' through state terrorism and bribery." We were also, he warmed, setting in place domestic forces which threatened our democracy.[6]

5. Porter, *Empire and Superempire*, 64.

6. Johnson, *Sorrows of Empire*, 284.

Many Americans of the nineteenth century, most notably, perhaps, Walt Whitman, envisioned an America of the future that might serve as a model for all humankind. This was true of the Whitman of "Leaves of Grass." But by the mid-1870s, in "Democratic Vistas," Whitman seemed to have lost all restraint as he excoriated his contemporaries for their frivolous talk, their vapid intellectual exchanges, their unrestrained greed and their total lack of noble purposes. Yet Whitman's hopes for a future America that would serve as a universal model of compassion, kindness, brotherly affection, and nobleness of mind would never suffer unqualified defeat.

I earlier commented on Richard Rorty's belief that Whitman and Dewey were correct in describing America's soul as encompassing both the struggle for social justice and the hope of substituting America for God; and I introduced William Appleman Williams who, in *The Tragedy of American Diplomacy*, describes with great accuracy why and how US diplomacy has so often led to ruinous consequences. But if our nation's diplomacy has frequently produced results that may accurately be described as "tragic," is it legitimate to describe the country's *history* as tragic?

In *The Irony of American History* (1952), Reinhold Niebuhr offers numerous reasons why American history cannot be described as "tragic." I believe, on the contrary, that "tragic" *may* be an apt term to describe a country that began with such extraordinary promise, with so many material, cultural and spiritual gifts and that ended up often acting like a spoiled, cruel child, invading lands from Nicaragua, to Panama, to Vietnam, to Iraq, leaving behind a trail of enormous suffering and waste. (Native Americans might argue that the European colonists acted like vicious, spoiled children from the start.) However one might judge the country in its infancy, it does appear true that at various points in its history, the United States has turned its back on the struggle for social justice at home and has acted, especially in international affairs, as if it has learned very little from its past that might point to a genuine maturing of its spirit and its soul.

In one of the essays in this volume, "America's Forgotten Wars," I write about a fact of American history that is seldom reflected upon by journalists and others who contribute to the creation of Americans' understanding of the country of which they are a part. We forget the sheer number of wars in which Americans have fought from the Revolution to Iraq and Afghanistan. It's a staggering number. If one includes all the interventions, the minor invasions—e.g., the Dominican Republic (1965) and Grenada (1983)—and the major conflicts, the number would surely run to several score. In *Killing Hope: U.S. Military and CIA Interventions Since World War II*, William Blum lists more than fifty occasions since 1945 when the United States has exercised its authority abroad, not usually as "policeman," which is what most Americans have been led to believe, but frequently as little better than a brutal thug.

Following on my contention that American history, not just its foreign policy, might be described as "tragic," I might observe that it has been precisely the grand success, in a material sense, of America that has been largely responsible for its decline in a spiritual sense. From the start, that success has necessitated one inescapable commitment—to war. Thomas Jefferson saw clearly what lay in store for the country:

> Our people are decided in the opinion that it is necessary for us to take a share in the occupation of the ocean . . . and that line of policy be pursued which will render the use of that element as great as possible to them. . . . But what will be the consequence? Frequent wars without a doubt. . . . Our commerce on the ocean and in other countries must be paid for by frequent war.[7]

As was generally the case, Jefferson here was prescient about America's future, and Williams, who taught history for many years at the University of Wisconsin at Madison, developed a thesis about the reasons for the tragic dimension in our relations with other nations, which I find irrefutable. In essence, Williams's argument consists of two fairly simple propositions: first, that among the Founders, perhaps especially James Madison, there was the confirmed belief that America was destined to expand and, in fact, to become an empire. Moreover, Madison and the other Founders held to the proposition that the new nation's success as an equal in the family of nations depended absolutely on such expansion.

There were many steps along the way toward complete global hegemony, which did not occur until after World War II—the Louisiana Purchase, the Monroe Doctrine, the war with Mexico, "Manifest Destiny," the elimination of millions of Native Americans culminating in the brutal "Indian Wars," the war with Spain, and the recognition at the end of the nineteenth century following the closing of the frontier that America's economic prosperity required expansion overseas. Annexing the Philippine Islands after a vicious war of conquest (1899–1902) was a perfectly logical step in the push for markets in Asia. Being the victor in World War II and in the Cold War made almost inevitable an attitude among America's leaders that the United States *deserved* to dominate the world.

Adding to that first cause of the tragedy, the endless wars, is the second cause, a strange amalgam of a missionary zeal to spread American values across the globe—liberty, democracy, Christian morality—which served to give a "spiritual" luster to the expansionist theme, combined with the

7. Williams, *Tragedy of American Diplomacy*, 18.

conviction that American economic enterprises could flourish in far-flung parts of the world with little or no reflection on how the latter flourishing might undercut the former values. No American leader was more committed to this double-barrel assault, aimed at the Chinese and others, than President Woodrow Wilson, ironically the great apostle of national self-determination. Wilson spoke of "battering down doors" of nations that did not welcome American products.[8]

According to Williams, the Open Door Policy had been designed by Wilson's recent predecessors in the White House. This was the theory that America could and should aggressively pursue trade with poor, undeveloped nations such as China, other Asian lands and the countries of Latin America. It was adopted enthusiastically by President Wilson. But always when Wilson spoke about the benefits that would accrue to American industries as a consequence of such trade, he left no doubt about his conviction that it was America's moral duty to use force whenever it was needed to *impose* American values upon the world's benighted masses, wherever they were found.[9] Considering himself and America to be "trustees of the world's welfare," Wilson gave voice to an attitude that would echo repeatedly in the rhetoric of US officials in the future. George W. Bush's fatuous claim that his policies would eliminate evil from the world was one such instance. In an address to the nation on September 16, 2001, Bush declared: "My administration has a job to do and we are going to do it. We will rid the world of evildoers."[10]

Wilson enunciated his "missionary imperialism," as it came to be called, perhaps most egregiously in the following declaration: "When men take up arms to set other men free, there is something sacred and holy in the warfare. I will not cry 'peace' as long as there is sin and wrong in the world."[11] For Wilson, the Calvinist, there was apparently no contradiction in pursuing a vigorous campaign to teach Latin Americans to love the products of US industries, even if this radically undermined their traditions and ways of life. Even invading those countries to inculcate North American values was not considered beyond the pale. Wilson could be quite explicit on the latter point. He once told an English diplomat that he intended "to teach the South American republics to elect good men."[12]

---

8. Ibid., 72.

9. Ibid., 69–70.

10. Perez-Rivas, "Bush Vows."

11. Williams, *Tragedy of American Diplomacy*, 69.

12. Ibid., 70.

Williams argues that this American propensity to believe that America was *the* elect nation among all of Earth's peoples and commissioned, as it were, to bring its values to all the world's millions living in spiritual and intellectual darkness led eventually and inexorably to repeated interventions and invasions and finally to Vietnam. After an analysis of how an isolated Washington political elite misread a struggle for national independence, then denied Vietnam a promised election, which Dwight Eisenhower said Ho Chi Minh would have won in a landslide, then turned the CIA loose in South Vietnam to organize a campaign to eliminate anyone suspected of disloyalty to the US-backed government, Williams asserts that "the CIA agents became the new ward heelers. Then, terror of terrors, the acceptance of the philosophy that power and freedom erupt from the muzzle of a gun."[13] As someone who spent many hours protesting what became a vicious, decade-long campaign of destruction, I can only say "Amen" to Williams's utterly damning analysis.

Using the word loosely as is normally the case in everyday parlance, that war was surely a "tragedy" for the people of Vietnam and Cambodia. However, that outcome and much else that has occurred subsequently in American political and cultural history call into question my earlier suggestion that America's history might be described as "tragic." Genuine tragedy traditionally has involved more than just the hero's fall from a position of high honor, respect and renown to a state of lowly defeat and failure. In *Tragedy Is Not Enough*, Karl Jaspers writes: "We find genuine tragedy . . . only in that destruction which does not prematurely cut short development and success, but which, instead, grows out of success itself."[14]

Arguing that the failure revealed in tragedy shows "the true nature of things," Jaspers writes that "in failure, life's reality is not lost; on the contrary, here it makes itself wholly and decisively felt." And now the critical element in true tragedy: "There is no tragedy without transcendence."[15] Genuine tragedy, in other words, requires a rejection of illusions, a clear-eyed embrace of reality, and an acceptance of responsibility that only mature judgment is capable of. Only if these conditions are met can real catharsis occur. Tragedy, in short, requires self-awareness.

Meeting these conditions is difficult enough for an individual; I seriously doubt that it is possible for a nation. In chapter 2, I suggest that to free itself of its addictions and illusions, America needs something similar to a "12 Step Program." Unfortunately, as Chris Hedges documents persuasively

13. Ibid., 8.
14. Jaspers, *Tragedy Is Not Enough*, 96.
15. Ibid.

in *Empire of Illusions: The End of Literacy and the Triumph of Spectacle*, we may have traveled too long on the "Yellow Brick Road" to recover. Our American romance with the fluff of infotainment, with the easy way of meeting most of life's challenges, from marriage, to producing essays for college courses, to the "dumbed-down" state of general public intelligence— our mastery as a people, in other words, of the arts of deception and self-deception may have rendered most of us incapable of the clarity of vision and the generosity of spirit that the cleansing of our national soul requires.

Having been assured for so many generations that the United States is in every respect superior to all other nations on Earth and being generally incurious about the truthfulness of what our government proclaims are its motives in dealing with other nations, many Americans probably cannot be expected to respond warmly to an invitation to examine the disturbing realities concerning our national life and our foreign relations that these essays reflect. A significant cause of America's soul-sickness, I am convinced, is the self-righteousness of our leaders which is inevitably reflected in many of our citizens. Americans have much to be proud of, but it is way past time for us to become adults willing to acknowledge the evils—slavery, ethic-cleansing of indigenous peoples, multiple invasions and occupations in the Western Hemisphere, the dehumanizing oppression of Jim Crow segregation, genocide in Vietnam and Cambodia, the near destruction of Iraq—to name the most egregious—of which our country has been guilty.

"CARRY A BIG STICK AND USE IT OFTEN"

One sign of our lack of maturity is our constant resort to force to get our way. In "America's Forgotten Wars," I have written about the relationship of the United States to the republics of Central America, focusing principally on Nicaragua. Although I have visited almost all of those countries, it is Nicaragua I know best, having spent extended periods there since 2000. John Brentlinger, who taught the philosophy of art at the University of Massachusetts at Amherst, came to know the country far better than I since he lived and traveled there extensively while doing research for a book which became *The Best of What We Are: Reflections on the Nicaraguan Revolution* (1995). On almost every page Brentlinger's love for this country—its mountains, its lakes and cascading rivers, its weather, its sounds (the thunder of a July storm or the surf on a Pacific-coast beach), its music and dance, but especially its people—is evident. In his imagination, Nicaragua seems to become an actual lover whom this sensitive and generous-hearted North American embraces with unreserved passion. He writes of the difference between how nature appears in Nicaragua and in the United States: "Nature, in Nicaragua, does not appear to be subdued and exhausted, poisoned and in withdrawal. Here it is powerful, fertile, rich, and assertive."[16]

It is in Brentlinger's reflections on history, however, the shameful account of America's vicious treatment of this small neighbor to the south (which can stand in for its treatment of many of the countries beyond the Rio Grande) that this gringo's compassion and ability to really *feel* the suffering of others is most fully revealed.

> To us North Americans, these strangers who stand in the sun, who create so much beauty, who defy all reason by defying us, live in darkness. But it is a darkness we impose to hide the sources of our wealth and the misery we cause. This darkness covers our own hearts. Our postures of innocence hide a history of terrible deeds and a present of indifference. To acknowledge this would be almost unprecedented. *It would require a revolution in values.* How could this be done? Nicaraguans have much to teach us. . . . We have to know and unite with them in the struggle to regain our own lost souls.[17]

These thoughts resonate with Adrienne Rich's conviction that to struggle for the soul of one's country is a duty that any true patriot might gladly embrace. And, as my dear, departed friend John Brentlinger so eloquently reminded us, the soul most in need of deliverance is our own.

16. Bretlinger, *Best of What We Are*, 9.
17. Ibid., 11, emphasis added.

CHAPTER 1

AMERICAN GLOBAL HEGEMONY VS. THE QUEST FOR A NEW HUMANITY[1]

ON MARCH 20, 2003, the day after the United States began its attack on Iraq, I was in Oaxaca, Mexico. Since it was a national holiday marking the arrival of spring, school children were everywhere. In the central plaza first-, second- and third-graders were performing—dancing and singing—for admiring parents, grandparents and other onlookers. How different our two countries are, I thought. While Mexicans celebrate new life emerging from the Earth, our government rains down death from the sky.

I had arrived in Mexico earlier in March, after a lecture tour down the East Coast, giving a talk to university students and others entitled "Toward a Politics of Justice, Compassion, Sustainability and Hope." I had organized this talk around four propositions: first, that the United States has become an empire, one that has caused great suffering to the peoples of what we once called the Third World since the beginning of the twentieth century when US forces brought about the deaths of hundreds of thousands of Filipinos, most of them civilians, and since 1945 has been responsible for what some critics call "the third world war."[2] Former CIA operatives calculate that during this time the number of deaths caused by US invasions, CIA-orchestrated coups, low-intensity wars, etc., amounts to "gross millions."[3]

My second proposition is that our country is in the grips of a profound pathology, which manifests itself in a number of ways, e.g., a kind of love affair with violence and an addiction to war, and that we are in denial about our addiction. The third proposition is that the Earth, our exceedingly

---

1. A version of this essay appeared in the *Ecozoic Reader* 3.2 (spring 2003).

2. Dorrel, *What I Learned*. In numerous books Noam Chomsky has documented the US onslaught against Third World peoples. See, e.g., *Pirates and Emperors*.

3. Stockwell, Q&A session at the University of Illinois at Chicago, August 25, 1987.

lovely but fragile home, is in serious danger of ecological collapse and that, instead of devoting untold billions to wars and preparations for wars our nation should undertake an effort, comparable to the Marshall Plan or John Kennedy's campaign to put a man on the moon, designed to develop a sustainable economy based on renewable energy sources. The final proposition argues that only a monumental transformation at a deep psychic and spiritual level is likely to prevent our self-destruction and that this transformation, if it occurs, must be accompanied by a political revolution if we are to avoid environmental meltdown in the decades ahead.

Moreover, I am convinced that today the United States constitutes the most serious threat to survival of life on the planet. The American way of life—4 percent of Earth's population consuming 25 percent of available resources and 40 percent of the petroleum, while squandering our national treasure on armaments wildly disproportionate to the need—is obviously not sustainable. Moreover, our gargantuan consumer appetite contributes directly to the poverty and suffering of 2.5 billion people in the less-developed countries. We insist on obtaining "our raw materials" at rock bottom prices, and when a nation such as Chile or Guatemala or the Dominican Republic has elected a government dedicated to obtaining a fair price for their copper or bananas or sugar, the United States has seen to it, through CIA-orchestrated coups or outright invasion, that such wayward nations learn the lesson that the American Empire tolerates no such opposition.

In addition, throughout the twentieth century, the United States has supported some of the world's most bloody and rapacious dictators. From Indonesia, to Haiti, to Nicaragua, to the former Zaire, where President Mobutu murdered hundreds of thousands of his people and stole enormous sums from the public treasury, American support for tyrants has been consistent. Though US leaders have claimed that such support has been critical in order to check the spread of communism or to create "stability" in the targeted countries, the inevitable result has been to vest economic and political power in oppressive, autocratic leaders subservient to North American elites and eager to cooperate with multinational corporations.

Invariably, these corporations are drawn to countries where wages are depressed, labor unions outlawed or where labor organizers are intimidated or assassinated, as was the case in El Salvador, Colombia, and Guatemala in recent decades, and environmental laws are lax or easily circumvented. There are hundreds of maquiladoras lining the Mexican-US border, where the labor force is made up almost entirely of young women. These women face wretched working conditions—including extremely long hours and low wages, as well as intimidation for sexual favors and rape by supervisors. The garments created in those sweat shops move across the border and sell at Wal-Mart and other outlets far cheaper than do comparable fabrics made in the United States. Chances are that few of those who wear these shirts and dresses give much thought to the *true* costs of producing them. This is but one example of the exploitation of Third World peoples with which the United States is complicit.[4]

Such disparity in wealth and freedom to pursue a fulfilling life as exists between the majority of North Americans and the peoples of the Global South, when added to our insistence upon consuming as much of Earth's limited resources as our omnivorous appetite can absorb, surely portends more political turmoil and war in the twenty-first century. The US government, in fact, in a document titled "Vision for 2020," has asserted that the gap between the haves and have-nots will widen in the new century and that therefore the United States must be prepared to conduct military campaigns from space in order to protect our "national interests." The militarization of space and its use in insuring the supremacy of the United States in any future conflicts—commercial or otherwise—has been documented by several authors, including Rosalie Bertell in *Planet Earth: The Latest Weapon of War* (2000) and Chalmers Johnson in *The Sorrows of Empire: Militarism, Secrecy, and the End of the Republic* (2004). Johnson's analysis of this issue is worth quoting at some length:

> The determination to militarize outer space and dominate the globe with orbiting battle stations armed with an array of weapons includes high-energy lasers that could be directed toward any target on earth or against other nations' satellites. The Space Command's policy statement, "Vision for 2020," argues that "the globalization of the world economy will continue, with a widening gulf between the 'haves' and the 'have-nots,'" and that the Pentagon's mission is therefore to "dominate the space dimension of military operations to protect U.S. interest and investments" in an increasingly dangerous and implicitly anti-American world. One crucial goal of policy should be "denying other countries access to space."[5]

---

4. There are many sources documenting the horrific conditions experienced by workers in the *maquiladoras* of Mexico and other Latin countries. See Nash, "Women in Between," and Wright, "Dialectics of Still Life."

5. Johnson, *Sorrows of Empire*, 81.

THE SPIRITUAL SICKNESS BEHIND OUR
CULTURE OF AGGRESSION

We are at a moment in our planet's and our species' history when there is an overwhelming need for global cooperation and global planning for humankind's entrance into the "ecozoic era" (a term coined by Fr. Thomas Berry for our period in evolutionary history), a time when many of our fellow inhabitants on Earth appear eager for the new beginning called for in the "Earth Charter." But America, once the "city on a hill" supposedly lighting the way for other nations, now seems blinded by its greed and its multiple addictions—to endless consumption, to military solutions to international conflicts, and to lies from leaders in government, industry and the military about the true state of our nation and of the Earth.

The failure of our educational institutions and other organizations involved in creating systems of value and meaning—churches, corporations, the media—to provide genuine alternatives to the dominant culture, which, according to E. M. Adams, the author of *A Society Fit for Human Beings* (1997), is radically deficient in those features which a fulfilling human life requires, makes inevitable the pathologies plaguing our national life. If, as the old saw has it, one cannot make a silk purse out of a sow's ear, neither can one expect to make a healthy individual out of the images and messages which a society such as ours, placing supreme value on wealth and power, communicates to its children.

In more than half a dozen books, Adams, for years professor of philosophy at the University of North Carolina at Chapel Hill, examined the evolution of Western societies since the early modern period and offered a persuasive diagnosis of the intellectual and spiritual sickness that he believed characterizes contemporary life in those societies. Put simply, having chosen an understanding of human reality almost exclusively in terms of what can be known through the senses—what can be observed and measured and tested—many thinkers in the West gave up the humanistic understanding inherited from the past. Science and the scientific method became supreme and with the development of highly sophisticated technology gave us the wonders of modern medicine and telecommunications that we now take for granted. But in the process, something critical was lost: a coherent vision of those elements that constitute a healthy human being and a vision of a society capable of sustaining emotionally and spiritually healthy individuals. Having subsumed all other human needs to the requirements of the economic order and having identified the acquisition of wealth and power as the ultimate goal of human life, the Western mind, as Adams once stated, has become deranged.

With the humanistic (i.e., the moral, civic, artistic, and religious) culture intellectually undermined and with the dominance of the economic order driven by the rationality of individual self-interest maximizers, the social infrastructure that nourishes the human spirit and supports the civic enterprise has progressively disintegrated. There is little wonder that many families are dysfunctional, that the crime level is high, that psychotherapy is a thriving business, and that antidepressant drugs are big money-makers.[6]

If Adams's analysis is correct, then our situation is indeed desperate. Because, as he states,

the values of our culture are inverted, the virtues required for the success of our economic and military systems are morally corrupting, [and] our dominant intellectual vision of humankind and the world generates a profound human identity crisis and undercuts the humanistic dimension of the culture that supports the human enterprise.[7]

In an ideal world, we, the United States, would take the lead in steering the planet toward a global community fit for human habitation. Unfortunately, rather than being a source of healing and nurture, we are too often the source of the sickness. We export our violence and our junk culture to the far corners of the Earth. The globalization and market economy our leaders seek to impose—through such agreements as NAFTA and the Free Trade Area of the Americas (FTAA), as well as the IMF and World Bank, both largely creatures of the United States—on the weak and the poor around the globe further concentrate wealth in the hands of the few and create more dispossession for the many.

What is at stake is not only the destruction of centuries-old customs and habits rooted in the belief that water, for example, rightly belongs to all the people of a given locale and ought not to be monopolized by private concerns. At stake also is the ultimate condition of the human mind and soul. For the forces seeking a global marketplace where all human activities are subject to the control of an elite made up of corporate executives, government officials and bureaucrats leave an indelible imprint not only upon villages and cities; they work a kind of perverse magic upon the inner life as well. Ultimately, they "colonize" the unconscious. The artist Elisabeth Garsonnin puts the case starkly:

6. Adams, *Society Fit for Human Beings*, xvi–xvii.
7. Ibid., xvii–xviii.

I can readily identify with the young people today; how trapped they must feel. The natural world is almost gone, and it's being replaced by this awful hard-edged commercial creation, with technohumans running it. They're already in Antarctica.

They're in all the jungles. . . . Their satellites are photographing everything. They know what's in the ground and what's on the land. Soon they'll be on Venus and Mars. And they're inside human cells. Where is there left for the mind to flee? They've even invaded the subjective spaces, the fantasy world. As an artist I feel that the sources of creation are being wiped out and paved over. It makes the only viable art protest art. . . . It means they already have us confined; we can only react to *them*. I am so sad.[8]

In *The Culture of Narcissism: American Life in an Age of Diminishing Expectations*, Christopher Lasch analyzed American society from numerous perspectives, revealing the degree to which narcissistic proclivities dominate the American psyche. The contemporary Narcissus, he writes, "demands immediate gratification and lives in a state of restless, perpetually unsatisfied desire," devoid of interest in the future and with a barren inner life characterized by a "pseudo-awareness of himself."[9] Like several other scholars and critics intent upon diagnosing the pathologies of contemporary American life, Lasch cites capitalism as the source of many of our national maladies. For under the conditions of advanced capitalism, everything tends to become a commodity and even the self does not escape the ubiquitous forces of an aggressive and all-embracing program of commodification.

In one chapter Lasch uses the thought of the Marquis de Sade to illuminate the stage of entrenched narcissism at which he believes life in the United States has arrived. Sade, Lasch reminds us, reduced human beings "to their sexual organs," suggesting that they are "interchangeable," a move parallel to "the capitalist principle that human beings are ultimately reducible to interchangeable objects."[10] Moreover, in Sade's "ideal society,"

pleasure becomes life's only business, pleasure, however, that is indistinguishable from rape, murder, unbridled aggression. In a society that has reduced reason to mere calculation, reason can impose no limits on the pursuit of pleasure—on the immediate

8. Garsonnin, as quoted by Mander, *Absence of the Sacred*, 138.
9. Lasch, *Culture of Narcissism*, 23.
10. Ibid., 132.

gratification of every desire no matter how perverse, insane, criminal, or merely immoral.[11]

One may argue, of course, with Lasch's conclusions, noting that many Americans would not agree that the pursuit of pleasure is life's ultimate purpose. Yet it is hard to deny that the narcissistic personality pervades our culture, ceaselessly demanding attention to the desires of the self and the satisfaction of its insatiable appetites. Trevor Turner, a psychiatrist, offers contemporary evidence supporting Lasch's theory. In "I Shop, Therefore I Am," he notes that there "seems to be a rising demand for 'lifestyle' medications and even several new 'conditions,'" for example, "sexual-addiction syndrome" for those whose sexual habits drive them from partner to partner in seemingly uncontrollable promiscuity.[12]

Why not, he asks, "malignant self-actualization syndrome" to designate the extreme preoccupation with the self so rampant in America today? Citing an abundance of evidence, everything from an "obsession with appearance" and the cosmetic surgery industry to an "increasingly privatized lifestyle," Turner contends that increasingly we are a people focused on the needs and desires of a self isolated from community and incapable of relationship with others. "Your own flat, your own car, your own space, your own 'personal' computer are the sacred must-haves of today."[13]

"Me" might be said to be the logo best characterizing contemporary American society. From Madison Avenue to Main Street, narcissism appears to have taken up permanent residence. Narcissism and addiction are, I believe, two sides of a coin. The capitalist marketplace, which in its present form cannot exist without manufacturing endless, insatiable desire, inevitably leads to an addictive society. Turner puts the case this way:

> If we take drug and alcohol addicts as the ultimate example of those serving their own needs to the detriment of others—ranting, robbing or ruining so as to ease *their* personal pain—we can also see how subtler addictions are fiercely reinforced by our highly controlled society. . . . We are so hooked on a thousand creature comforts, in the West at least, that we do not see the dependency downsides of coffee (anxiety), sugar (obesity), cars (heart attacks) or additives (tantrums).[14]

11. Ibid., 69.

12. Turner, "I Shop, Therefore," 13.

13. Ibid., 14.

14. Ibid.

HEALING OUR CULTURE

Any clear-sighted perception of the realities of our era must, I believe, acknowledge that we are at a crisis point. Decisions we make will determine the future for all other species and for the Earth itself. While this destiny places upon us a responsibility of almost unimaginable and unbearable weight, it also offers us an opportunity of breathtaking magnitude and consequence, a gift for which the only appropriate response is profound gratitude.

To properly acknowledge the true nature of this moment in the history of evolution, we humans ought, I think, to declare ourselves citizens of the cosmos. If that sounds too grand and too abstract, let us declare ourselves citizens of planet Earth, dedicated to its health and sustainability. And let us recognize that no matter what our race or religion, our nationality or profession, our social class or our economic standing, we are part of an interdependent whole. In metaphysical terms we are part of the web of Being, in more practical terms that collection of individuals we call the human family, each of whose health and happiness depends ultimately on the health and happiness of every other human being. As Martin Luther King Jr. reminded us, in his great "I Have a Dream" speech, quoting John Donne, "No man is an island . . . [each is] a part of the main."

To sustain such a vision, we—east and west, north and south—require a spirituality capable of embracing the marvelous diversity and complexity of this human family. A spiritual globalization is required, a globalization based on love, not hate, on cooperation, not exploitation, on hope, not fear. In contrast to the economic globalization already far advanced, the globalization of which I speak would honor the unique knowledge and skills of indigenous peoples everywhere, would strive to implement programs of health care for all, whatever their incomes, would see to it that water, electricity and other essentials do not become the property of corporations interested in maximizing profits instead of human welfare, would encourage small-scale economic ventures such as the micro-lending enterprises pioneered in Bangladesh, would work to insure that laborers were paid a fair wage for their labor and that work places were safe and environmentally friendly. In addition, a spiritual globalization would have as its ultimate goal a planetary society and culture "fit for human beings," one whose every feature tended to nurture human life and, indeed, all forms of life on the planet.

Utopian? Many will say yes. I say that the peril and the opportunity of our moment in history demand thinking so bold, so creative that only ideas once dismissed derisively as "hopelessly utopian" can answer the longing of billions of our brothers and sisters on the Earth for a just, peaceful and sustainable planetary society—and answer the call of the cosmos itself.

Fortunately, we are not without thinkers who possess the wisdom and the courage to articulate a vision of such a society. For example, implicit in everything Father Thomas Berry has written is the understanding that only if humankind can begin seriously to enter into a new relationship with the evolutionary processes that brought our species into being, one that acknowledges our kinship with all of the created order and deals with the rest of creation with respect and a deep concern for equity and justice, is continued human life on Earth likely to be possible.

Father Berry's challenge to the present generation—and those who come after—is indeed revolutionary. For he challenges this creature that normally fears fundamental social and intellectual change and clings tenaciously to habits of mind rooted in past experience, no matter how dysfunctional they may have been rendered by changes in the material culture due to science and technology. He calls upon us to make a leap of faith into an utterly alien mode of existence. (It is an alien mode of existence, at least, for us as inhabitants of the modern Western world.) Here is what he claims we must do:

> Our challenge is to create a new language, even a new sense of what it is to be human. It is to transcend not only national limitations, but even our species' isolation, to enter into the larger community of living species. This brings a completely new sense of reality and of value.[15]

As I understand it, Berry's vision encompasses something like a recovery of the experience of the sacredness of all creation as a *sine qua non* of "a new sense of what it is to be human." But in a society such as ours from which the very notion of the sacred has almost entirely disappeared, it will not be easy to convince large numbers of people that their way of life is itself a kind of profane desecration.

Jerry Mander's *In the Absence of the Sacred: The Failure of Technology and the Survival of the Indian Nations* provides a disturbing analysis of the forces in the modern world, often most fully developed in America, that conspire to render the experience of the sacred something that we may read about in anthropological texts or accounts of "native" life such as *Black Elk Speaks* but never hope to know for ourselves.[16] And, since we have never known what it is like to live within sacred space or perceive a manifestation of the sacred in an eagle or buffalo, we exist with only the faintest glimmer of what we have lost, or, more typically, no glimmer at all, of what our technological society has denied us, what our addiction to "progress," to wealth,

---

15. Berry, *Dream of Earth*, 42.

16. As told through Neihardt, *Black Elk Speaks*.

and to *things* places beyond our consciousness. In the absence of the sacred, we live radically diminished lives, immersed in a stream of sensations, desires, fears, hopes and uncertainties; and even our religions, since they too are largely devoid of a profound sense of the sacred, frequently become little more than palliatives assisting us in getting through the day—and the night.

As we examine the impediments that our society places in the way of the creation of the new consciousness, the "new humanity" projected in Thomas Berry's vision, we must emphasize the role of our technology-driven, commercial culture in deepening human alienation from the natural world and those feelings we associate with an experience of the sacred. Mander refers to the "drive of Westerners to convert wild, uncontrolled, and unexplored terrain into productive commodity forms."[17] Nothing is exempt; nothing, as we used to say, is sacred.

At the Earth Summit in Rio de Janeiro in 1992, Boutrous Boutrous-Ghali, then secretary general of the United Nations, said, "To the ancients nature was the dwelling place of the gods. The Earth had a soul. To find that soul and restore it, this is the essence of Rio."[18]

To find that soul and restore it is also the most pressing challenge of our time.

Going back is not possible, however, as Thomas Berry has said. We must go forward, moving human evolution toward a genuinely new understanding of our place in the cosmos. This understanding requires a profound metamorphosis in the direction of unity, sympathy, compassion, fellow feeling and awareness of a shared destiny. We must learn to love, as W. H. Auden put it, or die. We must, in short, transcend our normal ego-protecting, boundary-building anxiety and possessiveness and learn to live in a new reality where the old barriers to compassion are overcome. In the most extreme sense, I believe, Thomas Berry is calling us to emulate Jesus, Gandhi, Albert Schweitzer, Dietrich Bonhoeffer, Nelson Mandela and Martin Luther King Jr.

Something like their vision, it seems to me, may at times be held by the poor and dispossessed, who, having almost none of the things we North Americans consider necessary for a fulfilling life, still manage to share the little they do have. They live, moreover, close to nature and participate in the rhythms of the natural world in a way that we have long abandoned.

I understand how easy it is, however, when sitting in an air-conditioned study with a well-functioning computer at one's disposal, to romanticize the world's impoverished masses. For many millions of these, I'm sure, life is, as

17. Mander, *Absence of the Sacred*, 138.
18. Hull, *Earth and Spirit*, 8.

the philosopher Thomas Hobbes put it, "nasty, brutish, and short." But when visiting Nicaragua and Guatemala in the recent past, my wife and I *did* come to know individuals who appeared to have retained some of the "natural wisdom" which had come to them as an inheritance from generations of ancestors living in the pre-modern past.

In any event, we in the West will have to trust the emerging global spirit now manifest in dozens of ways and in dozens of places. And we will have to trust, I think, the people. The people organize. The people march. The people demand justice. In Latin America, for example, following centuries of colonialism, imperialist exploitation and brutal dictatorships, the people are stirring, electing former labor leaders and indigenous candidates to the highest national offices. In Argentina, whose economy was wrecked by adherence to neoliberal practices imposed by the IMF, unemployed workers have occupied abandoned factories, formed cooperatives, and begun the process of creating an economy independent of the international marketplace. In both Bolivia and Ecuador, governments have been elected on platforms stressing economic justice for the dispossessed masses. Brazil's former president, "Lula" da Silva, a socialist and one-time union organizer, adamantly declared his opposition to economic models imposed from abroad and in his commitment to a new Brazilian society, emphasized the elimination of hunger and attention to the needs of the country's poorest citizens.

We can take heart from such striking instances of human ingenuity and courage, and we may also be inspired by the struggles of indigenous peoples everywhere as they strive to maintain their habitats and traditional ways. An organization located near my home in western Massachusetts, the Sacred Earth Network, works with native peoples on two continents. Through the East-West Indigenous Exchange, Native Americans have visited the indigenous people of the Altai region of Siberia; and in the fall of 2003 a group of Altais traveled to the United States, visiting Native Americans in New England and Canada.[19] One hoped-for result of these exchanges is a deeper understanding of the wisdom that has permitted indigenous people all over the globe to survive for millennia, a wisdom that will be sorely needed as humankind enters the Ecozoic era.

There *is* an emerging global consciousness—"species consciousness" in the language of the psychiatrist Robert Jay Lifton—which has given rise to such documents as the "Earth Charter" and which was on glorious display in a host of countries as millions protested the expected US invasion of Iraq. And in this longing for justice and peace, the vision of a "new humanity" is evident.

19. Sacred Earth Network newsletter, spring 2003.

In the present moment (early 2015), hopeful signs for Earth's future are manifest all over the world. Some contemporary thinkers are, in fact, suggesting that we are witnessing a worldwide transition so momentous that it is, according to Joanna Macy, "the third major watershed in humanity's journey, comparable in magnitude and scope to the agricultural and industrial revolutions."[20] Macy argues that for those who know where to look, it is clear that something unprecedented is happening: on every continent there are people becoming active in the struggle for a different world.

> Be they teachers in favelas, forest defenders, occupiers of Wall Street, designers of windmills, military resisters (the list goes on . . .), the fact is that people from all walks of life are coming alive and coming together, impelled to create a more just and sustainable society. In his book *Blessed Unrest*, Paul Hawken presents this—what he calls The Movement With No Name—as the largest social movement of human history.[21]

What is most encouraging about this movement—Macy says it might be called the Great Turning, a phrase coined by David Korten—is that millions "are hearing the call to widen the notions of their self-interest and act for the sake of life on Earth."[22]

The profound spiritual authenticity of a Rachel Corrie, sacrificing her life to save the home of a Palestinian family from an Israeli bulldozer; the determination, patience and firm conviction of the rightness of their cause of the Grandmothers of the Disappeared, who have gathered outside the Presidential Palace in Buenos Aires, Argentine, once a week for decades testify to the determination of individuals and groups to defy the forces of repression and violence that have scarred human lives for ages. Such heroic self-transcendence is difficult for human beings at all times and in all places, but for rare individuals in the past it has been possible. The critical question for us North Americans today is this: Is it possible for substantial numbers of us who embody the character traits of the addictive consumer to come to care *deeply* about the needs of the billions of other selves on the planet?

In the past human beings *have* changed ways of thinking and behaving, taken new paths, and begun to approach life in radically new ways. Therefore I cling, stubbornly and irrationally perhaps, to the conviction that our destiny is not to obliterate ourselves or to become a global herd of self-absorbed consumers obediently responding to signals emanating from Madison Avenue.

20. Macy, "Five Ways of Being," 8.

21. Ibid.

22. Ibid.

THE PROMISE OF NEW LIFE

As I look out my study window this early June morning, my eye is ravished by the astonishing tapestry of colors nature has chosen to offer. Prominent among them are the lavender of lilac and the yellow of buttercups and dandelions. But the color that forces me to gasp is *green*, a green so lavish, so ubiquitous, so insistent upon my attention and admiration that I cannot conceive of a time when nature will have been so ravaged by human greed, moral blindness and carelessness that it fails to answer to our expectation of spring's return each year.

Well over a hundred years ago, the English poet Gerard Manley Hopkins, in "God's Grandeur," wrote: "The world is charged with the grandeur of God / It will flame out, like shining from shook foil." Later in this sonnet we read, "And all is seared with trade; bleared, smeared with toil . . . the soil is bare now, nor can foot feel, being shod." The poet's acute anguish over humankind's destruction of nature seems at first unrelieved. Yet in the poem's second part, we find these words: "And for all this, there lives the dearest freshness deep down things. . . . Because the Holy Ghost over the bent / World broods with warm breast and ah! bright wings."[23]

Today many of us have difficulty believing in the God of the Judeo-Christian tradition that was still possible for Hopkins. But we *do* believe. Whether our vision is influenced by Buddhist principles, by the beliefs of indigenous peoples, or by a more systematic intellectual understanding of the divine such as one finds in process thought—panentheism, derived from the thought of the philosopher Alfred North Whitehead—I expect few of us struggling for a new humanity would call ourselves atheists. Even numbers of scientists, working at the cutting edge of research in chemistry, physics and biology, are acknowledging the presence of a reality that eludes the scientific method.[24] Some name this presence "spirit." Fritz Hull writes:

> The word spiritual [today] . . . often refers to a more collective experience of the numinous or sacred quality of the universe, to God, and to the essential importance of a vision of life infused with a sense of the sacred. Increasingly this word suggests that which touches our deepest instincts, pierces our illusions, and opens us to everything in the world that expresses love and truth.[25]

23. *Poems of Gerard Manley Hopkins*, 66.
24. See, for example, Sheldrake, *Rebirth of Nature*.
25. Hull, *Earth and Spirit*, 8.

Thus, sensing the growth of such a spirituality around the world, I must acknowledge that the pessimism intimated earlier in this essay is tempered. An indigenous leader in Ecuador speaks for native peoples everywhere when he says, "We are like moorland grass that grows again after it has been uprooted, and from this grass we will sow the world."[26] In this promise and in these examples of extraordinary courage and imagination, I find hope.

When this essay was first drafted, more than ten years ago, that hope was extremely tenuous. Today, even with Paul Hawken and Joanna Macy prodding us to have faith in the power for renewed human compassion and communal struggle that the Great Turning augurs, that hope still remains elusive. But whether or not we realize the new humanity that Thomas Berry envisioned, I feel exhilarated to be alive today and able to participate in the quest.

26. Saavedra, "Growing from the Grassroots," 28.

CHAPTER 2

AMERICAN PATHOLOGIES &
THE RESPONSE OF FAITH[1]

AT A TIME WHEN France was perpetrating acts of great violence against the inhabitants of its colonies in North Africa and Indochina, Albert Camus wrote, "I wish that I lived in a country where it was possible to love justice and still love my country."[2] As noted in the previous chapter, Adrienne Rich defined a patriot as someone who "wrestles for the soul of her country."[3]

If these statements were epigraphs, I would add a third, from a book by Chalmers Johnson:

> From the moment we took on a role that included the permanent military domination of the world, we were on our own—feared, hated, corrupt and corrupting, maintaining "order" through state terrorism and bribery, and given to megalomaniacal rhetoric and sophistries that virtually invited the rest of the world to unite against us. We had mounted the Napoleonic tiger. The question was, would we—and could we—ever dismount.[4]

As implied in the previous chapter, in the talk I gave to student audiences in the spring of 2003, I attempted to end on an upbeat note. I'm afraid, however, that in this talk I gave short shrift to hope. For then as now (this essay was written in 2005), it has been difficult to find grounds for genuine hope. Everywhere one looks one sees wars, ethnic strife, poverty and oppression, as well as forces of enormous strength—multinational corporations, powerful governments, including our own, the World Bank,

---

1. A version of this essay was published in *Cross Currents* 54.4 (winter 2005).

2. Camus, *Resistance, Rebellion, and Death*, 5.

3. Rich, *Atlas of the Difficult World*, 23.

4. Johnson, *Sorrows of Empire*, 284.

the IMF, and the World Trade Organization—striving for total economic globalization, which, in my view, could spell disaster for hundreds of millions in what we used to call the Third World. Our new century and our new millennium, one might say, have not gotten off to a very good start. Thus I have to acknowledge that those feeling despondent about the world situation have ample justification for discouragement.

Yet there is another set of facts that offers support for a more positive vision. This reality was given a voice in the winter of 2003 by the millions who protested against the expected invasion of Iraq. It has also been expressed each year since 2000 by a gathering, first of thousands but in 2005 of more than a hundred thousand, of labor activists, representatives of indigenous groups, students, environmentalists and others who have met to share stories, strategies and plans for creating an alternative to the supposed inevitability of globalization. That gathering is the World Social Forum, whose slogan is "Another World Is Possible." One of their key spokespersons is the novelist and essayist Arundhati Roy. As she put it, "Another world is not only possible, she is on her way. On a quiet day I can hear her breathing."[5] Though it requires a leap of faith to embrace such a vision, I do believe that the human family is on the cusp of a great evolutionary move toward a planetary society that is more just, more peaceful, and more sustainable than our present world and that there are billions of Earth's citizens longing for such a world to come into existence.

I believe also that our country, once celebrated as an inspiration and as an example of enlightened democratic polity to be emulated by other nations, is perhaps the greatest impediment to the realization of such a global society. I have in mind as examples not only the Bush Administration's doctrine of preemptive war and its refusal to ratify the Kyoto Protocol on Global Warming or the International Criminal Court or the Treaty on Land Mines or other efforts of the world's countries to achieve a more humane, more rational ordering of the affairs among nations. I am thinking of the psychological and spiritual condition of our people that makes possible such aberrant behavior. During the Vietnam War era, Senator J. William Fulbright, one of our truly outstanding twentieth-century statesmen, spoke of our nation as "a sick society."[6] I fear that that is an apt description today. In my view we are a country suffering multiple pathologies, chief among them a kind of love affair with violence and, among our leaders and many of our citizens, an addiction to militarism and to war. Sadly, like all addicts, we are also "in denial."

5. Roy, speaking at the World Social Forum in 2003.

6. Fulbright, quoted in "Sen. Fulbright Blasts America 'Sick Society,'" 13-A.

I believe that we are addicted to much else as well—to ceaseless, omnivorous consumption of Earth's limited resources and to the lies of politicians and corporate executives about the true condition of our society and the planet. In addition, we cling compulsively to our ignorance of the crimes our country has committed against the dark-skinned peoples of the global South, especially in the period since 1945. Like mischievous children, we pretend to a moral innocence that is not rightly ours.

I acknowledge that such sweeping condemnation of our citizens' ignorance and "innocence" tends to paint all of our countrymen and women with the same brush.

Polling data, for instance, reveal that a majority of Americans view the US war in Vietnam not as a mistake but as "fundamentally wrong and immoral." Moreover, it is essential to any discussion such as this to note that those who control money and power in this country do not want an educated and well-informed electorate and spend millions of dollars each year to misinform voters and confuse them with half-truths and lies. Ignorant voters are much easier to persuade with witty slogans and hyped political propaganda.

There can be no doubt that knowledge *is* power, and in a democracy those who lack knowledge are at the mercy of others who are able to manipulate and twist facts, data, history itself for their own, normally financial, advantage. Just how widespread is the ignorance of our national history, for example, can be shocking. According to William Blum, the Chinese Premier Zhou Enlai once confessed that he found "amusing" the total lack of "historical memory" in the American population. Blum also reports on a judge in a California court who quizzed fifty prospective jury members regarding their knowledge of Adolf Hitler; not one of the lot even recognized the name.[7]

With an electorate as poorly educated as ours generally is and with journalists who appear unwilling to challenge officials from the president and the secretary of state down to minor officials in various governmental departments, it is not surprising that what viewers and listeners frequently receive as authentic "news" is, in fact, not much more reliable than the opinion of one's next-door neighbor. Lies, in fact, clog the airways.

I find it a delicious irony that an actor, Martin Sheen, who plays the part of the president of the United States in a TV series, "The West Wing," tells the painful truth about our society when the actual resident of the White House, George W. Bush, appears to be severely challenged in the area

---

7. Blum, *Killing Hope*, 15.

of truth-telling. Here is what Sheen has said, in an interview published in *The Progressive* in 2003:

> This supposed idyllic society we have is the most confused, warped, addicted society in the history of the world. We are addicted to power, we are addicted to our image of ourselves, to violence, to divorce, abortion, and sex. Any whim of human character is deeded in us 100-fold. We are number one in child abuse, pornography. . . .[8]

One may take exception to some of the particulars of Sheen's indictment but the evidence supporting his overall charge is too pervasive to be denied. Gary Kohls, a physician in Minnesota, provides some of the depressing statistics: in an average year "27,000 Americans commit suicide, a disproportionate number of which are gay teens"; each year approximately 85,000 Americans are wounded by firearms "with teens representing a disproportionately large number of the perpetrators and victims."[9] Moreover, according to a Health and Human Services (HHS) report, nearly a million children are reported annually to be victims of serious abuse and neglect.[10]

These are staggering figures. One might have hoped that the record of drive-by shootings, hostage-takings, adolescent rampages that leave a classroom or schoolyard littered with the bodies of teachers and classmates, the accumulated Columbines of our society—one might have hoped that when combined with the evidence of societal dysfunction that the figures just cited provide, there would have been a loud demand for a time of national mourning followed by a genuine national dialogue about the causes of the sickness that afflicts us. Of course, from time to time we do have debates in Congress concerning gun control. But I am talking about soul-searching, a genuine probing of the consciousness of this country in a quest for solutions to our appalling addiction to violence. But how do you tell a nation of more than three hundred million that it needs to initiate something like a national "twelve-step" program?

Since the sickness of our society is, at bottom, a spiritual sickness, any healing, to be efficacious, must be spiritual also. But I am not at all certain that the religious institutions of the country are capable of providing the necessary guidance and nurturing to bring about that healing. Too often they are part of the problem, too enmeshed in the dominant culture and too dependent upon the perks that culture offers to play the roles of prophet and

---

8. Sheen, interview by Kupfer, 38.

9. Kohls, "Teen Violence."

10. US Dept. of Health and Human Services, "Child Maltreatment 2002," 3.

healer that our times cry out for. I will have more to say about this matter in a moment.

Then there's the Vietnam War, which still haunts this nation, a war in which American forces killed more than two million Vietnamese and 150,000 Cambodians, dropping more tonnage of bombs on those lands than were dropped by the Allies during all of World War II.[11] How does a country atone for such crimes, especially when a good number of its citizens refuse to acknowledge that crimes were committed?

One is surely justified in also asking, how could our leaders expect to visit such destruction on the people of those lands without serious consequences here at home? One consequence is that, according to some reports, more Vietnam veterans have committed suicide than the total number of US personnel killed in the war, some 58,000.[12]

For a contemporaneous view, Noam Chomsky reports, in 2014, that "suicides in the military began to outpace combat deaths by 2011, with almost one suicide each day. The statistics for veterans are even worse—22 are lost to suicide each day. That's one every 65 minutes."[13]

Probably it should not surprise us that many of the men who have gone on a shooting spree in various parts of the country, terrorizing entire cities and communities, as in the case of John Muhammad, who for days terrorized residents of the Washington, DC, area, have been trained as killers and have honed their skills as marksmen while in the military. I would speculate that many of these men kill fellow citizens out of a deep, perhaps half-conscious rage at the country, and its presumably indifferent and uncomprehending citizens, who taught them in homes and schools and Sunday schools to honor human life, then sent them to Vietnam or Iraq or Afghanistan to take human life.

Chalmers Johnson, in *Blowback: The Costs and Consequences of American Empire*, writes regarding the "profligate waste of our resources on irrelevant weapons systems" and of terrorist acts against US installations. He sees them as

> portents of a twenty-first century crisis in America's informal empire, an empire based on the projection of military power to every corner of the world and the use of American capital and markets to force global economic integration on our terms, at whatever costs to others.[14]

11. Zinn, *People's History*, 469.

12. Pollack, "Suicides among Vietnam Veterans," 772.

13. Chomsky, "Letter," 3–4.

14. Johnson, *Blowback*, 7.

Dominating and controlling other peoples, it seems, has become our nation's destiny. We've been at it longer than most of us would like to contemplate. General Smedley Butler, when he retired as commandant of the Marine Corps in the mid-1930s, wrote that for more than thirty-three years he had been "a high-class muscle man for Big Business, for Wall Street and the bankers. In short," he declared, "I was a racketeer for capitalism," adding that he had taken part in the "raping of half a dozen Central American republics for the benefit of Wall Street." We must give up, he said, "the Prussian ideal of imposing our wills upon other people in distant places."[15] Imposing our will on others, unfortunately, has become such an ingrained habit among the elite who year after year staff the White House, the Department of State and the Pentagon, that I think it appropriate to call it an addiction for most of our leaders, as well as many among the general public.

Some years ago, I gave a talk at a local church that began with these words: "As children we are taught to love our country and that is proper, for there is much to love." To be healthy, however, love of country, like love of a friend, requires a certain restraint, a certain capacity for constructive criticism. Inordinate love of country, a love that tends to elevate the country to a semi-divine status beyond the reach of rational and ethical critique is, from the perspective of the religious traditions with which I suspect most Americans may still be affiliated, idolatrous. And it is often apparent, I think, that those claiming for their country a righteousness which they deny to other countries, experience by their vigorous assertion of the goodness of their nation a kind of vicarious righteousness of their own. (See chapter 8 for a discussion of this subject.) In the language that Christians have traditionally used, what they experience, I would guess, is something like a feeling of "justification." Also, because we love our country, it is often seen to be justified in the violence it commits.

For our times it may be critical to point out that such close identification between a nation and the individual citizen—the sort of thing that occurred in Nazi Germany—can have extremely deleterious consequences, among them a propensity to self-aggrandizement that includes an enormous degree of pride and rigid belief in the near-infallible correctness of one's judgments. A word often encountered in writings about George W. Bush and his administration, which describes the man and many who surround him more precisely than any other I can think of, is "hubris."

Extreme hubris, as the ancient Greeks believed, may be understood as a form of madness, and I do not think it entirely an exaggeration to suggest that some of the people who provided advice and policy formulations to

15. Quoted in Ali, *Clash of Fundamentalisms*, 260.

George W. Bush were a little mad. Two of these, David Frum and Richard Perle, have written a book entitled *An End to Evil: How to Win the War on Terror*. They make such extravagant claims for the righteousness of America and for the prerogatives of George W. Bush in his campaign against evil regimes that they deserve to be numbered among those who have been unhinged by their sense of America's victimization following 9/11. Lewis H. Lapham, the former editor of *Harper's*, requires only two sentences to expose their folly.

> Evil is a story to which not even Billy Graham can write an end; nor can the 101st Airborne Division set up a secure perimeter around the sin of pride. The War on Terror is a war against an abstract noun, as unwinnable as the wars on hunger, drugs, crime and human nature. . . .[16]

If Frum and Perle represent an extreme case of the addiction to the image of America as a "righteous empire," many millions more appear to share that affliction.

Another addiction which I believe greatly contributes to our distressed spiritual condition is our consumer lifestyle. We do well to remind ourselves that we North Americans constitute 4.5 percent of Earth's population yet consume 20 percent of Earth's energy resources and produce 17 percent of the greenhouse gases and other pollutants contaminating Earth's atmosphere and ecosystems. If only one quarter of the total world population consumed at our rate, we would need four additional planets. Our habit of consumption is so grand, so lordly, so wasteful, and so indifferent to its impact on the Earth and on the rest of Earth's inhabitants, 2.5 billion of whom live on $2.00 per day or less, one billion of those on $1.00 per day or less, that merely to contemplate it seriously makes one's head swim.[17] We middle class North Americans, I think it is fair to say, are Earth's spoiled children, snatching at anything we take a fancy to, assuming it is ours by right. Here it is critical to stress that there are many millions of Americans living in severe poverty who can only look on via TV, perhaps enviously, as more comfortably fixed citizens fill their shopping carts to overflowing, while the wealthy buy Cadillacs and Rolls Royces.

I would guess that most of our citizens have no idea that there is any connection between our affluence and the poverty and suffering of the 2.5 billion struggling to survive each day on what we blithely hand over for an ice cream cone. But there is a connection and those of us who care about

16. Lapham, "Notebook: Dar-al-Harb," 7–8.

17. Brown, *Eco-Economy*, 147. The World Bank estimates that 1.3 billion live on "$1 a day or less."

justice and fairness should remember and do our best to teach others that fact. Many good people—students, priests and nuns, labor organizers, journalists, farm laborers, and others—have been killed in countries such as El Salvador, Guatemala, Chile, and Colombia so that the we can have bananas, copper and oil at rock bottom prices.

This may be difficult for many of us to accept, but I believe it is essential for anyone struggling for social justice, peace and preservation of the Creation to recognize that the economic system that has made possible our enormous affluence and our technological superiority, namely capitalism, is also increasingly a major threat to the Creation. For capitalism recognizes no limits. But limits are real, as real as human mortality or our sorrow over the end of a love affair or a marriage. Today a thousand enormous corporations control the destiny of the human species and all other Earth species; and their exclusive emphasis on profits and such practices as clear-cutting mountainsides and monopolizing the use of natural resources, as Coca Cola is currently doing with water in parts of India, are jeopardizing the very foundations of life on Earth.[18]

Paul Hawken, coauthor of *Natural Capitalism: Creating the Next Industrial Revolution,* leaves no doubt as to the role of these corporate powers in undermining the interests of the rest of us. Hawken is not opposed to business; in fact, he has started businesses and written a book about the process. It is huge multinational corporations, with their narrow focus on profits and their paucity of imagination about the way in which all elements of the created order are part of an interdependent system, that threaten the Creation. He cites the meeting in 2000 at the Hague regarding climate change. There four governments—Australia, Canada, Japan and the United States—"managed to reduce a conversation about the fate of the world and the future of energy into concepts like 'restrictions' and 'protecting our way of life.'"[19] And, of course, these governments were fronting for oil, coal, gas and auto companies. This meeting provided clear evidence that the multinational corporations cannot deal in a sane fashion with the crises of global life in the twenty-first century.

Ecological sanity and social justice, Hawken implies, are like Siamese twins. One without the other is unthinkable. Every time a square mile of rain forest is clear-cut; every time drilling for oil occurs in the habitat of indigenous people; every time a dam is built which destroys wetlands and floods rivers where fishermen have for centuries gained a living—each time this sort of desecration of the environment takes place, human suffering is

18. Newton, "Let Them Drink," 6.

19. Hawken, as quoted in Badiner, *Mindfulness in the Marketplace,* 186.

increased. And, says Hawken, it is to the alleviation of suffering that our attention should be directed.

And here, I would suggest, is where we, those of us who are motivated by faith and by the ethical imperatives of our faith traditions, come in. During a 2005 visit to Guatemala I made a trip with a group of young persons to the Guatemala City dump where hundreds of people survive on what they can retrieve from the leftovers and discards of the city's more fortunate inhabitants. An organization that calls itself Camino Seguro, "Safe Passage," provides each day two meals and classes for several hundred children who otherwise would spend their days sifting through garbage, eating whatever they can salvage, with no opportunity for education. I heard of some families, not so lucky, who live literally *in the dump.*

Also in Guatemala I saw a T-shirt on which were written these words: "To transform this world that surrounds us in such a manner that everyone can live at least with dignity." Let me repeat: "To transform this world that surrounds us in such a manner that everyone—[*todo el mundo*]—can live at least with dignity." That, I suggest, ought to be the goal, the mission, the passion of all of us who claim any sort of allegiance to Judaism, Christianity, Islam, or to another religious faith. For me it is a source of indescribable sadness that the grand vision of the prophet Isaiah of a world healed, made whole, transformed in order to be a fit habitation for the human spirit has been reduced, in much contemporary Christianity, to "God loves you."

"People steeped in the culture of monopoly capitalism do not want what they need and do not need what they want."[20] These words, written by Paul Baran over fifty years ago, I take to be a kind of ultimate critique of our society and a key to our pathological state. We may agree that many people in our society do not need what they want, that, in effect, vast numbers are actually hapless victims of a system which works overtime and spends tens of billions to manufacture artificial needs. But can we agree on what they should want, what their true needs are?

First and foremost, I believe, we need a vision, a picture, if you will, of what a society fit for human beings would look like. No rigidly structured blueprint, mind you, no infallible Marxist prescription for creating a workers' paradise, but a set of ideas and principles on which a more just, compassionate, peaceful, and sustainable global society might be built. "The Earth Charter," which is the result of the collaboration of dozens of people from various nations, religious traditions, and nongovernmental organizations, provides such a set of ideas and principles.[21]

---

20. Baran, *Longer View*, 30.
21. Bertell, *Planet Earth*, 197–99.

Second, I suspect many of us need help in being rigorously honest with ourselves. We probably need to confess that we, like most of our fellow citizens, have been infected with the virus of consumerism. Our obscene opulence protects us so thoroughly from the pain and indignities that are the daily lot of the other two thirds of Earth's inhabitants that it is very easy to slip into the habit of thinking that the world and all its wonders exist only for our pleasure and satisfaction. The result is often, I think, a process known as infantilization, a mental and emotional condition that is not conducive to responsible action. Add to this what Bill McKibben, the author of *The End of Nature*, among many other books, has identified as "the inertia of affluence," the reluctance of most of us to make the kinds of radical decisions that are necessary if the Earth is to be spared catastrophic ecological damage in the decades ahead, and you have a prescription for disaster.[22] To overcome this inertia, I believe we need a national campaign involving millions. If led by America's churches, such a campaign might stand a good chance of success.

I have five grandchildren. Like the people of Samoa and other island nations in the South Pacific, my wife and I have begun to write letters to our grandchildren asking their forgiveness for the destruction of the Earth that our generation and our children's generation are causing. The Earth they will inherit, with possibly thirty percent of its animal and plant species driven to extinction by mid-century, will be a vastly diminished and far less beautiful inheritance than the one received by those of us born prior to, say, 1970.

Third, if we wish to be true to our religious heritage, whatever that may be, we will probably have to acknowledge just how compromised most of our religious institutions have been by a relatively uncritical acceptance of our dysfunctional culture. Colman McCarthy, who once wrote for the *Washington Post* and now teaches peace studies at universities and schools in the Washington, DC area, captures beautifully the contradictions in which we who are believers now find ourselves. Soon after 9/11, George W. Bush spoke to a joint session of Congress and ended with these words: "Freedom and fear, justice and cruelty, have always been at war, and we know that God is not neutral between them. . . . May God grant us wisdom and may he watch over the United States."[23] McCarthy comments:

> Two Roman Catholic cardinals, a Methodist bishop, a rabbi, and an imam rose to applaud Bush's war talk. It wasn't the God of peace—the God of forgiveness, of mercy, of reconcili-ation, of love—they invoked, but the God of War, who blesses America and its military arsenal of Cobra attack helicopters,

22. McKibben, *End of Nature*, 204.
23. McCarthy, "God on Our Side," 34.

F22 Advanced Tactical fighter planes, B-2 bombers, and nuclear missiles . . ."[24]

No one representing the peace churches—the Quakers, Mennonites, and Church of the Brethren—was present,

> nor were any summoned to the pulpit of the National Cathedral, where Bush, his war planners, and 3,000 invited guests prayed and sang five verses of "The Battle Hymn of the Republic." None of the five men of the cloth who were at the pulpit delivered a call to embrace nonviolent responses to the September 11 violence. As Christians Billy Graham and Cardinal Theodore McCarrick prayed with fellow Christians Bush and Cheney in a Christian cathedral where an image of the crucified Christ hung high above the clerestory, I couldn't help but remember an observation of the Hindu Mohandas Gandhi: "The only people on Earth who do not see that Christ's teachings are nonviolent are Christians."[25]

Even those who may not agree with a totally pacifist response to violence might consider the proposition that much religion in the United States has been hijacked by apostles of aggression, domination, and violence—in short, by militarists guarding the empire—and thus the choice for Christians, and I speak as one raised as a Christian, seems to me to be between Christ and Caesar. Hence as we struggle for the soul of our country, we are also struggling for the soul of our religion.

Most of us have so little experience of "speaking truth to power," to use the Quaker expression, that it may be quite difficult at first to summon the needed courage. But if we wish to be faithful to the principles of our faith, we must do our utmost to find that courage.

A fourth point. Those of us who are Christians need, I believe, to recover the prophetic legacy of the Hebraic faith out of which our faith grew. We need, specifically, to recover the centrality of the passion for justice that the Hebrew Scriptures enjoin upon us. Arthur Green, in *These Are the Words: A Vocabulary of Jewish Spiritual Life*, speaks, I think, for Christians as well as Jews when he writes:

> Spreading our basic moral message—that every person is the divine image . . . requires that Jews be concerned with the welfare, including feeding, housing, and health of all. The Torah's call that we "pursue justice, only justice" (Deuteronomy 16:20)

24. Ibid.
25. Ibid.

demands that we work toward closing the terrible gaps, especially in education and opportunity, that exist within our society
and undermine our moral right to the relative wealth and comfort most of us enjoy.[26]

Commenting on recent efforts to recover ancient Jewish spirituality,
Green says, "If you try to create a closed world and lovely Jewish piety and
build it on foundations of injustice and degradation of others, Isaiah and
Amos will not let you sleep."[27] We who are Christians can say the same,
though we'd want to add the name of Jesus: Isaiah and Amos and Jesus will
not let us sleep.

And now a final point. Those of us struggling for the soul of our country
will be aided by an emerging global spirituality that transcends all national
and ethnic differences, all religious distinctions, and all barriers of class,
economic background, and gender. This nascent spirituality, deeply rooted
in that passion for justice about which Green writes, as well as in the longing
for a more peaceful and more sustainable world to which I alluded earlier,
finds expression in a variety of movements and events. Surely the emergence of the World Social Forum, with all its sophisticated understanding
of the current geopolitical situation and its commitment to a genuine "new
world order" designed for the benefit of all of Earth's people, not just those
who heretofore have made the rules governing "all God's creatures," signals
new possibilities for a spirituality based on global cooperation, mutual respect, and the shared excitement of a struggle for a noble goal. This other
world, of course, is the people's alternative to the world envisioned by the
officials of the World Trade Organization, the IMF, the World Bank, and the
multinational corporations, a world where the interests of the people always
take second place to the interests of money and power.

The final section of "The Earth Charter" concludes with these words:
"Let ours be a time remembered for the awakening of a new reverence for
life, the firm resolve to achieve sustainability, the quickening of the struggle
for justice and peace, and the joyful celebration of life."[28] If we are fully
committed to the creation of a world where these principles are not just
utopian ideals but a reality for all our brothers and sisters on the planet; and
if we make the restoration of the Creation and the establishment of a society
where everyone can live at least with dignity a constant preoccupation, as
natural for us as breathing, then, I submit, the spirituality for which many of
us long will probably take care of itself.

26. Green, quoted in American Jewish World Service, *How Should We as Jews Respond?*, 90.

27. Ibid.

28. Earth Charter Secretariat, *Earth Charter*, 3.

CHAPTER 3

WHY I AM A CHRISTIAN SOCIALIST

When I feed the poor, they call me a saint. When I ask why there are so many poor, they call me a communist.

—Dom Helder Camara[1]

How serious is the threat to the environment? Here is one measure of the problem: all we have to do to destroy the planet's climate and biota and leave a ruined world to our children and grandchildren is to keep doing exactly what we are doing today, with no growth in the human population or the world economy. Just continue to release greenhouse gases at current rates, just continue to impoverish ecosystems and release toxic chemicals at current rates, and the world in the latter part of this century won't be fit to live in.

—James Gustave Speth[2]

Sustainable development will require a change of heart, a renewal of the mind, and a healthy dose of repentance.

—Herman E. Daly[3]

---

1. Rocha, *Helder, the Gift*, 53.
2. Speth, *Bridge at the Edge of the World*, x.
3. Daly, *Beyond Growth*, 201.

41

There is a growing recognition that the state of Earth's ecological integrity is not just one more concern to be added to an already long list of concerns. . . . The ecological situation is not a concern in the usual sense of word, nor is it a special interest. It is the foundation of all concerns and the most general and comprehensive interest possible. It is both the given and created context out of which everything we care about and work for develops. The human/Earth relationship is the context in which all concerns are situated. Justice, equity, and peace as well as spiritual well-being have no other home than the human/Earth relationship in which to flourish or wither, as the case may be.

—KEITH HELMUT[4]

SEVERAL YEARS AGO, IF an American had declared himself a socialist or even someone slightly drawn to socialist ideas, he ran the risk of being labeled insane. Decades after its flowering in America in the late nineteenth and early twentieth centuries, socialism fell into serious disrepute. Identified in the popular mind with the Soviet Union, North Korea, and other states ruled by ruthless dictators, socialism seemed about as popular in the United States as street gangs or the mafia. For the most part, ordinary Americans seemed to be convinced that capitalism was the only sane way of organizing economic life.

And, indeed, with the fall of the Soviet Union and the end of the Cold War, and the apparent permanent success of multinational capitalism and the globalization of finance that went with it, those who controlled the organization of economic life on the Earth appeared to have more than adequate reasons to celebrate a permanent victory.

A few short years later, however, to advocate continuing with our current multinational capitalist system may invite the charge of mental derangement. I would argue, in fact, that many features of US capitalism are themselves "insane." I will return to this part of my argument in a moment, but first I wish to make clear socialism's fairly lengthy history by commenting on several figures from the past, Jews as well as Christians, who have identified themselves as socialists and written critiques of capitalist economic principles. And I want, as well, to describe briefly the biblical vision of a just and sustainable society in order to illustrate how compatible the

4. Helmut, "Ecological Integrity."

moral and ethical teachings of the Jewish and Christian religions are with basic socialist principles.

INTELLECTUAL FOUNDATIONS OF MODERN JUDEO-CHRISTIAN SOCIALIST THOUGHT

IN THE FIRST ISSUE of *Monthly Review* (May 1949), Albert Einstein commented on the fact that humankind had not evolved beyond the "predatory phase," and that under the capitalist organization of economic life, the needs of the individual, especially of workers, are sacrificed to the wishes of the owners of capital and of the means of production.

> Production is carried on for profit, not for use. There is no provision that all those able and willing to work will always be in a position to find employment.... The worker is constantly in fear of losing his job.... Technological progress frequently results in more unemployment rather than an easing of the burden of work for all. The profit motive, in conjunction with competition among capitalists, is responsible for an instability in the accumulation and utilization of capital which leads to increasingly severe depressions. Unlimited competition leads to a huge waste of labor, and to [a] crippling of the social consciousness of individuals."[5]

Einstein, of course, could not have foreseen just how prescient his comment on technological innovation would prove to be, with robots today replacing workers by the thousands.

Einstein's major concern as far as this essay is concerned, however, is the harmful effects—psychological and spiritual, as well as economic— that the capitalist system has on the individual and his/her relationship to society. Throughout this piece the implication is that a capitalist society is a society characterized by *alienation*, as the "social consciousness" of individuals is undermined by the relentless pressure to compete. Our American "rat race," in which only those who adopt a ruthless strategy of demolishing competitors are likely to survive, is the inevitable outcome.

Another Jewish intellectual who has written extensively about the deleterious effects of a capitalist society such as ours upon the individual is Erich Fromm, author of *The Sane Society* and *To Have or to Be?* In the latter work Fromm, a psychoanalytic theorist, contrasts two ways of existing in the world, the "having mode" and its opposite, the "being mode." Clearly, our American

---

5. Einstein, "Why Socialism?" 49.

way of life is a major example of the former. Fromm writes: "The having orientation is characteristic of Western industrial society, in which greed for money, fame and power has become the dominant theme of life."[6]

The belief that happiness and personal fulfillment come by way of the accumulation of wealth and material possessions, Fromm argues, is shown to be false by empirical evidence. Here is Fromm's assessment of the state of the American psyche: "We are a society of notoriously unhappy people: lonely, anxious, depressed, destructive, dependent."[7]

A society in which having is given priority over being, Fromm contends, invariably leads to the development of a character type whose principal features are "radical hedonism" and insatiable desire. Omnivorous consumption becomes a way of life and ends as addiction. "The consumer is the eternal suckling crying for the bottle. This is obvious in pathological phenomena, such as alcoholism and drug addiction."[8] Our way of life, based on endless acquisition of things, the "stuff" that always fails to satisfy an insatiable desire for *more*, has brought forth, Fromm claims, a "sick society."

A critical question which emerges from Fromm's discussion is this: Ought the primary focus of attention for those who care about the health of a society be the individual member of that society or the society as a whole? Fromm's answer is *both*. That is, in his view it is never adequate to focus on the individual's health without at the same time striving to alter the values and socioeconomic structures of the society of which the individual is a part, for the two are inextricably linked. Common sense tells us that anyone raised in America will, while growing up, acquire those attitudes, values, and ways of dealing with life's experiences that characterize the "American way of life." There are exceptions, of course, but they are rare.

Like many other observers of our current national situation, Fromm, writing decades ago, recognized that a way of life based on endless, compulsive consumption was not sustainable. And like them, also, he made clear his conviction that only a radical change of mind and heart would be adequate to save us from self-destruction. What is needed is a new society, but "a new society can be brought about only if a profound change occurs in the human heart—if a new object of devotion takes the place of the present one."[9]

What is at stake here is nothing less than the survival of the human species and of the Earth as its home. Fromm puts the case starkly:

6. Fromm, *To Have or to Be*, 19.

7. Ibid., 5.

8. Ibid., 27.

9. Ibid., 133.

The need for profound change emerges not only as an ethical or religious demand, not only as a psychological demand arising from the pathogenic nature of our present social character, but also as a condition for the sheer survival of the human race. Right living is no longer the fulfillment of an ethical or religious demand. For the first time in history, physical survival of the human race depends on a radical change of the human heart. However, a change of the human heart is possible only to the extent that drastic economic and social changes occur to give the human heart the chance for change and the courage and vision to achieve it.[10]

Fromm, the Jew, challenges contemporary Christians to foreswear the practices which have characterized purportedly "Christian" societies for most of the past two thousand years—subjugation of women, wars of conquest, imperial domination of other people's lands and cultures. His claim is that, for the most part, it is the values of the pagan world, which Christianity supposedly supplanted, not those of Jesus, which have characterized life in Europe and America. "In a Christian culture," he writes, "the Passion Play would take the place of the Olympic games."[11]

CHRISTIAN SOCIALISM: AN ANSWER TO SEVERAL OF THESE PROBLEMS

Christian Socialism, at least in Great Britain, has a long and honorable history stretching back to the mid-nineteenth century. In 1848, a group of Christians met in London to discuss how to avert revolution following the rejection by the House of Commons of a petition addressing the grievances of the working class. The leader of this group was Frederick Denison Maurice, whose book *The Kingdom of Christ*, became the theological basis of Christian Socialism.

> Maurice argued that politics and religion are inseparable and that the church should be involved in addressing social questions. Maurice rejected individualism, with its competition and selfishness, and suggested a socialist alternative to the principles of laissez faire. Christian Socialists promoted the cooperative ideas of Robert Owen and suggested profit sharing as a way of

10. Ibid., 9–10.
11. Ibid., 142.

improving the status of the working classes and as a means of producing a just, Christian society.[12]

Subsequently, the Christian Socialists published books and pamphlets, established night schools for laborers, and in 1893 formed the leadership cadre of the newly established Independent Labour Party. During World War I, many Christian Socialists urged young Brits to become conscientious objectors. Following the war, the writings of one of their members, Wilfred Wellock, reveal a great deal about the temper of the times in Britain, as well as the spiritual basis of the socialism of the day: "The only organization that appeared to be advancing was the Independent Labour Party. . . . The rapid march of the socialist movement in Britain at this time, with the Independent Labour Party as its spearhead, owed its success to its essentially spiritual appeal." Wellock continues, stressing the spiritual foundation of socialism that appealed to him and to others with whom he spoke. "The ILP inherited the spiritual idealism of the early Christian Socialists and of the artist-poet-craftsmanship school of William Morris. . . . This was the only kind of socialism that appealed to me. . . . I am a socialist, provided you give a spiritual interpretation to the term." Wellock speaks of the possibility of "social transformation" due to the power of a spiritually infused Christian socialism.[13]

One figure prominent in the evolution of Christian social thought in America in the early twentieth century was Walter Rauschenbusch. For Rauschenbusch, "the essence of Christianity was not a theory of atonement or even 'the Fatherhood of God and the brotherhood of man.'" Rauschenbusch believed that the "spiritual reality of the kingdom" proclaimed by Jesus was at the heart of the Christian faith. In his day, he had concluded, the "churches no longer remembered what it meant to pray 'Thy kingdom come.' . . . The kingdom was the 'lost social ideal of Christendom.' It could be recovered only by embracing the teachings and way of Christ."[14]

And Rauschenbusch was convinced that the socialists of his time, even if they did not pray, "'Thy kingdom come,' much more than the churches . . . were struggling to fulfill the biblical vision of a just society."[15] Rauschenbusch was a central figure in the development of the Social Gospel in this country in the early decades of the twentieth century. Advocates of the Social Gospel condemned the human suffering caused by unbridled capitalism, making clear their preference for an economic system more in tune with biblical principles of justice, compassion, and shared wealth.

12. *Sparticus Educational.*

13. Ibid., 2.

14. Dorrien, *Soul in Society*, 27.

15. Ibid., 29.

Rauschenbusch and other Social Gospelers believed that they were heralding a rebirth of Biblical Christianity that would allow for the spread of the gospel message throughout the country, if not across the Earth. And Rauschenbusch held to the notion that there was a parallel between what was occurring in his day and the rediscovery of the message of Paul by the reformers of the sixteenth century. "Perhaps our generation," he wrote, "is called to go back to the synoptic Christ as Luther's generation was called to go back to Paul." Rauschenbusch, in fact, believed that "a new Reformation was brewing."[16] The Social Gospelers, in short, as they observed the changes in American society wrought by secular forces in the Progressive Movement, combined with the emergence of a radicalized form of social Christianity, came to believe that something like the kingdom of God was possible on Earth.

Reinhold Niebuhr, who in his early career as a pastor and writer was drawn to the Social Gospel, later became its harshest critic. Niebuhr, quite correctly, declared that there was an excess of idealism and even naiveté that clouded the Social Gospelers' vision. What was lacking was a realistic assessment of the proclivities of humans to pursue egoistic aims, and to compete in power struggles, not for the common good, but for individual or group advantage. In other words, the Social Gospelers had forgotten about the ubiquity of sin in human relations. The "Christian realism" that was born out of Niebuhr's writings of the thirties, forties and fifties influenced the thinking of an entire generation of American historians, diplomats, politicians, theologians and ethicists.

Dorrien argues, correctly, I believe, that while Niebuhr's corrective to the untoward idealism of liberal Christianity was justified, it had the effect of blinding some Christians to the clear injunctions found in the prophetic literature of the Old Testament and in the message of Jesus in the New Testament to work tirelessly to bring about a more just, more humane, more peaceful society *in this life.*

Another Christian scholar of the first half of the twentieth century, whose sympathies were definitely with those who advocated for an organization of economic life different from the capitalist model, was William Temple, an Anglican theologian who in the 1920s and 1930s "became an important advocate and theorist of democratic socialism." Temple, later to become Archbishop of Canterbury, "proposed that an excess profits tax could be enacted to create worker-and-community controlled enterprises." In *Christianity and the Social Order,* Temple argued for "subordination of profits to the end of fellowship,

16. Ibid.

withering capital investment, mutual export trade, economic democracy, a socialized monetary system, and the social use of land."[17]

It will surely come as a surprise to many Christians that the ecclesiastical head of a major branch of Christianity could be as radical as Temple clearly was. In the book cited above he wrote, "It is important to remember that the class war was not first proclaimed as a crusade by Marx and Engles; it was first announced as a fact by Adam Smith. Nothing can securely end it except the acquisition by Labour of a share in the control of industry."[18]

In preparation for a critical conference of Anglican leaders in 1940, Temple wrote regarding several "stumbling-blocks, making it harder for men to live Christian lives. We believe," he specified, "that the maintenance of that part of the structure of our society, by which the ultimate ownership of the principal industrial resources of the community can be vested in the hands of private owners, may be such a stumbling-block."[19] Once again, one of the leading Christian spokespersons of the twentieth century comes down on the side of the worker, not the industrialist. (It is worthy of note that the Archbishop wished to use "is" where "may be" appeared in the final draft but agreed to the change of wording in order to obtain several powerful voices in support of the statement.)

Though he did not wish to see the church identified with a particular political party, Temple "conceived democratic socialism as the form of political economy most consistent with Christian ethics and the democratizing logic of liberal democracy."[20] In Temple's view, economic justice and equity were linked to the development of local workers' cooperatives, an idea that is rapidly catching on in the United States today.

Among the American adherents of the socialist cause were Helen Keller and Dorothy Day, the cofounder of the Catholic Worker Movement. Both of them emphasized in their speeches and writings the degree to which a rapacious, predatory capitalism, an economic system which honors greed, inculcates greed, rewards greed, and cannot thrive without greed is antithetical to the basic teachings of both the Old Testament and the New.

AN ECONOMY OF GRACE

The good news to a hungry person is bread.

—ARCHBISHOP DESMOND TUTU[21]

17. Ibid., 283–84.

18. Ibid., 284.

19. Iremonger, *William Temple*, 431.

20. Dorrien, *Soul in Society*, 284.

21. Tutu, quoted in *God's Mission in the World*.

In *The Biblical Vision of Sabbath Economics*, Ched Meyers, an independent biblical scholar associated with the Church of the Savior in Washington, DC, makes available for contemporary Christians an understanding of how the principles and injunctions for the organization of economic life found in the Hebrew Bible, later reinterpreted by Jesus for his day, are critical for the health and sustainability of *our* society. Meyers examines the biblical teachings regarding both the Sabbath and the Jubilee year (the seven times seven year) and speaks of a "theology of Sabbath economics and its ethic of regular and systematic wealth and power redistribution." This practice, he asserts, was "most clearly summed up in the Jubilee release of slaves, deconstruction of debt and return of foreclosed land." Meyers describes this practice as "neither utopian nor abstract":

> It arose out of the concrete Hebrew experience of slavery in Egypt and so is both *corrective* and *preventive*. I believe it contin-ues to offer communities of faith today a way out of our histori-cal and persistent slavery to the debt system, with its competing theology of meritocracy and its alienating and cruel practices of wealth and power concentration and social stratification.[22]

Throughout this pamphlet, Meyers is at pains to make clear that from the creation story in Genesis to the prophetic literature and on to the parables and "miracles" of Jesus, there is a common thread of injunctions and practi-cal lessons drawn from the experiences of the ancient Hebrews: YHWH, the God of the Israelites, requires His people to deal justly with each other and, especially, to care for the needs of the poor. In fact, as Meyers argues, the account in the *Book of Exodus* of the Israelites gathering manna in the wilderness during their forty years of wandering reveals that the kind of society their God expects them to create is one in which there *are* no classes of rich and poor. What we have here is an early blueprint for the just and sustainable society that, according to Meyers, is again and again presented as the ideal throughout the Bible:

> The "instructions" in this narrative give us the three defining characteristics of this alternative economic practice. First, every family is told to gather just enough bread for its needs (Ex:16–18). In contrast to Israel's Egyptian condition of deprivation, here everyone has *enough*: "Those who gathered more had no surplus, and those who gathered less had no shortage." In God's economy there *is* such a thing as "too much" and "too little."[23]

22. Meyers, *Biblical Vision*, 6.
23. Ibid., 12.

The second injunction concerned surplus accumulation: the bread that came as a gift from YHWH was not to be "stored up." In imperial Egypt the Israelites had been forced to build "store-cities," where the wealth derived from plundering neighboring peoples was stored. The Bible, Meyers writes, "understands that dominant civilizations exert centripetal force, drawing labor, resources, and wealth into greater and greater concentrations of idolatrous power." In their new life as a community engaged in an "economy of grace," the Israelites are instructed to employ techniques of redistribution in order to keep wealth circulating rather than "concentrating through strategies of accumulation."[24]

The third instruction concerned Sabbath discipline. As Meyers explains this practice, it is much more than simply a demand that one not work on the seventh day as YHWH is reported to have rested on the last day of creation. What is at stake here is faith, i.e., the faith that a benevolent deity has *given* the good earth for human sustenance, but also the corresponding understanding that "attempts to 'control' nature and 'maximize' the forces of production"[25] violate the implicit covenant between this deity and his people. Meyers quotes from Richard Lowery's *Sabbath and Jubilee*: "Sabbath observance [requires] confidence that the world will continue to operate benevolently for a day without human labor . . . [and] promises seven days of prosperity for six days of labor. It operates on the assumption that human life and prosperity exceed human productivity."[26]

The economic and social imperatives inherent in the Sabbath logic also inform the practice of Jubilee. For if the land actually belongs to God and has come to the children of Israel as a gift, they in turn must act with generosity toward those in their midst who suffer from exploitation or deprivation. Having themselves been freed from slavery, they must now in the Jubilee year free *their* slaves. Moreover, during this period when the community was enjoined to redress injustices in their midst, "releasing each community member from debt" became a key element of Jubilee practice, as did restoring to original owners "encumbered or forfeited land."[27]

When we turn to the prophetic witness, we find that repeatedly Amos and Hosea, Jeremiah and Isaiah castigate the Israelites for their apostasy when they cheat their neighbors with false weights or oppress the poor by robbing them of their land. Isaiah declared: "Woe to you who join house to house and field to field until no space is left and you live alone in the land"

---

24. Ibid.
25. Ibid.
26. Lowery, as quoted in Ibid., 13.
27. Ibid., 15.

(Isa 5:8), a practice which sounds remarkably modern if we think of countries like El Salvador or Guatemala where less than twenty families own virtually all of the prime arable land.

Meyers claims that, "once we restore Sabbath economics to its central place in the Torah, we hear its echoes *everywhere* in the rest of scripture."[28] It should come as no surprise, of course, that Jesus, in his teachings and in his actions, exemplified dynamically the cardinal principles of Sabbath and Jubilee and posed a major threat to the leaders of Judean society of his day by repeatedly challenging their rigid, legalized interpretations and distortions of the demands of an "economy of grace."

It is not by chance that, according to the Gospel of Luke, Jesus began his ministry by reading from the prophet Isaiah passages that make unambiguous that his message and his mission are firmly rooted in Sabbath and Jubilee principles:

> The Spirit of the Lord is upon me,
> because he has anointed me to
> preach good news to the poor.
> He has sent me to proclaim release
> to the captives
> and recovering of sight to the blind,
> to set at liberty those who are
> oppressed,
> to proclaim the acceptable year of
> The Lord (Luke 4:18–19)

Here Jesus makes unmistakable that his message is for the *poor*, for those who are prisoners, for any of the Israelites who are "oppressed," as many of his fellow citizens were by debt and land foreclosures. "Only real debt-cancellation and land restoration could represent *good* news to the poor."[29]

Again and again in the Gospels, we find Jesus attacking a socioeconomic system that allows accumulation of wealth and land at the expense of "the poor," that distorts the legal system (in order to give advantage to the wealthy and powerful), described in the book of Deuteronomy, where it is written "Justice, only justice," and which turns religion into an arm of the banking industry. Witness Jesus' outrage when he throws the moneychangers out of the temple, one of the few occasions when he expresses real anger.

Meyers is especially helpful to contemporary Christians in explaining how Jesus' claim of authority to forgive sins is related to the economics of life in Judea of his day. In the language that Jesus spoke, Aramaic, "sin"

---

28. Ibid., 22.
29. Yoder, as quoted in ibid., 23.

and "debt" are the same word. In the Lord's Prayer that Jesus instructs his disciples to pray, the correlation is significant: "Forgive us our *sins*, for we ourselves forgive everyone *indebted* to us" (Luke 11:4).

Jesus' assertion that he has the authority to forgive "sins" can only lead to irreconcilable conflict with the religious and civil authorities, for in so asserting he is obviously announcing the beginning of a revolutionary "new" socioeconomic order, though it actually involves a kind of restoration of the community of justice, compassion and relative equality established in the "economy of grace" described earlier.

Early in the Gospel of Mark we read that Jesus performs healing "miracles," as in the case of the paralytic who is able to rise and walk after Jesus proclaims, "My son, your sins are forgiven" (Mark 2:3–12). The religious leaders are aghast that a human being presumes to forgive sins and are outraged a little later when Jesus instructs his disciples, who are hungry, to gather grain on the Sabbath. Clearly this upstart, this interloper, this self-appointed prophet, who claims authority from his heavenly Father, wishes, as the scribes and Pharisees view him, to overthrow the established order thereby challenging *their* authority.

In one of his most famous pronouncements Jesus answers them: "The Sabbath was created for humanity, not humanity for the Sabbath." In this episode Jesus makes clear his conviction that religious doctrines and religious practices are means, not ends in themselves. Meyers puts it this way:

> [This episode] reiterates the Sabbath as part of the order of God's good creation, and confirms that its purpose is to *humanize us* in a world where so much of our socio-economic reasoning and practice is dehumanizing. . . . In fact, Jesus' central struggle with the political leadership was not over theology, but over the meaning of Sabbath. . . . This "Human One," claiming the authority to cancel debts and to restore the Sabbath, is a Jubilee figure indeed.[30]

Anyone raised in a church of any denomination is almost certain to be familiar with Jesus' method of presenting his message—pithy sayings and parables. One of the best known of the former concerns wealth and the precondition for entrance into the kingdom. As Mark tells the story, a young man owning "great possessions"—in Jesus' day this would normally mean considerable land—approaches Jesus and asks what he must do to *inherit* the kingdom. As Meyers points out, the word "inherit" should tip us off: the young man is thinking that the kingdom is somewhat like property. And, as we've already seen, the large estates in Judea at the time were most often

30. Ibid., 25.

acquired "through the debt-default of the poor. Small agricultural landholders groaned under the burden of rent, tithes, taxes, tariffs and operating expenses. If they fell behind in payments, they were forced to take out loans secured by their land."[31] And it was the already-wealthy landowners who had money to lend; the system, therefore, was a stacked deck, greatly contributing to the economic inequality of Jesus' time.

In response to the young man's question, Jesus says, "You know the commandments" and then recites the last six, the so-called "ethical commandments." Meyers points out that instead of using the words "covet your neighbor's property," Jesus says "Do not defraud," a clear reference to a passage in Leviticus where their God instructs the Israelites regarding how they must conduct economic affairs in the Sabbath community: "You shall not defraud your neighbor; you shall not steal; you shall not keep for yourself the wages of a laborer" (Lev 19:13). The clear implication here, according to Meyers, is that the man's "great possessions," which he had no doubt inherited, came by way of fraud.

Jesus then makes clear how this no doubt proud and self-assured man can *receive*, not *inherit*, the kingdom of God, that is, by selling all his possessions, giving the proceeds to the poor and following Jesus. Meyers writes, "He must de-construct the fraudulent system from which he derives his privilege and restore to the poor what has been taken from them."[32] The young man, we recall, cannot part with his wealth and the privileges it provided, and therefore departs "sorrowful."

The disciples are astonished when Jesus proceeds to illuminate the problem that this young man and all the very wealthy have when attempting to enter the kingdom. Knowing that the disciples often have difficulty understanding his parables and sayings, Jesus reiterates three times the lesson he wishes them to derive from this encounter: "How hard it is for those who have riches to enter the kingdom of God." Then comes the saying that has perplexed so many modern Christians in the wealthy—when compared to the poor of the global South, obscenely wealthy—countries of the North. "It is easier for a camel to go through the eye of a needle than for a rich man to enter the kingdom of God" (Mark 10:26).

Meyers asserts that Mark never tells his readers precisely what the kingdom is but makes it very clear what it is not. "Whatever else the Kingdom of God may be, it is plainly where the rich are *not*!" Each of Jesus' repetitions "insist[s] that the Kingdom of God is simply the social condition *in which there are no rich and poor*. By definition, then, the rich cannot

31. Ibid., 33.
32. Ibid., 34.

enter—not, that is, with their wealth intact."[33] In advising the young man concerning what is required if he wishes to be admitted to the community of grace, Jesus is unambiguous. What is required is economic justice.

This story, like numerous others in the New Testament, contains echoes of the history of the Israelites and the laws given to the children of Israel as set down in the books of Deuteronomy and Leviticus. What becomes increasingly clear as one reads about Jesus' healings, his forgiveness of sins/debts, as in the case of the woman taken in sin, who has probably become a prostitute through economic necessity, or his miracles such as the feeding of the five thousands, when he instructs the disciples, "*You* feed them," is that those who "practice the Jubilee/Kingdom way will *receive* (not inherit) the community's abundant sufficiency—an allusion to the divine economy of grace."[34]

Meyers summarizes this interpretation of Jesus' teachings and actions thus:

> The biblical tradition in which Jesus stands asserts that only the divine economy of grace, not the market, can address the problem of deprivation. The practice of Sabbath economics, illustrated by manna in the wilderness . . . is the tradition that Jesus is "remembering" in a different wilderness in a different time, teaching self-sufficiency through the practice of sharing available resources (what we today might call "cooperative consumption.")[35]

In summary, the economic ethic that Jesus embodies and teaches is firmly rooted in the history of the Hebrew people—their escape from slavery, their wandering in the wilderness, their receiving the laws designed to govern their behavior as a people living in a good land *given to them* by a gracious and generous God, their repeated failures to live up to the principles and standards incorporated in the Sabbath and Jubilee traditions, which forbid accumulation of excessive wealth, which call for forgiveness of debts and redistribution of land so that extremes of wealth and poverty can be minimized, and a sincere, determined commitment to alleviate the suffering of the poor and, in fact, to strive for a society in which real poverty does not exist.

What becomes utterly clear as we reflect on the kind of society Jesus proclaims and then examine our contemporary capitalist society is a shocking contradiction between the two. Our society exhibits an addiction to

33. Ibid., 32.

34. Ibid., 36.

35. Ibid., 49.

accumulation of property of all sorts, an easy accommodation to scandalous extremes of wealth and poverty, a heartless treatment of some of its most deprived citizens, as in the case of elderly Native Americans living in tiny shacks without running water or enough fuel to heat their homes during a cruel South Dakota winter, and a blind faith in the "invisible hand" of the market to bring about something approximating just and rational economic outcomes. It bestows astronomical rewards on the most avaricious among us, and it has an obsession with the celebrity that riches and power create. As we examine contemporary America with eyes not misted over by the propaganda directed at us by the engines of capitalism, the realization becomes unavoidable that our capitalist way of life is the exact *opposite* of the vision of a just and sustainable society that Jesus teaches and exemplifies.

We may continue to be what we are and to do what we currently do; but we might at least acknowledge what we are—and what we are not. What Jesus teaches is redistributive justice, "high heresy," as Meyers puts it, to the capitalist mentality. But for Jesus such justice equals the kingdom of God.

DOUBLE, DOUBLE, TOIL AND TROUBLE

> The absence of trust is clearly inimical to a well-run society. . . . If we don't trust each other, our towns will look horrible and be nasty places to live. [As Jane Jacobs observed], you cannot institutionalize trust. Once corroded, it's virtually impossible to restore. And it needs care and nurturing by the community.
>
> —TONY JUDT[36]

Right-wing politicians frequently accuse liberal members of Congress of fomenting "class war." Anyone familiar with the history of labor-owner relations in this country during the past century and a half knows that, indeed, class warfare has been an endemic feature of our capitalist economy since the Civil War. For decades during the late nineteenth and early twentieth centuries, American workers fought against overwhelming odds, including hired Pinkerton guards and armed strikebreakers, in order to achieve the most minimal of rights, such as an eight-hour workday, prohibitions against child labor, and safe working conditions. Every inch of the way, those with great wealth—the Carnegies, the Rockefellers, the Morgans and their ilk—used the power their riches gave them, including "buying" senators,

---

36. Judt, *Ill Fares the Land*, 67.

representatives and judges, to block the reforms that a humane and just society would consider the right of every human being.

Today the class war has been extended from workers on the shop floor to the general public. As Jim Hightower, the former Texas Secretary of Agriculture points out, "Corporations are granted enormous legal and governmental privileges that the rest of us don't get" and therefore ought to recognize a "moral obligation . . . to provide good wages and ethical treatment for the larger society from which [they] benefit. This obligation is central to our nation's unifying principle of the common good—either we are all in this . . . or not."[37]

Until quite recently, it seemed that Hightower was correct when he claimed that the wealthiest among us had, for the most part, decided that they owe the 99 percent of their fellow citizens exactly nothing and had "monkey wrenched the system to separate their own good fortunes from the well-being of the rest of us—and from the well-being of America itself."[38]

While I believe that this claim is still largely correct, a good bit has happened in the recent past that might call into question such a blanket condemnation of America's richest citizens. Warren Buffett, with a net worth of $58.5 billion, is exhibit number one among those who have spoken about the harm done to American society by great wealth disparities. Another outspoken critic is Nick Hanauer, an early investor in Amazon, who supports a dramatic rise in the minimum wage to $15.00, while at the same time calling for an increase in taxes paid by the wealthiest Americans. A notable figure among these outspoken rich citizens is Leo Hindery Jr., described as "one of hundreds of wealthy people directly asking Congress to raise their taxes." He is active in a group called Patriotic Millionaires.[39]

Such altruism can only be applauded, though some of these contemporary Robin Hoods are not entirely altruistic in campaigning for more equal distribution of the nation's wealth, since they argue (correctly) that their businesses cannot thrive if working people do not have money to spend on the products their industries create. Despite the significant number of exceptions, it is still probably true that Hightower's indictment aptly describes the majority of this country's super-rich. Seemingly dedicated solely to the "bottom line" and apparently without moral scruples regarding the suffering their policies cause others, these titans of industry and finance now quite literally hold the rest of us—and in a real sense, the rest of the world—hostage to their whims, their phobias, their lust for power and

---

37. Hightower, *Hightower Lowdown*, September 2010, 2.

38. Ibid.

39. Associated Press, "From the Rich."

wealth. For their decisions influence everything from the availability of decent jobs for American workers to enactment of realistic legislation to avert ecological disaster. No wonder these mega-rich elites are called Masters of the Universe.

Numerous indicators—social, economic, political, psychological—would lead an unbiased observer to conclude that our society is far from healthy. For significant proportions of the public anything approaching clear thought and rational discourse appears to be impossible. Twenty percent of the public is reported to believe that President Obama is a Muslim, when, in fact, he and Michelle and their children were, before coming to Washington, active members of a *Christian* congregation on Chicago's South Side.

As a further sign of how far astray we have wandered, several candidates for major political offices have in recent years campaigned on platforms that included proposals to move toward a dismantling of the federal government, including eliminating Social Security, a program which has been remarkably successful and has the support of a majority of Americans. And some of those candidates have won. The virulent hatred of the federal government and seemingly almost any feature of a functioning government (except for the Defense Department) that has been brewing for a generation finally erupted in the Tea Party movement. The determination of the right-wing House Republicans to overturn the Affordable Health Care Act, even if that meant shutting down the government, as was done in the early autumn of 2013, may be only a dry run for the disruption and chaos that await us as the blue-red ideological divide among the states becomes a political Grand Canyon.

Fortunately, however, the messianic followers of Grover Norquist, who has campaigned for decades to shrink the Federal government to bathtub size, may have pushed their lunacy too far. Following the completion of a bipartisan budget agreement just before the holiday recess of 2013–14, some far-right conservatives described the agreement as a "sellout." Speaker Boehner responded in anger, accusing his Tea Party colleagues of denouncing an agreement they had not read and of forcing the Republican Party to adopt positions that are not supported by the general public. "They pushed us into this fight to defund Obamacare and to shut down the government. Frankly, I just think they have lost all credibility."[40]

Another Republican, Chuck Hagel, a former senator from Nebraska and one-time secretary of defense, was even more blunt when criticizing the Republican Party, in this case regarding their antics in the debt ceiling debate:

40. "GOP," *This Week*, 4.

The irresponsible actions of the Republican Party over this were astonishing. I'd never seen anything like this in my lifetime. . . . I was very disappointed. I was very disgusted in how this played out in Washington, this debt ceiling debate. It was an astonishing lack of responsible leadership by many in the Republican Party, and I say this as a Republican. . . . I think the Republican Party is captive to political movements that are very ideological, that are very narrow. I've never seen so much intolerance as I see today.[41]

The extremism of Tea Party politics may, in the long run, be felt more decisively and destructively at the state and local level than in Washington. In North Carolina, in 2013, for instance, the Tea Party–dominated General Assembly took a sledge hammer to program after program designed to aid those in the state who are most in need and most vulnerable. In what can only be described as an outrageous display of viciousness, they

eliminated 5,200 teaching positions and 4,480 teaching assistants, they cut pre-K classes for 30,000 preschoolers and diverted $10 million to a school voucher program. They terminated unemployment benefits for 170,000 out-of-work North Carolinians and denied Medicaid to 500,000 qualified recipients. They abolished the earned-income tax credit for 907,000 working class residents of the state—and they reduced taxes for the top 5 percent. Then to insulate themselves from voters, who might respond at the polls, North Carolina's Republican legislators passed the most restrictive ballot access law in the nation—specifically targeting minority voters.[42]

It is encouraging to know that a significant number of North Carolinians have responded with regular protest demonstrations called "Moral Mondays" at the capitol in Raleigh, with over three hundred arrested on one occasion. Amazingly, this movement has spread throughout the South, with comparable protests and arrests in South Carolina, Georgia and even Alabama.[43]

The Tea Party phenomenon and the astonishing rise of Sarah Palin's popularity after her choice as John McCain's running mate in 2012 both provide clues to the frightening fragility of the bonds of trust and belief in the necessity of treating one's political adversaries with civility and respect that hold a democratic society together. Some of Palin's most vociferous

41. As quoted in Werleman, *Crucifying America*, 59.
42. Dubose, "Politics of Faith and Fusion," 1.
43. Berman, "What's Next," 23–25.

supporters once described themselves as "barbarians"; I assume they had in mind the "barbarians" assaulting the gates of ancient Rome but it's hard not to recall in this context a slogan popular among American socialists in the early twentieth century: "Socialism or barbarism." (It is impossible in early 2016 not to lament in the Donald Trump phenomenon the popularity among masses of US voters of crude, vulgar and vicious attacks on political opponents. The barbarians have breached the gates of the new Rome.)

The failed effort of those who supported the shuttering of the federal government could be dismissed as only a small "lunatic fringe" of the Republican Party, posing no threat to American democracy. That, unfortunately, is not the case, since almost all of them represent "safe" seats where redistricting by Republican governors and state legislatures has ensured that the districts contain a majority of Republican voters. Hence the House of Representatives is likely to have a Tea Party–leaning minority into the foreseeable future, a certain recipe for acrimonious debates, meaningless delays, and legislative business unattended to.

But the Republican-dominated Congress that took office in January, 2015, seems ready to adopt slightly different tactics. Rather than waste time and effort as they did in 2014 on dozens of fruitless votes to overturn Obamacare, the Republican leadership appears to have decided that a more successful tactic is to attack that policy piecemeal, aiming to render legally invalid certain provisions of the bill. And they have pledged to take aim at Obama's executive orders granting to several million undocumented immigrants protection from summary deportation by underfunding the National Security Administration.

It is clear from statements by both the former speaker of the house, John Boehner, and senate majority leader, Mitch McConnell, that undermining President Obama's programs and thereby denying him the legacy of genuine progressive achievements that he hopes to realize in his last two years in office is their top priority. The failure to thwart Obama's negotiations to check Iran's development of nuclear weapons indicates, however, that, even with majorities in both houses, the Republicans' power to undermine a Democratic president's policies, especially when they are supported by a majority of voters, can run aground.

Partisan bickering may have subsided somewhat and at some point as we enter a new presidential election cycle Republican leaders will probably move to bridle the party's most outlandishly obstreperous naysayers. The United States will eventually have a federal government that works. The Great Recession has officially ended, with unemployment in the late summer of 2015 under 6 percent; yet there are still millions of our citizens without work or work commensurate with their training and talents. Among these millions are untold numbers of recent college graduates surviving on low-wage jobs and often living at home with parents. The hopes of finding an appropriate job for those over fifty who have been unemployed for more than a few months continue to be slim. And for the masses of black and Latino youth in our inner cities, the way forward must in many cases seem hopelessly blocked by poverty, near-illiteracy and dreams that frequently end as nightmares. It is also wise to remember that government figures on unemployment *always* underestimate the actual number of those without jobs, since there are millions who, after seeking jobs for months or years without success, have given up the search but are counted in no survey.

Although the national mood as of this writing is reported to be optimistic and the American economy does show signs of real strength when measured against the world economy, I believe that an honest judgment about the state of American society in its totality must be that it is far from healthy. During the past year or so, it's true, the majority of Americans have apparently awakened to the predicted devastation that awaits the Earth if humans refuse to undertake measures to dramatically reduce pollution of the atmosphere with carbon dioxide and methane gasses. Yet there are many millions of our citizens who have been led to believe that global warming is a "hoax," and almost every Republican member of Congress has indicated a readiness to block meaningful measures designed to abate humans' abuse of the planet's ecosystem and atmosphere. In addition, in surveys of potential voters taken prior to the Iowa caucuses and New Hampshire primary, among 8 or 10 major concerns mentioned, global warming did not even place last. One has to ask, do these voters live on another planet?

Fortunately, President Obama has recently signaled that protecting the environment will be a central concern of his final two years in office; and robust actions by his Environmental Protection Agency, such as regulations governing methane emissions from coal-fired electricity-producing plants, are a key example of his seriousness in that regard. But the administration's decision to permit Shell Oil to drill in the Artic is a strange anomaly for a president who says he understands the need for urgent action to protect the planet from irreparable damage in the immediate future.

With Republicans in control of the Congress at least until elections in 2016 and likely for some years beyond that date, it would be foolish to attempt predictions about whether America can begin to undertake the kind of *radical* policies desperately needed to prevent ecological breakdown later this century. Hurricane Sandy should have been all that was needed to remind us of what destruction nature can hurl at human beings, but our legendary American optimism, coupled with our outrageously short historical memory, leaves the nation exposed to frightening future disasters. The wild fires raging through the forests of California, Oregon and Washington in the late summer of 2015 ought to leave no doubt in anyone's mind that climate change is very real and that, as Naomi Klein has warned us, it "changes everything."

"DERANGED" SOCIAL AND ECONOMIC STRUCTURES AND A SANE ALTERNATIVE

> Providence has a way of punishing those who persist long
> and willfully in ignoring great realities.
>
> —GEORGE F. KENNAN[44]

Wendell Berry, a Southern Baptist farmer, poet, novelist and author of many books about American culture and the despoiling of our natural resources, especially our land, brilliantly analyzes the psychological and spiritual distemper that afflicts our people.

> The general reaction to the apparent end of the era of cheap fossil fuel, as to other readily foreseeable curtailments, has been to delay any sort of reckoning. The strategies of delay, so far, have been a sort of willed oblivion, or visions of large profits to the manufacturers of such "biofuels" as ethanol from corn or switchgrass, or the familiar unscientific faith that "science will find an answer." The dominant response, in short, is a dogged belief that what we call the American Way of Life will prove somehow indestructible. We will keep on consuming, spending, wasting and driving, as before, at any cost to anything or anybody but ourselves.
>
> This belief was always indefensible—the real names of global warming are Waste and Greed—and by now it is manifestly foolish. But foolishness on this scale looks disturbingly like a sort of national insanity. We seem to have come to a collective delusion of grandeur, insisting that all of us are "free" to be as greedy and wasteful as the most corrupt of kings and queens.[45]

The central thesis of Berry's argument is that we Americans, like Christopher Marlowe's *Doctor Faustus*, have made a pact with Satan, denying our condition as creatures existing in a reality in which our very existence is

---

44. Keenan, quoted by Bacevich, "Solving for X."
45. Berry, "Faustian Economics," 37.

defined by limits. To live without recognizing limits is, of course, to deem oneself as Godlike, perhaps the ultimate sin for a Christian believer.

Berry's suggestion that our society suffers from "national insanity" may remind the reader of my earlier contention that unqualified commitment to the American brand of capitalism, what the French call *le capitalism sauvage*, savage capitalism, bespeaks a form of "mental derangement"; and I do indeed believe that a number of features of our capitalist system are "insane" or are at least composed of extremely dubious rationality. A very plausible case can be made, in fact, that the entire capitalist system as we know it defies both rationality and common sense. And that it is utterly corrupt and probably beyond fixing.

David C. Korten has written a book, *Agenda for a New Economy: From Phantom Wealth to Real Wealth*, in which he argues this point of view quite persuasively. Korten's thesis is simple: There are two kinds of economy, Wall Street's economy and Main Street's economy; and two kinds of wealth: phantom wealth, which exists on paper and in computers and is moved around the world in seconds for the benefit of brokers, hedge fund managers, and bankers; and real wealth, which consists of land and natural resources and things people make and use. Those who control phantom wealth become fabulously rich operating a giant casino where, as in actual casinos, the house always wins.

Korten compares the super-rich of the Wall Street economy to the pirates of old:

> Wall Street's only business purpose is to enrich its own major players, a bunch of buccaneers and privateers who find it more profitable to expropriate the wealth of others than to find honest jobs producing goods and services beneficial to their communities.[46]

Having recently lived through the revelations of the manner in which Wall Street brokers and auditors, hedge fund managers, and officials of major banks colluded to swindle untold billions of dollars from unsuspecting investors, most of us are unlikely to find Korten's judgment extreme: "Wall Street behaves like a criminal syndicate."[47]

(For those who *do* consider his words extreme, the comments of an insider may be persuasive. Charlie Dupree, who graduated from Woodberry Forest, the same prep school I attended in the forties, is a vice president at JPMorgan Chase. About Wall Street he writes: "Here everybody thinks he's

---

46. Korten, *Agenda for a New Economy*, 45.

47. Ibid., 124.

an honest guy. He also believes that everyone he deals with isn't. The end result is that much of the time everyone lowers his standards and nobody is truly honest.")[48]

Because Korten believes that the local economy, what he designates the Main Street economy, serves the interests of individual producers and consumers, while the Wall Street economy works to exploit those individuals, Korten is adamantly opposed to globalization and to the development of single-crop economies worldwide. "Wall Street," he writes, "has learned that its ability to generate unearned profits is best served by a system that minimizes local self-reliance and maximizes each locality's dependence on distant resources and markets."[49]

The problems that arise from the practice of monoculture are most dramatically seen in the area of food production and distribution. Millions suffer when local self-reliance is sacrificed to the interests of multinational corporations. Korten puts it this way: "A weather disruption on one side of the world creates food shortages on the other. If the United States decides to convert its corn crop to ethanol, the price of tortillas in Mexico shoots through the roof."[50]

Looking more closely at this example, until recently Mexico was self-sufficient in the growing of corn, but with the passage of NAFTA, which took place at the height of the globalization frenzy, subsidized US corn entered the Mexican market, selling at a price below that of the locally grown crop. The results were predictable. Many local growers were driven out of business, making the Mexican public dependent upon corn grown in Iowa and Kansas and upon the dealers in Chicago and New York who manipulate prices to generate significant profits for themselves. Korten writes: "Wall Street's preference for a system of local monocropping everywhere not only leaves each community dependent on its predatory corporate intermediaries but decreases global food security."[51]

To escape the exploitative, life-destroying Wall Street economy which produces so much havoc in the lives of those who live on Main Street, we will have to create an entirely new economy, Korten argues, one that works for everyone, putting people before profits and using natural biosystems that recycle everything as our model. Korten summarizes this part of his argument thus:

---

48. Dupree, Woodbury Forest School promotional material, ca. 2005.

49. Korten, *Agenda for a New Economy*, 110.

50. Ibid., 111.

51. Ibid., 111.

Instead of maximizing the rate at which we turn useful resources into toxic trash, we will need to optimize the health and quantity of our stocks of real wealth, taking care to recycle and reuse in continuous production-consumption loops that convert the wastes of one activity into resources for another. To integrate our lives into Earth's biosystem, we must learn to mimic life's capacity for locally-rooted self-organization. To succeed in these efforts, we must reverse the processes of economic globalization that undermine the efficiency, balance, resilience, and adaptive capacity of real-wealth Main Street economies.[52]

If, as Korten argues, we need a totally new model for the organization of our economic life, what would it look like? Among his many suggestions, one of the most critical is "full-cost pricing." That is, under the current system, when a corporation builds a large shopping center, only the obvious costs of materials, fuel, labor, insurance, etc. are calculated to arrive at the cost of this activity. But there are "externalities," such as "worker, consumer, family, community, and environmental health" which should be factored into the calculations to arrive at a *real* cost. The cost of those externalities should be borne by the corporation, not passed on to the public.[53]

Another feature of Korten's "new economy" would be the elimination of corporate welfare. Corporations receive enormous financial benefits ranging from "resource-depletion allowances to subsidized grazing fees, export subsidies, and tax abatements." A sane economic system would surely force corporations to pay for the "externalized costs" of their doing business, i.e., the real-wealth losses now borne by the public. These include such things as "worker injuries, toxic contamination of land, air, and water."[54] (Here we might be reminded of how General Electric polluted the Hudson River for years and did next to nothing to protect this beautiful natural treasure. This example of the exploitation of public wealth by private corporate interests can be multiplied dozens of times, since it was for years the norm, not the exception, for corporations to pass on to the public the costs of cleaning up contaminated land and rivers.)

According to Korten, when external costs are factored in, "between 1998 and 2005, two-thirds of US corporations paid no US income taxes— zip. Tax loopholes, combined with trillions of dollars of direct subsidies and externalized social and environmental costs" made possible this fleecing of the public.[55]

52. Ibid., 116.
53. Ibid., 124.
54. Ibid., 126–27.
55. Ibid.

Despite the recent Supreme Court ruling in the Citizens United case, a corporation is not a person; Korten argues that to treat it as such is a travesty. Laws and regulations should be designed to force corporations to act in ways that benefit the public, not exploit the public, that protect natural resources, that reflect a concern for the health and well-being of future generations as well as contemporary society. Corporate charters should be rewritten, specifying that each corporation's performance is subject to "periodic review." A first step in making corporations responsible contributors to the common good of the republic would be to prohibit "all tax exemptions for corporate expenditures related to lobbying, public 'education,' public charities, or political organizations of any kind."[56]

A cardinal feature of the new economy would be the restoration of "national economic sovereignty." Given the current state of affairs, this is a truly radical proposal. Today corporate executives hide money offshore, move factories to whatever country offers the lowest wages and lax or nonexistent laws protecting the environment, and in other ways behave as if they owe absolutely nothing to the people of the country that provided the resources which made possible their own and their corporation's success.

Hence, Korten asserts, local self-reliance in meeting basic human needs is an essential part of the new economy. "Communities are best able to set their own economic priorities and achieve economic security when most of their basic needs are met by local businesses that employ local labor and use local resources to meet the needs of local residents for employment, goods, and services." Local owners are much more likely to care about the health and well being of their customers than are absentee owners whose principal or sole interest is profitability.[57]

Korten recognizes the necessity of the United States reindustrializing but insists that we need a new model for this process, one that emphasizes the development of "human-scale businesses," locally owned and dedicated to rebuilding communities. A key attribute of a sane and humane economy would involve the passing of laws that control or eliminate the power of corporations to ignore the needs of their workers and the public they supposedly serve:

> Eliminating absentee ownership, broadening ownership participation, and breaking up unaccountable concentrations of corporate power are all foundational elements of a New Economy agenda. A progressive tax on assets—combined with tax breaks for firms owned and managed on a cooperative model by their

56. Ibid., 128.
57. Ibid., 128–29.

employees, customers, and those who live in the communities where they are located—can create appropriate incentives to encourage the voluntary break-up of large corporations and their sale to workers or other community investors. Making absentee owners personally liable for harms caused by the corporations in which they hold shares would create another powerful incentive for such restructuring.[58]

An equitable distribution of wealth and income is, according to Korten, an indispensable aspect of the New Economy. He points out that this does not mean that everyone receives the same compensation for his or her work or contribution to the common good. It *does* mean that each citizen is assured of "enough to cover the essentials of a healthy and *dignified* life and that economic rewards beyond providing for basic essentials should be allocated fairly in proportion to one's contribution to the real wealth of society." Using this calculus, he offers a startling but invaluable proposal: "*Agricultural workers, janitors, elementary school teachers, hospital attendants, and many others would receive more than hedge fund managers, because they all make a greater contribution to the real wealth of society.*"[59]

Though I do not recall that Korten anywhere uses the word "socialism," it should be obvious that the New Economy he proposes is totally compatible with the agendas put forward by a variety of advocates of democratic socialism. His focus—and theirs—is always on liberating the individual from the oppression of concentrated wealth, on restoring to local communities control over the operations of their economic life, on insuring that the values of justice, compassion and cooperation are not undermined by powerful forces intent, for example, upon subverting the capacity of labor unions or workers' cooperatives to protect workers' rights. His emphasis, as well, is on creating a rational and just distribution of the rewards of creativity and labor and on bringing into being a society in which each citizen can live without fear of destitution, homelessness or the shame of being among the abandoned poor.

Like socialists old and new, Korten declares that a good society is one in which every citizen can live with *dignity*. When the price of wheat is manipulated by Midwestern brokers and Goldman Saks bandits[60] causing a dramatic rise in the cost of this product essential to hundreds of millions across the globe, which leads to "food riots" in numerous countries of the global South and also creates added hardship for America's poor, the result

58. Ibid., 131.

59. Ibid., 134, emphasis added.

60. Kaufman, "Food Bubble," 27–34.

is not just hungry bellies but an accompanying diminution of dignity. Both Christianity and Judaism teach that protecting the dignity of every individual is a key moral injunction of the faith. To ignore that imperative is, in effect, to expose oneself to the charge of apostasy.

This episode revealed contemporary multinational capitalism at its most naked viciousness. Adam Smith, who "envisioned a world of local-market economies populated by small entrepreneurs, artisans, and family farmers with strong community roots,"[61] would have been astonished and appalled at what the not so invisible hand of the market had accomplished, bringing great profit to Wall Street crooks and added misery to hundreds of millions of the world's most impoverished masses.

Korten maintains that what America most needs is a new story, one that provides a vision of an economic system that supports human beings in all aspects of their lives, a system infused with the humanistic values of justice, compassion and cooperation. His New Economy, if implemented, would revolutionize American life and without a doubt make possible a less anxiety-ridden, less competitive, less violent society. And a more just one, by far.

Most readers of Korten's book will, I suspect, agree that his ideas seem reasonable and for the most part desirable. But I would guess that the majority would add, "What he says sounds wonderful but it is hopelessly utopian. We will never have in the United States anything remotely resembling his New Economy." And, sadly, I fear they may be right. But like the proponents of liberation theology and others in Latin America who have allowed themselves to contemplate a society that really does *aim* to approximate the kingdom Jesus proclaimed, perhaps we ought to permit ourselves to "dream dreams" and to entertain visions. It is well to note, also, that some end goals may be unrealistic but that moving down the path toward them can result in progress that matters: that saves lives, lessens misery, and improves the environment. That's a worthwhile victory even if the ultimate success of specific goals does not come to pass.

Since writing the initial draft of this essay, I have realized that, although I still believe in the necessity of aspiring to the creation of a society that approximates the just kingdom that the early Christians hoped to create on Earth, I had allowed my "visions" to cloud my sight regarding what is actually *possible* in the world we live in today. This, I think, is a problem for any Christian who longs for a world where the poor and oppressed find their suffering relieved and where something resembling a just social order thrives.

---

61. Korten, *Agenda for a New Economy*, 119.

Martha Nussbaum sheds light on this subject when she says, "The world is beautiful but a mess." And the mess seems to spread almost daily from South Sudan, to the Central Congo Republic, to North Korea, to Syria, to Palestine, to Israel, to Ukraine, to Iraq. But wars, plagues, droughts, famines, and dislocations of whole communities of people—have these horrors not been the human lot more or less in every age of which we have a record? No doubt that is true. But there is a significant difference that must be reckoned with as we consider the state of the world in the early twenty-first century. Across the planet, gross millions of humans are being robbed of security, or of land, or of a life-sustaining diet or of even a reasonable semblance of what might be called home. This phenomenon, which includes much more than the masses of individuals driven from their original homes by warfare or famine, one scholar denominates "expulsions."

In *Expulsions: Brutality and Complexity in the Global Economy*, Saskia Sassen writes about how contemporary technology and financial practices are being used to deprive large populations of those things we usually consider necessary for a decent life, with such examples as the nine million Americans who recently lost their homes due to the deceptive practices of Wall Street operators. Other examples she cites are the experiences of peasants in some African countries who find that the land they have farmed for generations has been sold out from under them, bought by entrepreneurs to be used to grow food to feed middle class customers in wealthier countries.

In order to understand the significance of Professor Sassen's theories regarding contemporary expulsions, it is critical to examine her use of a key term—"subterranean trends." Subterranean trends, she argues, are forces at work in the economies of societies often with vastly different political structures. These trends normally elude the casual view of most people and even the steady examination of experts. Here she describes her hypothesis: "beneath the country specifics of diverse global crises lie emergent systemic trends shaped by a few very basic dynamics."[62] She uses China and the United States as an example: as different as the two countries are, one communist, the other sporting a long-standing capitalist economy, they may be more similar than is usually acknowledged in that "speculation-driven finance and a push for hyperprofits" are central features of both societies. And both experience significant expulsions—in China it's millions of peasants forcibly removed from their homes to make way for factories and even new cities, in the United States millions deprived of their homes by fraud.

One fact that Sassen emphasizes is that the processes of expulsion that she cites are *made*, that is, they derive from human ingenuity. "The

---

62. Sassen, *Expulsions*, 7.

instruments for this making range from elementary policies to complex institutions, systems, and techniques that require specialized knowledge and intricate organizational formats."[63] Sassen calls our attention to the ubiquity of expulsions across the globe and notes that such expulsions "can coexist with economic growth as counted by standard measures."[64]

As I write in the early autumn of 2015, the scenes of millions of refugees and displaced persons fleeing violence in Syria, elsewhere in the Middle East, and Africa seem a terrifying confirmation of Professor Sassen's thesis: expulsions in endless repetition are quite likely a permanent feature of life in the twenty-first century. Yet the causes of the steady stream of humans headed for Germany and other European countries appear to be the standard, "old-fashioned" ones—the violence of war or a simple longing for a better life.

As one looks at the state of the world at this moment, it would be easy to conclude that W. B. Yeats described precisely our time when, in his 1921 poem "The Second Coming," he wrote: "Things fall apart / The center cannot hold." It does surely appear that, instead of the "great transition" to a more sane, more peaceful, and more sustainable global society that Lester Brown, Joanna Macy, David Korten and others have speculated about, we are actually experiencing a "great unraveling."

So, how to deal with this dilemma? The advice I give myself is to adopt a dialectical stance: first, to assume with Reinhold Niebuhr the understanding that perfection in human affairs is an illusion, that with every good that is achieved there comes the possibility of evil, and that contradictions are an inevitable component in human affairs and history. But, second, one must attempt to maintain something like the tragic view, recognizing that noble ideals sustain the health and sanity of the human soul, yet are, as often as not, liable to betrayal or corruption. That is no reason, however, to abandon the struggle for a more just and humane society.

NEITHER PARADISE NOR THE KINGDOM BUT SANE

Any society, [Edmund Burke] wrote in *Reflections on the Revolution in France*, which destroys the fabric of the state, must soon be "disconnected into the dust and powder of individuality." By eviscerating public services and reducing them to a network of farmed-out private providers, we have begun to dismantle the fabric of the state. As for the dust and powder of individuality: it resembles nothing so

63. Ibid., 2.
64. Ibid.

much as Hobbes's war of all, in which life for many people has once
again become soltary, poor and more than a little nasty.

—Tony Judt[65]

Once upon a time, America had the makings of a genuine social democracy. Few would claim that a truly *socialist* society has ever stood much of a
chance of taking root here, though in the early thirties, as the Great Depression left one quarter of the work force jobless, some feared that it might.
But as Tony Judt argues in *Ill Fares the Land*, for a time, during the New
Deal and Great Society eras, we Americans were moving in the direction of
creating a society embodying economic and social features characteristic of
the social democracies of Europe.

In a review of Judt's book published in the October 2010 issue of
Harper's magazine, Terry Eagleton, an English literary scholar and critic of
culture, wrote:

> Even in the Land of the Free, Judt reminds us, "public" was not
> always a term of opprobrium, despite the fact that a churlish sus-
> picion of the state is in his view "uniquely American"; much of
> what was best in American legislation and social policy during
> the twentieth century was social-democratic in all but name.[66]

One example of this tendency in US policies that Judt cites was the
Tennessee Valley Authority, a large-scale public project that was hugely beneficial in bringing electricity to millions of Americans in the South, many of
them among the nation's most needy.[67]

In the European democracies following World War II, legislation was
passed protecting society's most vulnerable, with restraints placed on the
market to guard against outrageous inequalities among the citizenry. Prior
to 1980, in America as well as in Europe, Judt suggests that "everyone believed in the state," probably somewhat of an exaggeration for the United
States but for the most part true.

> Public ownership, large-scale public investment, and steeply
> progressive taxation were warmly welcomed from the New Deal
> to the British Labour Party. . . . Two generations of Americans
> enjoyed security and social mobility on an unprecedented scale,

65. Judt, *Ill Fares the Land*.
66. Eagleton, "What Is the Worth," 77.
67. Ibid.

while from Frankfort to San Francisco social inequalities shrank dramatically.[68]

From 1980 to today, Judt convincingly argues, a dramatic reversal has taken place. Margaret Thatcher in the UK and Ronald Reagan in the United States launched attacks on "big government," on labor unions, and on social programs designed to protect and assist those whom society was inclined to ignore or shun: unwed mothers, children living in poverty, black ghetto youth surviving on relatives' social security or welfare checks or, more often, on the one employment opportunity available to many of them—selling drugs.

With the sharp decline in federal financial assistance came a harsh, at times almost contemptuous condemnation of the recipients of government "hand-outs." The result of more than three decades of attacks on government programs that a sane society would consider necessary and appropriate has been an unraveling of the social contract that once bound Americans together. Privatization, almost daily, it seems, makes inroads in all aspects of our national life, from schools to prisons, to the waging of war. (Will we ever know how many individuals, employed by private contractors such as Blackwater, have been on the ground in Iraq and Afghanistan? I doubt it.) What has been lost for many has been a belief in America as a compassionate, genuinely communal society of shared benefits, shared pain. The rage that fuels the Tea Party movement is one aspect of the loss of trust resulting from decades of propaganda, most frequently funded by right-wing billionaires such as Sheldon Adelson and the Koch brothers, directed against "big government" and "socialist" policies.

A prophetic voice for our deeply troubled time, Judt offers this observation on the "symptoms of collective impoverishment," the legacy, one might say, of the so-called "Reagan revolution": "Broken highways, bankrupt cities . . . collapsing bridges, failed schools. . . . Even as the U.S. budgets billions of dollars on a futile military campaign in Afghanistan, we fret nervously at the implication of any increase in public spending on social services or infrastructure."[69]

Writing in *The Nation*, Katha Pollitt makes it clear that there are sane alternatives to our diminished health as a caring society. Upon returning from a year in Germany, Pollitt was immediately reminded of the differences between our free enterprise society and life in a social democracy such as Germany.

"Berlin is a poor city by German standards," Pollitt writes,

68. Ibid.
69. Ibid.

with homeless people and beggars and presumably mentally ill people as well. But it doesn't have the kind of destitution we take for granted in the United States, especially for African Americans. The strong German safety net keeps people from plunging into the abyss.[70]

Apparently she found nothing like the 43.6 million Americans living at or below the poverty line, nor the tens of thousands of homeless children who haunt the overcrowded homeless shelters in many American cities or live on our cities' streets, often turning to prostitution to survive.

In Germany unions are powerful and "Germans have job security, retirement pensions, free or nearly free education including college, and health care including nursing care." Americans should be filled with envy when they learn that in addition to all these benefits, Germans receive "six weeks of vacation and twenty-seven (!) paid holidays."[71] Michael Moore's delightful 2016 film, "Where to Invade Next," authored splendid documentation of the startling perks that the German system provides its workers.

One might believe that this extravagant largesse cannot continue for long. But an article by Thomas Geoghegan in *Harper's* reveals that the German economy is much *healthier* than the American. In a country where workers share in a significant way in corporate decision-making and where the divisions between labor and management are not nearly so egregious as in the United States, industry thrives, producing products that are desired by international customers. What Geoghegan calls "the colossus of European socialism," Germany, "has somehow managed to create a high-wage, unionized economy without shipping its jobs abroad or creating a massive trade deficit, or any deficit at all."[72]

Geoghegan describes features of the German economic model which make Germany a much more egalitarian society than the contemporary United States—especially "works councils" and "co-determination." These features provide power to workers in Germany that is unheard of in the United States, e.g., workers making up half of the boards of corporations. "With works councils and co-determination, everything in the firm gets discussed, rather than the CEO going to the mountaintop without ever seeing a worker and deciding to pull the plug."[73]

This arrangement does not mean that the workers can prevent outsourcing or block the sale of the firm, but they can cut deals:

70. Pollitt, "It's Better Over There," 9.

71. Ibid.

72. Geoghegan, "Consider the Germans," 7–9.

73. Ibid., 8.

> In the United States, people don't even know the plant is clos-
> ing until management calls a meeting and ushers everyone out
> under armed guard. But in a German firm, the workers are
> Cato-like guardians, able to look at all the financial records and
> planning documents as if they owned the place.[74]

If, for example, they learn that management intends to open a plant abroad, they can see to it that money is invested in a German plant or can "fight to get a better owner." As should be immediately clear, these features of German economic life make for a healthier, more robust political life as well.

In one European country, in short, the "socialism" and welfare state so despised by substantial numbers of Americans have led to a society that seems, if not the ultimate ideal of a just and humane society, at least a sane one. (It might be worth noting that in another, smaller European country, Finland, the CEO of a corporation is allowed to earn only fourteen times what a laborer in his plant earns!)

At this point in our discussion of Christian socialism, we might ask a question: If these advances are possible in Europe, are they not also possible in America?

LAISSEZ FAIRE AND A FEW INSANITIES

Despite some economists and men and women on Wall Street who may be singing "Happy Days Are Here Again," I still maintain that capitalist America is in deep trouble, and concerned citizens can be forgiven for asking some embarrassing questions. Why, for example, should we continue to endure the "boom and bust" cycle every twelve or fifteen years, as if it were our divinely ordained destiny? We are told by the cheerleaders for contemporary multinational capitalism that, while capitalism is not perfect, it is the best option available. That, I believe, is a dangerous falsehood. As David Korten has shown us, a reasonable alternative is surely possible. Now let us look in some detail at the devastation wrought by the existing system.

Our recent Great Recession—the noted economist Paul Krugman described it a true depression—ought to provide convincing evidence that the economic system with which we have lived for centuries is insupportable. There were reports several years ago from some of the unemployed that many months of sending out resumes with not one positive response had left them in despair. To give a couple of examples, one woman interviewed

74. Ibid.

on the PBS program "Need To Know" remarked that she had sent out re-sume after resume and in many cases learned that there were forty or fifty qualified applicants for each job. A man who appeared on the same pro-gram noted that he had been without work for more than ninety-nine weeks (the point at which unemployment benefits expire), had spent hundreds of hours searching for work with nothing but rejections to show for his effort. This person said he felt as if his life were coming apart.

The unemployment situation we have just lived through has been de-scribed as a "slow-motion social catastrophe"; long-term unemployment, it has been said, is "like the death of a spouse." The psychological and social costs of an economic system that tears at the fabric of our communal life, as witnessed by suicides, an increase in domestic violence and divorce, in-creasing rates of depression, etc., ought to convince even hardened skeptics to consider an alternative.

As noted above, the US economic situation, in 2014–15, *has* improved. The number of private-sector jobs added each month has increased substan-tially and the overall unemployment rate has come down steadily month after month. But this recovery has been painfully slow, leaving hundreds of thousands of college graduates either unemployed or reduced to taking two or three minimum-wage jobs to survive. Moreover, until this country returns to manufacturing as a major component of its economic activity, I doubt that anything approaching "full employment" will be possible. From the beginning, however, what has been lacking was genuinely robust invest-ment by the federal government in such projects as rescuing the nation's decaying infrastructure and developing a continent-wide light-rail system. Serious investment of that sort could have created millions of jobs and ended the agony of untold numbers of our citizens. But a pig-headed resis-tance to such investment on the part of large segments of the population, egged on by the apostles of austerity, such as the Koch brothers, insured the prolonging of what might have been a relatively brief period of suffering by the many who have been needlessly forced into idleness.

UNPLANNED PLANNING

It is instructive to examine some of the practices of our "unplanned" capi-talist economy. Does it not border on insanity to subsidize the growing of corn for ethanol when it has been established that more energy is expended to create a gallon of ethanol than the energy that gallon will produce? And how can such subsidies be justified when it is corn oil, used in most of the foods we buy, especially the "junk food" gobbled up by our children and teenagers, that is leading to a national epidemic of obesity? Over seventy million Americans have been diagnosed as obese, and the incidence of obesity in the population, though declining, is still alarming.

One commentator, the filmmaker Robert Kenner, has speculated that one-third of those born after the year 2000 will be seriously overweight before they reach adulthood, leading to a widespread incidence of diabetes and related diseases such as heart and kidney failure. This critic is hardly exaggerating in claiming that the costs of dealing with these diseases will likely "bankrupt" the nation.[75]

Another insanity concerns our use of fossil fuels. Since it is the exhaust from jet fuel that is one of the chief sources of the carbon dioxide poisoning Earth's atmosphere and contributing to global warming, does it not defy reason and practical wisdom to ship by air strawberries from California to Connecticut or kiwis from southern Florida to New York or grapes from Chile to Boston so that we can satisfy our craving for such fruit in the wintertime?

Now let's consider our romance with the automobile. How can it be considered anything but a totally irrational feature of our life style given the serious damage it causes that element of the natural world upon which our very lives depend—Earth's atmosphere. How's this for an example? When she was a child and teenager living in southern California in the forties, my wife could ride the trolley from Pasadena to Los Angeles in less than an hour. I have read that today LA commuters spend seventy (70!) days per year stuck in traffic.

In *The Long Emergency*, James Howard Kunstler describes the creation of the suburban sprawl and the massive destruction of public transportation systems that followed World War II as "sleepwalking into the future."[76] Neurotically allergic to the planning practiced by the "socialist" countries of Europe, we have been seduced into allowing those who focus on the bottom line to plan for us—those who made fortunes providing the cars, the rubber for their tires, the gasoline to power them, and the lumber for the homes built at increasing distances from the city center where most of the home buyers worked. The trolley tracks have long ago gone to the junkyard and our national infatuation with the automobile has seeped into our genes. It is true that Kunstler's prediction that Americans would face a major crisis around 2020 when readily available and relatively cheap oil would begin to disappear has been rendered passé by the discovery of massive oil and gas deposits in North Dakota and in the Arctic. But that means that as a

---

75. Kenner, *Food, Inc.*
76. Kunstler, *Long Emergency*, 1.

nation we are still committed to employing any technology that promises to provide relatively cheap energy from fossil fuels, no matter the cost in human health and damage to the environment. Fracking is the latest example.

Another sign of our societal sickness and the insanities to which it gives rise is the fact that every aspect of our national life of greed and waste gets counted as positive worth, i.e., as a contribution to the Gross Domestic Product (GDP). Thus when Peabody Coal destroys an entire mountain in West Virginia or Kentucky, filling neighboring streams with bulldozed trees and sludge, all the effort in both the destruction *and the cleanup* counts as a contribution to GDP.

A wonderfully acerbic but highly accurate assessment of this procedure is the following observation by David Korten:

> In taking the GDP as the measure of economic performance, economists are assuming that the faster resources flow through the economic system to become toxic waste, the wealthier we are. We could get much the same result simply by managing the economy to maximize the rate of growth of our garbage dumps."[77]

Socialist societies are not always paragons of sweetness and light, but it is impossible to account for America's history of military adventurism, invasions of nations with which the country is not legally at war, and oftentimes ruthless occupations apart from the distinctly capitalist spirit of the American brand of imperialism that emerged early in the life of the country.

It is no exaggeration to claim that many millions of lives have been the bounty forfeited by the peoples of the Global South to the Yankee obsession with control and domination—and lust for wealth, especially that of Latin America. For a heartrending revelation of the price Chile, Brazil, Argentina and other South American countries have had to pay for their location on the map, i.e., in the same hemisphere as the United States, few resources are superior to Eduardo Galeano's *Open Veins of Latin America*:

> Latin America is the region of open veins. Everything, from the discovery until our times, has been transmuted into European— or later United States—capital and, as such has accumulated in distant centers of power. Everything: the soil, its fruits and its mineral-rich depths, the people and their capacity to work and to consume, natural resources and human resources.[78]

77. Korten, *Agenda for a New Economy*, 104.
78. Galeano, *Open Veins*, 2.

It's pure speculation, of course, but I'm inclined to believe that had the US populace been mature and educated enough to place committed socialists in key positions of government during the past hundred or so years, they would not have permitted the development of our depressing history of militarism and violence. In general, socialists advocate nonviolent resolutions of conflicts; many have been pacifists. And had we been the "Christian nation" that many Fundamentalists like to claim we are, almost certainly it would have been Jesus, the Prince of Peace, rather than the Crusaders who would have served as our model for conflict resolution.

MORE! MORE! MORE! VERSUS SUSTAINABILITY

> A few hundred cars with good roads may be a great blessing. Yet when the number increases into the millions and hundreds of millions, the automobile is capable of destroying the higher forms of life on the entire planet. So with all human processes: undisciplined expansion and self-inflation lead only to destruction. Apart from the well-being of earth, no subordinate life system can survive. So it is with economics and politics: any particular activity must find its place within the larger pattern, or it will die and perhaps bring down the larger life system itself. This change of scale is one of the most significant aspects in the change of consciousness that is needed.
>
> —THOMAS BERRY, *THE DREAM OF THE EARTH*

It has long been a little-examined article of faith in America that growth is always desirable. "Grow the Economy!" has been a kind of mantra repeated by one administration after another. But as the ancient Hebrew writers and a number of contemporary Americans, e.g., the Quaker economist Kenneth Boulding and the economist Herman Daly, have argued, growth is not always a good thing. Often it is a positive evil, as it is in our case today. Our ever-growing economy, consuming increasingly scarce natural resources and producing greenhouse gases and toxic wastes contaminating Earth's atmosphere and ecosystems at alarming rates, is obviously not sustainable. Our economy and Earth's environment are on a collision course. Scores of scientists and thinkers from various disciplines, including, the Intergovernmental Agency On Climate Change, Bill McKibben, author of *The End of Nature* and *Deep Economy: The Wealth of Communities* and organizer of the 350.org campaign, James Hansen, formerly of NASA, and Naomi Klein in *This Changes Everything: Capitalism vs. the Climate*, have warned of the disastrous consequences of making growth the guiding principle of our economy.

In writing about the precarious state of Earth's health, James Speth, once dean of Yale's School of Forestry, quotes Hansen: "Our home planet is now dangerously near a 'tipping point.' Human greenhouse gases are near a level such that important climate changes may proceed mostly under the climate system's own momentum."[79] In short, very soon the destructive elements causing global warming will operate on their own irrespective of any corrective measures humankind may undertake.

> This warming has brought us to the precipice of a great "tipping point." If we go over the edge, it will be a transition to a "different planet," an environment far outside the range that has been experienced by humanity. There will be no return within the lifetime of any generation that can be imagined, and the trip will exterminate a large fraction of the species on the planet[80]

An additional sign of insanity in our capitalist way of life is the enormous amount spent by the corporations, $100 billion annually at last count, to propagandize ("brainwash" is the more accurate word) American consumers, persuading them to buy their products, many harmful to the citizens' health. As many Americans in various regions have discovered, it is not only the people of certain areas of Louisiana who suffer the consequences of the indifference and neglect of chemical and pharmaceutical corporate executives; we all swim in a "chemical soup," and lung cancer, breast cancer and other forms of that dread disease cannot be understood apart from the toxic chemicals we encounter every day of our lives no matter where we live. In a sane society, where the happiness and well-being of citizens always took priority over profits or the monetary compensation of corporate executives, individual citizens would not have to worry about which corporation was poisoning their air or their water.

The evidence that our capitalist economic system is dysfunctional, corrupt and corrupting, is revealed in every aspect of American society. If further evidence is needed to persuade skeptics, let this tidbit suffice. Millions of our citizens have been struggling to avoid foreclosures on their homes, to keep their children clothed and fed, and to hold on to their faith in America as a nation that still stands for justice and some semblance of equity in the distribution of wealth. Yet, in 2009 one CEO, David Tepper of Appaloosa Management, "earned" $4 billion. As Jim Hightower observes, no one *earns*

---

79. Hansen, quoted in Speth, *Bridge at the Edge of the World*, 27.
80. Ibid.

such an outrageous sum—roughly two million dollars per hour. "He might have grabbed, snatched, looted, absconded with and otherwise hauled off $4 billion—but no one can 'earn' that much, for earning implies a reward commensurate with some achievement."[81]

THE SOCIETY WE HAVE AND THE SOCIETY WE MIGHT WANT

Under capitalism we are deprived of the power to decide whether we want to produce more hospitals or more breakfast cereals.

—TERRY EAGLETON

The fundamental question Christians and Jews ought to ask themselves is this: In what kind of society do I want to raise my children and my grand-children? What are the major features of a society that lends itself to the creation of relatively whole, relatively healthy individuals? What are the principal values of such a society? For Christians and Jews the answers should be obvious, and it puzzles me that we so infrequently ask those questions. Is that because we take for granted the answers? Do we just assume that, because we have been taught from early childhood to love and admire its way of life and its (putative) values, the United States as we know it is the best society we can hope for or imagine? If that is true, we need, I believe, to reexamine our assumptions and to activate our imaginations. We need, as earlier noted, what David Korten calls "a new story."

Some years ago a group of thinkers produced a remarkable book entitled *Habits of the Heart*. Usually referred to as the "Bellah volume," after Robert Bellah, one of the six scholars who produced it, this study and a follow-up volume entitled *The Good Society*, provide a detailed analysis of where contemporary American society finds itself and what is required if America is to lay claim to being a truly *good* society. What follows here is taken largely from Gary Dorrien's *Soul in Society: The Making and Renewal of Social Christianity*.

From the beginning the Bellah group makes plain its understanding of how far America has strayed from its originating vision: "We have committed what for the republican founders of our nation was the cardinal sin: we have put our own good, as individuals, as groups, as a nation, ahead of

---

81. Hightower, *Hightower Lowdown*, May 2010, 3.

the common good."[82] (In theory, this statement might seem correct; a more accurate perspective is probably reflected in a comment of John Jay, the first chief justice of the Supreme Court: "Those who own the country ought to govern the country.")

These scholars are unequivocal in their belief that "if America is to build a future society worth living in . . . it will have to build upon the long-held social Christian vision of a *cooperative commonwealth*."[83] The Bellah group advances a vision of "economic democracy" that resonates with the thoughts of all those whose ideas we have already examined.

Here is Dorrien's summary: Economic democracy "would not sacrifice communities for economic growth."[84] Contrast that vision with the Wal-Mart phenomenon of mega-stores located on the outskirts of small towns draining trade from the Main Street economy of family-owned pharmacies, grocery stores, restaurants, and clothing establishments, thereby undermining the community that locally-owned businesses sustain.

A point that I have stressed throughout this chapter is made with stinging poignancy as Dorrien continues his summary of the Bellah group's argument. The modern capitalist addiction to "infinite accumulation" is utterly contrary to fundamental Christian teachings. "The prevailing American preoccupation with piling up money and material possessions is spiritually deadening." Dorrien concludes this part of the argument with words that, I believe, ought to hang on the walls of every church in America: "The readiness to defend ill-begotten privileges with force is immoral. The prevailing view of nature as a commodity to be conquered and exploited degrades the sacredness of creation."[85]

Dorrien describes the impact of *Habits of the Heart* with these words: "The book's portrait of an increasingly rootless and narcissistic middle class was widely heralded as a telling critique of the loss of genuine community in American life." He also notes its (almost exclusive) focus on professional, white and middle class citizens and comments on the book's general neglect of the feminist movement. In addition, Dorrien highlights two of the Bellah Group's important conclusions: first, that "many Americans no longer take moral instruction from character-shaping communities of any kind"; and second, that "American churches increasingly cater to the emotional needs

---

82. Dorrien, *Soul in Society*, 341.

83. Ibid., 342, emphasis added.

84. Ibid.

85. Ibid., 375.

of anxious, lonely, or stressed-out achievers, offering to provide communities of undemanding care for religious consumers."[86]

At a time when enormous wealth in the hands of a few threatens to create in America an all-powerful oligarchy, the warnings of the Bellah group are especially apposite: "Republican theory from Aristotle to the American founders has assumed that a free society can survive only if there is a 'rough equality of condition, that extremes of wealth and poverty are incompatible with a republic.'"[87]

Habits of the Heart sounded a warning more than thirty years ago. Much has changed in America since then, little of it likely to support reasons for contemplating the next thirty years with anything but apprehension (though elsewhere in this volume I comment on hopeful signs of a social and even spiritual awakening). It would be an exaggeration to claim that the ruthless, rapacious brand of capitalism that spreads its tentacles into every crevice of our national life is the sole source of our societal ills, but it would be foolhardy to deny its power as almost certainly *the* primary cause of our national soul-sickness.

On all sides there are voices calling attention to the fact that our society is in crisis, and the grotesque inequities in wealth distribution in America and the corruption of the political system resulting from corporate America's ability to use its billions to set the agenda in almost every area of our national life should make obvious the need for an alternative economic system.

Noam Chomsky describes the corruption wrought upon our society by unbridled capitalism as graphically as anyone I know. In a 2013 interview published in the *Progressive* he said:

> You can't call our system a democracy. It's a plutocracy, or what Jim Hightower calls a "radical kleptocracy." In the United States, the bottom 70 percent of the population in income level essentially has no influence on policy. They're disenfranchised, so it doesn't matter what they think. Political leaders don't pay any attention. You go up the scale, you get more influence. You get to the really top, the top tenth of 1 percent, they're basically designing the policies, so they get what they want.[88]

But would a socialist system cure all our social and political ills? Of course not. But the adoption of several major socialist principles could go a long way toward the creation of a sane society, and if not the ideal "good society," at least a society far better than the one we now have. Think of the

86. Ibid., 339.
87. Ibid., 341.
88. Barsamian, "Interview: Noam Chomsky," 37.

difference it would make if we eliminated money from politics or adopted a universal health care system. The Affordable Health Care Act is a good first step toward that goal but it is rife with needless complexities and concessions to insurance companies.

Let me be more specific regarding my own commitments. When I am asked why I am a socialist, I reply that I am a socialist because capitalism is destroying both my country and my home, the Earth. Because I believe Pope Francis speaks the truth when he comments on the destructive power of "the new idolatry of money." Because I think Robert F. Kennedy Jr. also speaks the undeniable truth when he claims that "we are now in a free fall toward old-fashioned oligarchy: noxious, thieving and tyrannical."[89]

When others ask what is my understanding of socialism, I answer that socialism is a system of ideas and practice that puts people before profits. In a socialist society serious efforts are made to discourage massive accumulations of wealth and limits are placed on the salary of every citizen, no matter what position she or he may hold. Under a democratic socialist ordering of politics and economy no one goes to bed hungry or is forced to sleep on the streets. Socialism encourages the development, from an early age, of instincts, values and habits that make for a peaceful, harmonious and sustainable society—compassion, especially for the less powerful citizens, a passion for justice, an abiding concern for the common good, and a willingness to sacrifice, when the occasion calls for it, one's own individual desires for the community's well-being.

I would add that, as noted above, those who adhere to a socialist vision of human society have almost always opposed wars and many, like Albert Einstein, have been pacifists. Among their heroes and models have been Leo Tolstoy, Albert Schweitzer, Gandhi, Dr. Martin Luther King Jr., Nelson Mandela and, of course, for Christians, Jesus. They denounce again and again the sickening futility of war. Without exception, they proclaim the brotherhood and sisterhood of all human beings, and they work for a global community of nations bound together by commitment to the principles of justice, peace and sustainability. This, at any rate, is my conception of socialism. The conception of socialism held by Karl Marx was a bit less idealistic.

In *Why Marx Was Right*, Terry Eagleton describes the reality of life under socialism as Marx understood it: "For Marx, socialism is the point where we begin collectively to determine our own destinies. It is democracy taken with full seriousness, rather than democracy as (for the most part) a political charade."[90] But Marx, Eagleton repeatedly stresses, was not, surely,

---

89. Quoted in McChesney, *Dollarocracy*, 6.
90. Eagleton, *Why Marx Was Right*, 76.

a "cockeyed optimist." Eagleton's point here is that Marx never envisioned a future society completely devoid of conflict. While "the free flourishing of individuals is the whole aim of his politics," it is well to remember that Marx understood that "individuals must find some way of flourishing in common."[91]

It is important to note Eagleton's gloss on this issue in Marx's thought: there "will always be conflicts between my fulfillment and yours or between what is required of me as a citizen and what I badly want to do."[92] Such contradictions, Eagleton stresses, are inescapable aspects of the tragedy that defines human existence and can never be resolved this side of the grave.

The cardinal issue here is that, contrary to the popular view, Marx had few illusions about human nature, and socialism as he envisioned it does not depend on super-virtuous individuals. Eagleton puts the argument this way: reaching Marx's goal of a more just, more humane society does not require that everyone be morally magnificent all the time.

> Socialism is not a society that requires resplendent virtue of its citizens. It does not mean that we have to be wrapped around each other all the time in some great orgy of togetherness. This is because the mechanisms which would allow Marx's goal to be approached would actually be built into social institutions. They would not rely in the first place on the goodwill of the individual. Take, for example, the idea of the self-governing cooperative, which Marx seems to have regarded as the key productive unit of the socialist future. One person's contribution to such an outfit allows for some kind of self-realization; but it also contributes to the well-being of the others, and this simply by virtue of the way the place is set up. I do not have to have tender thoughts about my fellow workers, or whip myself into an altruistic frenzy every two hours. My own self-realization helps to enhance theirs simply because of the cooperative, profit-sharing, egalitarian, commonly governed nature of the unit. It is a structural affair, not a question of personal virtue.[93]

Some will say, all that sounds very nice but isn't it hopelessly utopian? What strikes me as utopian is the belief that the human family can survive, even to the middle of this century, practicing the kind of ruthless capitalism the United States has long practiced and which has now taken root at the far corners of the Earth. For five thousand years we've tried that way of

91. Ibid., 86–87.
92. Ibid., 87.
93. Ibid., 88.

organizing our collective life, of which our savage American capitalism is the contemporary apotheosis: exploitation, oppression, domination. Maybe it's time we tried another way. Norway, Finland and Sweden haven't created the kingdom of God, but with mixed economies and reasonable limits placed on salaries, and universal health care and educational opportunities, they have eliminated the worst of the alienating and dehumanizing features of unbridled capitalism.

Now a word for the Christians among those reading this essay. If we heed the words of the authors of the Torah, of the prophets, of Jesus, of Walter Rauschenbauch, the Bellah Group, and Pope Francis, we will not be hard-pressed to decide what kind of economic system we are expected to favor. Being realistic, however, we have to acknowledge the unlikely prospect of a majority of Americans voting for anything like the "economy of grace" that Jesus urges upon his followers or that the early Christians practiced, as recounted in the Acts of the Apostles. Of course, one doesn't vote for such communities; individuals *form* them and they survive only so long as the individual members have faith that they are worth the effort. And it must be admitted that the experience of a number of such communities established in the United States in the nineteenth century, none of which survived very successfully or for very long, does not provide great hope for the success of such communities in the future.

But what kind of alternative economic system might American voters support? Several years ago, even with the widespread dislocations and heartaches afflicting so many of our citizens, I would have said that few Americans would find even a modified version of Scandinavian socialism acceptable. Times have changed, however. In late 2013, an avowed socialist college teacher, Ksama Sawant, won a citywide race for a seat on the Seattle city council and made national headlines. Her opponent was not a wild-eyed Republican but a veteran Democrat. And Sawant, whose campaign called for raising the minimum wage to $15.00 per hour, believes her surprise victory augers well for other socialist candidates. Polling suggests that she is correct. As John Nichols wrote in "Socialist in Seattle,"

> In a 2012 Gallup poll, 39 percent of Americans said they had a positive impression of socialism. Among Americans under thirty, the numbers go higher: 49 percent [are] favorable toward socialism in a 2011 Pew survey versus a 46 percent favorable figure for capitalism. For African-Americans, a majority claimed to "have a positive view of socialism."[94]

94. Nichols, "Socialist in Seattle," 14.

Responding to Boeing's threat to leave Seattle if the city voted for a $15 minimum wage, Sawant came back with a genuine socialist answer: "The only response we can have if Boeing executives do not agree to keep the plant here is for the machinists to say, 'The machines are here. The workers are here. We will do the job. We don't need the executives. The executives don't do the work; the machinists do.'"[95]

What, then, are the prospects for even a quasi-socialist socioeconomic society emerging in the United States? Skeptic that I tend to be, until very recently I would have said, "Not very promising." But Ms. Sawant is making me a believer when she reports that from all over the land people are contacting her, some saying, "Wow, I didn't know this could happen in the United States." Also, despite the major swing toward the Republican Party in the midterm elections of 2014, in state after state ballot measures supporting progressive policies such as raising the minimum wage won by impressive margins. (See my discussion in chapter 5 of the "irrationality" of the voters and the failure of the Democratic Party to offer a coherent alternative.)

If the overwhelming power derived from the billions of dollars for ad campaigns given to candidates by the multinational corporations, the chamber of commerce and the multibillionaires like the Koch brothers could somehow be neutralized and the truth about the real sources of the people's suffering could be told, then perhaps a mixed economy, with limits on wealth accumulation and the elimination of dog-eat-dog competition, might stand a chance.

Despite the figures cited earlier concerning positive attitudes toward socialism, I am wary of predictions about election outcomes in areas involving such a vast change as the move from a capitalist economy to even a modified socialist economy. We have become a pampered, self-indulgent breed, we comfortably-fixed, *middle-class* North Americans. But the middle class is shrinking and there are many millions of the desperately poor who, rather than being pampered, are largely ignored and forgotten. Hence I have to ask, have we lost, as Bellah and his colleagues argue, that ready willingness to sacrifice personal preferences for the common good that is, finally, a *sine qua non* of a healthy democratic society? Is it reasonable to believe that a majority of Americans might choose to give up the perquisites, damaging as many of them are to the individual and to the society at large, that our current capitalist system promises?

What would probably be required for such a major shift in economic structures to occur would be a lengthy period of education when citizens could examine alternatives and compare likely outcomes. Many skeptics

95. Ibid., 15.

would have to be convinced that an economy not driven by vigorous, even destructive competition could be productive and sustainable. As explained earlier by Terry Eagleton, in a socialist society it is the structures built into the economic system itself that allow for friendly competition among workers in an overall atmosphere of cooperation.

There *are* examples of such cooperative ventures from which Americans might learn, one of the chief of which is the Mondragon worker/consumer cooperative located in the Basque province of Spain, whose growth since its founding in the 1950s has been extraordinary.

> The essentials of the Mondragon story are simple. What arose in 1956 as a handful of workers in a disused factory, using hand tools and sheet metal to make oil-fired heating and cooking stoves is today a massive conglomerate of some 260 manufacturing, retail, financial, agricultural, civil engineering and support co-operatives and associated entities, with jobs for 83,800 workers, and annual sales in excess of $US 20 billion.[96]

Despite its size, Mondragon is a worker-owned enterprise, with workers making decisions about every aspect of the business. The benefits that flow from this kind of cooperative venture range from job-security to protection from the financial crises that cause so much anxiety to workers in enterprises organized according to capitalist practices. During the recent recession, in a country where national unemployment exceeded 25 percent and was 53 percent for its young people, Mondragon held unemployment to less than half the national average. Moreover, "co-operatives experiencing reduced demand are able to transfer members to one where it is increasing, without detriment to their rights or entitlements. And supplementary capital can be accessed from centrally held inter-co-operative solidarity funds."[97]

An important feature of the Mondragon cooperative venture is the idea of "labor-entrepreneurs," that is, members "who will receive community support for establishing and running *new enterprises*." Such direct initiative makes possible an enhanced sense of one's role in creating a truly democratic community of workers.[98]

At Mondragon, the total design of the enterprise contributes to the well being of the worker. For instance, "members can agree to forfeit or postpone entitlements such as one or more of their fourteen per annum pay packets

96. Matthews, "The Mondragon Model," 2.

97. Ibid., 3.

98. Krimerman, "Education-Shaper," 7.

or the payment of interest on their individual capital accounts, or in extreme circumstances authorize individual capital accounts draw-downs."[99]

Mikel Lezamiz, director of cooperative dissemination, sums up the spirit and practice of Mondragon: "Our purpose is to create wealth and jobs in society. Work with dignity. This is the goal."[100]

In America it is often taken as a sign of wavering patriotism not to sound hopeful, even after examining in detail a multiplicity of signs that make a hopeful outcome doubtful. My wife used to claim that I was a congenital pessimist, which may be true. But a certain kind of pessimism can be useful if it does not lead to a sense of futility and to ennui but instead to a serious assessment of dangers and of realistic prospects for positive change.

OUR BISHOP IN ROME

Of all the reasons for belief in positive change in the near future, I consider the election of Cardinal Jorge Mario Bergoglio as Pope Francis the most significant. He will not produce miracles; he won't raise the dead. And as head of a large, worldwide community of Christians, with a huge bureaucracy and centuries of theological and ethical teachings that he alone cannot alter, he does not possess unlimited power. But he has already demonstrated by the force of his warm, outgoing personal charm and the passion of his speech as he calls for compassion and justice for both the world's poorest inhabitants and for the Earth, that *he* is the miracle for which many millions have long waited.

Several things are clear about this new pope. First, as both his encyclical letter *Laudato Si'* and his earlier pronouncements make unmistakable, Pope Francis is not what we have come to expect from the Vatican. Francis is a radical. Spokespersons for the Vatican and some US journalists have attempted to blunt suggestions that Francis condemns capitalism with the fervor of the most dedicated Marxist. For example, John Allen Jr., writing in the *Boston Globe*, claimed that "he's not Che Guevara in a cassock." That is surely true. He does not call for violent overthrow of governments. But a careful reading of his writings leads to one ineluctable conclusion: Francis *is* a revolutionary.

Growing up in Buenos Aires, Francis could not help but observe the gross disparities that separated the wealthy few from the impoverished masses. As a priest he lived amongst slum-dwellers and thus came to know intimately the suffering to which their poverty condemned them. In the

99. Matthews, "Mondragon Model," 2.
100. Ibid.

seventies and eighties, moreover, he was influenced by the theological currents that flowed from Vatican II, signaling a major turn in Catholic thought that highlighted recognition of how much the practice of Catholic Christianity had veered away from Jesus' unambiguous rejection of an economy based on pitiless exploitation of those without political, financial or institutional power. Recognizing that too often the Church in the modern era had neglected Earth's destitute masses, the Catholic Church announced as a corrective a "preferential option for the poor." As a result, there began to emerge in the Global South but especially in Latin America a clear call for a recovery of the prophetic message of the gospels. What resulted from this intellectual and spiritual ferment came to be known as "liberation theology."

At the center of liberation theology is the conviction that preaching a message of *spiritual* redemption divorced from a deep concern for the conditions of life of those to whom the message is directed is a blatant betrayal of both the Hebrew prophets and Jesus.

In short, this new but really ancient interpretation of the gospel message is this: following Jesus, the church must struggle for liberation of the *whole* self—from hunger, from political oppression, from ignorance, and from fear of the future.

One of the earliest and most influential exponents of liberation theology was the Peruvian priest Gustavo Gutierrez. Soon after his election, Francis invited Gutierrez to visit the Vatican, and the influence of this theological radical representing the underside of history is everywhere present in the Pope's reiteration of a passionate concern for Earth's exploited and ignored masses.

In *The Power of the Poor in History*, Gutierrez declares that "salvation is a continuing process of liberation" and emphasizes the centrality of the struggle for justice in the ongoing achievement of a society where individuals "shall not build for others to live in or plant for others to eat (Isaiah 65:22)," a society, in other words, where "everyone profits from their own labor." On this point, Gutierrez is unequivocal: "To work for a just world where there is no servitude, oppression, or alienation is to work for the advent of the Messiah."[101]

Gutierrez can be wonderfully blunt when writing about the need in Latin America, and by implication, elsewhere, for Christians to adopt a view of the gospel message that leads to "a process of human emancipation," to a totally new way of being human. And that emancipation requires "a memory of the Christ who is present in every starving, thirsting, imprisoned, or

---

101. Gutierrez, *Power of the Poor*, 32.

humiliated human being."[102] It also requires a rewriting of history, since in the past history was written by and for members of the ruling class, with the poor and disenfranchised almost always excluded:

> *Rereading* history means *remaking* history. It means repairing it from the bottom up. And so it will be a subversive history. History must be turned upside down from the bottom, not from the top. What is criminal is not to be *subversive*, struggling against the capitalist system but to continue being "*super*versive"—bolstering and supporting the prevailing domination. It is in this subversive history that we can have a new faith experience, a new spirituality—a new proclamation of the gospel.[103]

Some American journalists have been more enthusiastic about the Pontiff's radical views regarding both the climate crisis and the scandalous conditions of life of Earth's billions of poverty-stricken and hungry humans than was John Allen Jr. Among them is Wen Stephenson who wrote in the *Nation*:

> It should be no surprise that Francis, the first Latin American pope and the first from the Global South, where the Catholic Church's center of gravity now lies, is the climate-justice pope, squarely on the side of the poor and the developing world—a region in which the concept of climate justice, far from being some marginal left-wing cause, is the mainstream majority view. In the encyclical, Francis frames the unfolding climate catastrophe as a fundamental issue of human rights and social justice for the global poor—as well as today's young people and future generations everywhere.[104]

In addition to Gutiérrez, another Latin American theologian whom Stephenson cites as a major influence on Francis is the Brazilian, Leonardo Boff. The author of *Cry of the Earth, Cry of the Poor*, Boff was probably responsible for Francis's decision to yoke the suffering of Earth's environment with the suffering of the world's poor. Boff begins his book with a biting condemnation of the capitalist mentality that "devastates the Earth and plunders its wealth, showing no solidarity with the rest of humanity and future generations." This is the same logic as that which "exploits classes and subjects people to the interests of a few rich and powerful countries."

102. Ibid., 21.
103. Ibid.
104. Quoted in Stephenson, "Climate-Justice Pope," 15.

Boff has no doubts about Francis's commitment to a subversive reading of history. Francis, he asserts, has "lived liberation theology."[105]

I need only add that as a socialist with Christian roots, I consider Francis one of the great inspirational figures of our era. Among his truly astonishing accomplishments has been an awakening of a largely latent spirituality not only among Catholics or among Christians of any stripe, but also among many millions who claim no allegiance to Jesus but recognize the spiritual power of a fellow human whose authenticity shines forth like a beacon for a floundering ship on a dark and stormy sea.

No less remarkable is Francis's skill in anchoring the call for a spiritual revival in a resounding critique of our "throw-away culture." In the recent encyclical he argues for "changes of lifestyles, production and consumption," criticizes any society that promotes "insatiable and irresponsible growth," and calls for a redefining of our idea of progress. He makes absolutely clear his rejection of "a magical conception of the market," that is, the notion held by many that somehow and in contrast to common sense and all available evidence, the market knows what's best for all of society. Always and everywhere in the encyclical, the man I call "our bishop in Rome," enthusiastic lover of humankind and of the Earth that he is, keeps his eye firmly on the common good.[106]

Vatican gatekeepers and American commentators may do their best to immunize Pope Francis from the taint of Marxism, but only the willfully blind will fail to see that in all but name, he is a rousing socialist.

But no matter how passionate an advocate for the ethical teachings of the prophets and Jesus a pope or any other church leader may be, nor how obviously "socialist" Francis's economic teachings are, the global overhaul that the world's economic system requires for a livable future depends on the efforts of committed individuals across the planet. And it's critical for success to emphasize that socialism comes in many flavors and as a system for organizing economic life is infinitely adaptable. What works in Nicaragua may not, without a good deal of pruning, work in Seattle.

Yet Christian socialism isn't radically different from other forms of socialism. The words of Jesus or Jeremiah, not those of Marx, may supply the initial catalyst for a believer to accept a socialist politics, but almost certainly his or her ultimate goal will be a more just, humane, and equitable way of providing goods and services than is found in the typical capitalist system, certainly the contemporary multinational capitalist system. And as with the Jewish, or Muslim, or Buddhist or secular socialist, he or she will

105. Ibid.
106. Pope Francis, *Laudato Si'*, sections 23, 193, 190.

bring to their commitment peculiar desires and peeves. But I suspect that at bottom they will be like Kshama Sawant, a socialist who has twice won a seat on the Seattle city council. They will reflect the "fed-up" feelings of millions at home and abroad.

John Nichols begins a *Progressive* interview with Sawant by calling attention to evidence of socialist or militantly progressive forces catching fire on both sides of the Atlantic: "Jeremy Corbyn [an avowed Marxist] has won the leadership of the British Labour Party, Syriza [the radical leftist Greek party] won again in Greece, Podemos is rising in Spain, Ireland is seeing mass protests, we have all sorts of radical politics developing in Latin America and South Africa, Bernie Sanders is shaking up the presidential race."[107] What's going on? Nichols inquires.

With this opening, the interview evolves as a discussion of "a mood of resistance" to economic policies and politics that have in the recent past led to recessions, massive accumulations of wealth by a tiny minority of citizens in country after country, and brutal imposition of austerity policies causing grievous suffering for vast numbers of people from Athens to Johannesburg. And social media have permitted protesters in Australia to communicate with protestors in Europe and North America. Nichols provides the details: "We're seeing people in different places recognize and support the struggles of others. People in Seattle are cheering on Jeremy Corbyn. People in Ireland are cheering on Kshama Sawant."[108]

What we are witnessing may indeed be a global movement, an insurgency of multitudes who will no longer remain silent as they are screwed by a tiny elite fraction of the seven-plus billion inhabitants of the planet. What appears to be happening is like a large family that's been scattered for generations, with many of its members living through horrific exploitation, losses and grief, with no common language, all suddenly finding a long-forgotten language that allows them to communicate and offer support and nurture to one another.

Sawant puts the case thus: "We are connected internationally. . . . Truly, national boundaries obscure the real connections. We have deeper connections with working people in Ireland and South Africa than we do with the elites in the United States."[109] Sawant emphasizes the critical place of organizing and developing tactics and strategy with an eye toward electoral success in her vision for a socialist future in America. As she scans the national scene and notes labor unions, fast food workers, environmentalists,

107. Nichols, "Mood of Resistance," 37.
108. Ibid.
109. Ibid.

graduate students and sundry others protesting in the streets—often with good results such as the $15 per hour wage hike in Seattle and elsewhere in the country—she is encouraged.

An alum of the Occupy movement, Sawant is a savvy political actor and is likely to play a major role in the development of a *national* and perhaps enduring campaign for a far more progressive America than the one we've inherited. There is even an outside chance that a socialist—Bernie Sanders—might become America's president.

This, however, is probably too much to hope for. But it is certainly true that at the present moment, *Christian* socialists have no reason to feel like odd balls. We are part of a global gang of intelligent, dedicated, and aroused individuals working for a cause about which we can be proud. The odds against our success are great. But we work alongside fellow humans who are great. Millions are discovering the joy of participation in this genuinely communal effort and that in itself is a boon of no small consequence.

So let us put our shoulders to the wheel and keep in the back of our minds the vision of an Earth made whole, where justice flows like water, where each of Earth's inhabitants lives with dignity. Let us be realists with visions. Let us give thanks for Jesus, and Isaiah, and Karl Marx, and Saint Francis, and Pope Francis. And let us dedicate ourselves to the worldwide struggle for the creation of a cooperative commonwealth where music and poetry resound from every hilltop and on city streets voices sing out the joyful anthems of Woody Guthrie and Pete Seager.

CHAPTER 4

A LETTER TO MY GRANDCHILDREN

February, 2015

Dear Ben, Hazel, Grace, Sam and Dakota—

The purpose of this letter is to ask your forgiveness—for myself, for my generation, and for the generation of your parents. I ask it because by our greed, our wastefulness, our carelessness and our indifference, we are destroying your inheritance, our beautiful but extraordinarily fragile home, the Earth.

This home, as you know, came to us through billions of years of evolution. It has gone through many stages of destruction and renewal, producing more and more evidence of its inexhaustible creativity. It is not only great poets and gifted painters who have turned repeatedly to the luxuriant beauty of the natural world for inspiration but also millions of folk like us.

Think of the Japanese cherry trees in bloom in Washington in April and the hundreds of flowering shrubs in Carroll Gardens in Brooklyn in May; or the lovely dogwoods in Oregon and redbuds in Virginia or the desert flowers of Arizona. If you can really visualize those dazzling specimens of Earth's fecundity and capacity for creating almost endless varieties of remarkably distinctive species, then you arrive, I believe, at only one conclusion: as a species we humans are blessed to have been given the gift of a home as glorious as the one we have received.

But let us listen to one of the greatest of the poets, William Wordsworth, who, in a poem written more than two hundred years ago, tells of his own response to Earth's beauty:

> I wandered lonely as a Cloud
> That floats on high o'er Vales and Hills,
> When all at once I saw a crowd,

A host of dancing Daffodils;
Along the lake, beneath the trees,
Ten thousand dancing in the breeze.

The waves beside them danced, but they
Outdid the sparkling waves in glee:—
A Poet could not but be gay
In such a laughing company:
I gaz'd—and gaz'd—but little thought
What wealth the shew to me had brought:

For oft when on my couch I lie
In vacant or in pensive mood
They flash upon the inward eye
Which is the bliss of solitude,

And then my heart with pleasure fills,
And dances with the Daffodils.[1]

A more recent poet, e.e. cummings, celebrated the gifts of the natural world in language very different from that of Wordsworth. Here is one of his most famous poems:

I thank You God for most this amazing
day: for the leaping greenly spirits of trees
and a blue true dream of sky; and for everything
which is natural which is infinite which is yes

(I who have died am alive again today,
and this is the sun's birthday; this is the birth
day of life and of love and wings: and of the gay
great happening illimitably earth)

how should tasting touching hearing seeing
breathing any—lifted from the no
of all nothing—human merely being
doubt unimaginable You?

(now the ears of my ears awake and
now the eyes of my eyes are opened)[2]

---

1. Wordsworth, from *Selected Poems*.
2. Cummings, *Selected Poems*.

I know that none of you believes in the supernatural, intervening God of traditional religion; neither do I. But I *do* believe that there is a spiritual force in the universe that in some way makes our lives—all life, in fact—possible and that prevents the universe and the Earth from flying apart into trillions of bits and pieces. Some scholars have suggested that this force also works to draw us humans to each other, in other words, that our desire for love and bonding has its parallel in the "glue" that holds the sun and its planets, the Milky Way and all the other galaxies in their fixed orbits.

And in our day it seems clear that, despite melting glaciers and rising seas, despite grasslands turning into deserts, despite the increase in the intensity of tornados and hurricanes, and despite record-breaking temperatures, there is a genuine hope around the globe for a more just, more peaceful and more sustainable earth community. If we concentrate only on the excessive heat of past summers or on the disappearance of thousands of species of plants and animals each year, it is very easy to despair. Some reputable scientists tell us that if we continue to pollute the atmosphere with carbon dioxide and other greenhouses gases as we have been doing for the past two hundred years, the earth will be virtually uninhabitable by the year 2100. So only the very foolish or the very insensitive can avoid being profoundly anxious.

Yet there are good reasons *not* to despair. One of the greatest of these is *your* generation. I have read lately of students, some still in elementary school, who are organizing to fight against climate change. Perhaps in your schools there are such organizations. If you go online you will surely learn more about what seems to be a national movement. In an article entitled "Youth Organize for Planetary Survival," I have read about high school and college students who are doing serious work to enlist other young people in a campaign to bring about meaningful changes in our national way of life and in our national policies to create a more sustainable planet for all Earth's creatures.

It is clear to me that we are at a critical turning point in the life of our species and of our planet home. For centuries we humans have treated that planet as if it were an inexhaustible source of everything we desired for our comfort and our pleasure—minerals, coal, oil, timber, land and water. And we in North America have been especially reckless in squandering those resources. Sadly, we have been equally reckless in contaminating our rivers and lakes, our ecosystems, and our atmosphere, though our country has surely not been alone in such careless treatment of our habitat. But now we seem to be awaking to the realization that there are limits to the abuse that Earth can sustain. Maybe, before it's too late, we can change our habits.

Perhaps you do not know that your Grandmother and I were fairly early advocates warning our fellow citizens about the dangers that climate change portended. In 2002 we organized a symposium on the ecological crisis and did so again three years later. At the latter event a featured speaker was Bill McKibben, who was just beginning to be recognized as one of the foremost spokespersons of an emerging national campaign, which later morphed into 350.org, to slow down, if not halt, the destruction of our planet home due to contamination of Earth's atmosphere and ecosystems.

Now, in 2015, I urge you all to join this fight, to do whatever you can—in your schools and wherever else you meet with friends and others in your age groups—to educate, to challenge, to demand genuine changes in political policies and in the practices of the gas, oil and coal industries to radically reduce emissions of greenhouse gases and to effect a transition to a green economy.

As children, you may think you have no power to bring about changes in a world where adults make all the important decisions. I think that is wrong. It is not my intention to place on you an impossible burden, but I do believe that all of you except Dakota, who is too young to fully understand the crisis we face, can do *something*. So put your keen minds to the task. My guess is that as you explore possibilities, you'll discover or create fruitful courses of action about which you had not previously dreamed. And you'll find the adventure exhilarating.

The spirit of the Earth, I'm sure, will thank you!

Before I close, I want to quote another poet, your Grandmother, Ann Hutt Browning, who surely loved the natural world as much as any of the great poets writing in the English language. Here is a little poem she wrote after the family's year in Macedonia in the late 1970s.

Journey to Treskavic

When I stumbled on the searing rock
Stones skittered under my shoes,
And there between my hands and knees,
I found a touch of color.
On the scrabbled sheep path
That was the hard way up to the monastery,
An autumn crocus pushed, purple and gold,
A petalled star rising from dust.

Skirting its leaflessness
I hurried along to catch the others.
What I know is that it came to be
A part of me and rises now,
Balm, like honey.[3]

---

3. Browning, *Deep Landscape Turning*.

Your Grandmother, I feel certain, would have fervently joined me in asking your forgiveness and in urging you to take part in the campaign to protect and maintain your inheritance—for your children and their children unto the seventh generation.

With much love and admiration,

Granddaddy

CHAPTER 5

STRUGGLING FOR THE SOUL
OF AMERICA

Civilized man chokes his soul.

—John Muir

PART I

THE REEDUCATION OF A SICK SOCIETY

One of the saddest features of this depressing tale is that in a country whose earliest European colonists were motivated by a religious faith whose scriptures teach that "love of money is the root of all evil," (I Timothy, 6:10) almost every aspect of our national life today has been corrupted by money. After armaments and security systems, hypocrisy is America's number one export.

America is sick. It is a society plagued by a plethora of illnesses that infect the very soul of the nation. The signs are everywhere—blatant, glaring, shouting for attention—but we have been so preoccupied with congratulating ourselves for our superiority to all other nations on Earth that we've hardly paused to notice. Each year three hundred thousand children, mostly African Americans and Latinos, go through the juvenile justice system. Every two minutes, an American woman is sexually assaulted. On reservations in the Dakotas and elsewhere in the West, thousands of elderly Native Americans survive through bitter winters forced to choose between medications and wood to heat their homes. Nicholas Kristof asserts, "More Americans have died from guns in the United States since 1968 than on battlefields of all the wars in American history."[1] We should hide our faces in shame.

Once again I quote Martin Sheen whose voice, perhaps more than any other, describes with utter precision the nature of our national sickness:

> This supposed idyllic society we have is the most confused, warped, addicted society in the history of the world. We are addicted to power, we are addicted to our image of ourselves, to violence, to divorce, abortion, and sex. Any whim of human character is deeded in us 100-fold. We are number one in child abuse, pornography. . . .[2]

We as a society have lost our way. Until very recently, we have appeared unable to do more than quarrel with each other or to wring our hands in despair, or to take up weapons and slaughter the innocents, as did Adam Lanza at Sandy Hook School in Newtown, Connecticut.

Following that massacre, many theories—some quite plausible—have been put forward attempting to explain why we suffer an epidemic of mass shootings. But generally absent from the discussion that followed Newtown and the many subsequent shootings has been the one truly vital question: What is *really* wrong with America? Sheen's words provide us many clues, most of them symptomatic. But what are the root causes? Who has examined the nation's soul deeply enough to give us light and guidance that might lead toward a more healthy psychological and spiritual condition? There are a number of scholars, public intellectuals, religious gurus and assorted others who might assist us in this challenging task but I have in mind principally four. The first is E. M. Adams, whose critique of capitalist ideology I touched on in chapter 1.

Because "the values of our culture are inverted," Adams wrote, "the modern western mind is deranged."[3] If we could look objectively at contemporary American life, in fact, with eyes not clouded by the propaganda our commercial culture spews at us from infancy to the grave, many would agree that human fulfillment and happiness do not come by way of accumulation of wealth and the things wealth can buy. However, at the heart of the so-called "American Dream" resides an image of success as precisely such accumulation.

Thus Adams concluded that the "virtues" required to succeed in our economic and military systems are "morally corrupting." It is here, I think,

---

1. Kristof, "Lessons from the Virginia Shooting," A23.

2. Sheen, interview by Kupfer, 38.

3. Adams, *Society Fit for Human Beings*, xvii.

that Adams approaches the crux of the matter, for at this point he identifies the critical damage wrought upon the human being whose self-image has been molded by capitalist ideology. We humans violate our basic nature, he implies, when we spend our lives clawing our way to the top, in the process leaving behind a battlefield strewn with the psyches, if not the bodies, of those we have cheated, deceived or exploited. According to Adams, allowing the economic dimension to achieve its current dominance in virtually every aspect of our social life has resulted in "a profound human identity crisis [which] undercuts the humanistic dimension of the culture."[4] Hence, Adams maintained, our society is not one truly fit for human beings.

A healthy society, a genuinely sane society, would recognize that its principal capital lies not in its skyscrapers, or its oil deposits or its grain elevators or its battleships—as important as some of these may be—but in its people. And thus it would strive day after day, week after week, month after month, and year after year to create citizens who are intellectually, morally and spiritually mature, responsible, self-directed, and compassionate. Instead, what we find in America today, Adams declares, are masses of "spiritually impoverished and morally dysfunctional people."[5]

If Adams' assessment is correct, "deranged" does not seem too harsh a word to describe our country's condition. Claiming that our civilization seems destined to self-destruct, Adams proposed a corrective:

> a radical transformation of our culture and social order by shifting our priorities from materialistic to humanistic values (those indigenous in the moral, civic, artistic, religious enterprises) . . . and by replacing capitalism as we know it with a *humanistic economy.*[6]

In order to achieve a culture in which our youth would be enabled to grow into citizens worthy of the freedom and responsibilities a democratic society promises and requires, Adams points to education as the indisputable *sine qua* non.

But not just any old education. As a philosophy professor for more than four decades, Adams watched American higher education move through various stages and emphases, quitting the nineteenth-century ideal of liberal education for what increasingly became training for a particular vocation. History, foreign languages, English and American literature, philosophy, religious studies, the visual arts and music increasingly were

---

4. Ibid.
5. Ibid., 99.
6. Ibid., xviii, emphasis added.

pushed aside in favor of more "practical" subjects, the chief of which in many universities has become business. I have read that at Harvard, for example, the Business School is awash in cash; and increasingly at colleges and universities across the country, students enrolled in business courses far outnumber those studying one of the humanities. But students are not dumb and realize that in this economy a major in English literature or the history of medieval painting is not likely to yield a career that will allow them to pay off the substantial debt most will accrue while at a university or college.

To address seriously the pathologies that corrupt the American body politic, Adams says only a "cultural revolution" will suffice. Philosophers, humanities scholars and critics, and students of society should work together concerning how our society can heal itself:

> But the healing is something the society must do itself, for healing can come only from within. A deranged culture and a disordered society, if left to blind historical forces, are likely to grow worse. Like the damaged self, a pathological society needs probing self-examination and reeducation.[7]

In practical, empirical terms, what does this society that Adams claims is unfit for human beings look like? Exactly like the society described by Sheen—wracked by addictions. On every side—whether it's addiction to prescription drugs or alcohol, to violent films and video games, to the pursuit of wealth, to celebrity adulation, to cocaine and other hard drugs (now an epidemic in many states, including my own, Massachusetts and neighboring New Hampshire), to what amounts to worship of America as a supreme depository of selflessness and high moral principles, and to mindless consumption and reckless squandering of limited resources on a finite planet—it seems indisputable that in this "land of the free" untold numbers of our citizens are bound.

Our second source of illumination, Erich Fromm, whose writings I commented on in earlier essays, places great stress on alienation when discussing American pathologies. Capitalism, Fromm emphasizes, works overtime to inculcate attitudes and habits that block our natural, healthy predisposition to cooperate, to share, to experience joy in community and communal ventures. To be truly "with-it" in an advanced capitalist country such as America today, one is constantly reminded, oftentimes in subtle ways, always to look out for Number One and to turn a blind eye to the damage such egotistical pursuit of success may do to one's competitors or

7. Ibid., 19.

to the common good. Apparently having been convinced by the Reagan era slogan that "greed is good," US bank officials involved in the corrupt practices that brought on the Great Recession illustrate in detail the havoc caused by individuals who seem totally oblivious to the suffering their obsessive accumulation of wealth causes millions of their fellow citizens. From Fromm's perspective, such nabobs of the capitalist marketplace are quintessential representatives of the "having mode," individuals who appear *alienated* from their fellow humans, from the natural world, and, finally, from their own deeper selves. In this context, it is worth noting that, according to the *Harper's* "Index" for April 2013, chief executive officers of corporations rank number one among "occupations likely to attract psychopaths."[8]

"Alienation" is a term that Fromm and other contemporary leftist intellectuals have borrowed from Karl Marx, who believed that it was one of the key social and psychological pathologies bred by capitalism. Robert L. Heilbroner provides a useful summary of one aspect of Marx's meaning when writing about alienation:

> Human existence loses its unity and wholeness before the division of class domination. . . . The working person becomes separated from the product of his own labor. His work, once the very expression and incorporation of his genetic being, now confronts him as a thing apart, indeed as a thing that commands him as property. Marx calls this subordination of the worker to the "reified" product of his labor, confronting him as an alien thing, *alienation.*[9]

In other words, in a capitalist economy, the product, the commodity created by a worker, is not his or hers but something that stands over against the worker, in a system in which they have no say in how the creation of their hands or brains is used or sold and, if the product is sold, little or no say in what portion of the sale price is returned to the maker.

In *The Sane Society*, Fromm discusses alienation from several perspectives. He includes the situation of vast millions who are the victims of the corrupt practices of Wall Street brokers, bankers, and hedge fund managers. Fromm considered alienation to be a general condition of life in contemporary capitalist societies, reflecting the impotence of the average citizen to have control over the forces that govern the conditions of his or her existence. Most citizens of the United States, Fromm contends, while believing they experience the "freedom" of a liberal democracy, are, in fact, for the most part guided in their choices by a fear of being thought odd or by the

8. Harper's Index, 15.

9. Heilbroner, *Marxism: For and Against*, 72.

persuasive forces of the advertising industry. If he were writing today, he would no doubt add talk radio hosts and Fox News.

Fromm's books were published decades ago and it is unarguable that the rebellious youth culture of the sixties changed American life in a multiplicity of ways that appear to be permanent. For instance, the pressure to conform to the image of a "well-adjusted" corporate executive, indistinguishable from his fellows, has been significantly altered. Yet the obsession among America's youth to own the latest version of iPads and smart-phones bespeaks a kind of group mentality just as damaging to authentic being (or self-awareness) as was the need to be lost in the "lonely crowd" that characterized an earlier generation of middle-class Americans.

For a depressing picture of alienation from the perspective of those at the farthest extreme from multimillionaire denizens of Wall Street, one need only get a glimpse of young African American students in a classroom in Chicago or Los Angeles or Detroit, who know in their bones that their chances of escaping the generational cycles of poverty and near-illiteracy their parents have experienced are probably hardly better than one in a hundred. Utterly disaffected and apathetic, these youths understand just how truly impotent they are and may turn to selling drugs as the sole means of achieving a semblance of status and personal worth on the streets where many have existed since early adolescence.[10]

In our national mythology, capitalism is celebrated as the giver of all good things. And indeed capitalism *has* provided much to celebrate: life-saving medicines, worldwide communications, air travel to distant places, freedom from backbreaking work for millions on every continent, and, after centuries of starvation affecting many hundreds of millions, a satisfying and generally healthful diet for most of the planet's inhabitants. (This is a qualified success, however, in light of the two billion of Earth's inhabitants who live on two dollars per day—or significantly less—around eight hundred thousand of whom go to bed hungry.)[11]

But Fromm believed that the price paid for these evidences of capitalism's success was way too high and the psychological damage too costly. In 1976 he wrote about Americans as an unhappy breed: "lonely, anxious, depressed, destructive, dependent."[12]

A recent discussion (autumn 2015) on the PBS "News Hour" focusing on college students seeking help for psychological problems revealed that a

---

10. Unemployment among African American youth is 50 percent, as reported by Jacobson, "Bernie Sanders Says."

11. UN Resources for Speakers on Global Issues, "Vital Statistics."

12. Fromm, *To Have or to Be*, xvii.

good percentage of these students mention anxiety as a major cause of their emotional distress.

Much has changed in the twenty-five plus years since Fromm's words were penned that might cause some observers to challenge his critique of American society as excessively pessimistic, although many more might declare that our condition has only worsened. It may be relevant to note that in *The World Happiness Report 2013* conducted by the UN Sustainable Development Solutions Network, the United States ranks seventeenth, well behind a social democracy like Finland, which ranks seventh, where "socialist" education policies and universal health care produce an extremely well-educated and healthy population.[13]

In 2000, Yale University Press released a book entitled *The Loss of Happiness in Market Democracies,* by R.E. Lane. Years of research led Lane to conclude that, contrary to conventional wisdom, in societies where capitalist theory and practice reigned, people were generally less happy than in societies where a more communal and cooperative spirit was dominant:

> Amidst the satisfaction people feel with their material progress, there is a spirit of unhappiness and depression haunting advanced market democracies throughout the world, a spirit that mocks the idea that markets maximize wellbeing and the eighteenth-century promise of a right to the pursuit of happiness under benign governments of people's own choosing. The haunting spirit is manifold: a postwar decline in the United States of people who report themselves as happy, a rising tide in all advanced societies of clinical depression and dysphoria (especially among the young), increasing distrust of each other and political and other institutions, declining belief that the lot of the average man is getting better . . . a tragic erosion of family solidarity and community integration together with an apparent decline in warm, intimate relations among friends.[14]

The views of both Adams and Fromm, now substantiated by those of Lane, tell us that societies where *possessing,* not *being,* is the normative value do not lead to a satisfying, fulfilled life. The being mode of existence focuses upon the inner self, but not in an egoistic or narcissistic way. Quite the opposite. Here is Fromm's description of what's involved in this way of life:

> [This] mode of being has as its prerequisites independence, freedom, and the presence of critical reason. Its fundamental characteristic is that of being active, not in the sense of outward

13. Helliwell, *World Happiness Report,* 22.

14. Lane, *Loss of Happiness,* 3.

activity, but of inner activity, the productive use of our inner powers. To be active means to give expression to one's faculties, talents, to the wealth of human gifts with which . . . every human being is endowed. It means to renew oneself, to grow, to flow out, to love, to transcend the prison of one's isolated ego, to be interested, to "list," to give. . . .[15]

Fromm claims that most of us cling to the *things* of this world for a sense of security, albeit one that always betrays us. As a significant number of our fellow citizens have discovered in recent decades, no collection of baubles, bangles and beads serves to still that gnawing feeling deep in our souls that we are incomplete and were made for more than a horde of insensate objects. Fromm's words call to mind one of Jesus' best-known sayings: "What does it profit a man to gain the whole world and lose his soul?"

Fromm's thought directs us back to Adams' conclusions regarding the antidote to the "deranged" mind of modern capitalist societies—a truly "humanistic economy." To bring the "being mode" into prominence, a cultural impulse for the humanities must be nurtured. Teachers around the country, in fact, *are* discovering the potential of reaching disaffected students by way of the humanities, whether through reading and composing poetry and fiction, listening to Mozart or Schumann, or studying the works of Plato and the classical Greek philosophers and dramatists.

For this project, the work of social critic and journalist Earl Shorris might serve as a helpful guide. His creation of the Clemente Course in Humanities, a one-year program of study for students from impoverished inner-city neighborhoods, provides an alternative to the vulgarity and triviality of American popular culture—to which we are all subjected the moment we begin to understand the English language and which American education has, for the most part, failed to successfully counter. This course has proven remarkably successful across the nation. Determined to attack an environment of poverty, crime, hunger, unemployment, and addiction, Shorris took a chance that denizens of dehumanizing locales in US cities were capable of reading Plato and studying "moral philosophy, art history, literature, history, critical thinking, and writing."[16]

Shorris's gamble paid off. In a posthumously published book *The Art of Freedom: Teaching the Humanities to the Poor*, Shorris brought together a collection of pieces by students who had completed the course. These personal testimonies confirmed that a major aim of the project, to stimulate in the students a sense of personal agency and a belief in their freedom to

15. Fromm, *To Have or to Be*, 76.
16. Shorris, *Art of Freedom*, 7.

participate in a democratic society where their belonging was not in question, had been realized. To my mind, this experiment certainly suggests that Adams's proposal for a "cultural revolution," emanating from a total overhaul of American education based in humanistic studies, is not so utterly fanciful as it might at first seem.

Attempted on a grand scale, however, this would be a daunting task, especially because the organization of the contemporary American university "discourage[s] critical thought." Theologian John B. Cobb Jr. argues that the average US university is little concerned with integrated learning, because scholars pursue knowledge indigenous to their own discipline with scant understanding of, or interest in, other disciplines.[17]

American universities, in fact, display slight concern to provide their students an education that can be described as holistic. Cross-disciplinary dialogue is seldom encouraged. Most students leave their university with, at best, a smattering of facts and ideas from several disciplines but no coherent "philosophy" or worldview. It is the lucky university student today who is allowed to put together her own research project, as Cobb was able to do at the University of Chicago Divinity School in the Hutchins era.

In addition, scholars normally pursue research in a manner that is supposedly unbiased. Most universities, in fact, tout the proposition that this quest for knowledge is not swayed by the values—moral, religious, aesthetic, or monetary—of the researchers. Cobb claims that this assumption is delusional. Most major universities, in fact, depend heavily on funding from corporations or the military, and a great deal of research is conducted with nary a thought about the possible consequences for society of the knowledge that research produces. It would be a rare occasion indeed if an American university refused grants from the Pentagon in order to make a statement opposing the immense waste of taxpayer funds by the military-industrial complex or to register opposition to America's propensity to engage in warfare with the regularity of the swallows returning to Capistrano.

As the Earth slides precariously toward chaos and possible collapse, Cobb challenges our universities to eschew their ostensibly value-free orientations and commit themselves to an education that aims to create citizens with broad interests and minds and hearts nurtured by deep immersion in the liberal arts, citizens who will use their educations for the greater good of Earth's inhabitants.

Cobb concludes his article with an unequivocal assessment of how the failure of US universities impacts not only the nation, but the world:

17. Cobb, "Anti-Intellectualism," 218.

The structure and assumptions of the university have a great effect on those who study and work there. The university understands itself to be entrusted with the task of producing experts, and the experts it produces generally see the world in the way the university has socialized them to see it. Overall, they contribute more to leading the world into catastrophes than to steering it away.[18]

Many Americans, I suspect, would agree that our country requires a serious program of reeducation and a good number would probably find Cobb's challenges to contemporary university faculty and administrators persuasive. In *Voltaire's Bastards: The Dictatorship of Reason in the West*, John Ralston Saul's critique of US higher education correlates neatly with John Cobb's thoughts on this subject. In contemporary society with its massive proliferation of specializations in every field of knowledge, the specialist becomes the "expert," a kind of custodian of knowledge in his or her field, able to communicate only with others who specialize in the same field.

Possession of expertise in a narrowly defined area of knowledge thus becomes the possessor's major source of identity and self-worth. To guard his turf, the specialist discovered "that he could easily defend his territory by the simple development of a specialized language incomprehensible to nonexperts." The consequences of this phenomenon have been disastrous, Saul emphasizes, "because the new specialized terminology amounts to a serious attack on language as a tool of common understanding."[19]

This tendency, Saul claims, has been especially pernicious in the institutions where one would expect to find the most vigorous efforts directed toward maintaining language as the crucial tool for communication of contemporary ideas, moral and ethical principles derived from the human past, and the wisdom found in ancient sacred texts and ancient and modern literary works—that is, the universities. In our universities those aspects of language that are essential for communication of knowledge extraneous to what Saul calls the specialist's "box," clarity and simplicity, have been sacrificed for the jargon of the experts. What the average student and the rest of society need most—memory and common sense—often go down the tubes in favor of the rhetoric of post-structuralism and arcane French theory. "The purpose of language," Saul writes, "is communication. A great civilization is one in which there is a rich breadth and ease of communication. When

18. Ibid.
19. Saul, *Voltaire's Bastards*, 475.

language begins to prevent communication, that civilization has entered into serious degeneration."[20]

Saul hits the nail squarely on the head when he accuses those responsible for passing on a holistic understanding of humankind's intellectual and cultural riches, the professoriate, of being the very individuals who have capitulated to the contemporary obsession with specialization. "They have turned their universities into temples of expertise, pandering to modern society's weakness for exclusivity. . . . They now devote themselves to the prevention of integrated thought."[21]

(I want to stress, however, that I do not consider all teaching of theory as misguided. It is surely appropriate to introduce students, at both the graduate and the undergraduate levels, to what the world's great thinkers are saying about any number of important issues. One of these, for example, is how the human self is largely constructed by language.

Other possibilities are an examination of the success of language in communicating deep feelings or how psychoanalytic theory can be used to interpret the behavior of fictional characters such as the principal figures in a book such as Dostoevsky's *The Brothers Karamazov* or Edith Wharton's *House of Mirth*. What I object to is allowing the passion for theory to become so dominant that it crowds out the study of literature as literature.)

I do not consider Saul's critique of our universities to be exaggerated. I watched this process unfold during almost thirty-five years in the classroom. I signed on to teach literature, to discuss texts from a variety of cultures and historical periods, and to model for my students as best I could the critical thinking that is the precious heritage of any university graduate who wishes to be considered "educated." In the mid- and late sixties I taught courses with titles such as Metaphysical Rebellion and Studies in Existentialist Literature in which my students and I discussed such works as the Book of Job, *Prometheus Bound*, Marlowe's *Doctor Faustus*, *Moby Dick*, *The Brothers Karamazov* and Camus's *The Stranger*, as well as texts by Kierkegaard and Nietzsche. Some of the most talented students I encountered during my teaching career were in those classes, and from student reports, both written and verbal, I had reason to believe that these courses were generally considered both challenging and intellectually rewarding. The English Department of the University of Illinois at Chicago, where I was a junior faculty member, permitted me to teach these courses under the "Humanities" rubric.

20. Ibid.
21. Ibid.

By the mid-seventies, this commuter university, whose charter speci-fied a particular mandate to serve the needs of the city and its young adults, many of whom were children of recent immigrants and the first-generation in their families to seek post-secondary-school education, began more and more to look like other American universities. Faculty members became, as Saul suggests, "specialists"; one was a Victorian scholar or a Renaissance scholar, an expert in Shakespeare or Milton. Since I had written a book on a twentieth-century American fiction writer, Flannery O'Connor, I eventually found myself teaching almost exclusively the fiction of that period. (It is important to note, however, that in many academic fields, be it subatomic physics or American literature, it's nearly impossible *not* to specialize be-cause the proliferation of knowledge today is so vast that keeping abreast of others' work in one's field is normally a full-time job.)

I am not complaining: I loved teaching Hemingway and Fitzgerald, Edith Wharton, Flannery O'Connor and Eudora Welty, William Faulkner and Zora Neale Hurston, as well as later writers like E. L. Doctorow, Saul Bellow, Toni Morrison, and Louise Erdrich. My point is simply that "hu-manities" courses had disappeared. Russian writers belonged to the Slavic Languages and Literature Department and Camus to the Romance Lan-guages and Literature Department. Also, very quickly, research, not teach-ing, became the major focus of the faculty.

Soon enough the university began to resemble a corporation. Admin-istrators, with whopping salaries, seemed almost as numerous on campus as teaching faculty and increasingly directed their attention to monetary concerns. Provosts, deans and department chairs quickly realized that a convenient means of saving money was to lure senior faculty—oftentimes some of the institutions' finest teachers—into early retirement and replace them with part-time instructors at much lower salaries. This distortion of the university's historical role in society amounts to a kind of capitulation to the capitalist imperative to maximize output at the lowest possible cost, making it difficult to see how a genuine renewal of American higher educa-tion can be accomplished.

Unless we can recover an earlier American tradition of educating our youth in humanistic studies, thereby instilling the values that Fromm asso-ciates with the "being mode," we are destined to remain trapped in a moral and spiritual swamp where thousands die annually—literally from gun violence—and many more from the psychological and spiritual deadening of poverty and hopelessness. (It is important to acknowledge that in earlier generations such humanistic education was available only to offspring of families of means. And female students were normally excluded beyond high school.)

I am increasingly convinced that the reeducation Adams and Cobb call for, presumably with adolescents and young adults, starts way too late. To be truly effective, it should begin at age three, earlier where possible. A sane society, I believe, would invest massively in pre-k education, stressing language development, poetry, music and the arts. It would seek above all else to stimulate children's imaginations; it would teach very little by rote but would encourage students to pursue individual interests using games based on geography, principles of arithmetic, and language. It would teach the values of cooperation and sharing by allowing children to participate and cooperate as individuals who will one day become citizens, not only of this nation, but also of the world.

At a Montessori school in Chicago in the sixties and seventies, I watched each of my four children learn math and geography at astonishingly early ages—three, four and five—subjects I didn't learn until the second or third grades. They delighted in the school routine and returned home each day with minds filled with ideas and "projects" that called on their experiences at school. Always their learning was infused with the more or less relaxed and unstructured atmosphere of the classroom. The highly trained teachers were, of course, critical to the success of the program. But they served primarily to answer questions, to make suggestions, and, when necessary, to adjudicate disagreements. In that atmosphere, my children, at a very tender age, were learning to be self-directed, responsible individuals, capable of independent thought.

Because it was a private school, sustained by parents with incomes sufficient to cover tuition costs, classes could be held to a reasonable limit. I believe no class ever held more than twenty pupils, and in each classroom there were both a teacher and an assistant. Hence no child wanting assistance was left dangling for long.

And because most of the parents were educated middle-class professionals, there was no difficulty in rounding up volunteers to assist in any number of projects in and out of the classrooms. There was no need, in short, for a formal PTA. Ancona School struck me as an ideal educational venture which I wish could be replicated thousands of times across the nation. Since the parents of a large majority of America's children could never afford the fees needed to maintain such a system, the only way it might be established would obviously be through government funding.

Although I was involved in education for most of my adult life and had the lucky opportunity to observe how beneficial a Montessori educational experience was for my children, it is only lately that I have begun seriously to reflect upon and read about early childhood education. My study has led to several conclusions. First, that the primary aim in educating children under the age of seven ought to be to nurture the child's curiosity, spontaneity, self-reliance, daring, eagerness to explore, sense of the adventure that life ought to be, and capacity to suffer disappointment without withdrawing from risk-taking. The entire purpose of early childhood education, in short, should be to foster and thereby liberate the child's innate creativity.

Without proper outlets for that creativity, most children will respond in one of two ways: they will either clam up, repressing the intellectual and emotional energy that longs for channels of creative self-expression; or they will explode. I suspect that in many inner city American schools, a significant percentage of children, forced to sit quietly and be drilled in subjects foreign to their experiences at home, initially choose the first method of coping. As they grow older, say, in middle school or early high school, unless they have encountered a very dedicated and talented teacher who finds the time to offer individual encouragement or have been introduced to an activity that invites a creative response—playing an instrument in a band or painting portraits of fellow students, for example—they tune out. And soon thereafter explode.

The explosion can take many forms: joining gangs, selling dope, going to prison or, for the girls, teen pregnancy. But one thing seems certain: the United States will never solve its problem of failing students and failing schools so long as it refuses to give up practices that work against the natural inclinations and innate drives of young humans. That repressed energy has to go somewhere, and if it cannot be used creatively in school, then dropping out is a rational choice.

In *Teacher*, Sylvia Ashton-Warner writes about discovering by trial and error the most productive means of teaching young children in a New Zealand school where both Maori (the native New Zealanders) and white pupils were among her charges. One technique she found effective was pairing students, that is, asking two students to take turns reading to each other. The listening child was asked to "correct" the reader, assisting him or her in a friendly, supportive manner, thereby learning the importance of cooperative effort.

Ashton-Warner again and again comments on the explosive energy of the Maori children and writes about her efforts to maintain a degree of order in her classroom without putting her foot on the throats of her charges, the method recommended—figuratively, of course—by one of her (male) colleagues. Describing the energy of the Maori students, she writes:

> It's . . . like a volcano in continuous eruption. To stand on it . . .
> with both feet and teach it in quiet orthodoxy would be a matter

of murders and madness and spiritual deaths, while to teach it
without standing on it is an utter impossibility.[22]

This supremely creative teacher describes her classroom methods: she
stands back and allows the pupils to teach themselves. One example of her
"style," as she calls it, is tapping into the pupils' imaginations by asking them
to keep a "book" in which they write each day and then regularly read their
compositions aloud to the entire class. Such practices are appropriate and
possible, of course, only in a class of limited number. But in the United
States, where we cram twenty or twenty-five or thirty children into a classroom, even the most talented and adventurous teachers are hard pressed
to do more than maintain order. In a more sane society, officials would do
the calculus and discover that building more schools and mandating much
smaller class sizes would be less expensive than building more prisons.

Which brings me to the mania for testing in our schools. It is, in my
judgment, criminal to test children before the age of seven. Children who
come from homes where there are few or no books or magazines and little
or no conversation about art or poetry or current events cannot be expected
to absorb facts and figures that in no way relate to their deepest urges and
imaginings—and their experiences beyond the classroom. Math and science and formal language instruction can come later, *after* a multiplicity of
opportunities for the child to direct her or his stored creative energy into
paths that lead to productions that truly express the child's own imaginative
promptings—paintings, sculptures, poems, plays, stories, dances, games,
etc. In the process, much learning of reading, writing and arithmetic will
take place. But no tests are likely to exist or to be designed in the future that
measure what a child has learned from painting a portrait or writing a story.

After third grade, testing may make sense; but the results ought not to
be used to bludgeon principals and teachers. Far too many dedicated, hard-
working teachers have been moved around or fired and too many schools
closed by officials avid for high scores but blind to the realities of life for
children from impoverished neighborhoods where cultural opportunities
are severely limited and home life is often chaotic, if not violent. It is very
difficult for young spirits to blossom in environments where families are
frequently fractured, streets are unsafe, and role models are scarce. As has
often been pointed out, it is simply irrational to expect our schools to per-
form functions that rightly belong to the family and to the community.

I turn now to a book that has radically changed my thinking about this
country and its soul, Paul Gilk's *Nature's Unruly Mob: Farming and the Crisis*

22. Ashton-Warner, *Teacher*, 103.

in Rural Culture. Gilk's central thesis is that once humans moved into cities and began exploiting rural culture for both sustenance and profit, something essential for human health was lost. Traditional communities everywhere have used the land to produce enough food to sustain the life of the village and thus have retained a close relationship to and profound respect for the Earth. But in the past two centuries, the increasing centrality in Western countries of science and technology harnessed to producing surpluses of all sorts from the Earth with a correlative loss of vibrant rural communities has robbed the human soul of elements vital to its healthy functioning. Here is Gilk's take on our precarious situation:

> Civilization, lured by a fantasy of immortality and crazed by the mirage of progress, slips further and further from its evolutionary and historical roots. The roots of civilization—broad-scale, decentralized rural culture and folk community—have been pulled out of the ground by modern industrial civilization and beaten into commodity-intensive obedience. Our great contradiction is precisely that social stability and ecological coherence must be based on just such rootedness as civilization, especially industrial civilization, has sought to exterminate. In working for cultural renewal and the reconstruction of the countryside, we must be aware that *we are struggling directly against* the primary thrust of industrial civilization.[23]

A major virtue of Gilk's analysis of the societal sickness explored throughout these essays, which I have generally associated with capitalism, is that it takes us beyond the hegemony of capitalism itself in America and increasingly across the globe to the very genesis of urban life millennia ago. In Gilk's view, it is industrial civilization spawned by cities that has become the enemy of healthy human existence. He continues his critique of "civilization":

> Science and statistical economics may find ways to keep international capitalism grinding along; but it will grind on only at the price of environmental degradation and social desiccation. The political wreckage of society and the economic devastation of Earth must eventually stop. Earth and human nature cannot sustain such prolonged degradation, such intense disgrace. Most seriously, we are faced with the deployment of real weapons whose use would kill all of us and leave Earth a charred, radioactive, and burnt-out planet. . . . The more dependent we become on the technocratic system, the more we are captivated

23. Gilk, *Nature's Unruly Mob*, 4–5.

by its promises and allurements, the more it replaces common culture, the more difficult it is to change in a truly positive manner and the more likely the system's breakdown will result in unparalleled destruction, carnage, and chaos.[24]

Here it should be emphasized that Gilk is not advocating that all city dwellers flee their urban habitats and learn to farm the land. What he does want us to understand is that humans were once able to thrive in self-sustaining environments nurtured by a common culture shared by all of the inhabitants of a particular locale. And that the industrial capitalism that has made possible the megacities dotting the globe has at the same time left humans bereft of those traditions, rituals and habits that provide coherence, focus, and a purpose to the human venture on Earth.

In practical terms, Gilk advocates smaller cities, a much slower pace of life and a conscious effort to curb the embedded propensity of those of us living in cultures of affluence to consume madly. We must, he insists, recognize the imperative *to dramatically reduce our consumption.* He is certainly not naïve about how difficult that will be for most of us. He is simply telling us the obvious truth: either we learn to live much more simply and consume a great deal less or we destroy our habitat.

What I find most impressive about Gilk's thought is its capacity to examine with startling clarity and precision the essentially *spiritual* dimensions of the crisis industrial civilization has brought us to while employing almost none of the religious jargon that analysis of this turning point in human history might evoke in a less subtle thinker. What follows makes that point brilliantly:

> At present, as our sophisticated technology produces a bewildering array of commodities at an increasing pace—a pace that can be continually hastened via the broader application of robotics—the affluent people of the world are incited by "scientific advertising" to quicken the rate of commodity consumption, with little regard for environmental degradation or human oppression. Consumers are to race after cleverly packaged commodities to the "scientific" cheerleading of the advertising "industry," a degraded commercial excitation that saturates human consciousness with images of voyeuristic titillation, seduction that ministers to "the spiritual side of the trade." Greed and gluttony hide beneath the cloak of progress and prosperity. This proves that "progress," as the civilized substitute for heaven, is a concept, construct, and doctrine larded with deformed values

24. Ibid.

antithetical to the cultural enfleshment of the kingdom of God, whose core values are sharing and conservation. The practitioners of "advertising psychology" have brazenly manipulated what we might call the collective unconscious of the past and drained it of cultural vitality. This sets the stage for politicians who are packaged as electoral commodities by those with money and the most Machiavellian public relations. As folk memory is lost and as hypnotic consumerism becomes normative, the brand-name corporation, sports team, and military strike force provide the locus of loyalty and excitement.[25]

To those who might protest that such restraint and self-sacrifice as these reflections seem to demand would probably be beyond the capacity of most Americans, certainly the middle class and the wealthiest among us, Gilk suggests that a genuine paring down of collections of stuff might lead to untold benefits, among them enhancement of "spiritual alertness and cultural vitality."[26]

Paul Gilk's meditations on the root causes of the maladies that inflict pain on our country's soul shed much light on the sources of the derangement of the Western mind about which Professor Adams wrote. As Gilk notes, in a society totally dominated by the drives of industrialized commercialization, everything may be seen as just one more commodity to exploit for profit. The Harvard sociologist Michael J. Sandel offers an interesting gloss on this subject in the opening sentences of his book *What Money Can't Buy*: "There are some things money can't buy, but these days, not many. Today almost everything is up for sale." Sandel then lists fifteen options, including "a prison cell upgrade" ($82 per night), and the "right to immigrate to the United States," going for $500,000.[27]

Of course, sex in one form or another is always for sale. One of its forms is pornography, a thriving business involving cameras, directors and actors. In *Empire of Illusion*, Chris Hedges devotes a chapter to the ten-billion-a-year porn industry. Almost by definition, I think, pornography, through its "public" portrayal of loveless and often brutal sexual encounters, not only degrades what, at its most elevated expression, should be an intimate exchange of affection and caring, it also involves a dehumanizing exploitation of the female actors, the "porn queens." And it reflects, Hedges suggests, a depraved mythology involving the violent use of force to satisfy diseased desires. Hedges ends the chapter on pornography with a stinging

---

25. Ibid, 158.
26. Ibid, 159.
27. Sandel, *What Money Can't Buy*, 3.

assessment of the depth of the sickness that afflicts our country in the twenty-first century.

> Women, porn asserts, whether they know it or not, are objects. They are whores. These whores deserve to be dominated and abused. And once men have their way with them, they are to be discarded. Porn glorifies the cruelty and domination of sexual exploitation in the same way popular culture . . . glorifies the domination and cruelty of war. . . . It is the belief that "because I have the ability to use force and control to make others do as I please, I have a right to use force and control." It is the disease of corporate and imperial power. It extinguishes the sacred and the human to worship power, control, force, and pain. It replaces empathy, Eros, and compassion with the illusion that we are gods. Porn is the glittering façade, like the casinos and resorts in Las Vegas, like the rest of the fantasy that is America, of a culture seduced by death.[28]

Hedges's indictment of pornography points to a critical linkage between the degrading treatment of the female actors in pornographic films and a general indifference to the suffering caused by such things as the warehousing of a couple of million of our citizens in prisons and the undeviating US support for Israel's assaults on Gaza, no matter how many civilians are killed. Such indifference is indicative of our society's loss of its capacity for empathy. Porn, Hedges declares, "reflects the endemic cruelty of our society."[29]

This loss is surely one result of a massive failure of imagination among our citizenry. Studying Sophocles and Shakespeare by itself will not save us, but I do not know of a better way for students to learn the invaluable lesson about "walking in another's shoes."

At another level of psychic learning and healing, Wyatt Mason's essay "You Are Not Alone Across Time: Using Sophocles to Treat PTSD" describes the powerful therapeutic effects of staged readings of Greek tragedy at military bases around the country. The director of these readings, Bryan Doerries, explains how tragedy works on the mind and soul of those suffering from loss or catastrophe. "I think tragedy is a delivery system that awakens us to the possibility of meaningful change." This is the "catharsis" mentioned in the Introduction, a "purification of one's emotions," as Mason describes it, "through vicarious experience, through drama designed to beat the drums of feeling, so that we might suffer openly, commonly, communally." Tragedy,

28. Hedges, *Empire of Illusion*, 87.

29. Ibid.

in other words, permits a kind of magical release of festering feelings of terror, hurt or sorrow—"the release of seized emotion—by giving suffering a form." In a society where so many report feelings of hurt because of betrayal of promises, or loss of loved ones due to drug overdoses or the destruction of homes and the death of friends and neighbors due to tornadoes or wild fires, experiencing that release of stored pain and sorrow can provide relief of suffering and understanding of how one's own suffering is related to the universal suffering that is an inescapable feature of human existence.[30]

Educating our youth and especially those likely to assume positions of leadership in education, government and business in humanistic studies cannot automatically guarantee that the United States will become a more sane, more humane, and less violent society. Yet there are many reasons to believe that it might help. However it is done, it is obvious that a complete overhaul of our educational system is required.

And I would place at the core of a revamped US education the teaching of history and poetry. In order to have mature, responsible citizens, a democracy requires not just a literate population, but a population familiar with its nation's past. By this I mean much more than a superficial knowledge of the actions of various presidents and political parties, but also of the causes of depressions and of wars. Ideally, students would study the ideologies and political passions of key figures in both government and civil society. They would be allowed to take part in debates that were modeled on actual historical debates, e.g., Lincoln-Douglas, and they would be required to write a serious paper about a contemporary political conflict showing how that conflict grew out of decisions made in the past—by a president, by Congress, by a public official, by a labor organizer, or union, by a powerful industrialist such as Andrew Carnegie, or another individual or group.

Such a program of study would require great dedication and concentration, but properly supervised it could lead to a much deeper engagement of students in their growth as thinkers and citizens. Many of our problems as a nation, I feel certain, are due to a dumbing-down that takes place in both public schools and charter schools. Any hope we may have of restoring democratic politics in America will depend on our ability to better educate and subsequently engage the critical thinking skills of future generations.

Several times in these essays I have emphasized the importance of stimulating students' imaginations. A person's life is only partially lived if their imagination is underdeveloped, stunted. Art, in one form or another, can do wonders to address that problem. But millions lack the means to

---

30. Mason, "You Are Not Alone," 65.

attend a symphony performance, to see a play performed, or to visit an art museum.

I am thinking especially of youths who spend their formative years in the "asphalt jungles" of our major cities. But there are millions more in small towns and on farms who similarly lack opportunities to hear a Mozart piano concerto or to watch a professional production of, say, *Death of a Salesman*, or August Wilson's *Ma Rainey's Black Bottom*, or Lorraine Hansberry's *A Raisin in the Sun*.

There is, I believe, no better way of nurturing the young person's imagination than through the study of poetry. Poetry, whether read silently, read aloud or heard when read, especially when it's the author doing the reading, can awaken in the listener buried emotions or visions that enrich the life, inspire the soul, and help develop the character. Since it is language that permits our full development as human beings, attending to the sounds and sense of the words of good poetry and perhaps thrilling to the magic of great poetry—a sonnet by Shakespeare, a stabbing verse by Langston Hughes or a love poem by Rita Dove, for example—can make all the difference in the sort of person we become.

Poetry, when genuinely attended to, is also likely to aid in developing a critical skill which I think is woefully underdeveloped in our population today. That is the skill of seeing. Unless we are unfortunate enough to have lost our sight, we all see. But I believe that many of us in America today miss a great deal of what the world presents for our eyes to feast upon, especially the marvels of the natural world. Hence poetry that celebrates animals and birds, the grass and the trees which they may feed upon or where they may build their nests—such poetry has the potential of increasing the scope of our awareness of our "relatives" that millions of years of evolution have created. And if it is the creation of a truly gifted and sensitive writer, poetry about the natural world can awaken in the reader or hearer a sense that the fully lived life must develop—the sense of wonder.

A New Hampshire poet, L. R. Berger, sheds light on the reason why being present to nature is important. "People think that nature is about scenery," she says. "But it's so much more complex than that. It's about what it is to live in a quality of deep engagement where there's really a conversation going on between crows and trees and human beings."[31]

During a two-week stay at the retreat for writers that I operate in western Massachusetts, Berger claimed that she engaged in a conversation with a crow that perched each morning on the branch of a tree outside her room's window. Such experiences can add immeasurably to one's sensitivity

---

31. Berger, quoted in Crapo, "Reclaiming Awe," D2.

to the extraordinary gifts that life on Earth offers those with the capacity to respond and can only intensify our feeling of wonder at nature's generosity.

Berger's poetry invites the reader to join her in experiencing that wonder but also in sharing feelings of sorrow or anger over the ways our language is abused and corrupted by much contemporary usage, especially when employed by the military to designate forces of destruction. As an example she cites the phrase "soft target," which really means, she insists, "murder." She is especially offended by the way the military appropriates "the language of the natural world" as tags for nuclear tests or other operations, offering as instances "Operation New Dawn" and "Operation Blue Jay." When we hear our language subverted in this fashion, the experience unsettles us: "In some way, it adds to the confusion we feel because when words are separated from their true meanings, it leaves us very unbalanced."[32]

In a quite witty poem, "The President and the Poet Come to the Negotiating Table," Berger imagines an occasion when the poet engages in a kind of contest as she bargains with the President—obviously George W. Bush—not for money, or power, or celebrity—but for words, in effect, the right to use certain words. The poem opens with these lines: "I only agreed to compromise when it became clear / they were already stealing them again out from under us: / words, one at a time." The president claims he's ready to bargain because *"there are far too many words anyway."*[33]

The poet opens the contest by offering CONQUEST and DOW JONES and sweetens the offer with BOMBS but insists on getting back SMART. This exchange continues for another dozen or more lines until the president says that GOD is not on offer. The poet agrees: *"God,* I said, *must be returned to God."*

The poet then surmises that what is really on the president's mind is SHOCK and AWE, and she responds as we might at this point expect: "SHOCK was the word to bring me to my feet, / because poets can rise up angry and shaking / for what they love too. / SHOCK, I said. *You can have SHOCK. / But AWE—over my dead body."*[34]

STUDIES IN AWE

Most of us, I expect, have never imagined that awe could be a subject for scientific investigation. We've been proved wrong by two psychologists, Dacher Keltner and Jonathan Haidt, who for several years have been

32. Ibid.
33. Ibid.
34. Ibid.

running experiments in order to determine how the experience of awe can affect human beings. In an article published in the *Sierra Magazine*, Jake Abrahamson describes how these two scientists have collected data allowing them to develop theories about the nature of awe. He quotes from an article published in 2003: "In the upper reaches of pleasure and on the boundary of fear, awe is felt about diverse events and objects, from waterfalls to childbirth, to scenes of devastation. . . . Fleeting and rare, experiences of awe can change the course of a life in profound and permanent ways."[35]

Abrahamson, who frequently takes groups of inner-city young people boating on rivers flowing through the canyons of the mountains of Utah and other western states, writes about those experiences in a way that brings into focus the powerful impact the alert individual may encounter with wild nature. After an extremely loud thunderstorm on the first evening of one such voyage, he and his young charges emerge from their tents "in perfect sync." Explaining that he's "not a spiritual person," he can only wonder what it was that brought about a "quasi-religious feeling that the mountains, people, and river were hanging together in ethereal balance."[36]

Perhaps the most significant among his reflections on his response to the storm is Abrahamson's recognition that his own experiences correlate exactly with the discoveries of the psychologists:

> Scientifically speaking, the storm brought me into a state of awe, an emotion that . . . can have profoundly positive effects on people. It happens when people encounter a vast and unexpected stimulus, something that makes them feel small and forces them to revise their mental models of what's possible in the world. In its wake, people act more generously and ethically, think more critically when encountering persuasive stimuli, like arguments or advertisements, and often feel a deeper connection to others and the world in general. Awe prompts people to direct concern away from the self and toward everything else. And about three-quarters of the time, it is elicited by nature.[37]

Public officials and educators searching for ways of reforming both primary and secondary education should take note: the experience of awe contributes to the making of more mature, responsible and compassionate citizens. Those responsible for the education of our youth would do well to seek opportunities to expose students to awe-inspiring adventures in the natural world. For those who live in a city and have no Sierras or Niagara

35. Abrahamson, "Science of Awe," 38.
36. Ibid.
37. Ibid.

Falls nearby, it should be possible to find some cultural event that will "blow the minds" of the young. Anything that represents a radical dissociation from what Elisabeth Garsonnin describes as "this awful hard-edged commercial creation, with technohumans running it" might do the job.

With a talented and inspired teacher, students everywhere can experience the adventure of learning the New Story, the narrative of how everything that exists came to be and of how all things in the universe, including human beings, are integral parts of a living, pulsating wonder—the cosmos. That story has been told by many, but no one tells it in its full splendor quite so brilliantly as does Father Thomas Berry.

In chapter 6, I return to Father Berry and explain why this Jesuit priest focused in his writings and lectures on creation—the creation that is the Earth and what Berry calls the "sacred universe." For now it may suffice if I note that Berry possessed an extraordinary fund of knowledge in three areas: Christian theology and history; contemporary science; and the beliefs and religious practices of indigenous peoples, including the American Indian tribes. Berry tells the New Story with great depth of knowledge and a passion that suggests that in his innermost self he has *lived* that communion with the cosmos that indigenous peoples everywhere have experienced but which is almost totally absent from human experience in the modern "civilized" world.

If told properly, as Berry tells it in *The Dream of the Earth* and *The Sacred Universe*, and if apprehended in its full grandeur and beauty, the very listening to or reading of this story has the power to raise goose bumps on one's skin.

I believe, in fact, that Berry's exposition of the significance of the present moment in the life of humankind and the cosmic drama can add an extraordinarily valuable component to any future plan to overhaul education in America. In the following passage, Berry makes clear the importance of the New Story for our time.

> The physicist Brian Swimme tells us, "The universe shivers with wonder in the depth of the human." From the tiniest fragment of matter to the grand sweep of the galactic systems, we have a new clarity through our empirical modes of knowing. We are more intimate with every particle of the universe and with the vast design of the whole. We see it and hear it and commune with it as never before. Not only in its spatial extension, but in its emergent process, we are intimate with the world about us. We experience an identity with the entire cosmic order within our own beings. This sense of an emergent universe identical with

ourselves gives new meaning to the Chinese sense of forming one body with all things.

This identity is expressed by physicists in terms of the anthropic principle. In this perception the human is seen as a mode of being of the universe as well as a distinctive being in the universe. Stated somewhat differently, the human is that being in whom the universe comes to itself in a special mode of conscious reflection. That some form of conscious reflection on itself was implicit in the universe from the beginning is now granted by many scientists. The difficulty presently is with the mechanistic fixations in the human psyche, in our emotions and sensitivities as well as in our minds. Our scientific inquiries into the natural world have produced a certain atrophy in our human responses. Even when we recognize our intimacy, our family relations with all the forms of existence about us, we cannot speak to those forms. We have forgotten the language needed for such communication. We find ourselves in an autistic situation. Emotionally, we cannot get out of our confinement, nor can we let the outer world flow into our own beings. We cannot hear the voices or speak in response.[38]

It is important to note in these final sentences the repetition of medical or quasi-medical terminology. Berry identifies the loss of our capacity to respond to the universe as a kind of illness. He's quite specific: we are in "an autistic situation"; we, like a TB patient, are in "confinement." We are shut off from the "outer world" and incapable of communication, much less communion, with the outer world. Our responses betray a "certain atrophy."[39]

Berry expresses the belief that the intensity of scientific investigation reveals a kind of "reverence for the mystery and magic of the earth" but goes on to acknowledge the final irony of the Western historical process, one that's been imbued with an intense faith in human progress: this faith "in an ever-improving human situation" appears to be "bringing us to wasteland instead of wonderland."[40]

This observation points to a corrective formulation in any curriculum designed to educate young people in America for a sustainable future. Learning ought to have as its cornerstone a thorough, age-appropriate familiarity with the New Story. Students should be led to appreciate "the mystery and the magic" of the cosmos and aided, in all ways possible, to hear the voices of the Earth. If a teacher has herself or himself heard those

38. Berry, *The Dream of The Earth*, 16–17.

39. Ibid.

40. Ibid., 17.

voices, I think it's quite likely that they will be able, with the help of Father Berry's writings, to enable their students to hear them as well. In the process, I believe they are likely to have a reaction like that of Jake Abrahamson on that stormy evening in the Utah mountains—a "quasi-religious feeling" when the self, the Earth, and the universe seemed to be "hanging together in ethereal balance."

BEYOND FACT AND THEORY:
READING FOR INSPIRATION

Richard Rorty's ideas regarding America's soul help clarify what's at stake for "reeducating" America. Drawing a clear line between knowledge and inspiration, Rorty takes to task scholars and teachers who cannot bring themselves to teach as if their work might be directed toward achieving the society of their dreams. In the post-Vietnam era many American academics with political views on the left no longer allowed themselves even *to have* dreams of an America that they and others might admire. The stains on the country's soul created by that brutal slaughter of fellow human beings in Southeast Asia was considered "ineradicable."[41]

I, too, at times also found little in our country's political and cultural life capable of offsetting the moral and spiritual blight represented by the Cold War and the depravity of US support for dictators around the globe, as well as the horrendous bloodshed in Vietnam, Laos, and Cambodia. But in my teaching I never spurned inspiration.

Knowledge, of course, is valuable; and in a democracy it is essential. One reason US officials have been able to lead the country into disastrous military ventures overseas—the most recent being the invasion of Iraq—is the abysmal ignorance prevalent in American culture, especially that of our legislators, regarding our place in history, as well as geography, political theory and almost everything else except sports and entertainment.

It is critical, however, to be clear about who bears the greatest responsibility for this ignorance. Individuals may be intellectually lazy and irresponsible, but in a culture awash with the allures of entertainment and thousands of promises of quick and easy gratification of every human desire, and a class of elite experts who think the "rabble" are better off when left in their ignorance, blaming the average citizen for their ignorance misses a key point. Those with political power and certainly top executives in the corporate world fear a well-informed electorate. The large and enthusiastic crowds drawn to rallies for Sen. Bernie Sanders, who tells the truth about

41. Rorty, *Achieving Our Country*, 95.

wealth and power in America, suggest a hunger for education about who rules and who suffers in these United States.

Rorty's major point here is that, because of radical disillusionment and even cynicism, many thinkers on the left became in the second half of the twentieth century disengaged from the struggle to create a truly good society, and, in the process, substituted fact and theory for inspiration. The renewal of our society, Rorty believed, requires teachers, students, and citizens capable of reading beyond the acquisition of knowledge: "It is only those who still read for inspiration who are likely to be of much use in building a cooperative commonwealth."[42]

But in a society such as ours where individuals are thoroughly manipulated emotionally and intellectually by commercial interests and the trashy advertisements they employ to create semi-catatonic consumers, genuine inspiration is frequently as rare as totally fulfilling occupations or fully blissful marriages. It *can* be found in books, as I have been arguing in my discussion of poetry—I'd want to include fiction and drama, history, biographies and memoirs as well—and surely in recounting the universe story à la the writings of some scientists and Thomas Berry. And despite the general validity of John Cobb's critique of US universities, America still has, I believe, talented and dedicated teachers who read for inspiration and pass on that inspiration to their students. They are found in small liberal arts colleges but also in our large universities, both public and private. (I surely knew some at the University of Illinois at Chicago where I taught for more than thirty years.) And their work sometimes finds its way into major journals such as *Harpers*, *The Atlantic*, *The Progressive*, and *The Nation*, allowing them to inspire not only their students but the rest of us as well.

Yet the radical overhaul of America's educational systems and institutions that Prof. Adams called for seems currently way beyond our grasp and is, I suspect, possible only as a major ingredient of something approaching a political and cultural revolution—and a humanistic economy such as the one that Adams urged his fellow citizens to create.

PART II

AMERICAN AGGRESSION & THE NEED FOR CULTURAL REVITALIZATION

The contemporary flight from the teaching of integrated knowledge, critical thinking and inspiration in our universities has catastrophic

42. Ibid., 140.

consequences—and not merely theoretical ones—exemplified most recently by the blatant carelessness and hubris of George W. Bush and his administration. Bush's war against Iraq promises to produce catastrophic consequences into the indeterminate future. Surely we have not come close to paying the full price for the suffering caused by that reckless and brutal assault on a nation that had done us no ill, which, among other things, has contributed greatly to the state of permanent warfare in which our nation seems trapped. President Obama, we thought, had gotten us out of Iraq but now, in the summer of 2015, the stunning successes of the ISIS forces in Syria and Iraq promise involvement of the American military continuing into the indeterminate future. Despite the president's obvious reluctance to commit ground troops to that conflict, I doubt that he can hold out indefinitely. The pressure from hawks in Congress, from "experts" such as retired generals appearing on Fox News (and other TV channels), and from currently serving military brass to put "boots on the ground" will no doubt continue to be unrelenting.

Jim Hightower offers a biting critique of this latest US military escapade in a region of the world where our leaders understand little about the ethnic and religious forces fueling this conflict.

> The warmongers are pushing our nation into the sticky web of a centuries-old religious conflagration that (1) we don't understand, (2) cannot resolve, (3) presents no clear threat to our national security . . . (5) offers no moral high ground, (6) positions us as destroyers (or worse, crusaders), (7) is creating a whole new generation of young Muslim enemies for us, (8) has no timetable or definition of "victory," . . . and (10) will further drain our treasury, strain our military, and divert our people and resources from achieving America's own, long-delayed democratic potential.[43]

According to a scholar at American University who studies military spending, a rough estimate of the financial cost to put the brakes on destructive historical forces that our country has had a major part in creating is fifteen billion dollars—for the first year. In addition, the Wahhabi sect of Sunni Islam that forms the leadership cadre of the ISIS force is what Hightower calls the "love child of our supposed ally Saudi Arabia." The Saudis, who have funded schools and mosques throughout the Muslim world where an extreme fundamentalist and puritanical version of the faith is taught, including bloody punishment of those who violate the dictates of the law, are doing next to nothing to restrain their offspring.

43. Hightower, *Hightower Lowdown*, November 2014, 1.

Hightower's comment regarding our own long-delayed attention to developing America's democratic potential echoes thoughts expressed by earlier critics of US foreign policy. During the sixties, Senator J. William Fulbright of Arkansas became one of the country's most forceful and eloquent critics of the war in Vietnam. Repeatedly, Sen. Fulbright identified the fallacies of the arguments advanced by the hawks advocating for ever greater US commitment of troops to the war. With a profound understanding of the perhaps uniquely American obsession with "fixing" the lives and policies of people in distant lands while neglecting to fix our own, he sounded a deeply moral and rational appeal for reflection and restraint:

> Maybe we are not really cut out for the job of spreading the gospel of democracy. Maybe it would profit us to concentrate on our own democracy instead of trying to inflict our own particular version of it [on others.] If America has a service to perform in the world, it is in large part the service of her own example. In our excessive involvement in the affairs of other countries, we are not only living off our assets . . . we are also denying the world the example of a free society enjoying freedom to the fullest.[44]

In *Empire as a Way of Life*, William Appleman Williams noted that nations with imperialist inclinations frequently concentrate on external issues as a way of distracting their citizens from internal problems, weaknesses, or stresses. I am not accusing President Obama of such devious motives. I'm sure he feels genuinely impelled to order bombing strikes on the ISIS forces and no doubt sees the potential of significant harm to Middle Eastern peoples if these jihadists are allowed to overrun one country after another. But America's involvement in this effort should not preclude major assistance in the form of weapons and troops from Turkey, Kuwait, Qatar, and Saudi Arabia, countries in the region which have most to fear. However, our long history of inserting military force in areas where we have no right to impose our ideologies suggests that historians, journalists, and others who have speculated about a lengthy conflict between the United States and Islamic warriors are likely to prove prescient.

Endless wars *do* seem our destiny. That destiny might be different if those seeking high office in this country were *truly* educated, studying not only Greek tragedy and Shakespeare, but also contemporary thinkers such as Andrew Bacevich and Chalmers Johnson. Johnson's trilogy lays out in precise detail the consequences of America's imperial intrusion into every corner of the globe—including Muslim lands where American soldiers

44. Fulbright, quoted in Bacevich, *Washington Rules*, 113.

and culture are decidedly unwelcome. The blowback from the bloodshed the US war against Iraq has already caused can only be intensified as new "crusaders" campaign against jihadists in an expanding area of the Middle East. Furthermore, a determined enemy obsessed with revenge is almost certainly going to find ways other than beheading US journalists and other captured Americans to inflict pain on the "Great Satan."

Drone strikes are a contemporary and relatively minor expression of America's military might bringing grief to inhabitants of Iraq, Pakistan and Afghanistan. The American public has, until recently, largely responded with indifference and boredom to the crimes *its* military forces are guilty of and become aroused only when two US citizens are brutally murdered. It may be useless to speculate about what, if any, impact upon the American soul many thousands of deaths in countries half a planet away may have caused. But I suspect that the soul of a nation cannot go unscathed indefinitely when its leaders indulge in the kind of reckless rush to war that has been a major feature of American history in the new century.

I return now to an examination of how our country's soul has been damaged by the domination of capitalist economic factors. In addition to alienation there is another salient feature of life governed by the dynamics of the market—commodification. Under a capitalist dispensation everything, including human beings, loses its intrinsic value. Thus rivers, lakes, minerals, trees, land, even mountains, have only the value that lies in their capacity to generate wealth.

Corporations may, with impunity, pollute rivers to the point of destroying all living creatures that once thrived in them or literally remove mountains as coal companies have done recently in Appalachia.

When Henry Ford and other captains of industry discovered the monetary value of mass production, the workers on the assembly line became interchangeable, merely cogs in a vast machine. Marx, of course, had observed this phenomenon in the nineteenth-century factories of England where young women worked the machines producing fabrics that provided major contributions to the riches of the British Empire. The owners of the factories grew enormously wealthy; the young women were interchangeable and imminently disposable. No longer valued as humans with emotions, dreams, intelligence and souls, they were considered to possess no more value than the commodities they created. Little wonder that Marx wrote about *alienation* when reflecting on the exploitation of humans in a class-bound society such as Victorian England.

For Erich Fromm, a major source of alienation in the modern world was the primacy given to *manipulative intelligence*. By this term he designated an intelligence dedicated to scientific and technological manipulation of matter, of sorting through information and creating formulae and structures for control of the natural—or human—world, isolated from the inner world of feeling. Fromm's quotation of Charles Darwin's lament for his lost interest in art and poetry and music after beginning his scientific explorations can bear repeating:

> My mind seems to have become a kind of machine for grinding general laws out of large collections of fact. . . . The loss of these tastes is a loss of happiness, and may possibly be injurious to the intellect, and more probably to the moral character, by enfeebling the emotional part of our nature.[45]

When discussing what he calls "marketing characters," normally found among officials of the corporate world, Fromm discerns an acute underdevelopment of emotional life. "Since it is not cultivated or needed, but rather an impediment to optimal functioning, emotional life has remained stunted and never matured beyond the level of a child's."[46] As one reads Fromm's description of this character type, it is impossible not to think of the CEOs of the enormous oil, gas and coal conglomerates who, in the face of overwhelming evidence that the carbon dioxide created by their industries is destroying the habitat their grandchildren will inherit, make little or no effort to curb greenhouse gas emissions yet insist that they, too, care about the health of the planet. Here, in such atrophied consciences, is found the rarified distillation of the alienated human being.

THE SURPRISE MENTOR: KARL MARX

Another figure in this group of thinkers who can assist us in understanding and possibly helping to correct some of the pathologies of contemporary America is Karl Marx—as interpreted by John Cassidy, a staff writer for the *New Yorker*, and Terry Eagleton, an Anglo-Irish literary and cultural critic. In this country it has long been fashionable to scoff at Marx, to dismiss his thought with a smirk laced with contempt. Today, as America slouches toward a destiny far different from the seemingly unchallengeable superpower imagined by Paul Wolfowitz and other neoliberal advocates of total US global hegemony, it appears that Marx may have the last word.

45. Darwin as quoted in Fromm, *To Have or to Be*, 135.
46. Ibid.

In "The Return of Karl Marx," Cassidy provides readers a fairly comprehensive picture of this nineteenth-century thinker who spent thousands of hours in the British Museum reading and writing about the history of economic theory and development in the western world. Cassidy, in turn, spent many hours reading Marx and concluded that Marx's writings on that subject are truly first-rate. He summarizes his conclusions in the following sentence: "He wrote riveting passages about globalization, inequality, monopolization, technical progress, the decline of high culture, and the enervating nature of modern existence—issues that economists are now confronting anew, sometimes without realizing that they are walking in Marx's footsteps."[47] Cassidy stresses Marx's clear-headed understanding well before the twentieth century of the tyranny of money in capitalist economies. He quotes one of Marx's most powerful ideas: "Money is the universal, self-constituted value of all things. It has therefore robbed the whole world, human as well as natural, of its own values."[48]

What I believe Cassidy is at pains to accomplish in this essay is to illuminate the genuine brilliance of Marx's thought as a historian who not only provided the story of capitalism's development but also a comprehensive analysis of the destructive effects of capitalism on individuals whose values have been largely shaped by capitalist ideology. Cassidy suggests that capitalism's growth is like an avalanche and quotes Marx regarding its destructive effects: "Nothing can stop the permanent revolution capitalism represents. 'Uninterrupted disturbance of all social conditions, everlasting uncertainty and agitation distinguish the bourgeois epoch from all earlier ones,' Marx wrote."[49] Marx, I am sure, would not have been surprised in the slightest by the pathologies that plague contemporary America—the drug addiction, the mass shootings, the addiction to accumulation—nor by the widespread reporting of loss of joy and purpose in life.

Terry Eagleton provides us a quite different slant on Marx's gifts. Many Americans, I expect, would be startled to discover that they might learn something of value from Marx concerning the current ecological crisis. Eagleton notes that Marx "insists that it is Nature, not Labour or production, taken in isolation, which lies at the root of human existence."[50] In other words, we humans are an integral part of nature and can continue to exist only so long as we honor and care for nature. We have a pressing obligation

47. Cassidy, "Return of Karl Marx," 248.
48. Ibid., 250.
49. Ibid., 251.
50. Marx, as quoted in Eagleton, *Why Marx*, 50.

to pass on to succeeding generations an environment healthy enough to support Earth's future inhabitants. Marx put it this way:

> Even a whole society, a nation, or even all simultaneously exist-
> ing societies existing together, are not the owners of the globe.
> They are only its possessors . . . they must hand it down to suc-
> ceeding generations in an improved condition.[51]

Eagleton's study of Marx, *Why Marx Was Right*, might, in fact, prove to be a book quite useful to any American concerned about correcting or at least alleviating the consequences of the social pathologies we have so far examined. As we have seen, Adams, Fromm, Gilk and others have declared the moral and spiritual bankruptcy of our current economic system; Adams called for its replacement by a "humanistic economy." It is time to ask, what exactly might this replacement look like?

The stock phrase, now almost a mantra, that predictably issues from the lips of corporate cheerleaders whenever questions are raised concerning the economic system they love to defend, is "capitalism is not a perfect system, but it's the best we have." That, of course, is a grotesque lie. There *is* a better system and it's in place around the globe, for example, in the social democra-cies of Europe and in most Latin American countries. Its name is *socialism*.

The American public has for decades been brainwashed about the ills of socialism. Everyone from political leaders to corporate heads to journal-ists hired by the corporate-owned press have loudly claimed that socialism inevitably threatens private property and diminishes freedom, making it nearly impossible to convince the average citizen of the extraordinary dif-ference between a ruthless, repressive regime such as Stalin's Soviet Union and a social democracy like Finland or Norway.

The social democracies of Europe—Norway, Sweden, Germany, Den-mark, for example—offer a modified form of socialism and a way of life that is both civilized and sane. Citizens pay high taxes but education from kindergarten to graduate school is free and available to all. As is health care, which, in almost all of the European social democracies, is equal to ours if not superior, and far less expensive to deliver. One of the most attractive fea-tures of life in a country such as Germany is that a serious commitment to the common good protects citizens from the worst features of our American "savage capitalism." In Germany workers collaborate with management, take part in critical decision-making, and are treated with dignity and respect.[52]

51. Ibid., 229.
52. See chapter 3.

The contrast with US practice could hardly be more glaring. Here, as any worker and even lower-level executive laid off by one of the large corporations can attest, the CEO, who has probably never met a worker, announces that the plant is closing, pink slips are issued, and Bingo!—out you go into a rather cold world. The process is heartless but, as the representatives of the "owning class" will tell you, there is no alternative. That's how the system works. No exceptions! Except, of course, for those in the top echelons of management, whose golden parachutes provide a safe and soft landing.

Critics of Marx isolate his predictions of the inevitable victory of the proletariat over the owners of capital followed by the establishment of a classless society—ideas that appear only in his late writings and are contradicted by his earlier more "humanistic" work. This is used as the basis for the charge that in Marxist ideology human beings have little or no freedom; the critics also argue that where his teachings are put into practice, humans are doomed to be oppressed. Those who point to Stalin's USSR as proof of this belief are undoubtedly ignorant of the fact that Marx would have been horrified to learn that his ideas had been so corrupted by Stalin and other totalitarian dictators claiming to be his devoted disciples. They might remind themselves also that among Hitler's most ardent supporters were the German *capitalists* of his day.

As indicated in the earlier comments concerning John Cassidy's analysis of Marx's work, if they bothered to read Marx, his critics might discover valuable ideas that almost never surface in popular attacks upon him and his thought. In a spirited discussion of the debate about "human nature" that's recently been going on among American academics, for example, Eagleton contends that from Marx's early writings, we can learn something useful about how we "can get from the human body to questions of ethics and politics."[53] What follows is Eagleton's summary of Marx's thoughts on the dilemma of the individual expressing his or her free will in a liberal society:

> If human beings are self-realizing creatures then they need to be at liberty to fulfill their needs and express their powers. But if they are also social animals, living alongside other self-expressive beings, they need to prevent an endless, destructive clash of these powers. This, in fact, is one of the most intractable problems of liberal society, in which individuals are supposed to be free, but free among other things to be constantly at one another's throats.
>
> Communism [Eagleton employs "communism" and "socialism" as interchangeable terms], by contrast, organizes social

---

53. Eagleton, *Why Marx Was Right*, 229.

life so that individuals are able to realize themselves in and through the self-realization of others. As Marx puts it in *The Communist Manifesto*, "The free development of each becomes the condition for the free development of all." In this sense, socialism does not simply reject liberal society, with its passionate commitment to the individual. Instead, it builds on and completes it. In doing so, it shows how some of the contradictions of liberalism, in which your freedom may flourish only at the expense of mine, may be resolved. This means an enrichment of individual freedom, not a diminishing of it. It is hard to think of a finer ethics. On a personal level, it is known as love.[54]

It is perhaps not entirely surprising that in a discussion of economic history, ruthless competition, alienation, class domination and exploitation, leavened by a vision of the good society based on Marxist theory, the argument should lead finally to love. Clearly, for any society to function with a reasonable degree of harmony and a chance of maximizing the good of each of its members, something approximating love must be at work in the social and political structures of that society. Call it what you will—compassion, generosity, kindness of heart, caring for the welfare of one's brothers and sisters. To create a system of justice that protects the life and health and dignity of everyone within the society—*something* must be present in the moral and intellectual milieu of a nation to permit an outside observer to say, "Here I sense that people really do care about each other. They are probably realistic enough to know that utopias are not possible, but have faith that they can build a more just, more equitable, more caring society than the kind of class-ridden, authoritarian, cruel society they have lived with for centuries."

On my first visit to Nicaragua in 1984, I found such a hopeful and vibrant society. And it was a thoroughly socialist one. It was the creation of the Sandinistas, mostly young, educated Nicaraguans—many were university students—who had fought in a bloody struggle to liberate their country from a rapacious dictatorship which had enjoyed the unwavering support of the United States. Some of the Sandinista leadership were dedicated Marxists, some not, but all were determined to create a society in which the poorest of the poor—perhaps 90 percent of the population were desperately impoverished *campesinos* (peasants)—might receive a basic minimum of health care, education and land. It should be noted that, like the majority of the population, almost all of the Sandinistas were Roman Catholic Christians, deeply influenced by the Second Vatican Counsel's dictum regarding the Church's preferential option for the poor and by liberation theology.

54. Ibid., 86.

During my three-week-long stay there, I explored various barrios of Managua, often walking late at night, never feeling that I must be on my guard for thieves lurking in alleys. One day I visited a hospital where I found an American doctor who volunteered to give me a tour of the hospital accompanied by a Nicaraguan nurse.

What I learned was revelatory. Under the Somoza dictatorship, I was told, medical services were restricted to the dictator and his family, to officials of the government and the National Guard, virtually Somoza's private army, and to the dictator's business associates. For the impoverished masses, there was nothing. No doctors, no nurses, no health clinics, and almost no medicine, since the great majority of the country's inhabitants were too poor and lived too far from a pharmacy to buy any. Many among the poor died from diseases that had been eradicated in the wealthy nations of the North decades earlier.

The Sandinistas had changed all that. Now health clinics staffed by nurses had been established throughout the country. Hundreds of young men and women had gone off to Cuba to train as doctors and nurses and had returned home to serve all Nicaraguans, no matter their social class or their wealth. No woman in labor, the nurse told me, was ever turned away from the hospital, even if three women had to share a bed. Most diseases such as small pox and malaria had been eradicated through nationwide inoculation campaigns and control of the mosquito population. Plans were afoot to begin training doctors at home.

A major element of the Sandinista government's plan to create a more equitable, more just and more prosperous society was the land reform project. As had been the case throughout much of Latin America for centuries, the majority of the land was held by a handful of families with no reluctance to use violence to protect their privileged way of life. Like blacks in the American south during the Jim Crow decades, *campesinos* were frequently at the mercy of large landowners for work paying subsistence wages, if work was even available. And like their black counterparts in places like Alabama and Mississippi, the Nicaraguan peasant was expected to approach *el patron* humbly, hat in hand. Dignity was reserved for the wealthy and powerful.

Since such a dehumanizing system was intolerable to the Sandinistas, the distribution of land to the millions who lived on tiny plots in shacks often made of little more than a few boards and tarpaper became a centerpiece of the planning for a new society. Another key element was the literacy campaign. Because most of the population was illiterate, hundreds of idealistic youths left Managua to bring a basic level of literacy to those for whom books, magazines and newspapers were as alien as diamonds and champagne.

I learned something about the importance of the literacy campaign on the day of my visit to the hospital. As I walked down a major street, I was accosted by a man whose clothing suggested that he was probably a day laborer or possibly a *campesino*. I greeted him and he returned my greeting. Then he pointed to the pen sticking out of my shirt pocket. My thought was, Well, why not? The pen probably cost me 25 cents. So I handed him the pen. Then he pointed to the pad I was carrying. Again, I thought, What the hell, I can replace the pad for less than a dollar. So I gave him the pad. All he did was write his name and then return the pad and pen.

At that moment I realized I was observing an enactment of the true meaning of this socialist revolution. And it could be represented by one word: *dignity*. Upon millions of Nicaraguans, once trapped in a state of poverty, ignorance and utter political impotence, the Sandinistas had conferred hope and faith in the future. And the man I had just met no longer had to remove his hat and abase himself when speaking to a North American who clearly enjoyed privileges this individual probably could barely imagine. He could address me as one free man to another. This one brief encounter helped me understand more fully why the Sandinista Revolution was already becoming a model for other nations in Latin America.

Years later I would meet John Brentlinger, the retired philosophy professor from the University of Massachusetts, about whom I wrote briefly in the Introduction. John had spent months in Nicaragua researching the origins of the revolution. He had been raised in Oklahoma as a Southern Baptist; in the sixties he became a part of the New Left, adopted a Marxist worldview, and considered his religious upbringing an impediment in the progressive struggle for a just society in which he and various friends and colleagues were engaged. But in Nicaragua he underwent a kind of conversion or spiritual awakening. For there he encountered priests utterly dedicated to the Sandinista project and was especially struck by the way many Roman Catholic Christians were interpreting "resurrection as the recurrent struggle in history for a kingdom of justice and brotherly/sisterly love."[55]

What I found most significant in Brentlinger's description of the things he learned from the Sandinistas and their followers was that "the brother/sisterhood that exists among those who struggle for change is a relation of spiritual bonding—as I define it—among those for whom community, as achieved in the process of struggle itself, has become an end in itself."[56] I, too, during my brief stay in the country, felt in the depths of my being that

---

55. Brentlinger, "Revolutionizing Spirituality," 26.
56. Ibid.

"spiritual bonding," something I had rarely encountered in North American Christian congregations.

Like John Brentlinger, there were tens of thousands of North Americans who traveled to Nicaragua in the eighties, many staying for months or years to aid in the building of this new society where a deep sense of community was perhaps the chief reward for their commitment and hard work. Brentlinger's essay from which I have quoted, "Revolutionizing Spirituality: Reflections on Marxism and Religion,"[57] emphasized that there is no basic contradiction between the socialist struggle for a just, humane society and spirituality. America might lessen if not eliminate the pathologies that now undermine its health by emulating certain aspects of the Nicaraguan experience, including foremost a campaign to educate the general public regarding the truism that no democracy can long survive if its economic system ruthlessly trashes the common good. And if the American churches could bring themselves to teach the ethics of Jesus—a radical idea, I know—they might learn something useful from the Nicaraguan experience and thereby contribute significantly to our nation's spiritual rebirth.

Struggling to end racism once and for all, to correct the obscene maldistribution of wealth in the country, to guarantee that every individual and every family have sufficient income to live with dignity, and to provide life-long education and health care to every citizen—that struggle would, of course, evoke outraged cries of "Socialism!" from the super-wealthy and from the millions who have been taught to fear government intervention into individuals' private affairs and the creation of a "nanny society." It might, however, do a great deal to reduce the desperation and despair that will only increase as we move into an uncertain future marked by climate change, scarcity of essential natural resources, including fresh water ("water wars" in the West are already disturbing evidence of this problem), food shortages worldwide, and increasing warfare and chaos throughout the developing world as millions are driven from their homes by rising sea levels and desertification of land once used for crops or animal grazing. In the best of all worlds, it might also go far toward the development of a spiritual base that inspired an authentic commitment to turning the now hollow pledge of "justice for all" into a reality of which the entire nation might be proud. I do not, however, believe in miracles or in utopias; instead I emphasize the constraints that humans face as they struggle to make sense of and act responsibly in a world fraught with moral conundrums and choices with unpredictable outcomes.

57. Ibid.

Speaking as a Christian, Reinhold Niebuhr declared that "the evil in human history is regarded as the consequence of man's wrong use of his unique capacities. The wrong use is always due to some failure to recognize the limits of his capacities of power, wisdom and virtue." Adding that "man is an ironic creature because he forgets that he is not simply a creator but also a creature," Niebuhr comments on how the Hebrew prophets warned both the great empires of the ancient Near East and the "righteous nation," Israel, against pretensions of uprightness. Will America, sometimes described ironically as a "righteous empire," ever heed such warnings?[58]

If America is to escape the disaster that now seems its possible fate, what is called for is a moral and spiritual revolution; Dr. King described it as a "radical revolution in values." One might say that what's required is something like a rebirth. Individuals experience rebirth all the time—whether by religious conversion or spiritual awakening. Whether a nation, especially one as divided as ours currently is, populated by so many angry and desperate citizens, can summon the wisdom and the courage to undergo the needed changes is more than uncertain.

A few things, I believe, *are* certain. First, as individuals and as a nation, we must grow up. We must become adults. For too long we have lived with illusions, especially the illusion that America is an exception to the fact that deeds have consequences and that no nation, no matter how seemingly blessed by historical circumstances, natural abundance or "Providence," can forever impose its will upon other peoples without paying a terrible price. Martin Sheen speculated that America's domestic ills might be a kind of retribution exacted by history for our country's numerous invasions, occupations, and CIA-orchestrated coups throughout the global South, which have led, according to one former CIA agent, to "gross millions" of deaths.[59]

Following 9/11, many Americans appeared to have awakened to the fact that a large proportion of the world's population hated us, although we did have the sympathy and support of many nations. Moreover, it apparently dawned on some that the hatred was due largely to the fact that America was bent upon total global domination. The "Bush Doctrine" certainly alerted the peoples of the Earth to the fact that America reserved to itself a "right" that no other nation claimed, namely, the right to strike wherever and whenever its leaders believed that America's "national security" was at risk. The American Empire, in short, had gone public.

Along with our military personnel and weapons, however, come Hollywood, Madison Avenue and the *National Enquirer*. Faced with an invasion

58. Niebuhr, *The Irony of American History*, 156.

59. Stockwell, Q&A session at the University of Illinois at Chicago, August 25, 1987.

of their countries by our tawdry, violent and sex-ridden popular culture, it's little wonder that some Muslim males are driven nearly berserk and are ready to sacrifice their lives to destroy the agents of such profanation of their own cultures.

Americans, for the most part, appear incapable of understanding this phenomenon. Here, as in other aspects of our dealings with the rest of the world, we are protected by our ignorance and our happy innocence. We find it hard to believe that not every member of the human family wants to be like us or to embrace our tawdry, mind-numbing popular culture. And, as noted earlier, the failure of American education to develop a vigorous, creative imagination in most of our students leads to a population largely incapable of identifying with others whose cultural and religious values are significantly different from our own. Thus a suicide bomber in Yemen or Afghanistan becomes merely another statistic, not a human with loves, loyalties and anxieties about the future of his country—and possibly his family.

The older brother in the Boston Marathon bombing provided clues that might lead to greater understanding of how the mind of a committed Muslim can work and might, in the process, shed light on the question of the sickness afflicting the soul of our country.

He was reported as saying, "These Americans, I don't understand them. They have no values." I would never contend that this judgment, coming as it does from a man willing to kill and maim scores of innocent onlookers at the marathon's finish line, should be taken as a totally true or definitive statement. Clearly there are many millions of Americans who *do* have values, quite admirable ones. There is a vast difference, however, between those who *have* values and those who possess the wisdom and the courage to *act* on those values.

Nor do I believe this allegation should be dismissed as merely the ranting of a deranged terrorist. It would be salutary, in fact, if we Americans could undertake a national dialogue about our values, starting perhaps with the question of how others see us and why so many of them hate us. With such a dialogue, if it could ever be initiated, the urgently needed process of moral and spiritual rebirth might begin.

But this effort to free the nation from the grip of its manifold pathologies, the "reeducation" that Adams declared necessary and the reversal of our addiction to consumption that Gilk described as essential, would possibly be a generation-long process, against staggering odds. And we do not have thirty years to change our bad habits. In *This Changes Everything: Capitalism vs. the Climate*, Naomi Klein makes unmistakable just how urgently radical change is needed. With quotations from a multitude of leading environmental scientists and organizations respected worldwide, she makes a case that I find irrefutable: if we are to avoid ecological breakdown and societal chaos, radical change is needed not twenty or thirty years in the future but *now*.

Klein discusses how increased global temperatures would almost certainly trigger "a number of extremely dangerous feedback loops"; many scientists are predicting a temperature increase later this century of at least 4 degrees Celsius. Already there are reports of major melting of glaciers and ice sheets in Greenland, Alaska, South America and the Himalayas.[60] The most worrisome prediction concerns melting ice in Antarctica: "In May 2014, NASA and University of California, Irvine scientists revealed that glacier melt in a section of West Antarctica roughly the size of France now 'appears unstoppable.'" Should that entire ice formation melt, the result would be a sea level rise of "between three and five meters." But, according to Klein, a number of "mainstream analysts think that on our current emissions trajectory, we are headed for even more than 4 degrees of warming."[61]

Now the really frightening news:

> In 2014 the usually staid International Energy Agency (IEA) issued a report projecting that we are actually on track for 6 degrees Celsius—10.8 degrees Fahrenheit—of warming, and as the IEA's chief economist put it: "everybody, even the school children, knows that this will have catastrophic implications for all of us."[62]

Also, it may be too late, even if the "green revolution," which quickens its pace almost daily, prevents the worst of the predicted ecological meltdown from happening.

It may be too late, that is, to prevent the more powerful of the multinational corporations and the titans of the military-industrial complex from exercising such absolute financial and political control over our national life that we lose our democracy.

In a final chapter of *Empire of Illusion*, Chris Hedges is unambiguous about where our addiction to illusions has brought us: the game is over, he claims, the multinational corporations have won. With their enormous wealth, with which they can employ an army of lobbyists and a host of skillful lawyers, as well as buy the loyalty of judges and legislators, they now have a hammerlock on power—political and financial. In addition, they have managed to acquire most of the large media outlets, thereby controlling the information that the general public reads, sees, or hears. Most American

60. Orlowski, *Chasing Ice*.
61. Klein, *This Changes Everything*, 14.
62. Ibid., 14–15.

journalists, according to Hedges, are no more than courtiers who "do not defy the elite or question the structure of the corporate state." They lie. "The most egregious lie is the pretense that these people function as reporters, that they actually report on our behalf. It is not one or two reporters or television hosts who are corrupt. The media institutions are corrupt."[63]

Hedges has won the hard way his credibility as a critic of America's media personalities. When asked by the *New York Times* to be "embedded" with the troops in Iraq, he refused and began operating as a freelance journalist. Previously he had reported from war zones in Africa, Central America and the Balkans, often with great risk to his life. He has watched from the inside the relentless growth of the corruption about which he writes. Hence it behooves responsible citizens to heed his warnings that our democracy has been almost completely subverted by corporate power.

Is Hedges' pessimism fully justified? Until quite recently, I would have said that it is. But today we are in the midst of a resounding progressive awakening, with signs everywhere indicating that the country's working people, joined by many from the middle class, are no longer remaining silent in the face of manifold abuses delivered by the likes of the Koch brothers and large corporations.

Perhaps the most encouraging feature of this movement is that groups and organizations that earlier acted separately and sometimes at cross-purposes now support each other. Labor unions, for example, are supporting fast food workers in their bid for a living wage, though those workers are not unionized; environmentalists now indicate a willingness to work with those involved in campaigns to bring about greater equity in wealth distribution; in the South, the Moral Monday movement is orchestrating a powerful challenge to right-wing politics on issues ranging from public education to taxes. After police killings of young blacks in Ferguson, Missouri, Baltimore, and New York, young white citizens joined the Black Lives Matter protests. And in New York State, the Working Families Party (WPF) has forced Democratic governor Cuomo to agree to several concessions including working to achieve a $15 per hour minimum wage.[64]

Daniel Cantor seems to speak not just for his party but for all of the groups that are part of this nationwide movement for progressive change. "The WFP doesn't just want to speak truth to power: we want the middle class, the working class and the poor to share in that power. . . . The task

---

63. Hedges, *Empire of Illusion*, 175.
64. Cantor, "New Progressive," 19–20.

of progressives is to move from grievances to governance, from protest to policy."[65]

After decades of conservative propaganda about everything from "tax and spend" Democrats to attacks on Medicare, Medicaid, Social Security and public schools, combined with legislation awarding enormous tax breaks to the wealthiest 1 percent, plus Tea Party takeovers of state legislatures, the movement of the masses in protest may cause even hardened pessimists to cheer. Again and again, I read about citizens who had previously given up on political solutions now taking matters into their own hands. Across the land they are organizing and marching. Hundreds of thousands appear to have learned the lessons taught by earlier generations of protestors: in a democracy, power lies with the people but almost always it has been protests in the streets that have prepared the way for change in legislation. Thus we have to remind ourselves, as Chris Hedges has warned, that massive civil disobedience and jail time may be required for actual return of power to the people.

Organizing is always a critical component of any successful effort for change. In Wisconsin, an organization was recently created by a man with no formal political experience. In a few months of hard work, Mike McCabe put together the "Blue Jean Nation," and in lectures and video presentations, he is stirring the political pot in his state. McCabe knows that many potential voters feel abandoned by those with political power, especially many potential voters who would normally be attracted to the Democratic Party. When challenged by a member of one of his audiences who spoke of the difficulty of overcoming voter apathy, McCabe shot back: "Don't confuse apathy with a sense of powerlessness. The question is: How do we empower the disempowered."[66]

McCabe has dreams of a revitalized US democracy but his feet are on the ground. He makes no effort to minimize the advantage that the forces of reaction in Wisconsin and across the country have with the Koch brothers and Sheldon Edelman backing them with the seemingly endless streams of dollars made possible by the Supreme Court's *Citizens United* decision. But he counters with a quick history lesson: "Past generations didn't beat organized money with money, but by introducing very provocative ideas and an ambitious agenda."[67]

McCabe has spoken to numerous county Democratic meetings telling his audiences that "their party is failing" and has received standing ovations.

65. Ibid., 20.
66. Comp, "Blue Jeans, Big Dreams," 25.
67. Ibid.

He comments that "there is a canyon separating the party's rank and file and the establishment."[68] McCabe's experiences prove what some critics on the left have been saying for years: Tell the truth and tell it over and over. Eventually people will listen.

If anyone in recent American political life has demonstrated the wisdom of that advice, it's Bernie Sanders. The Sanders campaign, with its slogan "A Political Revolution," caught both Beltway elites and political pundits napping. But Sanders, who knows his history of American progressive politics and listens closely to the people, the "commoners," understands that millions of Americans feel exploited and politically homeless and long for a champion who will tell them the truth. And across the country, from Portland, Oregon, to Cleveland, Ohio, to New Hampshire, they are turning out in record numbers to listen as Bernie, who has no trouble telling the truth.

In an interview with John Nichols published in *The Nation*, Senator Sanders provided an overview of his campaign, its philosophy and its strategies. When asked if the country is at a "pivot point" comparable to that of the 1930s, he acknowledged that there is no massive depression today but that

> the discontent of the American people is far, far greater than the pundits understand. Do you know what real African-American youth unemployment is? It's over 50 percent. Families with a member 55 or older have literally nothing saved for retirement. Workers are worried about their jobs ending up in China. They are worried about being fired when they're age 50 and being replaced by someone who is 25. They are disgusted with the degree that billionaires are able to buy elections. They are frightened by the fact that we have a Republican Party that refuses to even recognize the reality of climate change, let alone address this huge issue.[69]

On issue after issue, from Internet neutrality, to climate change, to mass government surveillance, to public funding of elections, to tax giveaways for the wealthiest, Sanders sounds a note of radical protest that millions of Americans appear to welcome. He is at his best when denouncing Republican generosity to the richest Americans: "The Republican budget gave over $200 billion in tax breaks over a 10-year period to the wealthiest two-tenths of 1 percent—massive cuts in Medicare, massive cuts in Medicaid, massive cuts in education."[70]

68. Ibid.

69. Nichols, "Bernie Sanders," 13–14.

70. Ibid., 16.

The Republicans repeatedly scam working Americans, he asserts, because Republican policies are not fully covered by the news media and often not properly explained by opposition politicians. Sanders says "the more we can confront Republicans about their ideology of tax breaks for the billionaires and cuts to every program that is a benefit to the American people, and can expose them for their subservience to the billionaire class—that wins for us every single time."[71]

Whether Bernie Sanders can win the Democratic nomination is a question about which I don't wish to speculate. That he has inspired millions of his fellow citizens and completely transformed the nominating contest in the Democratic Party is beyond dispute. The "progressive revolution" that his candidacy celebrates does not depend on his success, however. But from now until the convention in 2016, Hillary Clinton and other Democratic candidates must surely move to the left—in Hillary's case, it has already happened—as this socialist lays out a scenario whereby America might be transformed into a state resembling the remarkably *sane* social democracies of Europe.

But, as the old English epigram puts it, "There's many a slip twixt the cup and the lip." And while a new progressive era seems an inevitable outcome of the political awakening that Sanders's campaign taps into and intensifies, it's well to recall the warning of thinkers like Chris Hedges and Chalmers Johnson, who chose as the title of his final book *Nemesis*, the name of the Greek goddess of divine retribution. In that volume, Johnson argues that America faces a fateful choice: either we follow the example of Great Britain which decided after World War II to give up its empire in order to save its democracy or we choose the Roman way—save the empire and lose a democratic polity. Johnson is not sanguine about the wisdom of the choice America will make: "I believe that to maintain our empire abroad requires resources and commitments that will inevitably undercut our domestic democracy and in the end produce a military dictatorship or its civilian equivalent."[72]

Johnson writes about how the founders of the United States were keenly aware of such a possibility and contrived a form of government, a republic, that they hoped would prevent such an outcome. But, he claims,

> the combination of huge standing armies, almost continuous wars, military Keynesianism, ruinous military expenses have destroyed our republican structure in favor of an imperial presidency. We are on the cusp of losing our democracy for the sake

71. Ibid.

72. Johnson, *Nemesis*, 278.

of keeping our empire. Once a nation is started down that path, the dynamics that apply to all empires come into play—isolation, overstretch, the uniting of forces opposed to imperialism, and bankruptcy. Nemesis stalks our life as a free nation.[73]

From Maynard Adams to Chalmers Johnson we have heard from thinkers whose wisdom, if heeded, might save America from self-destruction. And might, in the long run, save lost souls like Adam Lanza from slaughtering their fellow humans and themselves as an "answer" to their loneliness, their desperate alienation, and their despair.

But running through the witness of most of the thinkers we have encountered is a note of extreme pessimism: capitalism, when allowed to operate without clearly defined and enforced rules and restraints, is a destructive force, ruining lives, families, and entire communities. At least two of these thinkers, Hedges and Johnson, state fairly conclusively that capitalism, in the form of the massively wealthy multinational corporations and the military-industrial complex, have already subverted our democratic way of life, perhaps beyond recovery.

It is a hard thing to give up on a country one loves. As much as I admire Hedges and Johnson and as much as I agree with many of their respective analyses of the dire condition in which America seems entrapped today, I find myself unable to agree with their pessimistic predictions. The Republican Party may be owned lock, stock and barrel by the super-rich 1 percent of Americans; a craven Senate may fail to approve legislation designed to prevent criminals and the mentally ill from having easy access to weapons that can kill a dozen fellow citizens in five seconds; and the military-industrial complex may waste tens of billions of dollars annually on redundant or outmoded weapons systems, dollars needed to repair our long-neglected infrastructure and also to provide jobs in life-supporting occupations such as those designed to make the nation self-sufficient in green energy production. Congress may seem hopelessly immobilized by Tea Party adherents and other legislators for whom compromise is as unthinkable as supporting a constitutional amendment to ban unlimited corporate money in political campaigns. Yet I find myself, if not wildly hopeful, not despondent either.

Because, as noted earlier, across the country there is abundant evidence that Americans are using intelligence and initiative to create another America. And it's not only in the political sphere that major changes are occurring. The spring 2013 issue of *Yes!* magazine is devoted entirely to articles about the cooperative movement under way from coast to coast. Everywhere Americans are creating cooperative enterprises. In Colorado

73. Ibid.

and elsewhere medical insurance cooperatives have been established; even unions are getting into the act. Borrowing ideas from the Mondragon experiment in the Basque region of Spain, the United Steel Workers have fostered the development of co-ops in the Rust Belt long abandoned by the major corporations. A report issued in 2012 describes how union co-ops operate: "A union co-op is a unionized worker-owned cooperative in which worker-owners all have an equal share of the business and have an equal vote in overseeing the business."[74]

In Detroit, in the South Bronx, in Pittsburgh and in Minneapolis, creative citizens are establishing co-op laundries, large-sale urban vegetable gardens, even a co-op restaurant. The editor of *Yes!*, Sarah van Gelder, writes that co-ops "are owned by workers, residents, consumers, farmers, crafts-people, the community, or any combination. What they have in common is that they circulate the benefits back to their member-owners, and these benefits ripple out to the broader community."[75]

And in the small village in western Massachusetts where I have lived for fifteen years, a local citizen has devoted hundreds of hours to creating what's known as the Common Good Bank, in which I and others have invested. This enterprise permits those who join to shop at a number of local businesses and to present as payment a card much like a credit card. Today this "rCredits" system has 100 active members locally, and "groups in 6 states are asking for . . . help to launch rCredits in their communities."[76]

Such cooperative enterprises will not drive Boeing or Wal-Mart or EXXON out of business; what they almost surely will do is rekindle in America a spirit of cooperation and communal effort that could eventually lead to a new model for US economic life. In article after article published in *Yes!*, the message that's highlighted is that in these cooperative ventures, alienation has been banished. As common sense and the experience of the race tell us, laboring together for a shared outcome brings joy, not feelings of futility, diminished confidence in one's self-worth, or hopelessness. In addition, the experience of successful co-op labor may also remind all who participate in or observe such enterprises that traditional capitalist struc-tures and practices are not divinely ordained. They were man-made, coming into being with the Industrial Revolution, and thus can be altered or elimi-nated when humans decide that they have outlived their usefulness or are too subversive of the human venture to be any longer viable.

74. Van Gelder, "Cooperative Way," 1.

75. Ibid.

76. Spademan, from a letter to members.

Where should this meditation on the soul of America end: with the pessimism of Johnson and Hedges or on the visionary initiatives of millions of Americans who are busy creating a new model for the American economy? Despite the almost despairing tone of some of Chris Hedges' reflections on the slim chances of America shedding its pathological illusions and regaining its moral and spiritual health, he ends *Empire of Illusion* on a note not of optimism, surely, but with a strange kind of hope and shall we say, *faith*. Not faith in a supernatural deity to save us from our foolish, reckless ways, but faith in the human capacity for love.

"Our culture of illusion is, at its core, a culture of death." So begins the final paragraph of this disturbing anatomy of our sick society. But this son of a Protestant minister leaves readers with a paean to that human capacity without which, his ancestors would surely have affirmed, the human soul is lost. "The power of love is greater than the power of death." Like a poet or like a very talented preacher, Hedges leads his audience to a spiritual height where the soul of a sensitive reader is almost sure to be profoundly stirred:

> It cannot be controlled. It is about sacrifice for the other. . . . It is about honoring the sacred. . . . Blind and dumb, indifferent to the siren calls of celebrity, unable to bow before illusions, defying the lust for power, love constantly rises up to remind a wayward society of what is real and what is illusion. Love will endure, even if it appears darkness has swallowed us all, to triumph over the wreckage that remains.[77]

Hedges' lyrical meditation on love prompts some final reflections on the failure of love as perhaps the most salient factor in our unhealthy condition as a nation. If, as the song has it, "It's love that makes the world go round," it is also true that thwarted love, or perverted love, or betrayed love, or lust masquerading as love can turn the world into a snake pit. Like "freedom," "equality," and "rights," "love" is a word we Americans like to bandy about. In country music, in rock and roll, in fiction and in films, in advertising and in millions of marriages and relationships, "I love you" is probably the most ubiquitous phrase heard in America. And there is no reason to believe that this expression does not reflect true feeling when spoken by one individual to another.

But the record of divorce, of spousal abuse, of violence against children and the rape of children and women tells a different story. So do the recent scandals regarding Ashley Madison, a business enterprise that

---

77. Hedges, *Empire of Illusion*, 192–93.

yielded millions of dollars aiding married individuals to commit adultery. In this entire record we encounter a history of love distorted, undermined, corrupted.

According to Erich Fromm, only those who have become *adults* can love genuinely. But, as we have seen, Fromm believes that achieving such adult status requires almost superhuman commitment and discipline. Those who are able to love, he maintains, do not need illusions. Those who genuinely love have a strong, secure sense of self and yet are capable of extending their love beyond the self—to all creatures, even to the universe itself. "In the act of loving, I am one with All, and yet I am myself, a unique, separate, limited, mortal human being. Indeed, out of the very polarity of separateness and union, love is born and reborn." For our sick society, Fromm, the physician, prescribes love. "In the experience of love," he writes, "lies the only answer to being human, lies sanity."[78]

In *The Sane Society*, he also explains why so many of our citizens do not achieve full adulthood. Most of us, he argues, never grow beyond an incestuous longing for and clinging to the pleasure and security that our mothers provided. But, in adulthood, he notes, this infantile dependency is normally grounded in another source of comfort and security—for instance, a tribe, a nation, a religion. We never grow into the "being mode," never move beyond attachment to a force, a structure, or a tradition that serves to shield us from the anxiety of authentic freedom that true personhood involves.

In America today, a great many of us seem to find security and fulfillment in embracing a vision of a nation that has never existed, that "idyllic society" of which Martin Sheen spoke. The members of the Tea Party and of the NRA and millions of others appear to embrace a mythological America, one guaranteed by a somewhat mythological Constitution. (I would guess that many gun enthusiasts have read the Second Amendment or heard it read and ignored completely the clause where in plain English it is affirmed that citizens are allowed to "bear arms" in order to insure that each state has a "well-ordered militia." Period!)

Fromm adds a note that further illumines the role of the mythological America in the lives of so may of our citizens: "Nationalism is our form of incest, is our idolatry, is our insanity. 'Patriotism' is its cult." It should be noted, however, that Fromm condemns only that kind of patriotism that "puts one's own nation above humanity, above the principles of truth and justice."[79]

78. Fromm, *Sane Society*, 33.
79. Ibid.

Our addiction to violence, I believe, correlates closely with the inability of many Americans to break free of the narcissism bred by an advanced capitalist culture, identified absolutely with the idea of and the nation America, which inevitably fails to deliver the happiness and wholeness it so stridently promises. A profound sense of betrayal, I would guess, could lie at the root of the apparent desire for revenge that motivated the mass murderers of Columbine, Virginia Tech, Tucson, Sandy Hook, Aurora and the scores of other sites of seemingly motiveless killing.

Even if they have no expectation of becoming true "wise men" or "wise women," most humans, I would guess, hope in their hearts to achieve as they grow old at least a modicum of wisdom. That, at any rate, has been my experience—the hope, certainly, and perhaps a bit of the reality. Now in my eighty-sixth year, however, I have no grand illusions about myself or about the human race. We may, as several of the writers I have cited suggest, simply destroy ourselves. We surely have the capacity and in many ways have shown an inclination in that direction.

So the final note of these reflections might very well be, "So long, it's been good to know you." At the risk of sounding somewhat self-contradictory, I intend instead to echo Chris Hedges *without* the deep pessimism regarding the future of human civilization that he voices in the concluding words of *Empire of Illusion*. He and the other writers from whom I have gratefully learned a great deal agree: it *is* love that is the key to a mature human life, to wholeness, to sanity.

It remains only to add that for me, the other side of love is forgiveness. Thus I end with the conviction that, whatever the outcome of Earth's experiment with the human family, some of our fellow citizens on this exquisite planet have over the millennia learned a little, about how to love as well as how to forgive—even the heartless, greedy megalomaniacs of Wall Street, the morally-stunted politicians who take us into unprovoked wars, the journalists who lie to curry favor with the powerful, the confused and angry lost souls like Adam Lanza who murder their fellow citizens, the tyrants, like Assad of Syria, who bring calamity upon their people because they are addicted to power. It is easy to hate. It is very, very hard to truly love. Even more difficult, perhaps, to forgive.

CHAPTER 6

RELIGIONLESS CHRISTIANITY
IN AN AGE OF SPECTACLE

OFF AND ON FOR several weeks I have been reading Bishop John Spong's *Jesus for the Non-Religious*. Spong is an intelligent, scholarly sort and has made a career of assuring believers that they must cease clinging to two-thousand-year-old myths or watch Christianity lose all credibility with intelligent, educated, contemporary individuals. One of his most popular books is *Why Christianity Must Change or Die*. I had read this earlier work several years ago and knew its author to be a persuasive thinker, one who comes armed with much historical knowledge and cogent arguments. I was not fully prepared, however, for the virtual onslaught of biblical scholarship that he mounts in this study of Jesus, in which he offers a view of the *man* Jesus of Nazareth that he believes will be acceptable to those who consider themselves "non-religious."

Spong examines passages in the three "Synoptic Gospels"—Mark, Matthew and Luke—and later in the Gospel of John, again and again revealing how the authors of these books contradict each other, provide information which the historical record flatly denies as possible, offer accounts of supposed "miracles" that our modern knowledge of the workings of the natural world and of human agency tell us are impossible (e.g., five loaves of bread multiplying sufficiently to feed thousands, blindness cured with the application of spit and dirt, or bodies dead for three days rising from the grave). Spong demonstrates, moreover, how each of the writers of the synoptic gospels rearranges events in the life of Jesus to correspond with the major holy days of the Jewish liturgical calendar, a strategy deemed essential in order to be persuasive to the audiences for whom each of these accounts was intended: those still worshipping in Jewish congregations.

Spong's central purpose in deconstructing the mythological language of the Gospels is to reveal how the church over the centuries virtually smothered the essential meaning of Jesus' life and teachings with doctrines and dogmas that are abstractions having little to do with the actual human being, Jesus of Nazareth. Those doctrines grew out of a first-century world-view that posited a supernatural, theistic deity residing above the sky, who had produced the Earth in an awesome and miraculous six-day work of creation. Since he (this deity was always conceived as masculine) had originated the creation, he was capable of intervening at will, altering the course of both natural and human events.

Jesus operated within that worldview, as did his disciples and the gospel writers. Spong perceives his task to be a kind of rescue operation, making available to twenty-first-century, postmodern individuals who dismiss as hopelessly outdated the Christian creeds, with their assertions of virgin birth, resurrection from the tomb and ascension into a heavenly kingdom, an understanding of the meaning of Jesus quite different from that embedded in orthodox teachings. What Spong focuses upon is the Jesus who reveals what a person living a fully *human*, not a supernatural, life looks like. Once the stories of miraculous cures of physical ailments and banishment of demonic spirits by means of incantations have been accepted as myths, not literal historical facts, it is then possible, Spong argues, to truly encounter the Jesus who manifests the full range of human possibilities.

Yet millions of Christians today refuse to acknowledge that the first-century imagery and language of the gospels and the creeds are literal nonsense. The result is that

> Jesus becomes the captive of the hysterically religious, the chronically fearful, the insecure and even the neurotic among us, or he becomes little more than a fading memory, the symbol of an age that is no more and a nostalgic reminder of our believing past.[1]

Among the qualities most essential to the being of Jesus that Spong identifies, the central one is perhaps Jesus' capacity to overcome all barriers to human intercourse; no one—not lepers, not adulterers, not the ritually unclean, not half-breeds, e.g., Samaritans, not tax collectors serving the hated Roman occupiers—is excluded from the blessed company of those who long to love and to be loved. It is this bountiful outpouring of love and acceptance that marks Jesus as special, a fully human person who reveals so completely what human beings are capable of that his followers could only

---

1. Spong, *Jesus for the Non-Religious*, 9.

use language normally reserved for a divine being to adequately express their experience of the Jesus they had come to know and to love. Here is how Spong describes what this man Jesus means for him:

> The call of Christ for me has thus become a call to journey beyond every barrier that shackles and limits our humanity and its potential. Jesus was not divine because he was a human being into whom the external God had entered, as traditional Christology has claimed; he was and is divine because his humanity and his consciousness were so whole and so complete that the meaning of God could flow through him. He was thus able to open people to that transcendent dimension of life and being that we call God.[2]

A JUDGMENTAL DEITY WHO INSPIRES SELF-TORTURE

What Spong strives to make unmistakable is the vast difference between the God of orthodox Christianity—whom he characterizes as harsh, judgmental and punitive—and Jesus. Repeatedly inveighing against the portrayal of YHWH, the God of Christian tradition, as a deity whose worshippers must constantly beg for mercy, Spong implies comparison with an oriental potentate, seated on his throne surrounded by fawning courtiers, who requires that supplicants prostrate themselves before his awful majesty.[3] And it is surely true, as Spong maintains, that at various periods of Christian history worshipers have been driven by their faith to extreme acts of self-abnegation, mortification of the flesh, confessions of unworthiness and even belief in their total moral depravity as depicted in the traditional doctrine of the Fall. A current bestseller, *Swerve*, by Stephen Greenblatt, provides a brilliant account of the cruel lengths to which medieval Christians were driven to punish their bodies and cleanse their souls, self-torture as "payment" required for salvation.

In the American colonies of the eighteenth century, Jonathan Edwards's sermons and his writings, e.g., *Sinners in the Hands of an Angry God*, aroused believers to frenzies of confession and repentance during a period in American history known as the First Great Awakening. In the mid-nineteenth century another episode of religious upheaval took place, with hundreds of revivals occurring across the land. Again, agonies of guilt

2. Ibid., 275.
3. Ibid., 234.

and terrors concerning eternal suffering in hell's blazing pits became central motifs in this peculiarly American ordeal.

KILLING ANGER

One feature of Spong's analysis that I find most compelling is his discussion of the anger that the Christian faith seems inevitably to breed. In commenting on the anti-Semitism that led to vicious persecutions, violent pogroms and, finally, the horrors of the Holocaust, Spong speaks of a "killing anger" that has haunted nominally Christian nations for centuries. And that anger was not limited to Europe and surely did not die at Auschwitz. Spong quotes, for example, the elected leader of the Southern Baptist Convention who once publicly claimed that "God Almighty does not hear the prayers of a Jew."[4]

There can be no doubt that Spong is correct in his assertion that deeply rooted in Christian faith and practice is a profound core of anger: "Scrape away from traditional Christian teaching the piety and the stained-glass attitudes, and one finds cesspools of anger, boiling cauldrons that have ignited religious violence in every generation. Christians need to own this part of their history."[5] There is surely no need here to recount in great detail this disgraceful history, involving such episodes as the church's slaughter, century after century during the Middle Ages and on into the early modern period, of supposed heretics; the torture and burnings of millions of men and women accused of witchcraft; the massive bloodletting of wars involving religious disputes, such as the Thirty Years War when Catholics and Protestants seemed to delight in butchering their adversaries by the thousands.

One of Spong's most disturbing observations is that this Christian anger is directed not only toward others but also toward believers themselves. Go to a Christian church and listen, Spong implies, and you will detect immediately manifestations of this anger turned inward: "One can easily document in the words of both Christian liturgies and hymns the presence of incredible levels of self-negativity, self-rejection. This is nothing more than debilitating hostility in the name of God." But, Spong claims, such self-hatred is still perceived in some churches as "a positive sign of true religion."[6]

If it is true that in recent centuries much of this wrathful judgment directed toward the self has been winnowed out of several of the Christian churches, it is yet a fact that as late as the mid-twentieth century, in the

4. Ibid.
5. Ibid.
6. Ibid.

Episcopal Church, one of the branches of Christianity least given to empha-
sizing human depravity, in celebrating the Eucharist the priest was forced to
utter these words: "We are not worthy to gather up the crumbs under thy
table." And even today, though in the contemporary Prayer Book appear
the words "I am wonderfully and perfectly made," there linger overtones
of an earlier time when both priest and congregation were required to acknowledge that from Adam and Eve until the present we humans are fallen
creatures, devoid of goodness, "saved" only by the mercy of a deity who
sent his only son to die as a substitute sacrifice since humans were utterly
incapable of making restitution for the sin of rebellion against the dictates
of their creator.

SPONG'S (AND MY) REJECTION OF UNPALATABLE
AND UNBELIEVABLE DOCTRINES

Toward the end of his book *Jesus for the Non-Religious*, Spong comments on
how he struggled for years with this intellectual and spiritual impasse, forced
to repeat words he no longer believed, until in 1974 he was able to preach a
sermon in which he confronted, before the congregation of a major Episcopal
church in Richmond, Virginia, the dilemma of a "man of God" who could no
longer believe in the God he had been taught to worship and to serve.

Some years before that date, I, too, had stopped believing in that kind
of God. As a student at the Divinity School of the University of Chicago
in the early sixties, I, like Spong, had studied the theology of Paul Tillich.
In addition, I had read Rudolph Bultmann's *Kerygma and Myth*, as well as
books by a group of writers known as the "death of God theologians." A
major turning point in my thinking about the faith *I* had been taught from
the time I began to understand the English language occurred when I read
Honest to God, a searching examination of Christian teachings by an English bishop, John A. T. Robinson. At about the same time I devoured many
of the writings of Friedrich Nietzsche, whose Zarathustra had famously announced in the mid-nineteenth century that "God is dead." Hence Bishop
Spong's writings did not descend upon me like a traumatic revelation. They
did, however, assist me in accepting the fact that I had long since ceased to
believe in the supernatural, interventionist deity of orthodox Christianity;
and had done so without becoming an atheist. Like Spong, I consider myself a-theistic, no longer believing in that supernatural, theistic deity of the
Bible, but still not ready to deny that there is a creative power in the universe
corresponding to what we have traditionally called "God." In *The Body of
God: An Ecological Theology*, Sallie McFague provides a description of this

power that reflects my own understanding: "a spirit theology suggests . . . that God is not primarily the orderer and controller of the universe but its source and empowerment, the breath that enlivens and energizes it."[7]

Spong speaks of himself as "God-intoxicated" and I believe he is. His life has been dedicated to helping others like himself, "believers in exile," as he describes those alienated from religious institutions that continue to teach and to preach things that both modern science and biblical scholarship have shown to be untrue ("lies," he calls them), to accept that Jesus is indeed "divine." But not because he incarnates an otherworldly, supernatural deity. Jesus' followers used the language available to them to describe someone such as Jesus whose words, and deeds, and very being seemed so utterly beyond the "normal" capacity of human life—embodying the power to love beyond measure, to reveal the full potential of human beings in their struggle for wholeness, to penetrate deep into the Ground of Being—that only language normally used when speaking of gods seemed adequate.

John Spong, in short, has sought to rescue Jesus from the theologians and the evangelists who have clothed him in such royal robes that it has been impossible for many contemporary would-be followers not to reject him as a kind of first-century magician promising "pie in the sky." What Spong believes is emerging in our time is the "religionless Christianity" predicted by the German theologian Dietrich Bonhoeffer, not a body of doctrines codified in creeds to be repeated by rote, but rather a way of life for those with the courage to live without the psychological security provided by traditional religious systems.

Early in this book Spong comments on how humans, once achieving self-consciousness and experiencing the anxiety of separateness and isolation as individuals and recognizing the inescapable finitude of death, had created gods and goddesses powerful enough to protect weak, vulnerable humans. But a price had to be paid for such protection; namely, an acknowledgment of human weakness and fallibility ("sin," in other words) and an acceptance of the burden of guilt that inevitably accompanies the imperative to assuage the anger of the deity sitting in judgment in some far-off realm. Early homo sapiens, Spong thus argues, sought to overcome their aloneness and fear of death by creating myths concerning powerful gods to be worshipped and propitiated and places or states of existence such as Paradise or Heaven where the gods resided and to which those who pleased the god or gods might go after death. Anxiety regarding separation from the source of one's being and the fact of death thus gave birth to religion.[8]

---

7. McFague, *Body of God*, 145.

8. Spong, *Why Christianity Must Change*, 51.

In his explication of what is entailed in rescuing Jesus from these ancient myths that have served for centuries more or less as "security blankets," Spong focuses, toward the end of this book, on the meaning of the cross on which Jesus died. Saint Anselm in the eleventh century gave the church an interpretation of the crucifixion that has colored doctrinal teachings through successive centuries. Humans, Anselm argued, had so offended that majesty of the righteous God who had created them and thereby incurred such an immeasurable moral debt that there was absolutely no way they could pay the price needed for their redemption. Hence only God himself could settle the score or, rather, it was his only son who was called into service to satisfy the Father's demand for ransom. Thus Jesus, the literal Son of God, was sacrificed on the cross, thereby freeing believers from the curse of Adam and offering hope of eternal life. In the twenty-first century this tale of moral debt and bloody payment strikes many as bizarre, if not utterly grotesque. But Spong is correct in claiming that traces of Anselm's version of the story have lingered into the late modern period. In the depths of his soul, Spong—and I, too—find this tale abhorrent and an utter distortion of the message Jesus' death conveys—or ought to convey. Here is how Spong explains the meaning of the cross:

> What does the Jesus experience reveal about life, about God, about purpose, about the eternal search for oneness and about what it means to be at one with God? Only if we can answer this question can the cross become for us a usable symbol instead of a sign of the theistic deity's sadistic nature, which required the sacrifice of the son to pay the price of sin. When that theology enters our liturgies, it contributes to human degradation and feeds the fetishes that Christians have developed around the cleansing power of the shed blood of Jesus. It is this external framework—with its language of sacrifice, its abusive, punishing picture of God and its definition of human life as fallen, sinful and broken, capable only of begging for mercy—that has become bankrupt and must now be dismantled.[9]

To summarize Spong's views, in *Jesus for the Non-Religious* he announces unequivocally that a new age is being born, that it is time to reject an interpretation of the life of Jesus that turns him into a "savior" who, in some sense, frees us from the anxiety of living authentically. In following Jesus, Spong emphasizes, one is called to recognize him as someone who rejects "security systems," whether they be race, or tribe, or gender, or ideology, or religion.

9. Spong, *Jesus for the Non-Religious*, 284.

To walk the Christ path is . . . to walk beyond all religious forms that bind our humanity in order to enter the religionless world of a new humanity. It is to seek divinity not externally but as the deepest dimension of what it means to be human. It is to enter divinity only when we become free to give ourselves away."[10]

What walking this path entails, finally, is the courage to pledge allegiance to the Jesus presence "that leads to a wholeness, a new creation, a new humanity and a new manner of living."[11]

It is normally painful, sometimes excruciatingly so, to relinquish "security systems," especially those that have proven serviceable to untold millions over the span of thousands of years. I therefore can understand the rage of the woman who used her umbrella to attack Spong during the burial service for his first wife, adding as she left the church that she had long been waiting to get at "this son-of-a-bitch."

Having just participated in several church services during the Christmas season, when we lustily sang, "Joyful all ye nations rise / Join the triumph in the skies" and "He rules the world / With truth and grace / And makes the nations prove / The glories of his righteousness" and a dozen or more other affirmations of the history-altering victory over sin and death that a baby's birth on a cold night two thousand years ago established, I, too, find it difficult to part with these consoling myths. But I know Spong is right. We homo sapiens have arrived at a time when we can no longer depend on an all-powerful deity, residing in a distant heavenly realm, to save us from our folly. Myths and fairy tales are fine for children. But for adults they may represent potential self-destruction for a race of beings possessing the tools to destroy both themselves and the habitat on which their very lives depend. Hence Spong's message possesses an existential urgency that transcends the question of any individual's or any group's beliefs regarding heaven and hell, sin and salvation, Jesus as divine savior or Jesus as a profound but fully human expression of Being Itself.

WHAT SPONG MISSES IN MYTH

Although by this point in my argument there can be no doubt concerning my sympathy with Spong's quarrel with the institutional church and with many traditional Christian doctrines, I confess to having misgivings regarding what seems to me a reductionist tendency in Spong's work, i.e., such an

10. Ibid., 286.

11. Ibid.

intense concentration on Jesus as the ultimate source of divine emanations as to exclude other manifestations of the sacred. In fact, one looks in vain in the two books dealt with here to find any real discussion of the Earth or the universe—or simple human beings—as loci of the sacred. Moreover, I am convinced that Spong's treatment of myth misses something essential. Belief has to do with more than cognitive functions, and myth, along with poetry, music, painting, and design, reaches into some almost hidden recesses of the human soul that rational discourse normally fails to penetrate.

The novelist and essayist Marilynne Robinson, a writer whose prose always gleams with shining illuminations of some of the darker patches of religious and theological controversy, has written an essay in which she argues persuasively for the power of myth to convey spiritual truths about grief, homesickness, loss and longing, love and death that only story, whether sung or chanted, or etched on a vase, or recited by poets can communicate. And thus she rebuts conclusively, I think, the belief that ancient myths were merely efforts, in an age without the aid of the scientific method, to explain natural phenomena—and nothing more. Robinson's point is made clear when she notes that in Virgil's *Aeneid*, there is a moment when Aeneas, a Trojan who has escaped the destruction of the city he loved, sees a painting of Troy and is

> deeply moved by it and by what it evokes, the *lacrimae rerum*, the tears in things. This moment certainly refers to the place in classical civilization of art that pondered and interpreted the Homeric narratives, which were the basis of Greek and Roman religion. My point here is simply that pagan myth, which the Bible in various ways acknowledges as analogous to biblical narrative despite grave defects, is not a naïve attempt at science.[12]

Myth, in other words, embodies critical truths about human nature, truths that science is incapable of calling forth. Hence Robinson's claim that the great Greek tragedians—Aeschylus, Sophocles, and Euripides—"would surely have agreed with Virgil's Aeneas that the epics and the stories that surround them and flow from them are indeed about . . . a great sadness that pervades human life."[13] The problem for contemporary believers and for those who preach to them or who attempt to make sense of scripture and traditional doctrine for twenty-first-century audiences is surely one of interpretation.

On Sundays millions of Christians around the globe repeat the following words concerning Jesus that he "ascended into Heaven and sitteth on the

---

12. Robinson, *When I Was a Child*, 12.
13. Ibid.

right hand of the Father." The creed continues to spell out the hopes of the faithful: "And he shall come again, with glory, to judge both the quick and the dead; whose kingdom shall have no end."

Understood literally, these words can hardly fall upon the ears of educated listeners as anything more than gibberish. What can possibly be revealed of value to human beings living in an age of space travel and telescopes that bring us news of millions of galaxies in a universe that appears to stretch forever by this image of Jesus sitting in heaven "on the right hand of the Father"? Here, I think, we confront an inescapable question: Shall we follow Spong and ignore Robinson's argument concerning the essential nature of the truths revealed by the "poetry" of mythological language? Or should we attempt to find some point of convergence between these two contending worldviews? This is not an easy task, certainly not for me, because Robinson's argument tends to reinforce reservations I have long held regarding Spong's basic premises and some key aspects of his argument.

What seems to me missing in Spong's analysis, among other things, is wonder, awe, amazement regarding the Creation, the sheer fact that we are here debating the meaning of Jesus. William Blake pointed us in the right direction, I think, when he wrote these lines:

> To see a world in a grain of sand
> And heaven in a wild flower
> Hold infinity in the palm of your hand
> And eternity in an hour.

I am disturbed, too, that Spong's exclusive focus on Jesus tends to reinforce the prevailing propensity of American Christianity to slight the communal in favor of the individual: "What does Jesus mean *for me*?" As I wrote in another context, I experience "an indescribable sadness that the grand vision of the prophet Isaiah of a world healed, made whole, transformed in order to be a fit habitation for the human spirit has been reduced, in much contemporary Christianity, to 'God loves you.'"[14] In this formulation, billions of years of cosmic evolution are reduced to an infinitesimal speck of "recycled stardust." As precious as each individual human life is, there seems to me to be at least a touch of hubris in this ignoring of the cosmic context that has made possible—and apparently inevitable—the human longing to be loved. But, of course, in some sense the Christian story without the dimension of divine love—either God's or Jesus'—for the individual loses its *raison d'etre*.

---

14. Spong, *Why Christianity*, 98.

In a book of essays entitled *I Win, We Lose,* John Hall Snow, an Episcopal priest and professor of pastoral theology, writes about Christian love with a profound understanding of its revolutionary power to free believers from the terror of death, as well as its universality. Snow emphasizes St. Paul's role in extending the reach of this love beyond the Hebrew people and in freeing those touched by this love from the iron grip of the Law. Snow's explication of the extraordinary force of this love is surely not a new understanding, but in a society where so much attention is paid to the desires and needs of the individual, his description of the radical universality of this love possesses the power to persuade.

> The writers of Christian scripture were even more aware [than the Hebrew prophets] that the Christ event had made all things new by the breathtaking inclusiveness it revealed in its power to break the iron rule of death. The Messiah himself had died, not just for Israel but for all humanity. The ultimate word to be spoken about Jesus was love, a love so transcendent that a brutal, tortured, humiliating death as a common criminal affected it not at all. But this love, as it manifests itself in the corporate life of those who, by faith, regard it as an expression of divine will, who live within its graceful limits, is itself something utterly new. It includes the weak, and the poor, and the sick, and the mad, and the hungry, and the unsheltered, and the imprisoned. It includes the self-declared enemy: it includes the rich and powerful. It goes beyond affection, and sexuality, and kinship bonds, and mutuality and has as its motivating center not survival, but gratitude. It is a kind of grateful wonder at the unearned gift of life itself and a need to share oneself and what one is given with one's neighbor out of this gratitude.[15]

FATHER THOMAS BERRY: PROPHET OF THE ECOZOIC ERA

Oddly enough, it is another North Carolinian, Thomas Berry, a Jesuit theologian (at one point in his career, Berry began describing himself as a "geologian," i.e., a scholar studying and writing about nature, evolution, the cosmos), whose writings over a career of many decades direct attention to exactly what Spong neglects—*The Sacred Universe.*[16] In a volume of that

15. Snow, *I Win, We Lose,* 121–22.

16. Thomas Berry was introduced in the previous chapter, but some repetition of his ideas appears unavoidable here in order to make clear the extraordinary contrasts in the thought of these two Christian intellectuals wrestling with basic questions of belief.

title, containing fourteen essays written between 1972 and 2001, I believe the name "Jesus" appears only once. His attention is directed as exclusively to the evolutionary drama as Spong's is to the experience of Jesus. Despite fundamental differences in the approaches of these two controversial thinkers, there are striking similarities. Both, for example, display a dogged determination to speak the truth as they have come to understand it. Both sense the need for new directions in Christian thought and practice. Both, in effect, challenge the established church. Berry, though lacking the occasional flamboyancy of Spong's attacks, is no less definite in his commitment to ushering in a totally new understanding of what is needed from the churches and, in fact, from all the world's religions, to protect the Earth and all its species from ecological destruction.

Among twentieth-century American intellectuals, Berry was uniquely qualified for the task he set himself. Although superbly trained as a Catholic theologian, he had studied most of the major cultures and religions of the world. His writings are studded with quotations from the Upanishads, from Buddhist texts, and especially from Chinese holy books and scholars. He possessed, in addition, intimate knowledge of Native American religious beliefs and rituals. But, and this is the rare feature of his scholarly background, Berry was also trained in science and was totally at home in the world of Einstein, Heisenberg, Planck and the other great figures of twentieth-century scientific speculation and discovery.

Hence he, more than any other scholar on the planet, I think, could bring together a profound understanding of the wisdom and healing power of ancient myths and rituals and the New Story, i.e., the common story of our era provided by modern science. Some of Berry's assertions will probably strike readers unfamiliar with his work as quite startling. For example, this one: "As the primary manifestation of the divine, the natural world is the primary sacred scripture and the primary sacred community." Frequently, Berry's language calls to mind the thought of a mystic, one with the skill of a poet, as evidenced by a statement such as this: In earlier times, a "pervasive religious rapport with the spirit powers of the natural world developed, and ritual enabled humans to enter into the grand liturgy of the universe."[17]

Throughout his writings, Berry is unequivocal about the universe being the primary reality. Everything that is starts there—and ends there. The universe is foundational, irreducible, and for humankind to recover its own deepest psychological and spiritual health and wholeness, it must enter into a profound spiritual relationship—a kind of communion, really—with the universe. For that, Berry emphasizes, a virtually new species is required and

17. Berry, *Sacred Universe*, 105.

surely a new religion. A critical moral dimension of this new religion will be the conviction that "our first obligation in any phase of our human lives is to preserve the integral functioning of the larger world we depend on."[18] And all religious organizations are charged, at this critical moment in the evolution of the Earth and of the human species, to wage a serious campaign to usher in the new age, what Berry denominated the Ecozoic Era. (In *The Sixth Extinction*, Elizabeth Kolbert suggests "Anthropocene" to describe our age, since it is so totally dominated by human activity.)

It was Berry's firm conviction that as humans, now the nerve center of the evolutionary process, begin to experience more fully the exciting drama of the development of the vast universe from its simple origins and experience with deep feeling the majesty of the process, "new religious sensibilities will emerge. . . . This new scientific story of the universe has a mythic, narrative dimension that lifts this story out of a prosaic study of data to a holistic spiritual vision."[19] Berry the poet hits full stride as he describes the spiritual possibilities when humans possess a deep understanding of and communion with the universe.

> Through this story we understand with new insight how every component of the universe is integral with every other of the universe community. To be is to contribute something so precious that nothing before or afterward will ever contribute that special glory to the created world. Through this story we learn something about how the primordial mystery of the universe brought the planet Earth into being as the most blessed of all the planets we know of. We learn how life emerged and took on such an immense variety in its forms of expression. We learn too how we were brought into being and guided safely through the turbulent centuries. In our contemplation of how tragic moments of disintegration over the course of the centuries were followed by immensely creative moments of renewal, we receive our great hope for the future. To initiate and guide this next creative moment of the story of the Earth is the Great Work of the religions of the world as we move on into the future.[20]

Thomas Berry's grand vision, to my mind, renders absurdly trivial many of the religious controversies of our time. And his emphasis on the spiritual value of ancient ritual and myth, which at one point toward the end of this volume are evoked in a call for contemporary rituals to celebrate the

18. Ibid.
19. Ibid., 86.
20. Ibid., 86–87.

natural world and the flow of seasonal change, while different in focus, is not antithetical to Robinson's argument about the salutary influences found in the myths of a distant past.

Berry's project, like Spong's, involves providing an utterly new sacred narrative, one quite different from the familiar narrative derived from the Bible and church doctrine. Simply put, the new story is about neither a supernatural deity nor about Jesus; it is about the drama of evolution from the Big Bang to the twenty-first century, about fifteen billion years of change and chance and development leading from the explosion of a tiny particle of matter to the expanding universe whose size the ordinary human brain appears incapable of finally grasping. To my way of thinking, Berry's vision, devoid as it may be of the icons and signposts that those raised in either the Christian or the Jewish tradition would find familiar, is a grander vision for a world desperately in need of a holistic interpretation of all created things and of our oneness in a blessed communion of offspring of the universe.

SPONG'S BACKGROUND—AND MINE

Geography and guilt may have something to do with Spong's nearly exclusive concentration on Jesus as the ultimate revelation of the sacred. Both he and I grew up in the South, a region of the country where the Christian church is deeply embedded in the culture and where heaven and hell, fall and redemption, the "saving blood of Jesus" are still ever-present realities in the minds and hearts of millions of southerners. In the thirties and forties when Spong and I were children and adolescents, a miasmic fog of religious piety hovered over the landscape. No matter what one might or might not have heard in church—and as an Episcopalian I never heard "hell-fire and damnation" sermons such as our Baptist and Methodist neighbors were sometimes treated to and we surely never held revivals—it was impossible not to absorb from the ambient culture messages regarding the gruesome fate that awaited the unrepentant. Nor was it uncommon to be accosted on the street by a self-ordained preacher training a frozen gaze upon his startled victim while inquiring, "Brother, are you saved?" The virtually unavoidable result was that some sensitive young people absorbed an inordinate dosage of the guilt that Spong accuses the Christian religion of inculcating in its adherents. This was certainly true in my case and I suspect that it may have been also in Spong's. At the very least, he must have often observed the pernicious effects of this artificially induced guilt in family, friends and parishioners. Spong, it seems, reacted viscerally—as evidenced by the bitter language employed in his criticism of the institutional church—having no doubt encountered at an early age Christian teachings of humankind's weakness and moral corruption and the power of those teachings to undermine an individual's sense of self-worth and the drive toward self-fulfillment.

For example, to describe the relationship existing between the institutional church and its followers, Spong uses the word "sadomasochistic." Some will argue that this term is extreme, but surely it is not when we examine many centuries of Roman Catholic life and teachings. To cite a contemporary example, Deirdre English, formerly the editor of *Mother Jones*, relates an episode involving her uncle, a Jesuit priest. At a Christmas dinner in her home when she was sixteen, her uncle told her that she would most likely become a prostitute! When she asked for an explanation, he replied: "It's inevitable since you've been raised with no morals." When she replied that she did, indeed, have morals, his retort was "No, you have been raised with no religion [her father had left the church when in college and she had not been reared in the faith], and so you have no morals. Morals are based in the fear of God. Without the knowledge of hell, people will all be sinners."[21]

Not all Catholics subscribe to such a harsh view, I'm sure, but anecdotal evidence supplied by female Catholic students in Chicago in the sixties and seventies regarding church teachings on sexuality does support the notion that "Mother Church" has traditionally used threats and fear to control the behavior of its communicants.

Nor is Spong's term of sadomasochism unjustly harsh when applied to some forms of southern Protestantism. William Faulkner captures brilliantly the tortured and convoluted strands of guilt, self-hatred and violent reaction which some of the church music of the South reveals. Here are the thoughts of one of his characters, Gail Hightower, the defrocked Presbyterian minister who plays a major role in the final action of Faulkner's novel *Light in August*:

> The organ strains come rich and resonant through the summer night, blended, sonorous, with that quality of abjectness and sublimation, as if the freed voices themselves were assuming the shapes and attitudes of crucifixions, ecstatic, solemn, and profound in gathering volume. Yet even then the music has a quality stern and implacable, deliberate and without passion so much as immolation, pleading, asking for not love, not life, forbidding it to others, demanding in sonorous tones death as though death were the boon like all Protestant music. . . . Pleasure, ecstasy they cannot seem to bear; their escape from it is in violence, in drinking and fighting and praying; catastrophe too,

---

21. English, "Rush Limbaugh, Rick Santorum, and the Pope," 2.

the violence identical and apparently inescapable. *And so why should not their religion drive them to crucifixion of themselves and one another?*[22]

Some may argue that this passage reflects the beliefs of a fictional character, and a deeply disturbed one to boot. True, and while I would never want to maintain that the thoughts of a character in a novel are to be taken as an *exact* replication of the beliefs of the author, it is nevertheless true that no fiction writer—or sociologist or philosopher—has understood the South and its pathologies more thoroughly than did William Faulkner.

I have no knowledge of Bishop Spong's popularity among southern Christians—I cannot imagine that it's very great—but he has an international following that must number in the hundreds of thousands. He has produced many books, writes a weekly article posted on his website, and regularly lectures throughout the English-speaking world. His message, in short, reaches untold numbers of persons who no doubt share his animus toward a religion which they also believe has misled them, caused them misery due to feelings of guilt the church has been so expert at creating, and has obscured the true meaning of the Jesus experience. And presumably many of these persons are prepared to embrace a religionless Christianity in the new age of "renaissance and reformation" that Spong himself has done much to bring into being.

Although I still attend the small Episcopal church in the western Massachusetts village where I have lived for more than a decade—I love the language and musical cadences of the liturgy, I sometimes hear splendid sermons there, and a few members of the congregation are dear friends—I welcome Spong's challenges to institutional Christianity, though, as noted above, I find his wholesale rejection of the ancient myths that the church propagates in its liturgies and creeds in need of correction. Let us not throw out so totally myth and symbol; let us explore them for their *meanings*, meanings understandable to contemporary individuals and capable of freeing them from the fears, anxieties and delusions that accompany human existence at any historical moment. The need for the help that ancient myth, properly interpreted, can offer for the development of a rich interior life is especially great in a time such as ours, a time when the individual is virtually drowned in an ocean of data, "facts," news, and the noisy goadings of a million hucksters intent upon relieving the wavering shopper of her money. In fact, in an age so corrupted by corporate manipulation of citizens' anxieties and gullibility, by political shell games, and by the disillusionment widespread in a society where lying appears to cause no more perturbation to

22. Faulkner, *Light in August*, 404–405.

millions than losing a quarter in a parking meter, a good dose of the poetry of ancient myth—Greek, Hebrew or Christian—may accomplish much in the way of emotional healing.

ANOTHER ALTERNATIVE: CHRISTIANITY AS LIBERATION

Harvey Cox, in *The Seductions of the Spirit: The Uses and Misuses of People's Religion*, provides a compelling alternative to Spong's all-or-nothing approach to Christianity's mythic and symbolic structures. For Cox, the core question for any religion is how it serves humankind in its struggle for *liberation*. Liberation, he declares, is the *"purpose* of Christianity." Cox supports this claim with the assertion that Exodus and Easter are the two central motifs in the Christian understanding of life's meaning, with Exodus signifying more than simple political liberation.

> The early Christians ... saw Easter as a kind of continuation and enlargement of Exodus. I suggest that Exodus and Easter add up to a vision of "God" as whatever is in the vast spectacle of cosmic evolution which inspires and supports the endless struggle for liberation, not just from tyranny but from all bondage. "God" is that power which despite all setbacks never admits to final defeat.[23]

Cox wrote these words at a time, the early '70s, when liberation struggles were underway throughout the Third World and liberation theology was making a significant impact on the thinking of many in the churches. He was drawn especially to Latin American thinkers and to religious movements in Central and South America that sought "to bring their traditions into the service of human fulfillment here on earth."[24] What excited Cox most, I think, was the realization that across the planet formerly enslaved or colonized or rejected and/or ignored human beings by the tens of millions were asserting *their* basic humanity in a struggle for political independence, while at the same time undergoing major changes in their religious beliefs and practices that also emphasized human dignity and the irrepressible longing for psychological and spiritual fulfillment in this life.

As a confirmed Protestant, who had often viewed many Catholic beliefs and practices as little more than products of a lingering memory of "superstitions" from the long ago past, I found myself surprised and at

23. Cox, *Seductions*, 152–153.
24. Ibid., 155.

times delighted by Cox's explication of the significance of such things as the reverence with which Catholics view "the blessed Virgin." Whereas Bishop Spong seems incapable of focusing his attention upon any religious figure other than Jesus, Cox writes about the role of Mary in Catholic piety with deep understanding and sympathy:

> Mary as woman, mother, queen, or comforter is a focal sym-
> bol for one of the largest minorities in the world, the women of
> Christendom. Mary is the central religious symbol in their lives,
> the spiritual energy center that gets them through many tiring
> days and trying years.[25]

Cox seems to intuit effortlessly the deeper meanings of religious prac-
tices utterly alien to the tradition in which he was raised, i.e., the (Northern) Baptist Church. Continuing his reflections on Marian piety, he notes that

> "God," in Hispanic popular piety is almost always pictured as
> dead: as Christ in a casket, being lowered from the cross, being
> placed in a tomb. Mary on the other hand is the radiant incar-
> nation of life and flesh. Her two main manifestations tell it all.
> *Concepcion* symbolizes the always mysterious *beginning* of life.
> *Assumpcion* personifies the anti-spiritualist . . . insistence that
> eternal life without flesh would be terribly dull.[26]

Cox's explications of several aspects of Catholic faith and practice have not only deepened my own appreciation of the spiritual riches of the Ro-
man Catholic Church but have enabled me to understand why several very highly educated and intellectually sophisticated friends and acquaintances have, despite the pedophile scandals and other evidences of official corruption in the church in which they were reared, resisted the temptation to bolt.

Cox's corrective to Spong takes another but closely related form. He stresses the critical role played by Christian faith in the liberation struggles of oppressed peoples from the American south, to South Africa, to Latin America, a role that Spong ignores. Cox was writing about "people's religion" at a moment when Paulo Freire and other Third World writers were giving voice to the long suppressed yearnings and dreams of the silent ma-
jority of Earth's inhabitants. In Africa, in Asia, in Latin America the millions who had never been permitted to speak their minds, being dominated by tyrants of one sort or another, or by colonial rulers, were demanding to be heard. Revolutions were taking place throughout the southern half of the globe, and inevitably the religion of millions longing to free themselves

25. Ibid., 182.
26. Ibid., 177.

politically had to reflect the liberation conflicts changing Earth's political landscape forever.

Whereas Bishop Spong's attention seems focused almost exclusively on Jesus and on those alienated Christians who might once again become "believers" when the "Son of Man" is freed from ancient myths in a Christianity without religion, Cox focuses on *religion* as a central element in the liberation of humans from bondage of every kind. Martin Luther King Jr. surely appreciated intently the power of faith in the righteous, transcendent God of traditional Christianity to sustain his followers through brutal battles for justice, against seemingly hopeless odds. Cox, writing at a time when liberation theology was just beginning to penetrate the consciousness of North American Christians, repeatedly emphasizes the necessity that we privileged and astonishingly wealthy—when measured against the abject poverty of billions in the Third World—members of US churches wake up and overcome our provincialism. That need is as great today as it was thirty or forty years ago.

BEYOND RELIGION

Despite several noted differences with Spong's critique of the church and its doctrines, I remain sympathetic to his insistence on the imperative that contemporary Christians give up dependence on a stopgap God or *deus ex machina* called upon to save us when human effort fails. With Dietrich Bonhoeffer, Spong declares, we must embrace a "religionless Christianity." But if we are going to take Bonhoeffer as mentor and model, it behooves us to be clear about exactly what he is asking of us.

In 1939, over the strong objections of colleagues and friends, Dietrich Bonhoeffer left a secure position at Union Theological Seminary in New York City and returned to Nazi Germany, knowing that this choice would almost certainly lead to his death. Subsequently, Bonhoeffer, once a pacifist, concluded that evil as monstrous as the Nazi movement justified the taking of human life and joined a plot to assassinate Hitler. Although he was arrested for reasons other than the failed plot, Bonhoeffer was tried, and, in the spring of 1945, hanged. Thus Bonhoeffer chose, it seems fair to say, the way of the cross, and in his *Letters and Papers from Prison* he explains his understanding of the God of traditional Christianity in a godless world and the implications of this new understanding for those who wish to be followers of Jesus:

> So our coming of age forces us to a true recognition of our situation *vis-à-vis* God. God is teaching us that we must live as

men who can get along very well without him. The God who is with us is the God who forsakes us (Mark 15.34). The God who makes us live in this world without using him as a working hypothesis is the God before whom we are ever standing. Before God and with him we live without God. God allows himself to be edged out of the world and onto the cross. God is weak and powerless in the world and that is exactly the way, the only way he can be with us and help us. Matthew 8.17 makes it crystal clear that it is not by his omnipotence that Christ helps, but by his weakness and suffering. This is the decisive difference between Christianity and all religions. Man's religiosity makes him look in his distress to the power of God in the world; he uses God as a *Deus ex machina*. The Bible however directs him to the powerlessness and suffering of God.[27]

Bonhoeffer summarizes this portion of his explication of what he calls his "worldly" interpretation with these words: "only a suffering God can help us." What a strange worldview! That, at least, must surely be the response of the average citizen and, I dare say, the average Christian. I believe that most of us, most of the time, if we claim to believe in God at all, want an all-powerful God who can support us in moments of crisis, rescue us in times of calamity. Bonhoeffer, however, seeing that there is no divine power ready to intervene in the "godless world" we modern humans inhabit, utters the following challenge:

Christians range themselves with God in his suffering; that is what distinguishes them from the heathen. . . . Man is challenged to participate in the sufferings of God at the hands of a godless world. He must therefore plunge himself into the life of a godless world, without attempting to gloss over its ungodliness with a veneer of religion or trying to transfigure it.[28]

Bonhoeffer's cryptic and often paradoxical assertions—about the God who has abandoned us being our only help, about being on our own in a godless world, about the requirement that Christians plunge into that godless world and suffer along with the suffering God whom we must not call upon for help—may lead to some confusion but surely all point to one necessary virtue: courage. And Dietrich Bonhoeffer exemplified that virtue in every decision of his short life, ever faithful to meet the challenge he laid down for the rest of us. Apparently fearless with respect to consequences, he plunged into life and participated fully in the suffering of the God to

27. Bonhoeffer, *Letters and Papers*, 122.

28. Ibid., 122–123.

whom he had pledged fealty. He would almost certainly not have wished it, but how can we avoid describing that life as "heroic"? And how would the majority of us, mostly comfortable, mostly white, mostly middle-class Americans—I am referring now to anyone reading these words and to John Spong's American audience—respond to Bonhoeffer's challenge?

Fortunately, to accept the challenge of aligning ourselves with the Jesus who turns his back on the comforts of ossified religious rules and to join the suffering God who can only aid us in his weakness does not normally require a sacrifice such as the one Bonhoeffer made. But if we are really serious about following Jesus, we may go to jail, or suffer in other ways for our actions. As I said recently to a group gathered in a local church to discuss Christian socialism, the time has come when Christians *must* be prepared to be arrested in the cause of social and economic justice. (I sometimes fantasize about what would have occurred if a million American Christians had descended on Washington in the winter of 2003 and blockaded the entrances to the Capitol, the White House and the Supreme Court, protesting against war with Iraq—and stayed there until arrested. I think it likely that hundreds of thousands of Iraqi and over five thousand American lives would have been spared. But we American Christians are mostly too addicted to what Bonhoeffer called "cheap grace" to undertake such "daring" actions.) It is courage, I believe, for which our age pleads and, as noted earlier, throughout Spong's work, one hears echoes of Tillich's *The Courage to Be*.

And no one can say that John Spong, too, has not shown immense courage—defending, while still an active bishop, gays and lesbians against defamation and discrimination; suffering attacks, often vicious ones, upon his personal integrity and upon his scholarship; even threats upon his life. Moreover, several years ago Spong wrote a blistering letter to the head of the worldwide Anglican Communion, the Archbishop of Canterbury, chastising him for refusing to invite an openly gay American bishop to the Lambert Conference, a convocation of Anglican bishops from every corner of the globe. No one in his right mind, I think, impugns the courage of John Spong. But as I've already implied, Spong's use of Bonhoeffer in his argument against the institutional church seems to call for further examination of this supreme virtue.

Another writer whose work embodies motifs from Paul Tillich is Ernest Becker, whose *The Denial of Death* must surely be counted among the more brilliant studies of the twentieth century concerning the challenges humans face in attempting to live meaningful, authentic, fully engaged lives when they "are doomed to live in an overwhelmingly tragic and demonic world."[29]

29. Becker, *Denial of Death*, 280.

Becker again and again alludes to the "eternal contradictions of the real world" and does not shun use of the word "evil" and herein, I think, lies a fundamental difference between his Weltanschauung and Spong's. For I find little in Spong's work to convince me that he is ready to acknowledge the unyielding grip that evil has on the human spirit such as is implied in Becker's description of our "demonic world." Elsewhere Becker, a sophisticated student of Freud, Adler, Jung, Otto Rank and other greats of the psychoanalytic movement, refers to "the Fall" in discussing the plight humankind finds itself in today and will, we can assume, in the future.

In *Why Christianity Must Change or Die*, Spong writes: "We human beings do not live in sin. We are not born in sin. We do not need to have the stain of our original sin washed away in baptism."[30] With certain reservations, I can affirm that this message needs to be heard in a church where parishioners are still, in 2015, expected to repeat the following words: "God of all mercy, we confess that we have sinned against you, opposing your will in our lives. . . . We repent the evil that enslaves us, the evil we have done, and the evil done on our behalf." When I first heard these words spoken by the congregation with which I sometimes worship, I cringed. These are good and decent people, I said to myself, capable of many foibles and even hurtful actions, no doubt, but surely not *enslaved* by evil. When I raised this issue with a dear friend, also a member of the congregation, she pointed out that indeed most of us *are* enslaved—by addictions, chiefly the addiction to consumption, if nothing else. And our general lifestyle, with its extraordinary waste and production of greenhouse gases contributing to looming ecological collapse, is surely a sign of a people who seem enthralled to participate in what must be described as *evil* social and economic structures.

Just how great is the evil of the American way of life may be adumbrated when one considers that we, with 5 percent of the world's population, have until recently consumed 25 percent of the Earth's natural resources and produced 25 percent of the carbon dioxide and other toxic gasses fouling the planet's ecosystems and atmosphere. Perhaps it is salutary to recall something noted in a previous essay: if the rest of the world's population consumed at the American rate, four additional planets would be required to sustain that consumption.

One begins to grasp the enormity of the systemic sin in which "innocent" citizens are implicated when contemplating the likely consequences of the United States refusing to lead a global campaign to establish enforceable international standards for reduction of CO_2 in the atmosphere. To take but one area of the globe, imagine the fate of literally billions of people living

---

30. Spong, *Why Christianity Must Change*, 98.

in India, Bangladesh, China, Vietnam and other countries in Southeast Asia. These countries rely on water from melted glaciers in the Himalayas that feed three rivers—the Ganges, the Mekong, and the Yellow. Life in those countries depends absolutely on these glaciers. Now they are melting permanently. What happens when the rivers are reduced to trickles? The horrific famines of Somalia and other countries in east Africa will pale in significance when compared to the devastation that will occur as this scenario unfolds.

This almost certain disaster for a significant portion of Earth's inhabitants, attributable in large measure to America's actions or, in this case inactions, serves as irrefutable evidence of our country's and, by extension, our own culpability. We are not, we need to constantly remind ourselves, so innocent of involvement in evil as I imagine most of us wish to believe. Thus I would assert that any argument, such as John Spong's, that we humans are not inevitably implicated in sin is shattered when the focus moves from the solitary individual to the social and political context within which the individual exists.

Yet, I have to acknowledge that in one sense Spong is correct; as noted earlier, the doctrine of original sin, as it was developed and often used by the church, suggesting that it is a part of our DNA, so to speak, *has* had many deleterious consequences, for it is definitely true that the church has employed that doctrine to create guilt-ridden followers, to intimidate and to control. But, granting all this, granting that the doctrine of original sin has often been wrongly used, how does one explain the indisputable *reality* of radical evil that covers the globe from east to west, north to south? To attempt to support the claim in that question by citing examples would be a fatuous exercise in exploring the obvious.

And for the radical evil of America's twentieth-century policies abroad, we might reflect upon the words of a Native American Vietnam veteran who has said, "We were told, 'If it moves, shoot it. If it doesn't move, burn it.' We were the bayonet point of American policy." Nick Truse's recent exhaustive account of the unspeakable atrocities perpetrated by the American forces during the Vietnam War ought to convince any thoughtful individual of the capacity for radical evil lurking just beneath the skin of our "civilized" human selves. Chapter 7, "America's Forgotten Wars," explores in some detail the often hidden reality of the evil involved in America's penchant for military conflicts in various parts of the world.

In my view, Spong's desire to correct the pernicious influences of the church's teachings on original sin amounts to a virtual dismissal of a reality which, as Becker repeatedly affirms, is too ubiquitous to be denied or minimized. And, as Spong well knows, Paul Tillich and other twentieth-century theologians are unambiguous about a factor in human life that approximates what is meant by the Fall. For example, Paul Ricoeur writes in *The Symbolism of Evil* that "myths testify that man's most moving experience [is] that of being lost as a sinner."[31] Reinhold Niebuhr was fond of saying that original sin is the only Christian doctrine susceptible of empirical proof.[32] If we humans are not *fallen* creatures, we are certainly deeply *flawed* creatures, implicated, consciously or unconsciously, in monstrous evil.

In *The Denial of Death*, Becker repeatedly calls attention to the difficulty we humans have in understanding ourselves and in coping with the mystery of creation and of our own existence. Describing the human being as "the impossible creature" and contrasting humans with animals, Becker writes: "But look at man. . . . Here nature seems to have thrown caution to the winds. . . . She created an animal who has no defense against perception of the external world, an animal completely open to experience."[33]

What's more, much of that experience mystifies and even terrifies the poor, naked creatures we humans are when divested of the myths, social customs, and self-serving falsifications we create to buffer ourselves from the reality of our existence.

Great thinkers from Aristotle to Kant, from Kierkegaard to Niebuhr have described the predicament that constitutes human life; none has done it with greater perspicacity than Becker. The human being, he writes,

> not only lives in the present moment, but expands his inner self to yesterday, his curiosity to centuries ago, his fears to five billion years from now when the sun will cool, his hopes to an eternity from now. He lives not only on a tiny territory, nor even on an entire planet, but in a galaxy, in a universe, and in dimensions beyond visible universes. It is appalling the burden that man bears, the *experiential* burden. Man's body is a *problem* to him that has to be explained. Not only his body is strange, but also its inner landscape, the memories and dreams. Man's very insides, his self, are foreign to him. He doesn't know who he is, why he was born, what he is doing on the planet, what he is supposed to do, what he can expect. His own existence is incomprehensible to him, a miracle just like the rest of creation, closer to him right near his pounding heart, but for that reason all the more strange. Each thing is a problem and man can shut out nothing.[34]

31. Ricoeur, *Symbolism of Evil*, 8.

32. Finstuen, *Original Sin*, 69.

33. Becker, *Denial of Death*, 27.

34. Ibid., 28.

Becker adds at this point a few words from Abraham Maslow that clinch the argument respecting the fearful puzzle that humankind faces in its own existence: "It is precisely the godlike in ourselves that we are ambivalent about, fascinated by and fearful about, motivated to and defensive against. This is one aspect of the basic human predicament, that we are simultaneously worms and gods." Or, as Becker puts it more colloquially, "gods with anuses."[35]

It is this "burden" of human experience, living on an unpredictable planet in a mysterious universe and having to "make up," as it were, the rules for living with any hope of equanimity and sanity, not to mention decency and fairness, that produces the angst and the guilt that are, Becker underlines, humankind's inescapable destiny. No wonder he so often refers to the "tragedy" of human existence.

As I read Becker's analysis of the seemingly insurmountable obstacles humankind faces in truly understanding itself and the terrors it encounters in an existence shadowed by demonic forces, and simultaneously reflect on Spong's single-minded focus on Jesus as the ultimate source of enlightenment and the most authentic human expression of the love and spiritual generosity Christianity *at its best* has associated with its God, I am haunted by this question: Is the demythologized Jesus vast enough, mysterious enough, to fill the psychological void left by the "death of God"? In short, is the demythologized, religionless "faith" that Spong and Bonhoeffer advocate adequate to carry us through a time when, as the existentialist thinkers, novelists, and playwrights of the mid-twentieth century kept reminding us, the critical threat to human fulfillment and even, in some sense, to human life itself was and perhaps still is meaninglessness?

To confront that terror, Becker suggests that "creative myths" are needed. But he also maintains that a "creative myth is not simply a relapse into comfortable illusion; it has to be as bold as possible in order to be truly generative."[36] And here, once again, Tillich comes front and center. In his reflections on the New Being, Becker asserts,

> Tillich means that man has to have the "courage to be" himself, to stand on his own feet, to face up to the eternal contradictions of the real world. The bold goal of this kind of courage is to absorb into one's own being the maximum amount of nonbeing. . . . As an extension of all Being, man has an organismic

35. Ibid., 29.
36. Ibid., 279.

impulsion: to take into his own organization the maximum amount of the problematic of life.[37]

This analysis *qua* analysis is brilliant; as an imperative for ordinary mortals, I find it terrifying. Becker continues in this vein, however, upping the ante as he proceeds to elevate this exercise in ultimate courage to the cosmic level. A human's daily life

> becomes truly a duty of cosmic proportions and his courage to face the anxiety of meaninglessness becomes a true cosmic heroism. No longer does one do as God wills, set over against some imaginary figure in heaven. Rather, in one's own person he tries to achieve what the creative powers of emergent Being have themselves so far achieved with lower forms of life: the overcoming of that which would negate life.[38]

Tillich's ideas, as filtered through the wonderfully acute mind of Becker, lead to an overwhelming question: Is this creative myth of the New Being something of which only a handful of individuals in each generation may be capable? Say, a Mahatma Gandhi? A Martin Luther King Jr.? A Nelson Mandela? An Archbishop Oscar Romero? A Dalai Lama? And a Dietrich Bonhoeffer? Clearly, to overcome the meaninglessness which, according to Becker, is the form that nonbeing takes in our era—*that* requires heroes of near-mythic stature. Becker puts the case this way:

> What we find in Tillich's ontology of immanence . . . is a creature who takes more of the world into himself and develops new forms of courage and endurance. It is not very different from the Athenian ideal as expressed in Oedipus. Tillich's myth of being "truly centered" on one's own energies is a radical one.[39]

Becker's *The Denial of Death* was published in 1973 and Tillich's notion of the New Being, as salient as it may have then been as an ideal image of human life at its noblest today seems, to echo the younger generation, a bit "weird." Becker, of course, being a thinker of consummate clear-sightedness, had no illusions regarding what most humans do with their intellectual resources and their freedom. As he notes, Tillich's myth "points to all the evasions of centeredness in man: always being part of something or someone else, sheltering oneself in alien powers."[40]

37. Ibid.
38. Ibid.
39. Ibid.
40. Ibid.

Summing up his argument, Becker asserts that the normal human being participates in a "universal betrayal of [his] own powers" through his inclination to seek protection from the angst of individual freedom by submerging himself in "the large structures of society. He contributes to the very things that enslave him."[41]

T. S. Eliot reminded us that "humankind cannot bear very much reality."[42] This dictum may apply equally to all eras and all peoples on some level, though it does seem, at least at this moment, to have special relevance when applied to the people of the United States. Whole swaths of the population appear eager to believe anything they hear on Fox News. For example, no matter how many distinguished scientists or how many national and international boards declare global warming to be an indisputable reality and underscore the human contribution to this planetary crisis, millions of Americans consider the very idea of global warming a "hoax."

Where, we may ask, do these reflections on the thought of Spong, Bonhoeffer, Becker, and Tillich lead us? For some they may lead to near despair. Certainly this seemed true for Chris Hedges when speaking to an interviewer in the summer of 2011. Alluding to the victory of corporations in their take-over of American institutions and centers of power, Hedges said: "Rapacious corporate business interests have shattered all kinds of regulations and controls. They have carried out a coup d'état in slow motion. And it's over; they've won."[43]

Hedges's words call to mind those of John Stockwell, a former CIA agent speaking in Chicago twenty some years ago, who declared, "They [the multinational corporations] own the earth." Now more than ever before, they do, in fact, own almost everything; they own much of the land, the minerals, the petroleum, and the timber, and the entire chain of entities in food production, from fertilizer and herbicides to seeds and their patents, to the grain elevators and railroads by which the grain is shipped, and the plants where the bread is baked, to the distribution centers. They own the stock markets where the grain is priced and traded. They own the banks and other financial institutions. They own a vast number of shopping centers and even portions of some cities.

What is more chilling is that they own legislators, judges, Supreme Court justices, and most of the media. Hence they "own" the information that the public is allowed to receive. And as Hedges documents in *Empire of Illusion: The End of Literacy and the Triumph of Spectacle*, through massive

41. Ibid.

42. Eliot, *Complete Poems and Plays*, 118.

43. Barsamian, "Chris Hedges", 37.

expenditures in such forms as endowed chairs and grants that support research for military or business interests, large corporations exercise inordinate control over US higher education, subverting the real purposes of education in a democratic society. The elite universities, Hedges maintains, "do only a mediocre job of teaching students to question and think."[44]

It would be reasonable to expect Hedges, after writing a book such as *Empire of Illusion*, in which he examines in minute detail the various areas of our national life in which reality is ignored or treated as a dismissible annoyance—it would be reasonable to anticipate his advising his readers to accept the inevitable total collapse of American democracy into a plutocracy ruled by corporate NGOs and their political lackeys. And settle, like Candide, for tending their private gardens. This seems especially true in view of the fact that he uses as an epigraph for his initial chapter, "The Illusion of Literacy," a chilling paragraph from John Ralston Saul's 1992 book, *Voltaire's Bastards: The Dictatorship of Reason in the West*. Saul's basic thesis is that for more than four hundred years Western societies have staggered from one crisis to another, one bloody war to another, always assuming that a specialized elite, armed with the latest *abstract* principles, the latest rationalized techniques, will restore order, solve problems, create a new era of health and happiness. In fact, nothing changes. Hence, if, after listening to Spong, Bonhoeffer, Becker, Tillich, and now Saul we are left in a deep quandary regarding humankind's chances of eluding ultimate collapse, we may not be fairly charged with undue irrationality.

This conclusion seems to follow logically from Saul's contention that the fundamental premise of Western thought of the modern era is flawed. Reason, Saul maintains, is amoral, not capable of telling us how to live:

> Reason is no more than structure. And structure is most easily controlled by those who feel themselves to be free of the cumbersome weight represented by common sense and humanism. Structure suits best those whose talents lie in manipulation and who have a taste for power in its purer forms.[45]

Saul's conclusions are given a high degree of persuasiveness when one considers the example of Robert McNamara, a superbly trained intellectual and expert manager, committed to a rationally conceived plan to force the North Vietnamese to surrender—by bombing them "into the stone age," as recommended by one US general. Common sense might have suggested that a people who had endured subjugation by one foreign power after

---

44. Hedges, *Empire of Illusion*, 97.

45. Saul, *Voltaire's Bastards*, 16.

another for centuries would not allow itself, in an age when former colonies around the globe were struggling for independence, to be once again forced into a form of servitude. But McNamara, like nearly all US leaders at the time, was, one might say, "enslaved" by reason, clinging to the plan even after he knew it had failed. Thus the bloodbath in Vietnam *had* to continue. I cite this episode as a prime example of the "insanity" that infects US society.

Ours is an age, Saul argues, when specialized experts are sought out for answers to a multiplicity of questions. And a torrent of answers is forthcoming from a million sources, though the result is simply increased confusion. "But what are answers," Saul asks, "when there is neither memory nor general understanding to give them meaning?" Supposedly based on rationality, paradoxically our national life is actually a case study of a society where in many respects unreason reigns. Saul puts it this way:

> Organized and calm on the surface, our lives are lived in an atmosphere of nervous, frenetic agitation. Hordes of essential answers fly about us and disappear, abruptly meaningless. Successive absolute solutions are provided for major public problems and then slip away without our consciously registering their failure. Neither the public and corporate authorities nor the experts are held responsible for their own actions in any sensible manner because the fracturing of memory and understanding has created a profound chaos in the individual's sense of what responsibility is.[46]

Saul's book was published in 1992 and in the meantime our national life has become anything but "organized and calm," yet his main point remains valid. Without an anchor in some "creative mythology" that champions those virtues that we humans seem to recognize intuitively as necessary for the health of the human soul and that make for happiness—generosity, compassion, valor, truthfulness, mercy, common sense, and the capacity for forgiveness—we are left exposed to those who employ reason to exploit us. The spiritual bleakness of our society, with its soul-deadening focus on the accumulation of wealth and on the creation of spectacles that serve as a very temporary anodyne numbing the pain of life without genuine purpose, adds immeasurably to the meaninglessness that both Becker and Saul identify at the heart of contemporary American culture.

A true picture of our situation would surely incorporate the conclusion that we are victims of our own success: using the tools that reason, in the form of science and technology, has given us, we have mastered nature, "conquered" space, penetrated to the very smallest particle of matter while

46. Ibid., 17.

at the same time failing to create a society where responsibility and common sense guide action. A kind of world-class forgetfulness has been at work in this process, reminiscent of Kierkegaard's critique of Hegel: the great philosopher had constructed a system in which all of human history had been analyzed, catalogued, and understood. Only one thing was missing: the living and breathing individual, in this case, the philosopher, who had to take down his trousers to defecate and must deal with the terrors and anxieties of existence—and was destined to face alone that last great moment of *his* history—death.

What, then, can be *our* creative mythology? As I implied earlier, the Tillichian hero capable of absorbing into his being great quantities of non-being/meaninglessness can hardly be a model for the average citizen. Or, I would guess, the average churchgoer. Most in both categories seem to prefer the cover of large groups where one can be "lost in the crowd" and where extraordinary courage is seldom called for. And will the Jesus of Spong's dramatic rendering, the "hero" of a religionless Christianity, survive and supply adequate energy for the long haul? I think it is too early to make a prediction, though, as I noted earlier, I have doubts about the demythologized Jesus possessing the magnetic force to appeal to the ordinary "Joe," who, I would guess, thinks rarely about the state of his soul but doesn't mind the notion of a little heavenly assistance in a crisis.

Perhaps a possible answer for us is a "secular" citizen hero who contributes to the overcoming of the spiritual and psychological anomie of the age by opposing the forces that oppress and disenfranchise the majority of their fellow citizens. It could be someone like Howard Zinn, who spent his academic career teaching America about the dark underside of American history and who dared to be arrested when protesting an unjust war. Or it might be a Daniel Ellsberg, who risked a lifetime in prison in order to alert the American public to the multiple crimes the Nixon Administration was committing in Vietnam. It could be a Bradley Manning or Edward Snowden, both of whom have taken enormous risks to inform their fellow citizens of governmental practices that threaten to undermine the basic principles on which American democracy rests.

It might be an anonymous black woman in Chicago or Los Angeles who devotes her entire life to rescuing young men caught in an endless cycle of drugs and prison. Or it could be Bill McKibben, who was one of the very first Americans warning about the ecological disaster just over the horizon—and who has dedicated his life to working tirelessly to avert that outcome. Or it might be a writer like Carolyn Forché, who risked her life in El Salvador in the eighties, documenting and writing poems about the bloodthirsty regime, fully supported by the Reagan Administration, whose death squads left bodies on the streets of San Salvador night after night. It might be someone like Chris Hedges who has reported from locations where few other journalists choose to go—Gaza, Argentina during its "dirty war," Pinochet's Chile, El Salvador during the bloody eighties, and the Bosnian war—and in such books as *War Is a Force That Gives Us Meaning* and *Death of the Liberal Class*, has become an irreplaceable voice of sanity and truth-telling as he plumbs the depths of the soul of America, examining the sources of our spiritual sickness.

And he ends the interview referred to above on a note not of despair but of defiance. Continuing the critique of the corporate take-over of American life, Hedges revealed some of the influence of his study at Harvard's Divinity School: "Corporations are, theologically speaking, institutions of death. They commodify everything—the natural world, human beings—that they exploit until exhaustion or collapse. They know no limits. . . . And what they want is for us to give up . . . to become passive."[47] As John Spong urged in a quite different context, Hedges calls for us to grow up.

> We have to become adults. And it's hard; it's painful. I struggle with despair all the time. But I am not going to let it win. It is incumbent upon all of us that at the same time we recognize how dark the future is, we also recognize the absolute imperative of resistance in every form possible.[48]

Whoever our citizen heroes may be, and I have named a few possible candidates, it is indisputable, I think, that we are entering a radically new era in the life of the human family, one involving new forms not only of economic and political organization but new modes of spiritual awareness and practice. The focus on "savings souls" that motivated much of the zeal of Christian missionary outreach of the past several centuries has outlived its relevance. The passion of millions of Roman Catholics and fundamentalist Protestants that drives their campaigns against abortion and homosexuality is a sad distraction from what should be the focus of followers of Jesus of whatever church or denomination—creating a global society in which every member is adequately fed and everyone's personal integrity and dignity are honored. And as I have suggested at various points in these essays, there is a clear connection between the spiritual malaise affecting the souls of huge numbers of Americans and the physical suffering of Earth's hungry billions. Whether we consciously reflect on this issue or not, the gross contrast between our relative opulence and their desperate want cannot help

47. Barsamian, "Chris Hedges," 37.
48. Ibid.

but contribute to the feelings of impotence and meaninglessness touched on earlier in this essay.

Our argument to this point forces us to consider a question: Will Christianity somehow survive even as the ecclesiastical structures which for centuries have allowed it to thrive as a *religion* diminish in number and power? I'm inclined to think that it will and that even many of the institutional structures might be with us for decades, but only if the churches of America are courageous, creative, and unafraid to listen to voices committed to radical change.

Outside the formal structures of the church—and sometimes within them, too—things are happening that suggest that Christianity, if it can shed its attachment to forms and language that fail to address the *psychological* and *spiritual* needs of those among us who are searching for purpose and meaning in their lives, may indeed have a future.

A dear friend, Mariel Kinsey, for more than ten years wrote a column for the Episcopal Church in the New England town where we both live that appeared in the local newspaper. These columns have been collected in a book entitled *Where Is This Music Coming From? Musings of a Failed Hermit.* Because they so boldly and precisely describe exciting things that are happening that may have an impact on us all, I shall quote several paragraphs from the column for December 2009.

After stating that something *is* happening and that we don't know what that something is, Mariel writes:

> This "something" is happening in science, education, the arts; in religion and churches; in communication and management systems; in individuals and communities a new way of perceiving and relating is emerging.
>
> I am particularly interested in how this is unfolding in many denominations of the western Christian church. Along with ongoing conversations with friends, my significant "informants" are Richard Rohr, a Franciscan priest, and retreat leader; Cynthia Bourgeault, an Episcopal priest and spiritual teacher; and Marcus Borg, a Jesuit scholar and writer. Sometimes referred to as the "emerging church" or "emerging paradigm," this movement is so natural, so various, and so controversial in some circles, that the opinion and resultant words about it are voluminous. It is at once hailed as the salvation of a faltering church and as a heresy inspired by Satan him/herself."[49]

---

49. Kinsey, *Where Is This Music*, 105.

In another column Mariel has written about "flow," a concept central to the emerging paradigm: "both scientists and theologians are coming toward the perception that since everything in the universe is mutually interacting, then the essence of life can be understood as a vast relational flow of giving and receiving. That flow IS reality, that reality IS what we mean by the word God. Nothing exists outside of that reality, not even stars or black holes."[50]

This emerging paradigm seems quite compatible with Thomas Berry's exposition of the cosmic drama in which humans play a key role, and I see no reason why John Spong would find this understanding of reality unacceptable since it surely frees the person Jesus from archaic and, for many, unintelligible imagery of divinity. Jesus brilliantly personified the "flow of giving and receiving" and taught it in his every action and parable.

This paradigm frees us as well, that is, we frustrated believers, and hanging-on Christians like me, and possibly millions of searchers who have found that what Paul Gilk calls "the industry of religion" is totally inadequate to fill the spiritual void created by life in the wasteland our "shoppers' paradise" has now become. By explaining how science and religion no longer battle over beliefs nor compete for adherents but rather provide a vision of reality that great numbers of contemporary individuals, especially, perhaps, the young, seem to know intuitively to be the case, the new paradigm offers what, for me, at least, is an exhilarating answer to a search of many years. I feel, in fact, as if I have come home.

I do have a question, however. Will this paradigm appeal only to an elite in the fields of science and theology, as well as lay persons with the education and intellectual flexibility, plus adventurous spirit, that grasping a totally new world view requires. As I reflect on the possible response of the major churches, I remind myself that most of the members of the congregations with which I am familiar are in middle age or older and thus likely to bridle at the suggestion that they forsake established beliefs and practices.

For those churches whose membership dwindles year by year, it is obvious that only if they can attract a goodly number of youths are they likely to survive. And America's youth have recently demonstrated that many are not nearly as "laid-back," or as self-indulgent, or as egoistic as they seemed to be just a short while ago. Whether it is to the churches that large numbers of our youth will turn for spiritual rejuvenation is questionable and almost certainly unlikely if these institutions refuse radical change.

As for the churches themselves, adopting the emerging paradigm would be a huge step in a process of accepting the "good news" that contemporary

50. Ibid., 104.

science is telling us about ourselves and about our relationship to what has heretofore often seemed a mysterious and sometimes threatening universe. *Giving* and *receiving* by every particle of matter throughout the cosmos leading to the harmony of the spheres and the quest for harmony in human lives—what a stunning and enthralling "new" understanding of the meaning of *everything*. Another word for the process is *love*. A lesson found at the heart of all religious traditions. And a pathway toward health, wholeness, sanity. It's a message a sick society *might* welcome if conveyed by institutions that could be believed.

Though I am thrilled by the vision, I worry about our youth; while some are dedicating time and energy to *Black Lives Matter* and campaigns for decent wages and paid sick leave, or protesting against fracking, many others seem lost souls—pulled this way or that by a cacophony of voices urging one or another solution to loneliness, confusion, anxiety, or despair. And a majority in both categories, I suspect, look upon churches as citadels of obscurantism, hypocrisy, and irrelevance—if they bother to think about churches at all.

American society at large will probably not provide our youth with what they need—a grand, awe-inspiring, life-changing challenge to which they can dedicate their idealism and their imaginations. The churches might. Indeed, if the churches wish to be truly relevant in the twenty-first century, if they wish to offer an answer to the spiritual malaise that afflicts so many of our adolescents and young adults, they have an extraordinary chance if they choose to take on a leadership role in the fight to stave off catastrophic climate breakdown in the near future.

Young people in general don't give a tinker's damn about sin and salvation. They do care about fairness, about justice. And the struggle for climate justice is exactly the sort of campaign that young Americans are committing to. The churches may not increase their collection plates by very much if they declare an all-out battle against the fossil fuels enterprises but they could at least indicate to Americans of all ages that they are honest. They should begin by divesting. (Some such as the Congregational Church have already done so.) And investing all the withdrawn funds in green energy utilities.

So my ideal agenda for the American churches in this century is two-pronged: first, listen to the voices describing reality-flow-God and take the emerging paradigm into your theology and liturgies; and second, infect our youth with a passion for climate justice. After all, it's their future that's at stake and many of them understand and are already responding.

Whether that fight can be won may at this moment be beside the point. Possibly the critical question is that of Ernest Becker: Can a society such as ours produce in any measurable number heroes capable of taking into themselves the nonbeing, i.e., the meaninglessness, that corrupts so much of our nation's life today? Individual heroes we do have; more will come as the urgency increases. But can institutions, especially one as conservative as the Christian church has been, break free of its lethargy and itself become heroic? (I understand, of course, that to speak of "*the* church" is to suggest a monolithic institution which it definitely is not.) Pope Francis is certainly asking all churches, not just the Catholic Church, to rise to the challenge.

My conviction is that to be worth its salt in the twenty-first century, any religion or system of beliefs that purports to offer its followers guidance and support in leading responsible, meaningful lives must assume as a major commitment diagnosing the sources of our culture's soul-sickness and providing "medicine" for a cure. John Spong condemns the established churches for clinging to ancient myths; I condemn the established churches for failure to identify, challenge, and repudiate those aspects of American culture that foster the feelings of spiritual emptiness that afflict so many of our citizens.

There are exceptions, of course, and it should be stressed that the national headquarters of the mainline Protestant churches have year after year issued intelligent, carefully researched, sometimes passionate reports and calls for action about such subjects as racism, homophobia, the greed and waste of the American way of life, and the threat of looming ecological calamity. At the local level, however, I sense a reluctance on the part of clergy to speak what by this point in our history seems an irrefutable truth: most of us, Christian or Jew, believer or atheist, are entrapped in a way of life that is soaked in trivia and mind-numbing spectacle, often breeding apathy, despair and violence.

Here I should say that, despite having written an essay entitled "Why I Am a Christian Socialist," I long ago gave up the hope, which so animated the Social Gospelers, of creating a society whose compassion and thirst for justice might serve as foreshadowings of the biblical kingdom. Yet I still adhere to the belief that it is possible to use science and technology and the best instincts of our citizens to dramatically alleviate human suffering and at least postpone some of the worst consequences of climate change. (In 2015, it is impossible not to acknowledge that we *will* experience some of the worse features of the devastation global warming will bring; and the pig-headed refusal of Republican legislators to accept the irrefutable evidence that the burning of fossils fuels is the major cause of global warming is simply further support for the argument that our existence as a workable democratic society is in great jeopardy.)

Clearly, this moment in our national history does not encourage facile optimism. Lewis Lapham is correct, of course, in reminding us that no period of our history has been free of threats to our democratic way of life.[51] But today, I would argue, our democracy is more fragile than at any time since the Civil War. During the past several decades, a number of US writers, including Noam Chomsky, Howard Zinn, and more recently Christ Hedges have warned against what has sometimes been described as "friendly fascism." Some years ago, Bertram Gross wrote a book by that title. That is, a slow but inexorable development in the direction of an authoritarian society where civil liberties are progressively chipped away, where the press is either in bed with those who control great wealth and political power or are too intimidated to seek out and publish unpleasant truths, where the moguls of commerce and finance hold sway over the legislature and the judiciary, and the public is captivated by the reflected image of itself, as suggested by Saul, or too apathetic to care. The United States as described by Hedges in *Empire of Illusion* and *American Fascists* increasingly resembles just such a society.

That, at any rate, would have been my assessment a few years ago. Coming totally out of blue, however, the Occupy Wall Street movement forced me to admit that, even amidst the apparently dysfunctional Congress, the bitter, at times vitriolic verbal battles between Republicans and Democrats, and the absence among most politicians of even modest discussion of what is *the* critical issue facing the nation, the certain ecological devastation that climate change will bring, there is hope. How can anyone feel anything but hope when in every city in the country and in small towns as well, great numbers of citizens, many quite young, are practicing grassroots democracy with intelligence, political savvy and verve? Can they help in bringing down the monopolies of economic power that threaten our democratic institutions; can they really force the one percent to relinquish some of the wealth they have accumulated, normally at the expense of the 99 percent; can they play a major part in facilitating political reforms that will rectify some of the gross inequities of this society, leading to alleviation of the suffering of the desperately poor in our inner cities and in many rural areas, including the Indian reservations in the West, where thousands live in scandalous poverty; and can they, most importantly, effect a radical change in American attitudes toward the commons and what we all owe each other? In short, can they play a decisive role in the development of a campaign for a *just* society?

51. Lapham, "Dar-al-Harb," 7–9.

The Occupiers, of course, have long since abandoned their campsites on Wall Street and other locations across the country. But they have not disappeared. Many thousands of them are hard at work in cities and towns all over the country, organizing opposition to fracking, for example, or protesting the transfer of public funds from support of local public schools to charter schools. And wherever they are, they seem to exude, in a quite uncanny way, an almost ineffable quality that is perhaps best described by the word "solidarity." That is, as I observed TV news programs and read newspaper or magazine articles outlining the activities, aims, and values of most of the Occupiers, what immediately struck me was the vision, the determination, the willingness to sacrifice and to suffer, and the conviction that change is possible, which I in the past have associated with the liberation struggles of the people of Central America. Granting the vast difference between pepper spray and the possibility of a night in jail on the one hand and the threat of a Salvadoran death squad on the other, it yet seems reasonable to assert that for both the occupiers and for Central Americans struggling for liberation, human existence appears to have real meaning only when lived in *solidarity* with one's sisters and brothers.

In order to broaden the comparison, I should note that many of the Central Americans are Roman Catholic Christians and almost certainly they believe that in their struggles for dignity and social and economic justice, the theistic, biblical God they worship is their constant support. American blacks, in their centuries-long battles for racial justice, also turned to the supernatural deity of orthodox Christianity to guide and inspire them through heart-rending suffering and sickening defeats. And in both cases, hope and a sort of transcendental love brought both peoples to a partial achievement of their dreams.

Although I doubt that many of those involved in the OWS movement are Christians—either traditional believers or adherents of the religionless faith in a demythologized Jesus that John Spong espouses—I don't think it is overreaching to describe many of them as "people of faith." They don't repeat creeds and they don't proselytize. Probably most do not pray. They *act*. They organize. They protest. They welcome strangers. They inspire. They give cause for others to hope. And thereby they help to dissipate much of the meaninglessness of a narcissist society drenched in trivia, mesmerized by spectacle, and seemingly destined to smother in its own excrement—if not trash, then spent uranium. And they provide inspiring models to those "dead souls" trapped in cycles of compulsive consumption or compulsive sex, fruitless attempts at filling the spiritual vacuum that haunts millions of Americans—models of the joy and the freedom that come through discipline and dedication. In all these ways, I believe, they may project a way of life beyond the despair that Chris Hedges and many of the rest of us wrestle with daily.

It would be foolish, of course, to expect miracles from this nascent movement. It might have devolved into quarreling factions. It could have led to violent reactions to police brutality. Most of these young people have shown remarkable discipline and remarkable courage, enduring tear gas, pepper spray, and jail to convey their message: "We represent the 99 percent of Americans who are exploited by the nation's most wealthy 1 percent and we will not relinquish our demands for greater equity in the distribution of wealth in this country." The occupiers were exceptionally wise in not allowing themselves to be co-opted by the Democratic Party and in not attempting to create a huge, unwieldy national organization. One of the most salutary aspects of their movement was its local, democratic character.

Kalle Lasn, publisher and editor-in-chief of *Adbusters*, whose visionary thinking provided the impetus for the Occupy movement, sums up its success in these words: "It was perfect in the way it played out: the fact that it was leaderless and demandless and mysterious and everyone was second-guessing what the hell do these people want. . . . And we were able to pull off a magical few months when we held the attention of the world. Even if nothing happens from now on, we've already done something truly wonderful."[52]

Writing in the *Nation*, Carne Ross, who was Tony Blair's expert at the UN General Assembly when the question of Iraq possessing WMDs was the issue of heated debate, is enthusiastic about what the Occupy movement provides in the way of ideas and models for organizing societies. Ross is convinced that "top-down government-dominated politics" no longer works. "Governments by their own admission are less and less able to control the massive, heterogeneous forces now making our world: dramatic economic transformations, mass migration and climate change."[53] What is needed is participatory democracy, such as he observed in Zuccoti Park.

> This was politics of the many, included at last. . . . Here I saw true respect, not the pretend respect of diplomacy. Here I saw involving and passionate debate, not the childish antagonism of Internet debate or the partisan rancor of Washington. The crowd was gripped by an unfamiliar emotion, a shared sentiment that others were listening and that their decisions truly mattered.[54]

Ross is convinced that only a politics involving "self-organized, non-violent action by the many" is competent to deal with the kind of extremely

52. As quoted in Middlewood, "The Spark," 34.
53. Ross, "Occupy Wall Street," 24.
54. Ibid.

complex, increasingly integrated, thoroughly interconnected planet we now inhabit.

> The rational models of neoclassical economics failed to take account of the influence of irrational human behavior, like that witnessed in the credit bubble's credulity. . . . Unpredicted and unmanaged economic volatility, mounting social fragmentation and grave environmental damage are now overwhelming the appealing but simplistic "internal" logic of equilibrium-seeking markets and utility-maximizing consumers.[55]

(Reinhold Niebuhr's reflections on the limits of humankind's "power, wisdom, and virtue" and John Saul's theories about the fallibility of human reason, had they been heeded by the apostles of the unrestrained free market, might have spared millions a good deal of grief—in Russia, in various Latin American countries, as well as here in the heartland.)

Perhaps, in their courage and determination, so totally unexpected in the indulged, "spoiled" kids of this spoiled society, we find foreshadowings of the citizen hero for which the age yearns. And perhaps by way of these brave spirits, a new creative mythology can emerge. There are many millions here and in every country on the planet working to make such a dream a reality.

Among them are novelists, playwrights, poets and other artists whose works in a variety of genres alert us to the destructive forces of our world and probably more importantly, provide balm for our weary spirits and aching hearts. The poet Carolyn Forché, mentioned earlier, is a consummate example of the writer who combines, in her life and in her poetry, those qualities that I earlier cited as typical of a life that provides succor and combats meaninglessness. In a recent issue of *Poetry*, Forché offers a close-up view of her present spiritual state, some years after her time in El Salvador. Those of us struggling for a new understanding of the Christian story may find in her words much to inspire and sustain us in the tough times ahead:

> The wonderful experiences I had in El Salvador transformed my thinking and my spiritual life. The time there returned me to something, but without the encumbrances of certain institutional aspects of the church that have to do with its earthly manifestation as an institution. It was very freeing. I didn't want to leave, but not because I wasn't afraid. Whenever I came close to being wounded or hurt or killed in El Salvador, and there were a few occasions, I was terrified. I would immediately be nauseated. I was not good at this. Other people were much better at it. But I didn't want to leave, nevertheless, because I didn't

55. Ibid.

want to leave this community. *I had recovered the presence of God, only this time it was in humanity. I was in El Salvador, living in a place full of horror, but also full of light.* That's where I wanted to stay.[56]

I am an octogenarian and have only a few more Christmases to celebrate. But I have five grandchildren and it is impossible not to feel considerable anxiety about the country—and the world—I and my generation are leaving them. I take heart, however, from the citizen heroes I have cited, and thousands of others like them, who demonstrate great courage in the struggle for the "Peaceable Kingdom," even though they may not use that term. And they may not find in Jesus the well of love and acceptance that Spong locates there, and yet it is clearly a profound love of their brothers and sisters that motivates them. And I know of no other meditation on the presence of this profound love in our world, which is surely as "godless" as was Bonhoeffer's, more moving than these words from the closing paragraph of Chris Hedge's *Empire of Illusion*:

> I am not naïve about violence, tyranny, and war. I have seen enough of human cruelty. But I have also seen in conflict after conflict that we underestimate the power of love, the power of a Salvadoran archbishop, even though he was assassinated, to defy the killing, the power of a mayor in a small Balkan village to halt the attacks on his Muslim neighbors. These champions of the sacred, even long after they are gone, become invisible witnesses to those who follow, condemning through their courage their executioners. They may be few in number but their voices ripple outward over time. The mediocrities who mask their feelings of worthlessness and emptiness behind the facade of power and illusion, who seek to make us serve their perverse ideologies, fear most those who speak in the language of love. They seek, as others have sought throughout human history, to silence these lonely voices, and yet these voices always rise in magnificent defiance. All ages, all cultures, and all religions produce those who challenge the oppressor and fight for the oppressed. Ours is no exception.[57]

These words, from a person for whom I have great admiration, permit me to end my reflections with no increased belief that Jesus or any other manifestation of the sacred "rules the world." But I don't believe that Satan or some other incarnation of evil rules the world either. Ernest Becker

---

56. Forche, "One Whole Voice," 461, emphasis added.

57. Hedges, *Empire of Illusion*, 192.

is right: human existence *is* tragic, but in genuine tragedy there is always revealed an essence of goodness. And much of that goodness resides in the courage and the defiance of evil that the hero demonstrates. I consider myself fortunate to have lived in a time when such heroes as Martin Luther King Jr. and Archbishop Romero have shown us how fully human a life dedicated to unbounded love for one's fellow humans can be. And I have lived long enough to recognize that every age has its citizen heroes, though it is often hard to see just who they are at the time. There are many active today and many more who have yet to discover their role.

Carolyn Forché and Chris Hedges, each of whom has looked steadily into the darkness that shrouds the human heart in so many places on our planet and yet can remind us powerfully of what love can do despite the horror, provide life-saving contemporary examples of the "citizen hero" whose witness affords the rest of us great strength in our own efforts to grasp the courage to be—in whatever milieu we find ourselves. Through these two fellow citizens, I, at any rate, feel connected to a love that transcends national boundaries and even global boundaries. Hedges' father was a Protestant minister; Forché grew up in the Roman Catholic Church. Neither, I gather, feels a strong bond to established religion. Yet both, I think, would understand Spong perfectly when he speaks of his "Jesus experience."

And for both I can only give thanks as I continue to seek a faith not based in ancient myths or contemporary illusions. I have never been much given to hero worship, but I confess to feeling blessed to have lived in a time and in a country that produced such heroes as Carolyn Forché and Chris Hedges who, in their courageous examples, offer inspiration for others to follow.

CHAPTER 7

AMERICA'S FORGOTTEN WARS

The day is not far distant when three Stars and Stripes at three equidistant points will mark our territory: one at the North Pole, another at the Panama Canal, and the third at the South Pole. The whole hemisphere will be ours in fact as, by virtue of our superior race, it already is ours morally.

—PRESIDENT WILLIAM H. TAFT[1]

Wars are God's way of teaching the Americans geography.

—AMBROSE BIERCE

Americans love to fight. . . . All real Americans love the sting and clash of battle.

—GEN. GEORGE S. PATTON JR.

War is a racket.

—GEN. SMEDLEY BUTLER, US MARINE CORPS

1. Taft, as quoted in Galeano, *Open Veins*, 107.

189

Lt. Thomas Jefferson Kilcourse, United States Marine Corps, was not happy. He had just buried five of his men and two members of the local militia. The place was a hamlet in northern Nicaragua. The date was New Year's Eve, 1927. In the following journal entry, he vented his anger and frustration.

"Sad ceremony—Americans giving their lives for no cause of their own. . . . Some New Year's Eve—and what a greeting on New Year's Day for the families and friends of the dead—slaughtered like rats in a trap." There is no way of knowing how long Lt. Kilcourse had been in Nicaragua—the first contingent of Marines had arrived there in 1909—but long enough to have a pretty good understanding of what his men were fighting and dying for: "to keep in power a man who, when he got himself in a mess, and about to be thrown out of office by a revolution—called for and got the aid of American Marines to keep him in power—which means nothing but with his snout in the trough of the public treasury."

This no doubt competent and brave junior officer cannot suppress his bitterness as he considers the reasons for the mess *he's* in: the Nicaraguan president secure in his palace

> guzzling champagne . . . while he should be out leading his forces against the revolutionists. . . . And the forces opposed to the government are revolutionists—regardless of the fact that we call them bandits . . . an effort to fool the public of the United States whose opinion would demand our immediate withdrawal were they to realize the true facts.[2]

The Marines would stay in Nicaragua for another five years, at times led by Smedley Butler, described by Douglas MacArthur as "one of the really great generals in American history." General Butler had a rather different take on his tenure as gringo "enforcer" in Central America. After he retired in the mid-1930s, he wrote an article in which he expressed sentiments that Lt. Kilcourse would no doubt have appreciated. After mentioning his thirty-three years of service, rising from second lieutenant to Major General, he lets loose: "During this period I spent most of my time being a high-class muscle man for Big Business, for Wall Street and the bankers. In short, I was a racketeer for capitalism."[3]

Smedley Butler was no literary artist, but his language in the following paragraph describing his activities as a "racketeer for capitalism" does possess a kind of zip and snap that one might expect to find in a would-be poet writing journalistic prose:

2. Kilcourse, "Diary," Navy Archives, Washington, DC.

3. Ali, *Clash of Fundamentalism*, 259.

Thus I helped make Mexico . . . safe for American oil interests in 1914. I helped make Haiti and Cuba a decent place for the National City Bank boys to collect revenues in. I helped in the raping of half a dozen Central American republics for the benefit of Wall Street. . . . I helped purify Nicaragua for the international banking house of Brown Brothers in 1909-12. I brought light to the Dominican Republic for American sugar interests in 1916. I helped make Honduras "right" for American fruit companies in 1903.[4]

America's Initial Military Conflicts Abroad

At about the same time that General Butler was preparing to turn Honduras into one huge plantation for the United Fruit Company, American soldiers were winding up a brutal campaign in the Philippines. The Spanish-American War, ostensibly fought to free Cuba of domination by the Spanish Empire, had come to a very swift conclusion with the easy victories of US ground forces in Cuba and naval forces in the Philippines. The Filipino people had fought for their independence with considerable success for several years prior to the arrival of the Americans, and declared their intention of setting up an independent government. Washington, where Teddy Roosevelt was now president, declared the idea beyond the pale.

The overt racism of those who argued for annexing the Philippine Islands may strike some today as astonishing, but no one should really be surprised that US leaders couched their arguments in the same sort of language that had been used to justify the virtual decimation of Native American tribes. In fact, many of the soldiers who fought in the Philippines had served in the Indian Wars when orders sometimes came down to kill not just the males but women and children as well.[5]

As early as 1893, in *The Winning of the West*, Roosevelt had written, "The most ultimately righteous of all wars is a war with savages." Such a conflict, he maintained, laid the "foundations for the future greatness of a mighty people." T.R. then expressed what is probably the single most definitive utterance guiding American policymakers dealing with dark-skinned nations in the twentieth century. "It is of incalculable importance that America, Australia, and Siberia should pass out of the hands of their red,

4. Ibid., 260.
5. Ibid., 258.

black, and yellow aboriginal owners, and become the heritage of the dominant races."[6]

This passage is a classic example of imperialist justification for appropriating other people's possessions, but perhaps is noteworthy only because it so innocently and glibly spells out the unexamined assumptions that have lurked beneath the American Empire's twentieth-century campaigns against peoples of the Global South from the Philippines to Nicaragua, Haiti, Panama, and the Dominican Republic.

Wars of aggression are "righteous" so long as the victims are not of our race. "Dominant world races" should fool no one. He means Anglo-Saxon or other European descent. And because we white people are obviously superior, it is by right that we take other people's land or impose on them a government of our choosing. The Social Darwinism of the day, in fact, virtually dictated such practices, and the arrogance of T. R.'s statements would almost certainly have gone unremarked in many circles of American society in the Gilded Age.

The overt racism of this early episode in America's rush to join Great Britain and the other imperialist powers in acquiring colonies, or what might be called "plantation dependencies," was not limited to its leaders, since many (white) Americans would have agreed with Senator Beveridge of Indiana that America was "of the ruling race of the world."[7] The soldiers sent to bring civilization and Christianity to the benighted Filipino people (of course, many of these "savages" were Roman Catholic Christians) were not shy about revealing the delight they experienced when shooting "gooks," a favorite epithet used decades later by US troops in Vietnam.

One soldier from New York writing home expressed these sentiments:

> Last night one of our boys was found dead and his stomach cut open. Immediately orders were received . . . to burn the town and kill every native in sight. About 1,000 men, women and children were reported killed. I am in my glory when I can sight my gun on some dark skin and pull the trigger.[8]

David Bain notes that some of the American soldiers were horrified at what they witnessed or even took part in, while others appeared to revel in the "fun" that war on foreign soil made possible:

> "We make everyone get into his house by seven p.m.," a California corporal wrote home. "If he refuses, we shoot him. We

6. Bain, *Sitting in Darkness*, 66.
7. Shalom, *Imperial Alibis*, 13.
8. Bain, 84.

killed over 300 natives the first night. They tried to set the town on fire. If they fire a shot from a house we burn the house down and every house near it and shoot the natives."[9]

The comment of one participant in this crusade to bring enlightenment to the "lower races" requires no gloss: "Our fighting spirit was up, and we all wanted to kill 'niggers.' . . . This shooting human beings beats rabbit hunting all to pieces."[10] But perhaps we should hear the words of one American, and there were many others, who saw clearly the true significance of this butchery in the Philippines and protested against it. The sociologist William Graham Sumner wrote, "We talk of civilizing lower races, but we have never done it. We have exterminated them."[11]

SOME "WARS" THAT WERE NOT WARS

Many of America's "wars" have not been wars at all, since that word implies a meaningful opposition. Rather, more often than not they have been attacks mounted against relatively defenseless civilians whose leaders have pursued policies viewed in Washington as inimical to US interests. Take, for example, George Bush Sr.'s 1989 invasion of Panama. The ostensible purpose of the invasion was to remove from office the Panamanian president Manuel Noriega, whom US officials accused of various offenses.

Noriega had indeed permitted drug dealers to operate in Panama and was himself involved in that enterprise, though money laundering was probably his major source of income. He'd also been on the CIA payroll for years and had cooperated with the United States in supporting the Nicaraguan contras. But lately he'd switched sides in that conflict, a mistake that no US flunky should ever make.

There had been, in addition, tensions developing between Panama and the United States over administration of the canal. During the Carter Administration, treaties had been negotiated that gave Panama control over operations of the canal, a fact that aroused hostile opposition among conservative members of Congress and in the media. Then there were incidents involving the killing of a US soldier and the roughing up of an American military official and his wife. As Stephen Shalom points out in *Imperial Alibis: Rationalizing U.S. Intervention After the Cold War*, Bush was afraid that his manliness would be in doubt if he allowed a two-bit thug like Noriega

---

9. Bain, *Sitting in Darkness*, 84.

10. Ibid.

11. Sumner, *War and Other Essays*, 34.

to thumb his nose at him and get away with it. Moreover, the issue with Noriega was a problem not just for President Bush, but for other American officials. As Shalom notes, if the United States failed to use military force to settle its disputes with such a weak and insignificant country as Panama, "how was US superpower status—based as it as on military might—to be maintained?"[12]

There was another reason for the United States to launch a military strike against Panama. According to Shalom, "the invasion of Panama also provided [the Pentagon] an opportunity to demonstrate the capabilities and utility of its new, expensive, stealth fighter-bomber, desperate to find a mission as the Cold War wound down."[13] Thus, a few days before Christmas in 1989, twenty-two thousand American soldiers and an untold number of fighter planes and helicopters descended on the totally vulnerable population of Panama City.

The exact number of Panamanians who died in the invasion has, from the beginning, been a matter of dispute. Some human rights organizations have claimed several thousand; the US government's count was under three hundred. I see no reason to doubt the figure given by Chalmers Johnson—"3,000 to 4,000."[14] What was reported by eyewitnesses is that shells were fired into apartment buildings, that road blocks were set up by US forces where civilians attempting to flee the city were shot point blank, and that many bodies were dumped into mass graves.

A report of a nongovernmental organization, the Commission of Defense [of] the Human Rights in Central America (CODEHUCA), contains testimonies regarding "Extra-judicial Executions," "Shooting at civilians," and "Persecution of medical profession," as well as other offenses committed by the invading forces.

The picture that emerges from these testimonials is not one likely to make any American with an active conscience proud. One person interviewed by the CODEHUCA delegation described the scene as US forces attacked the neighborhood in which she lived:

> I saw when the Dignity Battalion [Panamanian military] members were fleeing, and then came USA soldiers, and then the helicopters. They were shooting their guns and those laser–rays right at our wooden houses and at the multi-family dwellings.

12. Shalom, *Imperial Alibis*, 178.

13. Ibid.

14. Johnson, *Sorrows of Empire*, 69.

I can tell you it wasn't the Dignity Battalions that were burning the houses—it was the gringos.[15]

Another witness testified that in the chaos which followed the invasion, the American forces only watched as looting took place and civilians were being shot: "What was noticeable was their impassivity, their indifference to all that was occurring—to the fact that there were Panamanians being shot and killed in their presence."[16] In addition to those Panamanians killed by US personnel and by rioting and looting fellow citizens, more than twenty thousand were left homeless; but an American president could hold his head high, knowing he would not be viewed by his peers as a man who had to "squat to piss," as Lyndon Johnson had described one US official who turned dovish on Vietnam.

The invasion of Panama was, of course, illegal when judged by the standards of international law and the United Nations Charter, but the United States has seldom been reluctant to violate international law when its "vital interests" were at stake. Or when a president, be it Theodore Roosevelt, Richard Nixon, or George Bush *père* or *fis* needed a war for ego-boosting or domestic political advantage.

Just as the deeply ingrained racism of American society has had a powerful impact on foreign policy, so has an equally ingrained heterosexism. Again and again the record shows that American officials tend to respond to threats, real or merely imagined, to America's security with the language of male dominance and oppression. As Stephen Shalom argues:

> Lack of sentimentality for dark-skinned people has been part of
> an approach to foreign policy that prizes masculine toughness
> and disparages any human empathy as feminine weakness . . .
> The pounding of Cambodia did not save American lives, but
> in Barry Goldwater's words, showed, "we still got some balls in
> this country."[17]

Shalom speaks of "testosterone poisoning" as an ailment that has affected American policy-makers for generations and concludes that military actions have often been the preferred response to problems that might have been resolved by peaceful means.[18]

---

15. CODEHUCA.

16. Ibid.

17. Shalom, *Imperial Alibis*, 194.

18. Ibid.

PROXY WARS: THE NICARAGUAN CONTRAS

A number of America's twentieth-century wars have been proxy wars, fought not by US personnel but by the government of a US client state, e.g., Guatemala in the 1980s, against a large segment of its own population. One of the most vicious and destructive of the proxy wars was the contra war against the elected Sandinista government of Nicaragua.

When the US Marines were withdrawn from Nicaragua in the early 1930s, they left behind the National Guard, whose chief, Anastasio Somoza, soon became the country's president who ruled like any other Latin American "strong man." Somoza was both ruthless and greedy and eventually controlled major interests in dozens of enterprises, amassing wealth estimated at just under a billion dollars—this in a country where the great majority were desperately poor peasants. Those who openly opposed Somoza's greed and disregard for the needs of the country's majority might be kidnapped and subjected to merciless torture and, in some cases, thrown from a helicopter by members of the National Guard.

Eventually armed resistance emerged, including some leaders who had studied abroad. A good number of those who took part in the resistance were students; many were women and girls. The name they chose for themselves, Sandinistas, had special significance for those on both sides of this conflict, for it was derived from the name of the leader of the "revolutionists" that Lt. Kilcourse and his Marines had fought against, Augusto Caesar Sandino. Sandino's barefoot peasant guerrillas, armed with antique rifles and the courage born of the love of one's homeland, had fought the Marines to a draw. Thus for millions of Nicaraguans, Sandino, who had been tricked and murdered by Somoza, had become in the national mythology the ultimate symbol of heroic patriotism.

Like many other leaders of revolutionary movements of Latin America at that time, several of the key figures among the Sandinista leadership had studied Marx and were avowed Marxists. And why not? After all, Somoza and his cronies practiced a vicious form of capitalism. Their exploitation of *campesino* farm workers employed on their vast estates was pitiless, and they resisted with violence any attempts to create a more just and humane society. Hence the class warfare Marx had written about was too obvious to be ignored, and for many Nicaraguans it was clear that Marx had been correct: those with wealth and power seldom if ever relinquish their privileges in response to pleas expressed in the language of morality or religion. (As Archbishop Romero of El Salvador discovered, more likely they shoot you.) Frequently a violent revolution becomes the only path toward a society founded upon justice and recognition of the rights of all its citizens. I should note, also, that most of the Sandinistas were practicing Christians for whom the words of the Hebrew prophets and Jesus regarding the obligation to struggle to alleviate the suffering of the poor and oppressed were salient injunctions.[19]

The new society established after the defeat of the Somoza dictatorship in 1979 was very clearly a socialist one. The lands of the Somoza family and of many of the wealthiest supporters of the dictatorship were confiscated and thousands of peasants were awarded small properties, enough to support a family. Doctors, some from Cuba, began to treat the poor, almost none of whom had ever before received professional medical care. Health centers, staffed by nurses, were established in remote rural locales. A literacy program designed to equip the most ignorant and most poverty-stricken peasant with the rudiments of math and reading brought idealistic young people from the cities to remote areas of the country where schools were built. Fundamental to the ideology of this entire enterprise was the belief in the innate dignity of each human individual, regardless of his or her station in life.

Almost overnight the Sandinista revolution inspired millions—in Europe, in the United States, and in Latin America. And it drove President Ronald Reagan almost crazy. Soon after he entered office in 1981, Reagan's State Department and the CIA moved to blunt the effects of this socialist movement that had recently won a victory over a US client state. As it happened, there was no need to plan an invasion. The Sandinistas had won a stunning military victory, but many of the dictator's National Guard had escaped—to Miami or Honduras or other neighboring countries. Thus there came into being the contras (the Spanish word for "against"), former members of Somoza' *Guardia*, recruited, trained, armed and paid by the CIA. Their purpose was to create havoc among the civilian population and to undermine the economy, in the process destabilizing the Sandinista government so thoroughly that it would lose all credibility in the eyes of the populace.

Although Reagan lauded the contras as the "moral equivalent of the Founding Fathers," they were, in fact, thugs who used the methods of terrorists to achieve their ends. They raped nurses. They burned health clinics and schools. They bombed fuel dumps. And they murdered selected targets.

Bradford Burns, a professor of Latin American history at UCLA, provides reports of extensive contra atrocities committed against the civilian population: "The International Human Rights Law Group published a report . . . containing sworn statements from witnesses to murder, torture, and rape committed by the contras. The chairmen of both the Americas Watch

19. Ibid., 96–97.

and Helsinki Watch visited Central America . . . and witnessed "a planned strategy of terrorism . . . being carried out by the contras."[20]

I suspect that few today except Noam Chomsky and historians writing about US relations with Central America remember the contra war. It lasted for about a decade and cost hundreds of thousands of lives, and, along with a US embargo, virtually destroyed the Nicaraguan economy. And it led to scandals in this country, especially the so-called Iran-contra affair—"trading arms for hostages"—with money from arms sales going surreptitiously to the contras after Congress had voted to suspend financial support. It was an extremely ugly affair but hardly more than a blip on the American consciousness, especially after Reagan assured the nation that he knew nothing of the skullduggery going on a few yards from the Oval Office.[21]

But for Nicaragua, the war had been a disaster. The United States, as always, simply went about its business of making the world "safe for democracy." (It was President Woodrow Wilson who gave this handy phrase to US officials teaching recalcitrant nations proper behavior.) When Nicaragua took its case to the World Court, seeking indemnities for material damages to its infrastructure, it was awarded $17 billion. The United States ignored the court's ruling. It likewise ignored two votes in the UN General Assembly condemning its brushing off the World Court's judgments.

GUATEMALA

Limpieza: Ethnic Cleansing Big Time

The case of Guatemala provides another example of what might be described as a "proxy war," this one possibly bloodier than the Nicaraguan contra war. Stephen Shalom describes the US role in a massive killing of Guatemala's indigenous population:

> In 1954, the United States overthrew the elected government of Guatemala and organized a brutal security apparatus to maintain the status quo. Over the next three and a half decades, the U.S.-backed security force . . . was responsible for as many as 200,000 killings, with the help of intelligence files set up by the CIA.[22]

Organized resistance to the brutal regime that followed the coup launched what soon became a civil war, in which the Mayan descendants

20. Burns, *At War,* 71.

21. Johnson, *Sorrows of Empire,* 130.

22. Shalom, *Imperial Alibis,* 134–135.

living in the highlands became the principal targets of the terror. Tens of thousands of these indigenous fled their homes, some to the jungles where they managed to survive for months or even years; some to Mexico; some to the United States. But anyone who might in any way have been thought less than totally loyal to the military junta that ruled the country—including professors, students, human rights lawyers, judges or journalists—might be snatched off the street, interrogated, tortured and then murdered. To make identification difficult, heads were often disfigured and hands cut off.

Kate Doyle, a Senior Analyst at the National Security Archive, a nongovernmental organization that "campaigns for the citizen's right to information," is the author of a document which presents in detail the story of Guatemala's years of terror, "THE ATROCITY FILES: Deciphering the archives of Guatemala's dirty war." Here she writes, "When Guatemala's thirty-six year civil war ended, in 1996, the country was a vast unmarked grave. More than two hundred thousand people had died or disappeared in the conflict, most of them unarmed civilians."[23]

Information from the army and the national police force regarding those who had been killed or disappeared was thought to be nonexistent until 2005, when quite by accident a huge trove of National Police files was discovered. At that point it was possible for Doyle and Guatemalan colleagues to begin investigations, identifying many of the victims and locating mass graves where bodies had been dumped. Eventually sufficient evidence was accumulated to allow for a trial in the spring of 2013 of former President Ríos Montt, who as the head of the Guatemalan army and later president of the country had overseen the scorched-earth policies in the countryside and the capture and murder of thousands in urban areas who were suspected of supporting the guerrilla movement. At one point, a trial in Madrid, Spain, was planned but because it was impossible to extradite Ríos Montt, he was tried in Guatemala—and found guilty of genocide.

Though a judge discovered irregularities in the proceedings and ordered a retrial, this author of untold suffering for millions of Guatemalans—if one includes the families and friends of the dead—will hereafter be known for what he is: a mass murderer. And a great many Guatemalans can rest a bit easier knowing the fate of a father or a brother or other relative or friend and having been able to provide a proper grave for the murdered ones. (The remains of many of those who were disappeared have been exhumed.) Moreover, some of those directly involved in the perpetration of atrocities have been arrested, tried, and are serving prison time. So a kind of justice has been achieved.

23. Doyle, "Atrocity Files," 52.

But such a resolution is extremely rare. And what of those in Washington or Langley, Virginia, who plot or organize and support the coups—from Iran, to Chile, to Indonesia, to Zaire, the former Belgium Congo, and to almost a dozen other countries, as well as the proxy wars—that have led to countless deaths? These often esteemed and well-paid planners of US policies designed for "policing the world," as many legislators and pundits like to put it, will naturally never be held accountable. And presumably few of them have sleepless nights due to the mayhem and bloodshed their policies have caused. Stephen Shalom's frank comments indeed represent the truth:

> Moral and legal rhetoric have been constant features of U.S. foreign policy, but morality and legality have been essentially irrelevant to those making policy. As Henry Kissinger explained in closed testimony after betraying the Kurdish minority in Iraq, "covert action should not be confused with missionary work."[24]

How is one to explain this sad story of America's aggression against so many of its neighbors on the small planet we share? Here I employ a metaphor: America often acts like a very naughty boy who bullies his chums, giving black eyes whenever one of them annoys him. And because he's bigger and more aggressive, he gets away with it. He's done it so often—and his bullying provides pleasure, for it confirms his feelings of superiority—that it's become an addiction.

He, quite literally, can't help himself.

A doctor in Panama City complained after the US invasion about *impunity*. The Americans come here, he said, and they kill our people and cause much destruction and they do so "with impunity." Why is the United States allowed to kill people and pay no price for its crimes? He was right, of course; no one pays a price for such crimes—except the civilians working in the Twin Towers and the firemen and policemen who died attempting to recue those trapped inside. And officials and Marine guards at US embassies in countries like Libya, when they are attacked in occasional episodes of "blowback."

When John Forster Dulles, secretary of state, and brother Allen Dulles, CIA chief, plotted with the UK to overthrow a democratically elected government in Iran and return to power a murderous kleptomaniac, the Shah, retribution was surely not on their minds. And they were rewarded a few years later when a major airport was named for them. But in Iran and elsewhere in the Middle East people did pay a price—many thousands slaughtered by the Shah's secret police—and American hostages were held

---

24. Shalom, *Imperial Alibis*, 6.

for months. And the United States has been portrayed not only in Iran but elsewhere in the region as the "Great Satan," not a very desirable moniker in such a volatile part of the world. As always, excuses are offered, though sometimes hardly thought necessary, lies are told, and quickly such "business of state" fades from popular memory. Almost no American remembers the coup in Iran and virtually no journalist working in print or on radio or television bothers to tell American readers or listeners about the significance for Iranian-American relations of this violation of Iran's sovereignty and the substitution of a violent, thieving government for a popular, democratic one.

VIETNAM: AMERICA'S SOUL IN PURGATORY

An American war that no one is likely soon to forget is the Vietnam War, although it really should be called the "Vietnam-Cambodian War" because after Richard Nixon declared that he would honor the neutrality of Cambodia, he ordered a merciless bombing campaign against that country. More explosives, in fact, were dropped on Cambodia than on Japan during the entire Second World War.[25]

Of America's many wars, Vietnam is surely likely to be judged by future historians as the most ruthless. As of this writing, it is certainly not forgotten and is likely to haunt the imaginations of millions—veterans and their families—for generations. Yet, given the extremely short attention span of most Americans and the general flaccidness of historical memory in this country, I would guess that after the last Vietnam vets have died, for most Americans Vietnam will be remembered little more than the invasion of Panama.

However, the publication in 2013 of Nick Truse's *Kill Anything That Moves: The Real American War in Vietnam* may render that prediction incorrect. For in this book Truse documents in painstaking detail the stark depravity of the American onslaught against the civilian population of Vietnam.

The most notorious massacre of civilians occurred in March 1968 at a village called My Lai. Here a US army unit moved into the village and did, indeed, kill anything that moved: chickens, pigs, cows and water buffalo, and any human being they could find.

> They gunned down old men sitting in their homes and children
> as they ran for cover. They tossed grenades into homes without

25. Ibid.

even bothering to look inside. An officer grabbed a woman by the hair and shot her point blank. . . . A woman who came out of her home with a baby in her arms was shot down on the spot. . . . Over four hours, members of Charlie Company methodically slaughtered more than five hundred unarmed victims."[26]

They even took a lunch break, then returned to the killing. In addition to the killing, these men raped girls and women and "mutilated the dead and fouled the area's drinking water."[27] For these atrocities, one junior officer was tried and spent a couple of years in prison. No senior officer was charged.

Truse makes it unmistakably clear that during the years when American personnel were present in Vietnam, many My Lais occurred. "They were no aberration. Rather, they were the inevitable outcome of deliberate policies, dictated at the highest levels of the military."[28]

The French philosopher and journalist Simone de Beauvoir offers supporting evidence documenting the charges of war crimes leveled against the United States in Vietnam. De Beauvoir served on a Vietnam War Crime Tribunal that was modeled on the Nuremberg trials. The testimony of several former US military personnel left little doubt that torture and slaughter of civilians were common practices in this conflict. An African American veteran said that "he had been present both at torture sessions and massacres. On the orders of an officer he had killed a woman who had not joined the group gathered on the village square quickly enough." Had he not done so, "he would have been shot at once."[29]

> "Our officers think the only good Vietnamese is a dead Vietnamese." He also said, "Another very common thing was that if we were fired on from a village we had our 'crazy moment'—the tanks and machine guns blazed away for quite a while, firing at everything in the village, living or dead." He was asked how many of these "crazy moments" he had witnessed, and he replied "I've seen them so often! . . . It was what you might call quite usual."[30]

This same soldier also spoke of the "strategic villages" to which the US forces moved hundreds of thousands of Vietnamese peasants and said, "All

26. Truse, *Kill Anything That Moves*, 3.
27. Ibid.
28. Ibid., 6.
29. De Beauvoir, *All Said and Done*, in Gioseffi, *Women on War*, 112.
30. Ibid.

the people I saw looked as though they were starving, and they were all in rags." Another American, a former "green beret," stated that "the Americans massacred all prisoners in Vietnam except for officers," who were turned over to government forces. Their fate was no better, however, since they were transferred to "death camps."[31]

De Beauvoir reported that "the unanimous decision [of the tribunal] was that the Americans did make use of forbidden weapons, that they treated prisoners and civilians in an inhuman manner, contrary to the laws of war, and that they were committing the crime of genocide."[32]

Officers insisted on almost daily "body counts" and the men involved in "search and destroy" missions knew they were expected to turn in impressive numbers. Hence they often killed civilians and reported them as enemy soldiers simply to meet imagined quotas or to impress superiors. Perks of various kinds, including leaves and promotions, depended on body counts; and officers' careers could be made or wrecked by body count arithmetic. According to Truse, a fair estimate of Vietnamese deaths, most of them civilians, is three million.[33] "Gooks," in short, were fair game, and the American "liberators," spurred by glib rhetoric at home and the collusion of their superiors, once again as in the Philippines, brought wholesale destruction in their train.[34]

WHY WE FIGHT

We might take a look at other American wars, "police actions," and interventions—a depressingly lengthy list—but I'd like instead to examine briefly some questions about why nations and individuals fight, in other words the psychology of war broadly understood. We might begin with the obvious fact that almost always it is men, not women, who instigate wars and have, in the past, normally fought them.

In a chapter entitled "The Sources of U.S. Foreign Policy," Stephen Shalom includes a section with the heading "Sexism, Heterosexism, and U.S. Foreign Policy." Shalom notes that those who make foreign policy in the United States are most often men attracted to power, who fear nothing more than being thought of as wimps, who frequently prefer the use of force against another nation rather than taking a dispute to the United Nations.

31. Ibid.

32. Ibid., 114.

33. Truse, *Kill Anything That Moves*.

34. A more recent account of the American war in Indochina is Christian G. Appy's *American Reckoning: The Vietnam War and Our National Identity*.

Some members of American officialdom during the Kennedy-Johnson Administrations spoke of the "hairy chest syndrome."

And in the eighties, when I joined more than six hundred protestors who sat down to block the entrance to CIA headquarters in Virginia, one of the favorite terms of derision used to describe men like me was "pinko-limp-dicks." When he issued orders for the bombing of North Vietnam, Lyndon Johnson was reported to have remarked, "I didn't just screw Ho Chi Minh. I cut off his pecker."[35]

Many of us who were adults or teenagers during the sixties and early seventies watched on the nightly news the destruction of the rain forests with Agent Orange, the fire-bombing of village after village, the virtual incineration of children with napalm. And then the saturation bombing of Hanoi. And we were sickened. Although the public reaction to those horrors seemed agonizingly slow, eventually the majority of Americans came to question the sanity—and the morality—of the war policy that Lyndon Johnson and Robert McNamara attempted to justify. So it is possible to say that in time the American public did, finally, understand that the American war in the former Indo-China was fundamentally wrong and morally indefensible. The revulsion felt by millions—which policy makers likened to a disease they labeled the "Vietnam syndrome"—was palpable. One might think that a powerful moral objection to the mass killing of civilians by the government one may have helped elect and to which one paid taxes would be considered a sign of psychological and spiritual health.

That was not the case. By the eighties, America's leaders had decided that such a "sickness" was not fitting for the world's major superpower. So the public had to be softened up by Reagan's invasion of Grenada, a tiny Caribbean island, in 1983 and by George H. W. Bush's invasion of Iraq in 1989. And in these cases, a cardinal mistake of the Vietnam era was carefully avoided: the nightly TV news coverage did not show American viewers the wanton carnage on Iraq's sands. In *War Is a Force That Gives Us Meaning*, Chris Hedges, a master of the English language, does the job for us: "War usually starts with collective euphoria," he writes.

> It is all the more startling that such fantasy is believed, given the impersonal slaughter of modern industrial warfare. I saw high explosives fired from great distances in the Gulf War reduce battalions of Iraqis to scattered corpses. Iraqi soldiers were nothing more on the screens of sophisticated artillery pieces than little dots scurrying around like ants—that is until they were blasted away. Bombers dumped tons of iron fragmentation bombs on

35. Shalom, *Imperial Alibis*, 19.

them. . . . Helicopters hovered above units like angels of death in the sky. Here there was no pillage, no warlords, no collapse of unit discipline, but the cold and brutal efficiency of industrialized warfare waged by well-trained and highly organized professional soldiers. It was a potent reminder of why so many European states and America live in such opulence and determine the fate of so many others. We equip and train the most efficient killers on the planet.[36]

Most Americans do not want to hear this story. It is too painful to learn that many of the tales of heroism and glory associated with America's wars are myths. Besides, for multitudes in this country, the emptiness of life in an artificial paradise of commodities can be filled with patriotic dedication and passion. For those able to pull aside the Wizard's curtain, however, the pumped-up, commercialized expressions of love of country that Fox News orchestrates, with military personnel front and center, at events like the World Series and the Super Bowl, tricked out with a crescendo of off-key renditions of "God Bless America" and "America, the Beautiful," reinforce the air of hypocrisy that increasingly surrounds public events in this country.

In *War Is a Force That Gives Us Meaning*, Hedges exposes the attraction that war has for multitudes of people, especially young men, but vicariously for many others as well. He describes war as "a drug," which can easily become an addiction.

It is peddled by mythmakers—historians, war correspondents, filmmakers, novelists, and the state—all of whom endow it with qualities it often does possess: excitement, exoticism, power, chances to rise above our small stations in life, and a bizarre and fantastic universe that has a grotesque and dark beauty.[37]

One of the things that I find most compelling in his description of war is its capacity to transform not just those who participate in war but also the reality that surrounds the death and destruction. War, Hedges asserts, "dominates culture, distorts memory, corrupts language, and infects everything around it."[38] Furthermore, his discussion of the effects of war on the individual participant sheds a good bit of light on why the psychological pull of war can be so seductive:

36. Hedges, *War Is a Force*, 84–85.
37. Ibid., 3.
38. Ibid.

The enduring attraction of war is this: Even with its destruction and carnage it can give us what we long for in life. It can give us purpose, meaning, a reason for living. Only when we are in the midst of conflict does the shallowness and vapidness of much of our lives become apparent. Trivia dominants our conversations and increasingly our airwaves. And war is an enticing elixir. It gives us resolve, a cause. It allows us to be noble.[39]

Earlier, I commented on the phony display of patriotism that Fox News creates for major sporting events. The Pledge of Allegiance, the music, the military uniforms, the unmistakable air of dedication to *our* brave fighting men and women who are prepared to sacrifice their lives for our safety and freedom—all are an irresistible attraction to many young citizens whose lives are utterly devoid of drama, purpose, and inspiring goals. Furthermore, not only do many of these youths lack challenging goals, they lack challenging opportunities. Hence for tens of thousands, a few years in uniform offer enticing opportunities—to travel, to acquire valuable skills, to learn work habits that can be useful when they return to civilian life. And if they take part in combat, they *may* have stories to tell their grandchildren.

THE COSTS OF WAR

It is more likely, however, that they will have nightmares. If they have seen buddies killed or have themselves killed members of the enemy forces—or have taken part in deliberate slaughter of civilians—unless they have been turned into professional killers who murder for pleasure, they will almost certainly never recover from the trauma of war. The experiences of veterans of Vietnam, Iraq or Afghanistan frequently leave indelible scars that can eventuate in drug addiction, violence against a spouse or children, broken marriages, self-inflicted wounds, lifelong psychological problems, and suicide. (See chapter 2 for a discussion of the post-war lives—and deaths—of Vietnam veterans.)

The personal costs of America's wars borne by those who have participated in the fighting clearly can be enormous. The financial costs, too, are staggering. According to a study reported by the American Friends Service Committee, the US government is still paying benefits to descendants of veterans of every American military conflict since the Civil War. And the costs to taxpayers of overall preparation for and participation in war—the Department of Defense, actual wars, and the nuclear weapons program—is 57 percent of the federal budget. In addition, veteran's benefits account for

39. Ibid.

5.5 percent. While it is true that major reductions in force sizes and other defense budget cuts have been undertaken by the Obama Administration, they do not represent a change in our militaristic direction. Instead of an army of over half a million, the United States will have *only* a little more than 400,000 soldiers to staff its bases around the globe.[40]

Now well into the second decade of the twenty-first century, America might appear to be in a position to limit, if not terminate, its historic propensity to engage in warfare of some sort every few years. US forces have left the Iraqis to fight amongst themselves and the great majority of American troops have departed Afghanistan.

Are we about to witness a miracle, Uncle Sam without a major enemy to engage in combat? Obviously, not. Chalmers Johnson's prediction regarding blowback has proved quite accurate: the spread of American popular culture, commerce, and military installations into every part of the world, especially into Muslim countries, has virtually guaranteed that any number of militant groups will push back. Someone, I think it was George W. Bush, has said that the fight against "terrorism" could last for a century. And with the large-scale use of drones likely to be the option of choice wherever possible, America can rain down destruction from the skies, in Yemen, North Africa, and Pakistan, for example, with minimal costs in (American) lives. This surely is the Pentagon's scenario for the future: fewer and fewer American lives lost as the United States wages high-tech military operations against states and collections of individuals thought to be associated with terrorism.[41]

The previous two paragraphs were written before the summer of 2014 when ISIS launched its campaign, conquering territory and cities in Syria and Iraq. It now seems almost certain that, no matter what President Obama may intend, the US military will be involved in that conflict in some capacity for years to come.

As is frequently the case, Chris Hedges provides one of the most provocative analyses of the historical background of ISIS. "The Islamic State of Iraq and Syria (ISIS) is our Frankenstein." So begins his article with the title "ISIS—the New Israel," posted on *truthdig* on December 15, 2014.

> The Unites States after a decade of war in Iraq pieced together its body parts. We jolted it into life. We bathed it in blood and trauma. And we gave it its intelligence. Its dark and vicious heart of vengeance and war is our heart. It kills as we kill. It tortures as we torture. It carries out conquest as we carry out conquest.

40. American Friend's Service Committee report
41. Coll, "Unblinking Stare," 98–109.

It is building a state driven by hatred for American occupation, a product of the death, horror and destruction we visited on the Middle East. ISIS now controls an area the size of Texas. It is erasing the borders established by French and British colonial powers through the 1916 Sykes-Picot Agreement. There is little we can do to stop it.

ISIS, ironically, is perhaps the only example of successful nation building in the contemporary Middle East, despite the billions of dollars we have squandered in Iraq and Afghanistan. Its quest for an ethnically pure Sunni state mirrors the quest for a Jewish state carved out of Palestine in 1948. Its tactics are much like those of the Jewish guerrillas who used violence, terrorism, foreign fighters, clandestine arms shipments and foreign money, along with horrific ethnic cleansing and the massacre of hundreds of Arab civilians, to create Israel. Antagonistic ISIS and Israeli states, infected by religious fundamentalism, would be irreconcilable neighbors. This is a recipe for apocalyptic warfare. We provided the ingredients.[42]

The regular news media fail, as is usual, to supply details of the backstory that supports the accuracy of Hedges' indictment. For instance, the use by the invading American forces during the First Gulf War of weaponry containing highly toxic "spent uranium"; and the "No Fly Zone" imposed by the George H. W. Bush's White House and continued by the Clinton Administration that prevented delivery of desperately needed medical supplies to Iraqi hospitals and clinics, leading to as many as five hundred thousand deaths among the country's infants and children.[43] When asked if she believed the "no fly" policy was worth the cost, Secretary of State Madeline Albright's answer was "Yes." Such glib affirmation of the cruelty of national policy need not condemn an entire population, but it sheds light on the reasons for hatred of America expressed by many millions, not all of them Muslims.

We Americans like to think of ourselves as kindhearted people, and when dealing with one of our own—especially one of our own "tribe"—we can be extraordinarily warm and emotionally generous. But in the small world we now inhabit, we mostly fail as neighbors. As Hedges' little anatomy and history lessons teach us, the havoc our nation creates in a distant part of the world can have significant repercussions for others on the planet, some our friends. It serves at the least to remind us of a lesson we should all have

42. Hedges, "ISIS—the New Israel," 1.
43. Arnove, "Scenes from Iraq," 34.

learned as children, that, though they often dawdle and take a devious route, the chickens do, finally, come home to roost.

THE "NEW" WORLD DIS-ORDER

Returning to a proposal regarding America declaring peace and removing its military bases from scores of countries from Yemen to Japan, I should stress that I believe my argument is strengthened when we recall that John Kennedy announced a desire to pursue a similar goal during the height of the Cold War, in his United Nations speech in 1963. I understand, however, how "utopian" such a suggestion sounds today. But as I wrote in "Why I Am a Christian Socialist," I doubt that the nations of the world can survive even until mid-century without nuclear weapons being acquired by terrorists groups intent upon destroying those they perceive as their enemies. And then all bets are off. In the earlier essay, I claimed that my suggestion that a truly sane society would "declare peace," withdraw all its troops from foreign soil, disband its military and devote the trillions of dollars thus saved to eliminating gross poverty and hunger from the Earth was not so utopian after all. I speculated, in fact, that, if the United States initiated such a plan, recruiting by various militant groups intent upon destroying the United States would dramatically decline or disappear entirely.

A much more practical proposal than the one I've put forward was recently tendered by Lester R. Brown of the Earth Policy Institute. Brown suggests reducing the Pentagon's annual budget by $185 billion dollars each year, a sum adequate "to eradicate poverty [worldwide], stabilize population, and restore the economy's natural support systems—forests, soils, aquifers, and so on. . . . The $185 billion is less than a third of the U.S. defense budget."[44]

Even *my* proposal might still strike me as reasonable except for the fact that what was once a more or less secular campaign to punish a neocolonial power for its repeatedly brutal meddling in Near Eastern affairs and for pushing its tawdry popular culture upon traditional Islamic societies has morphed, as Hedges emphasizes, into a *religious* crusade to establish an Islamic state throughout the entire Muslim world. This, obviously, is a radically transformed and much more threatening scenario; and now, willy-nilly, America and dozens of other countries are being drawn into the conflict.

There is a lesson here which US leaders might take to heart although there is little evidence to indicate that they will: Before you initiate a war in a region of the world where there are centuries-old ethnic and religious

44. Brown, *Breaking New Ground*, 166–167.

divisions, think long and hard about possible consequences of your actions. Talk to those who know the "sociology" of the area. Refrain from the use of military force until you have absolutely exhausted all diplomatic options for reducing conflict. If you decide that you must use force, plan carefully. Study the aftermath of the 2003 invasion of Iraq, where you'll find an unbroken record of incompetence, one disastrous failure following hard on the heels of another. Above all else, read Chalmers Johnson about the inevitable blowback to be expected when any country insists on using its superior power to work its will upon other nations. And read Andrew Bacevich.

In a sane society, Bacevich's *Washington Rules: America's Path to Permanent War* would be required reading for students in all college and university courses in American history and political science. It would certainly be required reading at West Point, Annapolis and at the Air Force academy. It would be required reading for the country's generals and admirals. It would be required reading for all members of Congress. And if members of Congress actually read this extraordinarily persuasive book and took to heart its message, that, in itself, would qualify as a miracle beyond measure; and then, perhaps, at least a variation on the kind of America that I have been calling for throughout *my* book might stand a chance of coming into being.

But none of the above is likely to happen. As Bacevich demonstrates with brilliant lucidity, the tentacles of the national security state have burrowed so deep into the country's consciousness and secured such firmly fixed anchorage in the society's institutions—political, military, educational, journalistic—that freeing America from their iron grasp does appear to be beyond reasonable expectations.

In *Washington Rules*, Bacevich, who served as an officer in the Marine Corps in Vietnam, leaves few stones unturned as he analyzes the rules that govern US foreign policy in the twenty-first century. Those rules, in fact, have been securely fixed since the end of World War II and were hardened in place by the Cold War. Essentially, what Bacevich wishes his reader to grasp is the totally unquestioned supremacy of those rules, accepted as absolutes by most politicians of both parties, by the military, by many intellectuals, by a vast majority of journalists, and by the American public at large.

The rules consist of what Bacevich calls a "credo," that is, a fundamental article of faith, and a "holy trinity." The credo has been articulated hundreds of times by those called upon to describe America's mission vis-à-vis the rest of humanity: "to lead, save, liberate, and ultimately transform the world."[45] And always it is understood that America alone can fulfill that mission.

Having laid out the principle, Bacevich then describes the practice: "to maintain a *global military presence*, to configure its forces for *global power projection*. And to counter existing or anticipated threats by relying on a policy of *global interventionism*."[46]

It cannot be happenstance that Bacevich's choice of language to describe the rules for America's domination of the entire world is saturated with religious overtones. For the complete and unchallengeable nature of the commitment that loyalty to America's global hegemony demands is very like that of unwavering belief in the realm of religious practice.

It cannot be chance either, I think, that oftentimes it is those who embrace religious doctrines without one flicker of doubt who are most susceptible to a form of patriotism characterized by rigidity and inflexible certitude that America has been called by God or Providence to rule supreme on the Earth.

That kind of certitude makes it extremely difficult for adherents of this quasi-religious political faith to discern the fallacies that such arrogance and hubris give rise to. As Bacevich notes, when US policies aimed at "saving" the world fail, as they do with disconcerting frequency, the result is not reassessment of the validity of the rules but rather a search for a guilty party to blame, somewhere else on the planet, and frequently a repetition of those policies that ought have been judged as unworkable and hence discredited. Such aberrant behavior in an individual would normally be described as a neurosis.

To carry the religious analogy a bit further, we might consider Bacevich's suggestion that the Pentagon is much more than a huge, five-sided building; it has become the embodiment of an idea, of a virtual myth, and a kind of temple—a symbolic representation of this rather mad notion that one country can lord it over the rest of Earth's peoples in perpetuity and with impunity.

And what should be obvious to all but the willfully blind is that in pursuing this belief that Washington has an inalienable right to rule the Earth, America sacrifices its own economic, social, moral, and spiritual health. Bacevich calls our attention to the fact that this self-righteous obsession with imposing our nation's ideas and values upon others, most often with military force, evoked in the postwar era some dissenting voices. In this context he quotes the US diplomat George Kennan who pointedly

45. Bacevich, *Washington Rules*, 12.
46. Ibid., 14, emphasis in original.

called his fellow citizens' attention to their tendency to neglect the needs of their own society: "It seems to me that our country bristles with imperfections—and some of them very serious ones—of which we are almost universally aware, but lack the resolution and civic vigor to correct." Kennan then underscores what is critically at stake here: "our duty to ourselves and our own national ideals."[47]

Kennan criticized his country's constant focusing on external threats, principally the Soviet Union, while refusing to address in a serious manner the imperfections and failures of its own society. He advocated "a genuinely healthy relationship both of man to nature and of man to himself." Then, he said, Americans might, "for the first time, have something to say to people elsewhere." It was even possible, he avowed, that they might become "a source of inspiration" to other inhabitants of the Earth.[48] In short, it was his hope that America might model freedom rather than attempt to impose it on others.

Christopher Lasch, whose thoughts about America's pathologies I invoked in chapter 1, also spoke about the authentic mission of America: "The real promise of American life," he asserted, resides in "the hope that a self-governing republic can serve as a source of moral and political inspiration to the rest of the world, not as the center of a new world Empire."[49]

Once again I find myself balancing, precariously, on the horns of a dilemma. Throughout this volume, I have called into question the chances of America turning from the path it has followed for decades, a path that has led to what seems an irreversible commitment to endless wars, ever-increasing power vested in the men and women who staff the military-industrial complex, and a population of uninformed and often disengaged individuals, easily swayed by propaganda from the military or from the hired acolytes of the super-wealthy one percent, and little inclined to fight to defend their rights as free citizens. And, to complicate the country's plight, it is threatened by a looming environmental disaster which neither the government nor our citizens seem prepared to address with the full-scale and urgent action the conditions of the moment call for. Thus I have more than once indicated that, much as I wish to affirm its opposite, I find it hard to avoid the conclusion that America is headed inexorably toward a crack-up of some sort or, at the very least, transformation into a society ruled by oligarchs and military brass.

47. Bacevich, *Washington Rules*, 236.
48. Ibid.
49. Ibid.

But then, as I've reflected on widespread evidences of renewal, of a major paradigm shift promising both political and spiritual renewal among various segments of the population at large, I have found my spirits lifting and my hopes for America at least somewhat restored.

In addition, as I've watched the nightly news following grand jury failures to indict white police officers for killing African American males in Ferguson, Missouri and New York City, the moral force of America's youth, clearly determined to bring about a radical shift in the functioning of the country's legal system with respect to protection of *all* its citizens, has generated in me a renewal of hope for America's soul. When viewed side by side with the Occupy Wall Street movement and other examples of organizing for social change led by the under-thirty generation, this new expression of idealism, courage and determination strongly suggests, to my way of thinking, that all is not lost.

So, once again I am left dangling between hope and utter despondency. Given our long history as a nation seemingly in love with war, coupled with the enormous power of the military-industrial complex and the billions of dollars to be earned by those maintaining our outlandish war-making capacities, and the seemingly permanent establishment of the rules for US global hegemony as described by Bacevich, the idea of our nation overcoming its addictions and undertaking an experiment as challenging as radically reducing its massive war-making machine in order to feed Earth's hungry masses does, I confess, sound a little absurd.

But those serious about the survival of the human family on the Earth must act on this idea. As I have asserted repeatedly since the early pages of this book, it seems clear to me that a radical paradigm shift, involving more than just changes in thought but, more importantly, changes in hearts, is required if we humans are to avoid destroying ourselves—either with bombs or with sizzling temperatures that will turn our planet into an overheated oven where no human will want to live.

And now, in 2015, there is indisputable evidence, I feel certain, that the human family *itself* is on the cusp of a paradigm shift of incalculable proportions. Kevin Danaher, the cofounder of Global Exchange, describes it this way:

> For the past 500 years our world has been dominated by a paradigm of money values/violence/God-is-on-our-side. But a new paradigm is rising from the grassroots around the world that can be characterized as life values/nonviolence/God-does-not-take-sides-in-intra-species conflicts.

This new paradigm seeks to shift from the current system that subordinates the life cycle to money values, to a new system where the money cycle will be subordinated to life values. Our young species is leaving our adolescence and entering adulthood. We are realizing that we cannot treat people and nature as commodities.

The contrast between the world-that-is and the world-that-could-be grows more stark every day; the world-that-is keeps getting worse, and the world-that-could-be keeps getting better. When a person realizes that they don't need to stay stuck in the world-that-is and they can make a pilgrimage to the world-that-could-be, it releases spiritual energy, the best renewable energy there is.[50]

Given the tenaciousness and the centuries-tested durability of the money paradigm, it would be unwise to count on its disappearance in the near future. Leaving behind adolescence and all the illusions that tag along, thereby freeing oneself to embrace genuine adulthood, is generally not an easy achievement—for an individual. For a species, it hardly seems possible.

And what about a country as trapped in illusions, myths of omnipotence, and narcissism as contemporary America seems to be? Is there reason for hope here? Can the life-affirming paradigm blossom in our land? When I think back on the evidence I have mounted since early in this volume my head says "Not likely!"

In addition to a head, though, I have a heart. And my heart remembers the words of Drs. Jill Stine and Margaret Flowers: If even approximately 3 percent of the US population became truly engaged in campaigns to bring about radical change in critical areas of our national life, meaningful progress toward a sane society would be possible.[51]

My heart also remembers the words of young Americans in St. Louis, and Detroit, and New York City, and Ferguson, Missouri, who, standing in the cold, declared their intention to keep organizing and keep protesting until it is safe for black males to walk the streets of our cities without fear of being shot or strangled by a police officer. And my heart remembers many occasions in the sixties and seventies marching with young Americans, including two of my daughters, both under age ten, down State Street in Chicago vigorously protesting the slaughter taking place in Vietnam. And returning month after month to repeat the slogans and the songs until, at last, we were heard.

50. Danaher, "Paradigm Shift."
51. Moyers & Company, November 2013.

So in this competition of head and heart, trying my best to be neither a cynic nor a Pollyanna, and acknowledging how foolhardy it is to attempt to outguess history, I still want to choose the heart. I want to declare that there's a "saving remnant" of Americans capable of sparking a true regeneration of the American spirit, freeing the country's soul from its infernal pathologies, propelling the nation beyond its neurotic clinging to childish illusions of omnipotence and moral purity. With this scenario, the story of the United States might move into a middle phase during which the nation could indeed become an inspiration to other nations.

That, sadly, is an affirmation I can no longer make. I don't repudiate it entirely, however. As I do in the realm of religious belief, so here, too, I remain a reluctant agnostic.

But that does not let me—or any serious citizen—off the hook. Even in the face of almost certain disaster, one keeps struggling. So, if you've been with me from the start, and have not decided that I'm daft to hold on to hope, no matter how attenuated, join me again. Let's get busy. Let's be creative, and adventurous, and dedicated, and hopeful and prove America's youth and Drs. Stine and Flowers and some of my fellow octogenarians and all in between who embrace the "life paradigm"—let's prove them right.

And Chris Hedges, whom I admire greatly but who, along with many other clear-eyed analysts, believes the game is over and that the multinationals have utterly destroyed our democracy and will eventually destroy the Earth—let's prove Chris Hedges and all those understandably despairing of our chances wrong. Chris will forgive us. If we don't try, I doubt that our grandchildren will.

CHAPTER 8

AMERICAN DYSTOPIA: COLD WAR, THE CIA, AND JOHN F. KENNEDY AS SACRIFICIAL VICTIM

Ninety-nine percent of the imagery imposed on the human mind in our society is seriously intended to deceive. Massive doles of fraudulence have damaged the collective sensibility perhaps beyond repair. ... The result, more and more obvious, is loss of faith in the power of any imagery whatsoever, whether visual, aural, or verbal.

—HAYDEN CARRUTH[1]

They [the Americans] are always right.

—VLADIMIR PUTIN

What can the world or any nation in it hope for, if no turning is found on this dread road? ... The worst to be feared would be a ruinous nuclear war. The best would be a life of perpetual fear and tension; a burden of arms draining the wealth and labor of all peoples; a wasting of strength that defies the American system or the Soviet system to achieve true abundance and happiness for the peoples of this earth.

Every gun that is made, every battleship that is launched, every rocket fired signifies, in the final sense, a theft from those who are hungry and not fed, those who are cold and not clothed.

---

1. Carruth, "Intentional Alligator," 247.

> We pay for a single fighter plane with a half million bushels
> of wheat. We pay for a single destroyer with new homes that could
> have housed more than 8,000 people. This is, I repeat, the best way
> of life to be found on the road the world has been taking. This is not
> a way of life at all, in any true sense. Under the cloud of threatening
> war, it is humanity hanging from a cross of iron.

—PRESIDENT DWIGHT D. EISENHOWER[2]

PERHAPS MORE THAN ANY other nineteenth-century American writer, Walt Whitman loved America. This is a truism that scarcely needs repeating. His love was passionate, unreserved and, one might say, unrequited.

I do not mean that American poetry lovers have not greatly admired Whitman's verse and ranked him near the top of the company of treasured native literary artists. They surely have. I mean simply that Whitman expressed, in both poetry and prose, extraordinary hopes for America, so extraordinary, so exaggerated, really, that no country could have possibly fulfilled them. Again and again in *Democratic Vistas*, for example, Whitman projects a vision of the possibilities of America as the progenitor of what is virtually a new humanity, a humanity characterized by brotherly love nurtured by the virtues of a genuinely democratic commonwealth.

Whitman had fond hopes for a flowering of the arts as an integral component of the future America and expressed a profound faith that the ongoing progress of human culture in America would prove to be the ultimate realization of the goal inherent in evolution itself:

> We see, as in the universes of the material kosmos, after meteorological, vegetable, and animal cycles, man at last arises, born through them, to prove them, concentrate them, turn upon them with wonder and love—to command them, adorn them, and carry them upward into superior realms—so, out of the series of the preceding social and political universes arise these States. We see that while any were supposing things establish'd and completed, really the grandest things always remain; and discover that the work of the New World is not ended, but only fairly begun. We see our land, America, her literature, esthetics, &., as, substantially, the getting in form, or effusement and statement, of deepest basic elements and loftiest final meanings, of history and man.[3]

2. Bacevich, *Washington Rules*, 225–226.
3. Whitman, "Democratic Vistas," 425.

Yet Whitman was surely no naïf and in *Democratic Vistas* he acknowledges how far the America of the 1870s has strayed from the idealized image he portrays sometimes on the same page. At one point he describes the contemporary American scene as a "sort of dry and flat Sahara." A bit later he writes that if the creative forces in the American character do not prosper, "our modern civilization, with all its improvements, is in vain and we are on the road to a destiny, a status, equivalent, in its real world, to that of the fabled damned."

Whitman, in short, was at the same time an ecstatic believer in America's grand (spiritual) destiny and an acute observer of the "pervading flippancy and vulgarity, low cunning, infidelity" found everywhere in American society of his day. He *did* project in his writings what might be described as a kind of utopian society of the future at the same time that he gave warnings against belief that such a society could come to pass without herculean efforts to overcome the moral and spiritual corruptions he observed on every hand. Thus one might say that Whitman's love of America was tempered by a realistic understanding of the manifold ways in which the loftiest of mankind's hopes and ambitions can be debased and betrayed by the waywardness of human desire.

Richard Rorty, I think, loved America as much as did Whitman. He also loved Whitman. Rorty was one of America's greatest philosophers during the latter part the twentieth century. He wrote many books and broke important ground in a number of areas of contemporary philosophical discussion, though perhaps his greatest contribution was a thoroughly compelling argument against any belief in a fixed, unchanging entity whether "God" or "reality" independent of human consciousness or human language.

In his 1989 book *Contingency, Irony and Solidarity*, Rorty identified two types of thinkers and, really, two types of human beings: "metaphysicians" and "ironists." Metaphysicians—he locates theologians in this group—believe that there is something or someone "out there" and that it is their job to come to know and to describe as best they can what that something is. This type of individual "believes in an order beyond time and change which both determines the point of human existence and establishes a hierarchy of responsibilities."[4] In essence, such individuals seek to *discover* truth of one sort or another.

In contrast, the ironist seeks to *create* truth. That is, following in the tradition of such American pragmatists as John Dewey, ironists believe that "truths" emerge out of the contestation of ideas bumping against each other in the marketplace of lived experience. But these "truths" are always

---

4. Rorty, *Irony & Solidarity*, xv.

contingent, less than absolute, always subject to revision. Here is how Rorty defines an ironist: "I use 'ironist' to name the sort of person who faces up to the contingency of his or her most central beliefs and desires." Knowing that there is no way to *prove* the validity of their dearest desires, liberal ironists, according to Rorty, nonetheless struggle to bring into being a society where "suffering will be diminished . . . [and] the humiliation of human beings by other human beings may cease." Rorty identifies himself absolutely with this latter kind of individual, the ironist.[5]

As the title of his book implies, Rorty is at pains to convince his readers that solidarity among humans is possible, and he argues strenuously that, rather than debating theories about human nature or the nature of human consciousness, or the reliability of language as humans' means of communication, liberal ironists ought to be "getting on [as he stated elsewhere] with what Dewey called trying to solve 'the problems of men.'"[6] Rorty, in fact, had little patience with the post-Vietnam generation of scholars and academicians who had been so thoroughly disillusioned with America that they no longer struggled as they had in the sixties for its restoration to sanity and health but retreated to debating arcane theories, more often than not French in origin.

In *Achieving Our Country*, Rorty lays out a sort of pattern for that restoration. The "cultural liberals," whose pessimism and cynicism Rorty challenges, need, he asserts, to reaffirm "common dreams." He calls upon all of us on the political left to accept "deriving our moral identity, at least in part, from our citizenship in a democratic nation-state, and from leftist attempts to fulfill the promise of that nation."[7]

In the introduction, I commented on Rorty's endorsement of Whitman's and John Dewey's hope that a utopian America might become a substitute for God. At that point I challenged such a notion, describing it as idolatry. Now I feel compelled to assert that I am totally perplexed that a thinker as brilliant and clear-headed as Rorty believed that any country could fulfill the role of the deity that Americans have traditionally worshipped—or any deity, for that matter. I am no less astonished that he believed that utopias anywhere, much less in the land lying between Canada and Mexico, are possible. As I've reflected on that proposition, some of the words of Martin Sheen, cited earlier, invaded my consciousness, insistently demanding attention: "this supposed idyllic society . . . the most confused,

5. Ibid.
6. Rorty, *Achieving Our Country*, 97.
7. Ibid.

warped, addicted society in the history of the world."[8] Sheen's words support
my conviction that any proposal that the United States is a fit candidate for a
future utopia requires a strong rebuttal. As I write in the spring of 2015, the
news reflecting upon the health of our country is anything but encouraging.
Let's begin with race relations in America.

Fifty years have passed since historic legislation was enacted outlawing
the worst of Jim Crow segregation and insuring voting rights for all our citizens. And we have a president of African American ancestry. In addition,
today there are tens of thousands of African Americans holding positions of
responsibility in business, in education, in medicine and law, and in government. Enormous strides toward justice and equality for black Americans
suggest that a majority of Americans *can* be moved to correct the crimes
perpetrated against African Americans in the past. But that's the half of the
glass that's "full." There's a glaring half that's "empty."

An article in the *Nation* presents an unsettling picture of the reality of
life for millions of black Americans.

> The world that young black people have inherited is rife with
> race-based disparities. By the age of 23, almost half of the black
> men in this country have been arrested at least once, 30 percent
> by the age of 18. The unemployment rate for black 16-to-24-
> year olds is around 25 percent. Twelve percent of black girls face
> out-of-school suspension, a higher rate than for all other girls
> and most boys. Black women are incarcerated at a rate nearly
> three times that of white women. While black people make up
> 14.6 percent of total regular drug users, they are 31.2 percent
> of those arrested on drug charges and are likely to receive lon-
> ger sentences. According to a report issued by the Malcolm X
> Grassroots Movement, which used police data as well as news-
> paper reports, in 2012, a black person lost his or her life in an
> extrajudicial killing at the hands of a police officer, security
> guard or self-appointed vigilante like George Zimmerman every
> twenty-eight hours.[9]

Those of us who have lived near one of the crowded, sweltering, rat-
infested black neighborhoods of our major cities, as I did for almost forty
years in Chicago, are not likely to be shocked by these figures. In Woodlawn,
the black neighborhood south of Hyde Park where I began graduate studies
at the University of Chicago in 1960, the unemployment rate for black males
was near 50 percent. The schools of that area were woefully neglected by city

8. Kupfer, "An Interview with Martin Sheen," 38.
9. Smith, "The New Fight for Racial Justice," 14.

authorities, with substandard maintenance of buildings and underfunding of staff and faculty. Police harassment of residents of the area was commonplace, and an air of hopelessness was pervasive, with men of various ages seen sitting in doorways with a bottle of whiskey ready for use in hand.

This was not the whole story of black life in our inner cities, of course, but it was, and continues to be, sufficiently true to serve as an indictment of the indifference and cruelty of our country's treatment of its black citizens. After the killing of an unarmed African American teenager, Michael Brown, shot six times by a police officer in Ferguson, Missouri, following the shooting of Trayvon Martin in Florida some months earlier, the evidence for a fairly consistent trend of shootings of black youths by white law enforcement personnel, who normally act with impunity, seems undeniable. It does not strike me as much of an exaggeration to say that it's open season on young black males.

For pure sadistic cruelty, the following account of the treatment of prisoners in solitary confinement in a Wisconsin state prison is not likely to have much competition. The following paragraphs are excerpted from an article by Glenn T. Turner that appeared in the summer 2014 *Resist Newsletter*.

> I am a prisoner in the Wisconsin Department of Corrections at the state's most secure institution, that being the Wisconsin Secure Program Facility (WSPF). I am presently on a status called Administrative Confinement (AC) which is allegedly a non-punitive indefinite solitary confinement status. Thus far I have been on this since May 10, 2010. I speak not as a passive observer, nor from hearsay or second, third, or fourth hand information. I do not imagine the things I speak of, for I personally live it daily.
>
> I've been incarcerated since October 18, 1991 and I have completed to date a total of nineteen and a half years of my bit in solitary of one sort or another with very brief moments in general population. . . . I have completed every form of program available to me while in solitary confinement and DOC officials have continued to maintain me on AC.
>
> What has now become a convenient cause to put prisoners on administrative confinement for indefinite segregation in solitary confinement for years on end is to label the prisoner a "gang leader." In this prison system that has never had a history of serious gang activity, this practice is suspect. I've seen prisoners who were unable to endure such long terms of confinement attempt to commit suicide, smear their fecal matter over their bodies, cells, and even eat their body waste. I've witnessed them

cut themselves, and some who—lacking any sharp object to cut themselves with, use their teeth to rip their flesh so as to expose their veins and rip those out to spray their blood all over their doors, windows, floors, etc.

I've seen yet others simply cry like unfed, hungry babies, all day and all night, and some lash out yelling and screaming all day, all night, banging on walls and cell doors, trying to get some form of acknowledgement from their jailers that they are human beings, only to be sprayed with various forms of chemical agents, left incapacitated in their cells. Only then to be taken and have their cloths cut from their bodies and put nude into a yet more restrictive type of segregation status. . . . There, they have nothing in their cell but a concrete slab to sleep on, a stainless steel sink and toilet combo, a surveillance camera and 24 hours a day of bright light illumination.[10]

I do not know the race of Glenn Turner but in a response to a letter I have written to him, he implies that he is an African American. I think it is safe, in any case, to assume that at least half of his fellow inmates suffering the heartless treatment he describes are black.

Rorty's hope for achieving our country as a utopian society gets smashed, I believe, as it encounters any number of stubborn facts of life in contemporary America. Vicious racism is merely one of the most obvious. The exponential growth of the prison-industrial complex is another. The catastrophic failure of the "war on drugs" is yet another. Cocaine and other hard drugs are found everywhere in the United States, and there is an epidemic of heroine use in parts of the country, notably New England. Many users no doubt buy drugs merely for the ecstatic high they produce. But a good number of users surely turn to drugs as a means of escaping—if only temporarily—feelings of worthlessness and spiritual emptiness. Or the thwarted longing for affection and the terror of abandonment.

The figures cited earlier revealing the ratio of blacks vs. nonblacks incarcerated for drug offenses, when combined with the picture Glenn Turner provides of the savage dehumanization of inmates in one American prison, lend force to my contention that our country is unlikely any time soon to become the near-perfect society that the word "utopian" suggests.

For further evidence, I might speak in this context about abandoned children, numbering in the tens of thousands, wandering the streets of our cities; or the millions of our citizens who deny the significance of threats to life on Earth represented by increased numbers of heat waves, tornadoes, wild fires, and droughts, and by melting glaciers and rising sea levels; or

10. Turner, *Resist Newsletter*, 1.

the rulings of the Supreme Court in the *Citizens United* and other cases when five of the justices have made unmistakable their intention to give preferential treatment to corporations over individual citizens; or the outrageous maldistribution of wealth in contemporary America, with the top 10 percent of the population controlling 85 percent of all wealth.[11]

But I'd like instead to conclude this part of my argument by saying that I find Martha Nussbaum's ideas about imagining a *good* society—not a utopian one—far more convincing than Rorty's vision of a society from which greed and envy and hatred and cruelty and other vices and imperfections of the human heart have been banished or at least significantly mitigated. Rorty approved of John Dewey's desire to eliminate the use of the word "sin." One may surely do away with the idea of sin and the use of the word, but the reality, unfortunately, is here to stay.

(At this point it may be useful to recall a comment of Norman O. Brown who suggested that psychoanalytic research and theory lead to the conclusion that humankind suffers from a neurosis from which no individual is entirely free and that "the doctrine of universal neurosis is the psychoanalytical analogue of the theological doctrine of original sin.")[12]

Despite my admiration for Rorty's work, I am disturbed by what seem to me two fallacious propositions in his writings; the first I commented on in the preceding paragraphs. The second is his statement that America was correct in pursing the Cold War and would have been guilty of a dereliction of duty in not attempting to defeat the USSR:

> I am still unable to see much difference between fighting Hitler
> and fighting Stalin. I still find nothing absurd in the idea that, if
> the reformist Left had been stronger than it was, post-World War
> II America could have had it both ways. Our country could have
> become both the leader of an international movement to replace
> oligarchy around the world, and the nuclear superpower which
> halted the spread of an evil empire ruled by a mad tyrant.[13]

I find three aspects of this argument unconvincing. First, it ignores the exceedingly crucial role of the struggle for independence of former colonies in Asia and Africa in determining the direction taken by global geopolitics in the postwar period. The European colonial powers—England, France, Portugal, and the Netherlands—were in no great hurry to give up their overseas possessions, and in the struggles that ensued, it was not surprising that the black and brown peoples fighting for independence turned to

11. Inequality.org, "Wealth Inequality."

12. Brown, *Life Against Death*, 6.

13. Rorty, *Achieving Our Country*, 63.

the one country on the planet that was willing to offer them support—the Soviet Union. (I do not wish to ignore China but during much of the period, China was preoccupied with consolidating its own successful struggle for independence from the European powers and limited its assistance to its very close neighbors, e.g., North Korea.)

It soon became clear in the post-World War II era that the United States would not support the liberation efforts of colonized peoples in the global South. Repeatedly, whether it was in Africa or Southeast Asia, the United States either gave material support and political cover to the colonial powers or went to war, as in Vietnam, to defeat the struggles for national liberation that emerged in country after country.[14]

Thus it is extremely difficult to take seriously the charge against the Soviets for their designs to spread *their* evil empire around the world when the United States was continuing to spread its empire by means of numerous CIA-orchestrated coups, invasions, and support for bloody tyrannies from Iran to Indonesia. Hence, given the history of America's support for oligarchs both prior to WWII and subsequently, the suggestion of a US-led worldwide campaign to defeat oligarchical political structures sounds, in my judgment, absurd.

It should be remembered, as well, that the United States had been invading and occupying the lands of dark-skinned peoples for some years before the birth of the Soviet Union in 1917 and continued to do so following World War I. I find, therefore, rather ludicrous the self-congratulatory explanations of America's policies in the Cold War period that were proffered by government officials, journalists and academicians. Some were so outlandish and so blind to the realities of America's actual ruthlessness in its dealings with such countries as Guatemala, the Dominican Republic and, especially, Vietnam as to strain credulity to the breaking point.

Elsewhere I have suggested that, after armaments, hypocrisy is America's number one export. Nowhere has this hypocrisy been more in evidence than in the fervid encomiums of the Cold War period celebrating America's selfless dedication to bringing her enlightened, civilizing virtues to Earth's inhabitants trapped in poverty and ruled by tyrants. Dozens of members of the intellectual class and the pundit elite pounded their drums in the public realm touting the nation's disinterested dedication to spreading freedom and democracy across the globe, with nary a word about the millions slaughtered in CIA-supported coups that overthrew democratically elected governments in Argentina, Chile, Iran, Zaire, Guatemala and a dozen other

14. See Herman, *Real Terrorist Network*; Fulbright, *Arrogance of Power*, 69–105; Chomsky, *Deterring Democracy*. See also Dorrel, *What I've Learned about U.S. Foreign Policy*.

countries; the proxy wars such as those discussed in chapter 7; and unwavering support for murderous tyrants, such as the Samozas of Nicaragua.

Let's listen to how America's pursuit of its aims in the Cold War was assessed by three eminent Americans. The first statement is by Professor Paul Kattenburg of the University of South Carolina. Writing about the "Vietnam trauma," Prof. Kattenburg alleges that America approached its role as a superpower "devoid of artifice or deception" and with "the mind set of an emancipator." Moreover, armed with such a self-understanding, "one need not feel or act superior, or believe one is imposing one's ethos on others, *since one senses naturally that others cannot doubt the emancipator's righteous cause* anymore than his capabilities."[15]

James Reston, a highly respected writer for *the New York Times*, was not sparing in his praise for America's noble campaigns to bring freedom wherever on the planet it did not exist: "I don't think there is anything in the history of the world to compare with the commitments this country has taken in defense of freedom."[16] In the late-sixties, while the United States was, in the words of Noam Chomsky, *"demolishing what was left of the South Vietnamese countryside,"* Reston declared that the US war was being pursued "on the principle that military power shall not compel South Vietnam to do what it does not want to do";[17] and hence, one has to assume, it was morally justified for many hundreds of thousands of Vietnamese peasants to have their homes, their rice patties, and their water buffalo destroyed, their jungles poisoned by Agent Orange, and, if not shot dead by US soldiers, forced to live in compounds little different from concentration camps.[18]

For official corroboration of the obvious nobility of America's policies in the Cold War period, one need only peruse the report of the National Bipartisan (Kissinger) Commission on Central America: "The international purposes of the United States in the late twentieth century are cooperation, not hegemony or domination; partnership, not confrontation; a decent life for all, not exploitation."[19] My discussion in chapter 7 of proxy wars in Central America might cast a shadow of doubt over the accuracy of this claim.

Samuel Huntington, a Harvard professor of great renown, added his voice to this chorus of true believers when he asserted that "the overall effect of American power on other societies was to further liberty, pluralism, and

---

15. Quoted in Chomsky, *Deterring Democracy*, 17, emphasis added.
16. Ibid.
17. Ibid., 18.
18. Chomsky, *Rethinking Camelot*, 54.
19. Chomsky, *Deterring Democracy*, 18.

democracy."[20] What is remarkable about these and other accolades assuring readers of the purity and nobility of America's actions, as opposed to the Soviets' perfidious and aggressive ambitions, is the total ignoring of historical reality.

Another highly regarded scholar, Hans Morgenthau, explained why the facts were to be ignored. Chomsky elucidates the reasoning behind this startling bit of twisted logic:

> The facts are irrelevant, because . . . to adduce them is "to confound the abuse of reality with reality itself." Reality is the unachieved "national purpose" revealed by "the evidence of history as our minds reflect it," while the actual historical record is merely the abuse of reality, an insignificant artifact. The conventional understanding is therefore self-justifying, immune to external critique.[21]

Chomsky can be wonderfully precise and pungent as he unpacks the authentic meanings of such attempts to whitewash our country's motives and actions in the arena of international politics. The following passage is a classic example:

> Though the sophistication of traditional theology is lacking, the similarity of themes and style is striking. It reveals the extent to which the intellectuals serve as priesthood. The more primitive sectors of Western culture go further, fostering forms of idolatry in which such sacred symbols as the flag become an object of forced veneration, and the state is called upon to punish any insult to them and to compel children to pledge their devotion daily, while God and State are almost indissolubly linked in public ceremony and discourse. . . . It is perhaps not surprising that such crude fanaticism rises to such an extreme in the United States, as an antidote to the unique freedom from state coercion that has been achieved by popular struggle.[22]

A second reason for challenging Rorty's thesis regarding America's pursuit of the Cold War is that it locked into place—seemingly as a permanent fixture of American society—the military-industrial complex, thereby insuring astronomical annual increases in the federal debt. Moreover, the Cold War gave legitimacy to the CIA as a rogue entity of our government. The CIA's efforts to assassinate heads of state such as Cuba's Fidel Castro and

20. Ibid.
21. Ibid., 19.
22. Ibid., 18.

its involvement in the overthrow of leaders such as Allende of Chile, whose government was up to that time the most democratic Chile had ever known, were fairly typical episodes in this shameful chapter in American history.[23]

One fact about the CIA that can be stated without fear of contradiction is that it has grown. Established in 1947 by President Harry Truman, its original purpose was to gather information from international sources that would aid the president in making decisions regarding the nation's security in the postwar era. Plots to assassinate other countries' leaders were definitely not a part of its mandate. Nor was subjecting to "enhanced interrogation," i.e., torture, prisoners suspected of terrorism. Nor was organizing and funding armies to wage war.

In a detailed portrayal of the Company's growth into what is virtually a parallel government, Scott Horton describes what Truman's modest intelligence-gathering agency has become. (The occasion for his *Harper's* article was the release in December 2014 of a report on torture by the Senate Select Committee on Intelligence.) The picture that emerges from that report can only be described as shocking. The CIA today has "a titanic budget, as well as its own army and, thanks to a fleet of missile-equipped drones, its own air force. It wages war directly in Pakistan, Somalia, Yemen and across the nations of the African Sahel, and it mobilizes proxy armies to do its bidding—arming Afghan warlords to topple the Taliban in 2002, seconding the Ethiopian military invasion of Somalia in 2006, and recruiting Libyan exiles to battle Qaddafi in 2011."[24]

Much of what Horton relays about CIA skullduggery and violations of international law as well as US laws is not in the report, nor, of course, is there commentary on the way Company officials thumb their noses at the State Department or treat members of Congress, whose requests for information are frequently answered only after long delays—or simply ignored.

Although there are, I'm sure, honest and honorable individuals employed by the CIA, it is surely no exaggeration to say that, as an institution, the Counter Intelligence Agency is a criminal appendix to the United States government.

One of the most disgraceful features of the CIA's history was its collaboration with seedy and corrupt underworld figures all under cover of defending America and saving other countries from the menace of international communism. Many articles and several books have been written about the subject.[25] Repeatedly one reads, for instance, about the part the

23. Johnson, *Blowback*, 28–29. See also, Zinn, *People's History*, 543.

24. Horton, "Company Men," 84–88.

25. See Stich, *Drugging America*; and Kwitny, *Crimes of Patriots*.

CIA has played in the drug trade. Dennis Dayle, who was once head of a unit of the Drug Enforcement Administration (DEA), wrote the following: "In my 30-year history in the Drug Enforcement Administration and related agencies, the major targets of my investigations almost invariably turned out to be working for the CIA."[26]

Wherever hard drugs have been produced, processed or forwarded to the United States since the 1950s, the CIA's fingerprints are on display. One of these locations was a remote section of Burma called the Golden Triangle, where a part of the Nationalist Chinese Army, after its defeat by the Red Army, settled and became "the world's largest source of opium and heroin. Air America, the CIA's principal proprietary airline, flew drugs all over Southeast Asia."[27]

Central America became, in the 1970s and 1980s, another player in the international drug trade. As noted in chapter 7, Panama's Manuel Noriega, while on the CIA's payroll, was heavily involved in laundering money from drug dealers. But it was the Nicaraguan contras, the CIA-recruited and -financed bands raiding villages and towns in both northern and southern Nicaragua, who led the pack in drug trafficking. Then Senator John Kerry headed a subcommittee that issued a report in 1989 containing the following statements:

> There was substantial evidence of drug smuggling through the war zones on the part of individual contras, contra suppliers, contra pilots, mercenaries who worked with the contras, and contra supporters throughout the region. . . . U.S. officials involved in Central America failed to address the drug issue for fear of jeopardizing the war efforts against Nicaragua. . . . In each case, one or another agency of the U.S. government had information regarding the involvement either while it was occurring or immediately thereafter. . . . Senior U.S. policy makers were not immune to the idea that drug money was a perfect solution to the contras' funding problems.[28]

A variety of schemes and ploys were devised for shipping cocaine to the United States. One involved a one-time CIA company, Southern Air Transport; planes loaded with cocaine "flew to Florida, Texas, Louisiana, and other locations including several military bases. Designated as 'Contra Craft,' these shipments were not to be inspected." Occasionally the relevant authorities had not been forewarned; thus if an arrest was made, "powerful

26. Blum, "The CIA, Contras, Gangs, and Crack."
27. Ibid.
28. Shalom, *Imperial Alibis*, 177.

strings were pulled to result in dropping the case, acquittal, reduced sentence, or deportation."[29]

Some of the most damning evidence of CIA involvement with drug dealers supplying the US market appeared in "Dark Alliance," a three-part story in a California newspaper, the San Jose *Mercury News*, in August of 1996. The reporter, Gary Webb, made claims that aroused angry cries for more information and legal actions from the black population in America's major cities, especially Los Angeles, and led eventually to a Senate investigation. In essence, the story alleged that urban African Americans had been targeted by a Central American gang marketing cocaine subsequently turned into "crack." The following excerpts suggest the sensational character of this story.

> For the better part of a decade, a San Francisco Bay Area drug ring sold tons of cocaine to the Crips and Bloods street gangs of Los Angeles and funneled millions in drug profits to a Latin American guerrilla army run by the U.S. Central Intelligence Agency . . .
>
> This drug network opened the first pipeline between Colombia's cocaine cartels and the black neighborhoods of Los Angeles, a city now known as the "crack" capital of the world. The cocaine that flooded in helped spark a crack explosion in urban America and provided the cash and connections needed for L.A.'s gangs to buy automatic weapons.
>
> It is one of the most bizarre alliances in modern history: the union of a U.S.-backed army attempting to overthrow a revolutionary socialist government and the Uzi-toting "ganstas" of Compton and South Central Los Angeles.[30]

Webb's allegations were at first more or less ignored by the major US news outlets. Subsequently, the *New York Times*, the *Washington Post*, and the *Los Angeles Times* ran brief pieces on Webb's revelations and even briefer ones on the Kerry Committee's report. Eventually the three major newspapers one after the other sought to discredit Webb's reporting, suggesting that many of his accusations lacked credible sources or that what Webb had presented as evidence of a CIA-contra alliance actually proved very little. Doyle McManus of the *Los Angeles Times*, for instance, wrote: "This goddamn thing is full of holes." A *Washington Post* "investigation" concluded that "available information does not support the conclusion that

---

29. Blum, "The CIA, Contras, Gangs, and Crack."
30. Webb, "Dark Alliance."

the CIA-backed contras . . . played a major role in the emergence of crack as a narcotic in widespread use across the United States."[31]

A major article entitled "Crack, the Contras, and the CIA: The Storm over 'Dark Alliance,'" by Peter Kornbluh, while supporting the general thrust of Webb's allegations, does point out a number of inconsistencies and failures to supply reliable sources to back up several key charges. Webb himself was forced to acknowledge that his articles did not claim that an agency of the US government was actually involved in the peddling of crack cocaine in our cities.

The pressure to discredit Webb and his story from both the government and the media was eventually sufficient to cause Webb's bosses to back-peddle regarding the reliability of his reporting. Just how far some of the newspapers went to attack the credibility of his work is suggested by these examples:

> The McManus piece credulously painted a portrait of the CIA as a law-abiding, conscientious agency. It included an abundance of denials from prominent CIA and Justice Department officials—while failing to inform readers of their role in some of the scandals of the contra war—that the CIA would ever tolerate drug smuggling or that there had ever been any government interference with prosecuting drug smugglers connected to the contras. This despite documentation to the contrary.[32]

Kornbluh's article makes abundantly clear that most of the journalists who paid attention to "Dark Alliance" were more committed to protecting the CIA and other government agencies than to helping readers understand the seriousness of the charges Webb had leveled. Some of the exposés of malfeasance by the journalists covering this story are almost as shocking as Webb's original charges:

> all three papers ignored evidence from declassified National Security Council [a nongovernmental agency] e-mail messages and *The New York Times* and *The Washington Post* ignored evidence from Oliver North's notebooks, which lend support to the underlying premise of the *Mercury News* series—that U.S. officials would both condone and protect drug traffickers if doing so advanced the contra cause. The October 21 *New York Times* piece *didn't even mention the Kerry Committee report*.[33]

31. Kornbluh, "Crack, the Contras, and the CIA," 38.
32. Ibid.
33. Ibid., emphasis added.

Demoted and disrespected by his editor, with his marriage and his life in ruins, Gary Webb committed suicide in 2004. In an online essay entitled "Gary Webb's Death: American Tragedy," Robert Parry tells this story of a corrupt journalistic community bending to political pressure:

> By the mid-1990s, a powerful right-wing news media had taken shape and was in no mood to accept the notion that President Ronald Reagan's beloved contras were little more than common criminals. That recognition would have cast a shadow over the Reagan legacy, which the right was busy elevating into mythic status.[34]

Even Senator Kerry's report, which is replete with testimonies connecting contra members with drug trafficking, was not immune to trashing, with *Newsweek* describing the senator as a "randy conspiracy buff."[35]

After almost a decade of bloodletting and who will ever know definitively how much waste of American taxpayers' money, the contra war came to an end in 1990. The CIA, however, has been free to plot, and spy, and syphon off funds from the national treasury in subsequent years pretty much as it did during the Cold War. And as Chalmers Johnson predicted, blowback from the US empire's provocative activities in a dozen or more locales around the globe has insured that "enemies," in a steady stream, will preoccupy new cadres of initiates at the Company's headquarters in Langley, Virginia.

The contra insurgency against the Sandinista government of Nicaragua was one of Ronald Reagan's costly obsessions. Another even more extravagant obsession was "Star Wars." The American public is not likely ever to know how many billions of dollars were wasted on such needless boondoggles as Reagan's anti-missal project, which never survived successfully even one serious testing.[36]

Nor are we likely to learn the cost of turning Honduras during the Nicaraguan contra war into what some in the military jokingly referred to as "the world's only land-based aircraft carrier." Honduras was used as a vast staging area for the contra forces, with barracks, airstrips and ammunition dumps all funded out of the US Treasury. At the time, I got in touch with my senior senator, Paul Simon, of Illinois, and asked whether he or anyone on his staff could tell me how much had been spent on that misadventure. He replied that he had not the slightest idea and did not expect ever to be able to enlighten me.

34. Parry, "Gary Webb's Death," 3.
35. Ibid., 2.
36. Bertell, *Planet Earth*, 87–89.

A scholar such as Andrew Bacevich could no doubt extend almost to infinity examples of the squandering of taxpayers' funds during the Cold War. Possibly more important is the overwhelming evidence, normally ignored by the media and the general public, that the Cold War could have been avoided or, if not avoided entirely, lessened in length and intensity.

In *Deterring Democracy*, Chomsky offers a wealth of information regarding how an inflexible conviction on the part of American officials that the USSR was in its very DNA an inherently evil state bent upon world domination made even the thought of compromise impossible. A 1950 document, National Security (NSC, 68) spelled out in detail the battle that *had* to be fought between America, understood as a benevolent champion of freedom and enlightenment, and what was perceived in America as essentially a "slave state." North Korea's invasion of the South, for instance, is offered as "the first step in the Kremlin's conquest of the world—despite the lack of compelling evidence, then or now, for Russian initiative in this phase of the complex struggle over the fate of Korea."[37]

The trillions of dollars that the Cold War added to the national debt set in motion the surge that continues to this day:

> The memorandum [NSC 68] calls for a huge increase in armaments, while recognizing that the slave state was far weaker than the champion of freedom by any measure. Relevant data are presented in such a way as to obscure direct comparisons and selected to exaggerate the enemy's strength, the standard pattern throughout the Cold War era. Nevertheless, even the data presented showed the US military budget to be double that of the USSR and its economic power four times as great.[38]

Arguing that the Soviet Union which, a few years earlier, had lost well over twenty million of its citizens in the Nazi invasion, needed a defense force far smaller than the one it then possessed, the author of NSC 68, Paul Nitze, justified the proposed substantial increase in US military spending as needed "to support our foreign policy," though, as always when such policies have been presented to the public, it was the moral crusade that was emphasized.

Chomsky discusses a moment in US-Soviet relations when there was a possibility for a dramatic reduction in tensions between the two superpowers. In 1952, the Kremlin put forth a proposal for reunification and neutralization of Germany, with no conditions on economic policies and with

37. Chomsky, *Deterring Democracy*, 11.
38. Ibid.

guarantees for "the rights of man and basic freedoms, including freedom of speech, press, religious persuasion, political conviction, and assembly"

> and the free activity of democratic parties and organizations. In reply, the US and its allies objected that the West did not recognize the Oder-Neisse frontier between Germany and Poland, and insisted that a reunified Germany be free to join NATO, a demand that the Russians could hardly accept a few years after Germany alone had virtually destroyed the Soviet Union.[39]

How different world history might have been had the United States accepted the Soviet offer. An immense amount of grief and violence would presumably have been avoided since a unified, democratic Germany would have posed no threat to the USSR, else the Kremlin would never have made the offer. And concluding such an agreement, with no demand that Germany become part of NATO would surely have alleviated the Soviets' anxieties regarding America's desires to best them at every turn. The US obsession with destroying the Soviet Union, however, precluded any move that betrayed an understanding that the Russians might have legitimate security concerns of their own that necessitated honest negotiations.

Although the Cold War came to an end in 1989/90 with the coming down of the Berlin Wall and the breakup of the Soviet Union, it appears today that a second Cold War may be developing. Several US scholars, including Stephen Cohen and Andrew Cockburn, have argued persuasively that repeatedly American officials have in the intervening years advocated policies that in the Kremlin can only be interpreted as provocative. Chief among these, perhaps, is the insistence upon pushing NATO to Russia's very borders. Since there is no unambiguous evidence that Putin has plans to invade Russia's European neighbors, why insist on placing nuclear missiles in Poland? And why such loud insistence that Ukraine, with its centuries-long association with Russia and its significant Russian-speaking population, join NATO, a western military alliance?

Writing in the *Nation*, Stephen F. Cohen accused the Kiev government of creating "a reign of terror" in the eastern sections of Ukraine, sending after May 2014, a growing number of "armored personnel carriers, tanks, artillery, helicopter gunships and warplanes to southeastern cities." Cohen notes that at first, the government forces limited their campaign to rebel check points, but that soon cities and neighboring towns were attacked and increasingly "urban areas . . . and even villages look[ed] and sound[ed] like agonized war zones." Cohen speaks of "deeds that are rising to the level of war crimes" about which the hawks in America have for the most part

39. Ibid., 24.

remained silent.[40] Washington's unrelenting blaming of Moscow for the bloodshed in eastern Ukraine certainly lends support to the notion that US officials are still intent upon pursuing something like a Cold War with the Russians. It's interesting to note as well that in recent testimony before a Senate committee, General Martin Dempsey, then chairman of the Joint Chiefs, declared that Russia, not ISIS or Iran, is America's major enemy.[41]

An in-depth essay on this subject by Andrew Cockburn makes clear how profoundly provocative American diplomatic and geopolitical decisions and actions since 1991 have been. In negotiations with the Soviets concerning withdrawal of tactical nuclear weapons from Europe, then-Secretary of State James Baker made promises, absolutely critical from the Russian point of view, to ending the mutual suspicion and hostility that had driven the Cold War for almost twenty-five years. Mr. Baker had unequivocally spelled out Washington's end of that bargain in a private conversation with Mikhail Gorbachev in February 1990, pledging that NATO forces would not move "one inch to the east" provided the Soviets agreed to NATO membership for a unified Germany. In the intervening years, again and again the United States has brazenly violated that commitment.

In a speech in 1996, just before the November election, Bill Clinton, ever mindful of how a shrewd politician could woo ethnic voters in the cities and towns of the Midwest, announced that after admitting Poland, the Czech Republic and Hungary, NATO would then extend membership to the Baltics and the "new democracies of central Europe."

In what would appear to be a wish to rub its defeated enemy's nose in the *merde* left over from their bitter competition, US officials flirted with a proposal to include in NATO a former Soviet state, Georgia.[42]

Against this background of duplicity and hardly-disguised contempt for the feelings of Russian leaders, it is not surprising that Vladimir Putin should vent in public his anger: "What happened to the assurances our Western partners made after the dissolution of the Warsaw Pact? Where are those declarations now? No one even remembers them."[43]

Perhaps what's most revealing in Cockburn's depiction of America's betrayal of commitments made to the Soviets are his revelations concerning how this entire episode in US diplomacy was driven, in part, by the military-industrial complex. When the Cold War ended, gloom descended on the officials of Lockheed and other manufacturers of the fighter jets

40. Cohen, "Kiev's Atrocities," 12–13.

41. PBS, *News Hour*, July 2015.

42. Cockburn, "Game On," 67–72.

43. Ibid., 68.

and assorted military hardware the Defense Department routinely orders. But the depressed mood lasted only a few months. Soon representatives of the defense contractors were schmoozing with politicians in Warsaw and Budapest, urging that the former Warsaw Pact nations prove their serious intentions as full-fledged members of NATO by arming themselves with F-16s. Even tiny, bankrupt Romania, where many of its citizens lived in ramshackle houses without running water, was not immune to the pressure. Eventually, after difficulties in obtaining an IMF loan, it, too, could claim an air force with more than a dozen F16 fighter jets.

According to Cockburn, one knowledgeable informant spoke about this chapter in our country's dealings with another major state with the following revealing observation: "'Fuck Russia' is a proud and long tradition in U.S. foreign policy. It doesn't go away overnight."[44] Today it seems clear that the night has been a long one. Perhaps Mr. Putin will succeed in communicating to influential officials in Washington that there are consequences for such contemptuous treatment of a powerful nation with which America shares this small and vulnerable planet. But any American leader, Barack Obama or some other, is powerfully constrained by tradition and by ingrained habits of mind that militate against a recognition that America's decision-makers are fallible and that the country's behavior may at times be both reckless and reprehensible.

Andrew Bacevich, whose ideas I discussed in the previous chapter, wrote in 2002 about the tendency of America's elected leaders and officials to become effusive when expatiating about the role of America in human history. Supporting that view, he quoted Bill Clinton regarding the respective positions of the United States and China in this matter, claiming that China was on the "wrong side of history" with the United States, as always, on the right side.

"America itself," Bacevich wrote, "had come to define 'the right side of history.' It had blazed the trail that others followed. Progressive, forward looking, divining the spirit of the age, America epitomized the destination toward which all humanity is inevitably travelling."[45]

Identical sentiments were expressed by Secretary of State Madeleine Albright: "As Americans, we have our own duty to be authors of history."[46] These contemporary Americans were, of course, simply reiterating self-congratulatory motifs that had been staples in the national mythology for generations. (Is it not striking how the obligatory "God bless America,"

44. Ibid., 71.
45. Bacevich, *American Empire*, 33.
46. Ibid.

when spoken by our presidents and other officials, frequently sounds more like a command than a petition?)

America's self-love, which was wonderfully invigorated by winning the Cold War, knows no bounds. It is monstrous. And in a world with thousands of nuclear weapons and well over a billion Muslims, a goodly number of whom have reasons to fear and hate us, it's a very dangerous feature of the national character. It certainly does little to assist clear thinking in diplomacy.

I think it noteworthy that after the Cold War ended, American officials were soon searching for a replacement for the USSR as Enemy Number One. A "peacenik" whose campaign to reduce nuclear armaments I read about at the time described an interview with a NATO official, whose national identity was not indicated but can, I think, be easily guessed. In response to a question about possible threats to the western alliance that necessitated maintenance of NATO's military capabilities, this official replied: "The fact is, we haven't got a threat—we're looking pretty hard though and you can be sure we'll come up with something." The 9/11 attack on the Twin Towers supplied enough enemies to keep American officials and military personnel occupied for more than a decade. And now it does look quite likely that we are in for a reprise of the conflict that kept the US munitions industry humming and the "spooks" at Langley on high alert. How else to interpret Obama's and John Kerry's haughty dismissal of Russia's concerns in the Ukraine dispute? Unless you want to start a second Cold War, you do not bully a great nation and former superpower such as Russia. But that is exactly what some officials in the State Department and White House do seem to wish.

As suggested above, the first Cold War probably could have been largely avoided. As it was, its lengthy duration provided more than enough opportunities for officials in the CIA, the State Department, and the White House to hone their skills in manipulating news reports, withholding key facts that might cast a negative light on policies of the United States or its allies, and in outright lying.

Which brings me to my third reason for opposing Rorty's suggestion that pursuing the Cold War was a necessary and laudatory course of action. Simply put, the Cold War atmosphere intensified a habit of mind that fighting World War II had already and unavoidably created, namely, the propensity to use any tactic, no matter how vicious and disreputable, to defeat the enemy. When the enemy represents pure evil, as the Soviets were made out to be, then you deceive, you fabricate "facts," you sacrifice innocent people in countries where the enemy's message might be gladly received. And you corrupt innocent people at home as you train them to become accomplished liars.

I have cited elsewhere examples of American officials distorting reality to fit the propaganda needs of a "democratic" empire. But during the Cold War the practice became so commonplace and was elevated to such a position of professional accomplishment that offering several examples here seems justified.

When doing research for the play mentioned in the introduction, I encountered the following statements in the State Department's annual report on Central America for 1986. Concerning El Salvador, the document sounds innocent enough. Here is what it says about the treatment of prisoners of the state: "The government's Normal Operating Procedures require humane treatment of prisoners by the police and the military." Furthermore, we are informed that "human rights form part of police training and officer's classes."[47]

At that time, it's important to remember, El Salvador was little more than a charnel house where death squads funded by the CIA left bodies on the streets of San Salvador or on the city's dump night after night; and where the military engaged in what amounted to a scorched-earth campaign in the countryside, searching for and exterminating anyone suspected of sympathy with the guerrillas.[48] In addition, members of the armed forces committed such atrocities as raping and murdering three American nuns and a fourth American woman, as well as killing six Jesuit priests and their housekeeper and her daughter. It was a member of the Salvadoran military who assassinated Archbishop Oscar Romero.[49] Clearly, the training provided to Salvadoran military and police personnel contained some significant lacunae.

Whatever may have been the training received by army officers in their home countries, many in the military forces of El Salvador, as well as of Guatemala, Colombia and other countries of Latin America, were trained during the Cold War era at Fort Benning, Georgia, at what was once called The School of the Americas, nicknamed by protesters "The School of Assassins." That the US government has maintained this outrageous facility, among whose graduates are some of the bloodiest criminals of the Western Hemisphere, long after the Cold War ended, suggests just how addicted to controlling the affairs of other nations US officials really are.[50]

47. Dept. of State, *Country Report*, 491.

48. Lernoux, *Cry of the People*, 61–80.

49. Johnson, *Sorrows of Empire*, 125–126.

50. Ibid., 136–137.

The School of the Americas is one of the more obscene legacies of the Cold War. Its traditional purpose, no matter what the official explanations may be, has been to prevent the development of genuinely humane, socialist or semi-socialist governments in Latin America. Fortunately, that aim has been thwarted by millions of the voting citizens of Chile, Argentina, Bolivia, Ecuador and other South American countries. Yet American taxpayers will, no doubt, continue to foot the bill for this mastodon inherited from an ideological and political conflict that most American citizens have hoped—and believed—had been finally resolved years ago.

Another legacy of that conflict has recently erupted in the form of thousands of children and adolescents fleeing their homes in Central America and risking robbery, rape, and death in order to reach a safe haven in the United States. Largely missing from news reports of this phenomenon is the fact that the country that was the bête noir of the Reagan Administration, an outpost of the "evil empire" where "a reign of terror" supposedly existed, i.e., Nicaragua, is missing from the list of countries from which these youths are fleeing. It's countries where the United States has invested billions in overthrowing democratically-elected governments and supporting coups— El Salvador, Guatemala, and Honduras—that have become too violent for their young people to live there free of the fear of being murdered. In stark contrast, Nicaragua's youth are staying at home and helping to build a "new society," based on those socialist principles that for decades have driven US administrators and politicians nearly berserk.

Are there realistic prospects that American policies will change? Evidence from the recent past does not support such a hope. When a right-wing coup took place in Honduras in 2009, removing from office a president elected in what had been widely declared a free and fair election, Hillary Clinton's State Department, surely with President Obama's approval, rushed to recognize the new government. Later on, Secretary Clinton acknowledged the United States' part in that event.[51]

My research on drug trafficking from Central America and Southeast Asia, including confirmed CIA collusions with the traffickers, has forced me to an inescapable conclusion: the CIA is an entity of our government whose crimes have grievously undermined the health of America's soul. But drug trafficking is far from the worst of those crimes. The worst crime is murder. The very worst of these crimes is collusion to murder and implication in the actual assassination of an American president.

I have never been a devotee of conspiracy theories and I had read none of the books that purported to reveal the ultimate truth behind the

---

51. Weisbrot, "Hillary Admits Role in Coup."

assassination in Dallas. I have no taste for murder mysteries, either. So I was somewhat reluctant, despite the urgings of friends whose tastes and values I trust, to pick up James W. Douglass's: *JFK and the Unspeakable: Why He Died and Why it Matters*. I should not have worried; although the book reads at times like a thoroughly researched and beautifully crafted work of fiction, there is nothing here that might be described as sensationalism.

The research alone is staggering. The notes run to just under one hundred pages. Again and again, Douglass quotes sources ranging from letters exchanged in secret between Soviet Premier Nikita Khrushchev and President Kennedy, to notes of conversations that took place between Fidel Castro and unofficial emissaries reporting to Kennedy, to extensive coverage of Kennedy's 1963 American University commencement speech, as well as an address at the UN in which the president made unmistakable his urgent desire to avoid a war with the Soviet Union.

Both speeches, in fact, make clear something that I expect many Americans have forgotten or never knew, i.e., that Jack Kennedy was, early in his presidency, committed to exploring ways to change Cold War attitudes and beliefs and was willing to alienate many in the US military establishment and the CIA by so doing. He was also aware that he was risking his own life in the cause of peace, for he had no illusions about how far some powerful individuals in the upper echelons of the Pentagon and the intelligence community would go to silence a president they considered a traitor for advocating détente with America's ultimate enemy.

The narrative that Douglass creates in this book is remarkable in several respects. First, because he highlights the truly *heroic* quality of Kennedy's life story; second, because he weaves into that story descriptions of and quotations from persons whom most readers would not expect to encounter there, Pope John XXIII and the Catholic monk, Thomas Merton; and third, because he sets up near the start, as any good storyteller must, a central conflict—between the young president and antagonists in the CIA and the military establishment who early on began to distrust him, then to hate him, and finally decided to kill him.

The decision to include Thomas Merton was a bold stroke. This cloistered monk had no direct communications with Kennedy, but he did write letters to Kennedy's sister-in-law, Ethel, in which he expressed his horror at the prospect of a nuclear conflict. This prospect he called "the unspeakable," and it was from Merton that Douglass borrowed the term for his title. Merton called attention to a similarity in attitudes on both sides of the Cold War divide: "Each believes that we have only two choices: appeasement or war, suicide or surrender, humiliation or holocaust, to be either Red or dead,"[52] a favorite expression of fervent Cold War advocates often used to taunt "peaceniks."

Kennedy may have never seen these letters but, as Douglass makes clear, the Catholic monk was praying that his fellow Catholic would be moved by *his* Christian faith to have the courage to resist, with all his moral fiber, allowing America to be drawn into a nuclear conflagration.

Readers of this essay may, in fact, be surprised to discover in Jack Kennedy a deep spiritual quality that his public life and abbreviated term in office did not always reveal. There was, I think, a significant parallel between Merton's agonizing about "the unspeakable" and Kennedy's deep dread of the Cold War terminating in a massive exchange of nuclear weapons that could end human life on Earth once and for all. He thought especially of the children, both Russian and American and elsewhere on the planet, who would never have the opportunity to learn, to grow up, to fall in love and to marry and have children of their own.[53]

From Douglass's accounting, I find it hard not to conclude that it was indeed Kennedy's Catholic-nurtured sensibilities and ethics that created in him the fortitude and determination to resist the staggering pressures from the Joint Chiefs, the CIA, and some civilians in his administration to fight it out with the Soviets using nuclear missiles. On more than one occasion he walked out of a meeting at which top generals and admirals assured him that America could "win" a nuclear war with the Soviets![54]

Once he was urged to resort to nuclear weapons in a dispute—this one over the Berlin Wall—when Soviet and American tanks faced each other in a stand-off that was settled at the last minute by negotiations. What Douglass presents unambiguously is Kennedy's growing realization that in opposing the military brass and officials of the intelligence establishment who were committed to winning the Cold War at any cost, including an all-out nuclear conflict, he was digging his own grave. In fact, he revealed to confidants, including his brother, Bobby, and Ted Sorenson, that if there were two or three Bay of Pigs episodes—that is, occasions when he refused to do the generals' bidding—there would be the possibility of a military coup in the United States.[55]

There were five occasions when the president's actions—or failure to act—infuriated the ranking officials of the CIA and the military: the Bay of Pigs, the Cuban missile crisis, the confrontation at the Berlin Wall, erected

---

52. Douglass, *JFK and the Unspeakable*, 19.

53. Ibid., 279–280.

54. Ibid., 109.

55. Ibid., 13.

by the Soviets to prevent residents of Soviet-occupied East Germany from escaping to the West, a dispute over permitting Laos, Vietnam's next-door-neighbor, to become a neutral state, and the question regarding the withdrawal of US troops from Vietnam in 1963.

Kennedy had no illusions about the chances he was taking in defying the generals. He was smart enough to realize from the first that these confirmed Cold Warriors had no intention of being deterred in their quest for total victory over the enemy. What probably enraged them most was the president's refusal to demonize the Russians. He, in fact, came increasingly to believe that the Soviet leader, Nikita Khrushchev, was a rational being with whom it might be possible to negotiate a resolution of disputes. But Kennedy also perceived that Khrushchev's situation precisely matched his own; he realized that in the Kremlin there were hardliners every bit as bent upon victory as were the generals he had to deal with.

One of the things I found most fascinating in Douglass' telling of this dramatic conflict between two societies with extraordinary differences in political philosophies and world views is the way the two leaders, due largely to the secret exchange of letters, but also face-to-face meetings, reached a mutual understanding and a genuine appreciation of his opposite number's authentic desire for peace. And each fully appreciated the dilemma the other faced, i.e., having to contend with forces in his own country determined to scuttle any efforts for a negotiated peace.[56]

Like no other American president, I believe, save Lincoln and Franklin Roosevelt, Jack Kennedy sought to "educate" his fellow citizens, to turn their minds from the Cold War imagery, rhetoric, myths, and clichés that he was convinced had to be exposed as fraudulent messages if peace was ever to be achieved.

In two key speeches, one at the UN, the other a commencement address at American University, Kennedy spoke not only to his immediate audience but also to the American people. Douglass quotes extensively from the American University speech, in which Kennedy laid out a kind of *apologia* for his peace campaign.

At this juncture it may be helpful to comment on the importance of a strategy Douglass employs throughout this book, i.e., quoting, as earlier noted, from the writings of Kennedy's fellow Catholic, Thomas Merton, but also from others who might at first glance seem extraneous actors in this drama. Pope John XXIII, especially in his papal encyclical *Pacem in Terris* (*Peace On Earth*), is a significant example of this practice. In so doing, Douglass provides a brilliant intellectual and ultimately spiritual misè-en-scene

---

56. Ibid., 383.

that allows the reader to apprehend much more fully than otherwise might be the case the profound changes that were taking place in this young and inexperienced president who at times before his election had sounded like a fervid Cold Warrior himself.

As one reads Douglass's summary of the American University speech, it is not difficult to understand why many in the Washington security-state establishment had long since come to distrust Kennedy, who must have seemed to many of them a super-idealistic do-gooder who refused to face reality, if not a turncoat who advocated a humiliating "defeat."

The president began his speech by stating that the basic element of peace was self-examination. "First: Let us examine our attitude toward peace itself. Too many of us think it is impossible . . . [or] unreal. But that is a dangerous, defeatist belief. It leads to the conclusion that war is inevitable—that mankind is doomed."[57]

Kennedy then noted that despair would indeed probably lead to human extinction but explained that there was a way out of the temptation to succumb to the nuclear war option—focusing "on a series of concrete actions and . . . agreements" that were in the interests of all parties.[58]

The president's second point was that self-examination included an injunction to "examine our attitude toward the Soviet Union." As a Catholic who would have heard Sunday after Sunday passages from the four Gospels, Kennedy had to be familiar with Jesus' words about examining the mote in one's own eye before castigating a neighbor for a beam in his eye. Then the president drew a distinction between a political system and the people who lived under that system, a distinction the Cold Warriors appeared incapable of making: "No government or social system is so evil that its people must be considered as lacking in virtue."[59]

The president then called attention to Soviet propaganda that portrayed the United States in distorted and fraudulent terms but added that it would be a tragic error if the American people made the same mistake as the Soviets. Describing the Soviet situation as a "warning," he urged his fellow citizens not to fall into the same trap: "to see only a distorted and desperate view of the other side." He further warned against viewing "conflict as inevitable, accommodation as impossible, and communication as nothing more than an exchange of threats."[60]

57. Ibid., 41.
58. Ibid.
59. Ibid., 42.
60. Ibid.

Kennedy's appeal was directed not only to the American people but to the Russian people as well. Quite cognizant of the suffering of Russia's citizens during WWII, he was signaling sympathy as well as reason and prudence. If these adversaries blundered into a nuclear exchange, he said, "all we have built, all we have worked for, would be destroyed in the first 24 hours." There follow concluding statements that drive home Kennedy's thesis that if humankind is to be spared the "unspeakable" horror of likely total destruction, "both the United States and its allies, and the Soviet Union and its allies, [must acknowledge their] mutually deep interest in a just and genuine peace and in halting the arms race."[61]

As the president ended his eloquent plea for sanity and recognition of common interests, I find it not hard to imagine the feelings of his student audience, especially as he uttered his final words: "For, in the final analysis, our most basic common link is that we all inhabit this small planet. We all breathe the same air. We all cherish our children's future. And we are all mortal."[62]

It is also not hard to imagine the responses of those at the CIA and elsewhere in the security state apparatus who had come to believe that it was their patriotic duty to eliminate this supposed threat to America's safety and values. Many of them, I'm sure, had so concluded after two crises that revealed the young president's resolve not to allow himself to be manipulated by those in the government who were itching for a fight with the Soviets.

The first crisis was the Bay of Pigs invasion. Kennedy had allowed himself to be convinced by CIA officials that a small brigade of Cuban exiles could invade the island and quickly defeat Castro's military forces. The invasion took place on April 15, 1961, and it became clear almost immediately that the hoped-for victory was an illusion. The organizers of this scheme had assumed that when it became obvious that the invasion was not going to succeed, Kennedy would be forced to order bombing by US planes and to send in ground forces to knock out Castro's army.

Kennedy quickly understood that he'd been tricked, that the CIA and military officials who had urged him to permit the invasion *knew* this venture would fail. Kennedy was not pleased. He responded immediately by removing Dulles as director of the CIA, as well as the second in command at the Agency, thereafter assigning a Pentagon general as his chief intelligence source.[63] Following this event, his reputation at "the Company," as the CIA

61. Ibid., 43.
62. Ibid.
63. Ibid., 13–16.

was known to those in the inner circles of government, ranked just above horse manure on a scale of likeability.

The second event that tested Kennedy's will almost to the breaking point and urgently called upon his political savvy was the Cuban missile crisis. When it was learned in October 1962, that the Soviet Union had installed missile launching pads in Cuba capable of landing nuclear weapons on US East Coast cities, Kennedy was faced with what seemed an impossible choice. He knew he could not avoid challenging Soviet Premier Khrushchev. And yet he wanted desperately to avoid the nuclear war being urged by his advisors.

In his memoir, Khrushchev said that his reason for installing the missiles with nuclear warheads was to prevent the United States from attacking Cuba a second time, for he was convinced that the Bay of Pigs invasion was only the beginning: "The installation of our missiles in Cuba would, I thought, restrain the United States from precipitous military action against Castro's government." Also Khrushchev was thinking that Russian missiles aimed at American cities were a logical response to American missiles aimed at Russian cities from bases located in Italy and Turkey.[64]

For more than a week Kennedy wrestled with this dilemma under enormous pressure from the generals. He ordered a blockade of Cuba before calling a meeting with the Joint Chiefs of Staff, at which Gen. Curtis LeMay all but ordered the president to act: "This [blockade and political action] is almost as bad as the appeasement at Munich. . . . I just don't see any other solution except direct military intervention *right now.*" For the post-WWII generation of the US military, the British capitulation to Hitler's demands at Munich represented the ultimate in "shortsightedness and cowardice."[65]

Rather than caving in to the military brass, Kennedy decided to use secret communication with Khrushchev which resulted in a compromise: the Soviet leader agreed to withdraw his missiles from Cuba in exchange for the United States withdrawing its missiles from Italy and Turkey, but only if Kennedy pledged that the United States would not invade Cuba in the future. To facilitate the agreement, he even committed his government not to publicize the terms of this compact, in order to allow Kennedy to announce the withdrawal of the Soviet missiles without revealing the strings attached to the agreement.[66]

A lesser man than John Kennedy, I feel sure, would have been cowed by LeMay and the other military leaders, as well as by congressional hawks

64. Ibid., 20.

65. Ibid.

66. Ibid.

screaming for action. Later in his brief term in office, some of the generals pressing for a first strike on the Soviet Union claimed that in a nuclear war with the USSR about thirty million Americans would die.[67] Such talk chilled Kennedy's blood. Henceforth he strove body and soul to avoid any use of nuclear weapons and devoted much of his remaining time in the White House to what he called, in his UN speech in 1963, "concrete collaborations for peace."[68]

In this speech Jack Kennedy expressed thoughts that reflected a depth of ethical and spiritual maturity that must surely have been the results of profound soul searching during the previous crisis-ridden months in office. Note the deep longing for the happiness of the human family expressed in the following passage:

> Never before has man had such capacity to control his environ-
> ment, to end thirst and hunger, to conquer poverty and disease,
> to banish illiteracy and massive human misery. We have the
> power to make this the best generation of mankind in the his-
> tory of the world—or to make it the last.[69]

Following the Cuban missile crisis, Kennedy continued off and on secretly to exchange letters with Khrushchev, and only months before his death, he and the Soviet leader negotiated a treaty eliminating atmospheric testing of nuclear weapons. On a speaking tour of the western states in the summer of 1963, the president discovered that his speeches about establishing peaceful relations with the Soviet Union were generally popular with voters. Even his appeals for universal disarmament, when subject to all the required stipulations and checks to insure compliance, did not seem to arouse great opposition. Thus Kennedy began to think about elections a year off, which he was now sure he'd win, and then a second term.[70]

Others in various positions of the US government had already begun to think of means for a violent end to his *first* term. The planning was elaborate, involving a significant number of persons both in and out of government, though mostly the former. Douglass' telling of this story is a kind of tour de force because he had to keep his reader's interest while marshaling an incredibly large trove of evidence, including incidents involving an apparent Lee Harvey Oswald look-alike in Mexico City at the consular offices of both Cuba and the USSR, where he loudly declared his desire to renounce

67. Ibid.
68. Ibid., 176.
69. Ibid.
70. Ibid.

his US citizenship.[71] And, in addition to pulling together recorded testimonies from dozens of persons present at the Dealey Plaza where Kennedy was shot, he himself interviewed a number of individuals able to shed light on numerous aspects of the assassination.

Since it is impossible here to provide *my* reader with more than the briefest summary of Douglass' argument concerning the planning for the killing of the president, the actual assassination, and the various efforts to identify the major actors in the crime without turning this essay itself into a book-length narrative, I shall begin by affirming that I find utterly convincing Douglass' conviction that the principal culprit in this crime was an agency of the government John Kennedy headed—the US Central Intelligence Agency. Although great efforts were made to conceal the CIA's involvement, again and again the evidence leads to the CIA.

We might begin with the understanding that Lee Harvey Oswald did not kill John Kennedy, that he was, as he proclaimed after being arrested, a "patsy." In fact, the available evidence leads to the conclusion that Oswald was in the employ of the CIA. After service in the Marine Corps, he supposedly defected to the Soviet Union where he expressed a desire to give up his American citizenship. The actual purpose for this move was for Oswald to begin functioning as a double agent, reporting to a handler at the CIA. James Botelho, who had been Oswald's roommate at the Santa Ana Marine base in California, told Mark Lane that Oswald was "not a Communist or a Marxist" and that Oswald "was on an assignment in Russia for American intelligence."[72]

After living in the USSR for several years and marrying a Russian woman, Oswald returned to the United States where he became the perfect scapegoat to be manipulated by those plotting Kennedy's murder. One aspect of the plot was the desire to blame the assassination on the Soviets or Castro's government. Hence it was necessary to have Oswald exhibit in public behavior that made clear his attraction to those two communist countries. In New Orleans and in Mexico City Oswald or someone of strikingly similar resemblance did just that.[73]

The real Oswald revealed a strong affection for the United States and approval of President Kennedy. In fact, he explained to his wife, who knew little English, that "he liked and approved of the President and believed that for the United States in 1963, John F. Kennedy was the best President the country could hope to have." Oswald added that "some critics blamed

71. Ibid., 75–82.
72. Ibid., 40.
73. Ibid., 335, 179–180.

Kennedy for 'losing Cuba,'" though actually the president wanted to "pursue a better, more gentle policy toward Cuba," but was not free to do so. Douglass adds this gloss: Oswald understood how constrained Kennedy was in this matter, having personally observed the "CIA's marshaling of anti-Castro, anti-Kennedy sentiment among its paid Cuban exiles."[74]

In Dallas on November 22, the Oswald look-alike was spotted by various witnesses both before and after the shooting. The similarities were so strong that some who saw this individual claimed that he could have been Oswald's identical twin. He, by the way, was "arrested" in the same movie theater where the real Lee Harvey Oswald was arrested and brought out the front door. The look-alike was taken out the back door and disappeared.[75]

Moreover, the actual Oswald was seen in the lunchroom of the Texas School Book Depository, on the second floor, by two witnesses only minutes before he supposedly shot the president from the sixth floor. Although the Warren Commission found that Kennedy had been killed by a lone gunman firing at the president from the rear, the fact that the rear of his skull was blown off by a bullet that had to have entered the head from the front points decisively to the killer having fired from the "grassy knoll," as many witnesses insisted.

Douglass cites witnesses whose reports leave not one iota of doubt that the fatal shots came from that site. One young woman, Judith Ann Mercer, who was on the sidewalk waiting to view the president's motorcade, observed a vehicle driving into the area; the driver stared at her and she later identified him as Jack Ruby, who, it was subsequently revealed, had connections with the criminal underworld and the CIA. It was he who killed Oswald. The passenger, carrying what appeared to be a rifle in a case, alighted and proceeded to climb to the grassy knoll.[76]

Another witness, a deaf-mute who was near the railroad track that ran behind the grassy knoll but close enough to have a clear view of two men whose presence there attracted his attention, watched the actual shooting of the president. This man, Ed Hoffman, reported that one of this couple was dressed in a suit and tie while the other wore clothes that suggested he might be employed as a workman on the railroad. In telling what he then observed to his father and others, Hoffman referred to these two individuals as the "suit man" and the "railroad man."[77]

74. Ibid., 329.
75. Ibid., 291–292.
76. Ibid., 255–258.
77. Ibid., 264.

According to Hoffman, as the president's limousine entered Dealey Plaza, the "suit man" knelt down, picked up an object and then looked over the fence that ran across that area. Hoffman could hear nothing but he saw a puff of smoke as the "suit man" tossed a rifle to the "railroad man," who broke it down and placed it in a tool bag, before disappearing. The "suit man" mixed with the crowd and when stopped by a police officer, pulled from his pocket identification of some sort, most likely that of the Secret Service, before getting into the vehicle, a Rambler station wagon, later identified as the vehicle seen by Judith Ann Mercer delivering a passenger with what she believed was a rifle less than an hour earlier. Douglass writes that "the Warren Commission went out of its way to ignore the obvious evidence of Secret Service imposters at a source of the shots."[78]

When Hoffman tried to tell his story, his father and uncle urged him to reveal nothing of what he had seen lest he too be killed. When some time later he attempted to explain to a Dallas FBI agent his knowledge of the assassination, this man offered to bribe Hoffman, using his fingers to signal silence and $500. All of Hoffman's subsequent attempts to find someone who might believe his account of the assassination were unsuccessful until Jim Marr published *Cross Fire* in 1989.[79]

A number of other persons had significant information which, had it been revealed soon after the assassination, would have forced the Warren Commission to dramatically alter its report. One of these was an Air Force sergeant, Robert Vincent, who had come to Washington, DC, on November 22, to inquire about a stalled promotion and hitched a ride on a C-54 back to his home base in Colorado. The plane had no markings except for a small emblem on its tail that he recognized as identification for CIA property. When the plane took off, Vincent was its sole passenger. When it landed several hours later, he assumed he was in Colorado, until he looked at the skyline and recognized it as Dallas, Texas. The plane had landed not at an airport but on a deserted spot that seemed to Vincent to be possibly a strip of partially-completed highway.

Immediately two men boarded the plane. One was tall, heavy-set, and dark, possibly a Cuban, Vincent thought. The other, a much shorter man, was, Vincent discovered when back in his home and watching the TV news, Lee Harvey Oswald.

Or, rather, the Oswald look-alike. When the plane landed a bit later, not in Colorado but in New Mexico, the two men alighted and disappeared.

---

78. Ibid., 264–265. See Douglass ch. 6, 235: "All the evidence points to the conclusion that there were no genuine Secret Service agents in Dealey Plaza immediately after the assassination, only imposters bearing Secret Service credentials."

79. Ibid., 266.

The tall man fit the description offered by several witnesses, including Hoffman, of the "suit man."[80] The planning for the assassination had proved worthy of a gang of "patriots" with years of experience plotting the elimination of heads of state from Africa to Chile.

(The best of plans, of course, can be marred by small errors as was true in this case when Lee Harvey Oswald was spotted on that Friday afternoon in Dallas in two different locations *at the very same time.*)[81]

We'll probably never know with absolute certainty how high up in the CIA and the branches of the US military the knowledge of the plotting went, but Douglass presents evidence that surely raises serious questions. The circumstances of the autopsy, which occurred not in the hospital in Dallas where the President was taken immediately after the shooting, but at Walter Reed Hospital in Maryland, was marked by features that were unusual, indeed strange enough to raise suspicions about the likelihood that high-level military officials were at least aware of the conspiracy. In Dallas, a number of medical personnel present when frantic efforts were made to save the president's life, affirmed that the bullet that had penetrated Kennedy's neck *had* to have entered from the front. But the report to the Warren commission omitted that fact.[82]

One of the doctors assisting in the autopsy was army Lieutenant Colonel Pierre Finck. In testimony under oath after being subpoenaed by New Orleans district attorney Jim Garrison, Dr. Finck said the autopsy room was filled with admirals and generals and that when the doctors wanted to probe the neck wound, a general who seemed to be in charge of the procedure ordered the doctors to examine the head and chest wounds but not the neck.

A Navy corpsman, Paul O'Connor, explained why the neck wound was not examined: "It got very tense. Admiral [Calvin] Galloway [the chief of the hospital command] started getting very agitated again, because there was a wound in his neck . . . and I remember the doctors were going to check that out when Admiral Galloway told them, 'Leave it alone. Don't touch it. It's just a tracheotomy.'"[83]

Another corpsman, James Jenkins, confirmed O'Connor's description of how the autopsy was "controlled" by the upper-level military, puzzled as to why the autopsy took place at Bethesda, a military hospital, and not at the civilian hospital in Dallas. "In retrospect, I think it was a controlling factor.

80. Ibid., 296–300.
81. Ibid., 293.
82. Ibid.
83. Ibid., 313.

... They [the military doctors] were controlled. So were we. We were all military and could be controlled."

He added that this experience caused him thereafter to feel that America was no different from a "third world country" and that, after the event, he had "no trust, no respect for the government."[84]

As I have stressed earlier, Douglass does a superb job of providing his reader a remarkable portrayal of the profound changes taking place in the heart and mind of America's young leader in the early days of his presidency. Kennedy had begun to understand the legacy of America's domination of its neighbors in this hemisphere and the suffering caused by its support for rapacious and corrupt oligarchs. When speaking to Jean Daniel, a French citizen who became a go-between in communications with Castro, Kennedy spoke these prophetic words:

> I believe there is no country in the world, including all of the African regions, including any and all of the countries under colonial domination, where economic colonization, humiliation, and exploitation were worse than in Cuba, in part owing to my country's policies during the Batista regime. . . . I approved the proclamation which Fidel Castro made in the Sierra Maestra, when he justifiably called for justice and especially yearned to rid Cuba of corruption. I will go even further: to some extent it is as though Batista was the incarnation of a number of sins on the part of the United States. *Now we shall have to pay for those sins.*[85]

Castro was impressed when he heard those remarkably frank words as repeated by Jean Daniel. The Cuban leader also spoke of Kennedy's Alliance for Progress, which, though not as grand as the term suggested, nevertheless indicated that at last there was a US leader in the White House who might be willing to challenge the banks, the trusts, and the multinational corporations that for so long had fed off the sweat of the masses of Latin America. He was also aware, of course, of the risks Kennedy was taking in speaking of peace with either Nikita Khrushchev or with this very outspoken critic of US policies who promoted socialism on this island once America's juiciest solely-owned "plantation dependency."

Repeatedly in his book, Douglass leaves no doubt in his reader's mind that Jack Kennedy was fully aware of how each of his speeches and actions was leading inexorably to his death. Early in the Kennedy story, Douglass cites a saying recited by Abraham Lincoln, which Kennedy also often repeated: "I know there is a God—and I see a storm coming; If he has a place

84. Ibid.
85. Ibid., 73, emphasis added.

for me, I believe I am ready." Kennedy was obviously ready, and when he announced plans, only months before his death, to withdraw a thousand US troops from Vietnam that year and the remainder before the end of 1965, he fully understood the consternation—the fury, really—with which this plan would be greeted by the CIA and the generals.[86]

A good deal of debate has surrounded the question of Kennedy's sincerity regarding ending military involvement in Vietnam. In *Rethinking Camelot: JFK, the Vietnam War, and US Political Culture*, Noam Chomsky mounts a high-powered attack, arguing that the president, despite public statements to the contrary, had no genuine intention of concluding the American involvement in Vietnam, until, that is, military victory had been achieved. Chomsky quotes from many internal documents supporting that conclusion. But he downplays Kennedy's expressions of desire to end the Cold War and is inclined to ignore the pressures JFK was under from the military establishment to achieve a victory in Vietnam. In fact, he slights the general atmosphere of tension between the president and many officials of his government that had existed almost from his earliest days in office.

Regarding ending the Vietnam conflict, I think Douglass gets it right:

> But how does a president of the United States try to end a war, when virtually his entire Cold War bureaucracy wants to continue it? That was the problem John Kennedy was trying to work through in the fall of 1963.[87]

Although correct, I believe, in almost all of his criticisms of US policies of the post-WWII era—and about the hypocrisy of American officials when defending America's support of murderous regimes around the globe—in this case I think Chomsky misses the intricacies of Kennedy's untenable dilemma. Douglass quotes numerous comments made by Kennedy in private conversations, as in this exchange with an old friend, Charles Bartlett:

> We don't have a prayer of staying in Vietnam. We don't have a prayer of prevailing there. Those people hate us. . . . But I can't give up a piece of territory like that to the Communists and then get the American people to reelect me.[88]

I think, in short, that Chomsky either did not have access to or chose to ignore the many occasions when Kennedy made very clear to friends, confidants, and members of Congress, e.g., Senator Mike Mansfield, that he had no choice but to end the US commitment in Vietnam. Yet, as a practical

86. Ibid., 12.
87. Ibid., 180.
88. Ibid., 181.

politician, he also knew that he had to engage in some deception to achieve that end.

Jack Kennedy exhibited great courage in every major episode of his life, and those who knew him best have said that in those last years he often spoke of death but apparently had no fear of his own death. He was no saint, and there were aspects of his character—the infidelity and womanizing, for instance—that were less than admirable. Yet I think it's pretty clear that had he not stood fast against the warmongers attempting to ignite a nuclear conflict with the USSR, chances are that none of us would be around to read or write about his remarkable life.

I believe, in short, that John Fitzgerald Kennedy was a sacrificial victim who gave his life for all humankind. Had he lived, the Cold War had a very good chance of ending at least two decades before it did. And the deaths of millions of Vietnamese, Laotians, and Cambodians, not to mention hundreds of thousands of Americans, might not have occurred. But history mocks our yearnings to replay past events as if they were moves in a video game, and it's a very risky business trying to guess what might have been.

What I *know* is that reading James Douglass's book and writing these few pages about John Kennedy's life and the plot to kill him have changed *my* life. I also like to think that if he had lived long enough to read Douglass's narrative and to contemplate JFK's heroic wrestling with the Cold Warriors, Richard Rorty would have joined me and others who believe the Cold War was a mistake which could have and should have ended much earlier than it did.

But such speculation is no doubt fruitless and we are left with only this: an increasingly fragile planet, a home that requires our love and our courage to rescue it from the greed and the shortsightedness and the lack of imagination of those who seek to exploit the Earth and its people for power and "filthy lucre." John Kennedy may warn us from the grave, but we have other extraordinary *living* spirits who, if we are wise enough to pay attention, can surely point the direction toward sanity and what may still be a reasonable human future. To achieve that future, we could do a lot worse than to turn a ready ear to another Catholic Christian, a man named Francis.

CODA

After the final draft of this essay had been completed and shortly before the entire manuscript was due at the press, I discovered on a friend's coffee table an extraordinary book, David Talbot's *The Devil's Chessboard: Allen Dulles, the CIA, and the Rise of America's Secret Government.* Any lingering skepticism about who was responsible for the assassination of President Kennedy after I had studied James Douglass's book was laid to rest by Talbot's exhaustive study of the legendary CIA head, Allen Dulles. Talbot's book makes clear, beyond all possible doubt, that the CIA, almost certainly with Dulles's knowledge if not his active involvement, orchestrated the murder of President Kennedy.

The portrait of Allen Dulles that emerges from Talbot's book is of an arrogant, cold and ruthless man whose driving ambition led him to use the CIA to undermine the president he had pledged to serve. Once Kennedy sacked Dulles over the Bay of Pigs fiasco, Dulles became Kennedy's implacable enemy, turning his home "into a center of anti-Kennedy government in exile."[89] A steady parade of CIA officials visited Dulles in the months after his dismissal from the Agency, and he even met with a Cuban exile who had been a "henchman" of the deposed Cuban dictator Batista. This anti-Castro character, whose activities were "underwritten by the Mafia," later "fell under Secret Service suspicion in a conspiracy against President Kennedy."[90]

As Talbot draws together the cardinal features of Dulles' personality, it is hard not to believe him capable of allowing his animosity toward Kennedy to bring him to a point at which he could believe that his enemy was the enemy of the country and that it was his duty to join in plotting to eliminate this threat for the good of the country.

Talbot's analysis of Dulles certainly supports such speculation. And it also lends credence to the notion that Dulles was psychologically able to take part in "the crime of the century" with little or no loss of sleep: "Dulles was capable of great personal cruelty. . . . Allen was less troubled by guilt or self-doubt than any of his siblings. He liked to tell people—and it was almost a boast—that he was one of the few men in Washington who could send people to their deaths."[91]

Talbot supplies a trove of circumstantial evidence, including the fact that Dulles spent the entire assassination weekend at a secret CIA facility in northern Virginia. But the hard evidence that leads to the CIA as the principal source of plotting to kill Kennedy was supplied by the "confessions" of Howard Hunt, one of the burglars involved in the Watergate scandal. Hunt was an old CIA hand who had played a part in the coup that overthrew a democratically-established government in Guatemala in the fifties. Toward the end of his life, Hunt began to reveal to his son Saint John

89. Talbot, *Devil's Chessboard*, 7.

90. Ibid., 7–8.

91. Ibid., 9.

what he knew of the plotting for the assassination of the president, including meetings in Miami of Agency personnel. He gave names, including one David Morales. According to a diplomat who knew him well, Morales "did dirty work for the agency," adding, "If he were in the mob, he'd be called a hit man."[92] In 1973, Morales's attorney Robert Walton reported that after an evening of hard drinking, Morales boasted, "We took care of that son-of-a bitch, didn't we?"[93]

The detailed and often complicated story that Talbot tells about events leading up to the assassination and its aftermath could easily furnish a master fiction writer material for a best-selling novel. This tidbit might serve as appoint of departure. In late 1978,

> as the House Select Committee on Assassinations entered the final stage of the probe, a former CIA official named Victor Marchetti published an eye-opening article in *Spotlight*. . . . Marchetti wrote that if the assassinations committee crept too close to the truth, the agency was prepared to scapegoat Hunt and some of his sidekicks.[94]

The agency often dealt with embarrassing events by leaking enough information to entice journalists and legislators to assume they had the full story when the really damaging facts remained hidden.

Allen Dulles died in January of 1969 and his funeral oration, read by a Presbyterian minister (Dulles's father had been a Presbyterian clergyman), had been written by the CIA. In the eulogy, the life of Allen Dulles was celebrated as a boundless campaign in the "defense of freedom and liberty." Talbot offers a somewhat different interpretation of that life. "Dulles's funeral oration was a celebration of the lawless era he had inaugurated. Under Dulles, America's intelligence system had become a dark and invasive force—at home and abroad—violating citizens' privacy, kidnapping, torturing, and killing at will. His legacy would be carried far into the future."[95]

This history of Allen Dulles and the national security agency he almost single-handedly created ought to serve as adequate warning to all Americans who feel anxious about the way American life has been distorted and corrupted by the Cold War and the subsequent "war" against terrorists. Together with James Douglass's *JFK and the Unspeakable*, Talbot's book ought to be read by millions of our citizens. If we are very lucky, we as a nation may escape further development toward a state in which "national

92. Ibid., 500.
93. Ibid., 501.
94. Ibid., 505.
95. Ibid., 617.

security" trumps truth, decency, and democratic processes. The loud and enthusiastic responses to the jingoistic, nativist, and clearly unconstitutional pronouncements of Donald Trump and other Republican candidates regarding barring non-Christian refugees from the United States do not, however, give great reason for hope.

CHAPTER 9

————

CLIMATE CHANGE &
OUR SHARED EARTH

Some years ago, in preparing notes for a future essay, I wrote: "I do not wish to sound hysterical. Brooklyn and Washington, DC, (two of my grandchildren live in the first of these cities, one in the second) will not be totally flooded in the next 25 or 30 years. *My* grandchildren will be safe. But *their* children will almost certainly witness catastrophic alterations in every aspect of Earth's ecosystems and climate." New York City will not be *totally* flooded by the year 2040 but significant portions of low-lying areas in Brooklyn, Manhattan and Long Island almost certainly will be.

Today, with predictions of increasingly ferocious storms battering the Atlantic and Gulf coastlines, betting on which American cities are in the greatest danger of flooding is a hazardous occupation. Few coastal cities will escape some degree of flooding in the decades ahead. Florida is probably the state likely to suffer the greatest damage due to rising sea levels. The February 2015 issue of *National Geographic* carried a special section devoted to Florida's projected future. Under the heading "An Altered South Florida," this rather frightening projection appears: "The coast would be radically changed by five feet of sea-level rise in 2100. This projection is on the high end of the plausible scenarios—though not the highest—under consideration by multiple agencies planning for Florida's future."[1] The favorite vacation spot of millions, the Florida Keys will experience sea level rises that call into question their viability for residents as well as tourists: "Just a few feet of sea-level rise would shrink the Florida Keys, to a fraction of their current size and submerge portions of the Overseas Highway, which links them to the mainland."[2]

1. Parker, "Treading Water," 111.
2. Ibid., 124.

While Miami and other Florida cities are rushing to prepare for the inevitable, even bringing in engineers from the Netherlands to advise local officials on ways to keep the ocean from overwhelming their shops, their residential housing and their playgrounds, Rick Scott, the new Florida governor, has issued an edict prohibiting the use by state employees of the words "global warming" and "climate change." "Bart Bibler, a respected employee of Florida's Department of Environmental Protection, used the term 'climate change' in a public forum. . . . His breach of ideological correctness earned him an official reprimand, a two-day suspension and an order to undergo a doctor's evaluation to verify his mental 'fitness for duty.'"[3]

(As the waters rise, I urge Governor Scott to advertise Miami as "Denier's Paradise." Turn it into America's Venice, bring in gondolas and expertly trained gondoliers and hire Donald Trump as barker. He could make a fortune, perhaps even put Disney World out of business. There is, however, one hitch: Miami may become rather uncomfortable for the visitors since the projected increase in excessively hot days—over 95 degrees F—may go from 8 to 140 per year throughout the southern states.)[4]

Although the dislocations and costs due to climate change experienced by our cities and citizens will be huge, other countries will suffer much greater disaster. As the Earth's glaciers predictably melt and large parts of Greenland and Antarctica slide into the ocean, sea levels will continue to rise—just how much is uncertain but some scientists are calculating in yards, not feet.[5] Millions living along the coasts of India, Bangladesh and other South Asian and African countries will be forced to join refugee populations farther inland. Michael Klare, in *Resource Wars: The New Landscape of Global Conflict*, has described the future struggle for increasingly scarce resources that will no doubt be exacerbated by hordes of displaced populations competing for such simple things as firewood to cook the evening meal, not to mention rice for the meal itself. The human rights group DARA has estimated that tens of millions will die of causes related to climate change between 2012 and 2030 and that truly massive starvation will occur in following decades.[6]

Few writers have described more accurately the frightening reality of the breakdown of Earth's support systems than James Gustave Speth, former Dean of Yale University's School of Forestry:

3. Hightower, "Republicans Just Sick," 62.
4. Parker, "Treading Water," 117.
5. See the documentary *Chasing Ice*, and Klein, *This Changes Everything*, 13.
6. Fundación DARA Internacional. "Climate Vulnerability Monitor."

> Human activities have pushed atmospheric carbon dioxide up by more than a third. . . . Everywhere earth's ice fields are melting. Industrial processes are fixing nitrogen, making it biologically active, at a rate equal to nature's; one result is the development of over two hundred dead zones in the oceans due to over-fertilization. Human actions already consume or destroy each year about 40 percent of nature's photosynthetic output, leaving too little for other species. Freshwater withdrawals doubled globally between 1960 and 2000, and are now over half of accessible runoff. The following rivers no longer reach the oceans in the dry season: the Colorado, Yellow, Ganges, and Nile, among others.[7]

Until recently, the United States contributed the greatest percentage of greenhouse gases to the atmosphere, though China has recently taken over the number one spot in this competition. Along with India and Brazil, the two other countries in the developing world experiencing rapid economic growth, China appeared to be dragging its feet regarding serious efforts to limit greenhouse gas emissions, despite some of its cities being blanketed with smog both day and night. It was only when Barack Obama visited China in the fall of 2014 that the Chinese leader committed his nation to targets for reduction in CO_2 emissions, but the delayed schedule raised questions about whether China's actions will prove to be really efficacious since the predicted "tipping point" in dramatic atmospheric changes is likely to occur before China begins in earnest to curb greenhouse emissions.

In most recent international conferences where representatives of the world's nations gathered to negotiate terms for global reduction of toxic emissions, the United States has failed to provide leadership. Barack Obama did not bother to attend the conference in Copenhagen in 2009 until the final day and has given scant evidence—until very recently (summer 2014)—that he plans to seriously undertake major efforts to forge an enforceable international agreement on greenhouse pollution before the atmosphere passes the tipping point beyond which Earth's climate progresses on its own toward irreversible catastrophe irrespective of human efforts to avert disaster.

At this moment (late summer of 2015), we can all rejoice that President Obama has apparently decided to undertake significant changes in his handling of this critical issue. New standards governing greenhouse gas emissions from coal-fired electricity plants were issued months ago; and Obama has just completed a trip to Alaska where he made climate change

---

7. Speth, *Bridge at the Edge*, 2.

a major focus of his visit. Many signs indicate that there's a new seriousness about his determination to make climate change a key issue of his remaining time in office.

Like many another concerned citizen, I watched for months the proposed completion of the Keystone XL pipeline that would have brought, over the country's most important aquifer, the Ogallala, the world's dirtiest crude oil from Canada to Texas, where it was to be refined and sold to overseas buyers. This was a foolhardy enterprise from the start, especially so with the discovery of huge oil deposits in North Dakota. Because this was an international enterprise, a decision from the Obama Administration was required to permit the pipeline's completion. That decision was delayed again and again, at one point awaiting a judgment by the State Department regarding the pipeline's possible impact on the environment. Astonishingly, John Kerry's State Department issued a preliminary assessment suggesting only a slightly negative impact. The outcry from environmental experts and organizations and from the broader public no doubt weighed heavily on Barack Obama's conscience—and his usually savvy political judgment—when he decided in 2015 to scotch the whole loony business. Count a major victory for Earth's atmosphere and ecosystems and for our grandchildren.

It must be noted as well that the country is not standing still in response to the challenge of reducing CO_2 in the atmosphere. According to a spokesperson for the fossil fuel industries, emissions of greenhouse gases have been reduced by five hundred million tons during the last decade.[8] And Lester Brown of the Earth Policy Institute has written that "of the 500-plus U.S. coal plants that were generating electricity at the beginning of 2010, 180 have closed or are scheduled to do so, leaving 343 plants in operation." Brown notes in addition that increased use of natural gas has been a factor in the decline in coal plants' production of electricity but warns about a serious danger that comes with widespread use of natural gas, "because of extensive leakage of methane—a much more potent greenhouse gas—from wells, pipelines, and tanks."[9]

The recent hustle for additional petroleum sources may have been rendered moot by the dramatic drop in the price of crude oil during the summer of 2015. As of August 21, crude oil closed at near $40 per ~~gallon~~. _barrel._ There is a reported glut of crude worldwide, along with a reduction in demand, and if the price lingers under $50 per barrel, the costs of drilling and then pumping from new wells may deter the likes of EXXON and BP from exploring new fields. SHELL's decision to withdraw its equipment from a

8. _News Hour_, PBS, Sept. 2, 2015.
9. Brown, _Great Transition_, 8–9.

site off the coast of Alaska might be taken as a sign of sanity on the part of executives of the petroleum corporations were we not convinced by previous behavior that their decisions are *always* dictated not by concerns for Earth's climate or its people but solely for the bottom line.

Whatever encouraging news we may have lately received about developments in the international effort to ward off climate disaster, we need to be absolutely honest with ourselves: we face a crisis that demands nothing less than radical changes in our economy, our habits of consumption, and in our life style generally. In fact, if we want to save our planet from becoming a sweltering oven for future generations, we have to start *in this decade* to do what a few years ago would have been unthinkable. We have to begin to transform nearly every aspect of human activity on the planet.

Naomi Klein has provided the road map. In *This Changes Everything: Capitalism vs. the Climate*, she is unambiguous: an increase in global temperature beyond 2 degrees Celsius means disaster. Kevin Anderson, a British scientist she cites, has argued that what is required to prevent temperature rises in excess of that threshold is for the developed countries to begin to reduce greenhouse gas emissions on the order of 8 to 10 percent per year!

Klein comments that such extreme reductions would have once seemed unthinkable; but repeated postponements of decisions by the world's leaders regarding binding and enforceable targets have led to this moment of crisis. Major increases in CO_2 emissions in recent years have pushed the climate near that dreaded tipping point about which climate experts have repeatedly warned. Either we act boldly now or we risk going over a cliff. To make the point as dramatically as possible, Yvo de Boer, once the UN's leading climate scientist, declared that "the only way" that negotiators will be able to "achieve a 2-degree goal is to shut down the whole global economy."[10]

Obviously such dramatic change is neither possible nor desirable. But *radical* change has to take place. It won't be easy. Klein has warned us, "climate change will test our moral character like little else." But there is a very positive side to this crisis, as explained by Miya Yoshitani:

> The fight here in the U.S. and around the world is not just a fight against the biggest ecological crisis of all time. It is the fight for a new economy, a new energy system, a new democracy, a new relationship to the planet and to each other, for land, water, and food sovereignty, for indigenous rights, for human rights and dignity for all people. When climate justice wins we win the world we want. We can't sit this one out, not because we have too much to lose but because we have too much to gain. . . . We

10. Klein, *This Changes Everything*, 87.

are bound together in this battle, not just for a reduction in the parts per million of CO2 but to transform and rebuild a world that we want today.[11]

Not only in Klein's impressive analysis and challenge but also in Pope Francis's encyclical letter *Laudato Si´: On Care for Our Common Home* do we hear this prophecy and this promise. Again and again the Pope emphasizes the necessity of understanding that the vision he harbors for the Earth includes a longing that every aspect of life on the planet, both natural and human, be made healthy and whole.

The Pontiff writes about the value of small changes in personal habits that can lead to reduced harm done to Earth's ecosystems and atmosphere; but he is unequivocal regarding the need for a thorough overhaul of our current economic system and way of life in the developed countries. Almost compulsively he refers to reckless and unbridled consumption, suggesting that it is *the* feature of life in the United States and other nations of the global North that must be altered, not merely for the sake of our "common home" but for the sake of humanity.

We do well to attend to his words as he bluntly summarizes his understanding of the current world situation: "We know how unsustainable is the behavior of those who constantly consume and destroy, while others are not yet able to live a way worthy of their human dignity."[12]

It is in the section on "Spirituality" where we find some of Francis's most provocative admonitions. Real change, he declares, "calls for rethinking processes in their entirety" and a willingness to "question the logic that underlies present-day culture."[13] He also writes about "ecological conversion" and quotes a source who has offered this insight concerning the interconnection of the Earth's sickness and humanity's sickness: "The external deserts in the world are growing, because the internal deserts have become so vast."[14]

Thus this spiritual leader of many millions of Christians around the globe is making clear his belief that a new era for humankind is possible but only if a "conversion" of significant numbers of humans to the struggle for climate justice takes place. Climate justice, of course, includes justice for the billions of Earth's poorest inhabitants who are often those suffering most acutely the effects of climate change.

---

11. Yoshitani, as quoted in Klein, *This Changes Everything*, 488.

12. Pope Francis, *Laudato Si´*, 193.

13. Ibid., 197.

14. Ibid., 217.

Miya Yoshitami's vision for remaking Earth as a dwelling place characterized by ecological sanity, careful attention to water resources and land use, harmony, democracy, and caring for one's brothers and sisters may be an illusion, but it is a vision shared by Pope Francis, whose faith in the goodness of creation and his fellow creatures owes a great deal, I think, to his namesake, Saint Francis.

The present Francis has already, it seems clear, made numerous converts. The longing for a new era for the Earth and for humanity is palpable. We would be fortunate if the climate crisis provided the occasion for a genuine change in lifestyles and worldviews of if enough of us two-legged creatures to lead to the peaceful "revolution" that many of the writers I have earlier quoted are calling for.

I have written at one point that I don't believe in miracles. But . . . if ever we needed a miracle, now is surely the hour of our greatest necessity.

Jonathan Schell wrote during the nuclear scare of the eighties that "a society that systematically shuts its eyes to an urgent peril to its physical survival and fails to take any steps to save itself cannot be called psychologically well."[15] *Mutandis mutatis*, Schell's warning is no less relevant for us than it was for Americans thirty years ago. Christianity and Judaism both teach that we are the children of a loving father. This believers know with the eyes of faith. Nature teaches that we are the children of a loving mother. This we *all* know with the eyes of experience.

And like our actual human mother, she teaches us the basic principles for living a successful life—about respect, and fair play, and limits, and honoring restraints. If we are capable of listening and learning, she can be a gentle teacher. But if we are pig-headed, willful and rebellious, she can be severe and harsh in her punishments.

We humans, unfortunately, have been all of these—pig-headed, willful, selfish and rebellious. And we are now beginning to pay a very heavy price for our undisciplined behavior. So long as corporations, national and multinational, continue to exploit the most vulnerable of Earth's inhabitants, an ever-increasing scarcity of essential natural resources in the near future will bring a critical time of testing for peoples on every continent. As noted earlier, the one absolutely essential resource that is likely to be in short supply in the not distant future is fresh water. In this country, as is the case around the globe, anxieties about adequate water supplies for future populations are a growing reality.

An article in *Sojourners* magazine highlights the problems we in the United States face: aging and wearing-out water systems; a diminution of

15. Schell, *Fate of the Earth*, 8.

federal funds to assist local governments in dealing with increased demand and malfunctioning systems; and the effects of climate change. "Climate change may pose a serious risk to water supplies in about 70 percent of U.S. counties—a third of these counties will be at high or extreme risk of water shortages."[16]

As is normally the case in a capitalist economy, when crises of this sort occur, private corporations move in quickly—to "solve" the problem and, of course, to use the problem as an occasion for profits. The results in many communities is that water prices go up—sometimes dramatically:

> On average, private financing costs one-and-a-half to two-and-a half times as much as public financing. . . . Water prices are regressive. When households are unable to pay for service, private players usually respond by cutting connections. This deprives low-income households of their human right to water, with potentially disastrous health and social welfare consequences.[17]

The likelihood of such an eventuality occurring in millions of households around the country raises a critical question: Does every human being have an innate right to water adequate for his or her survival? The logic of contemporary multinational capitalism would seem to dictate a negative reply. That, at any rate, is the answer of Peter Brabeck-Letmathe, chairman of Nestle Corporation, which is "aggressively pursing water privatization." Acknowledging that there are two opinions on this question, Brabeck-Letmathe asserts that "one opinion, which I think is extreme, is represented by the NGOs, who bang on about declaring water a public right. That means that as a human being you have a right to water. That's an extreme solution."[18]

Such a position amounts to granting control of a natural resource critical to all human life to a group of private citizens, thereby, in essence, giving them a life-and-death decision over millions of fellow humans. From the point of view of Nestle and other multinational corporations, that, apparently, is not an "extreme" opinion.

16. Barlow, "Great Water Crisis," 18.

17. Ibid., 19.

18. Ibid., 18.

ECOFEMINISTS AND OTHER ADVOCATES
SPEAK FOR OUR MOTHER

In the past three or four decades there has emerged in our universities and seminaries a growing number of scholars self-defined as "ecofeminist" theologians or philosophers. Their writing has contributed to radical changes in the thought of those who reflect on the grand issues of the day—in religion, social thought, cultural evolution, politics, relations between the sexes, etc. As the term suggests, these are feminist thinkers who believe that the ecological crisis of our era must be understood in the context of many millennia of male obsession with control and domination—of women, of women's bodies, and of the Earth, which has traditionally been associated with the female sex.

One of the major figures who fits this profile is Sallie McFague, who begins her seminal volume, *The Body of God: An Ecological Theology*, with a chapter entitled "The Ecological Crisis" and uses as the heading for an early section "A Lament for the Planet."[19] McFague offers in this book a comprehensive overview of possible ways of understanding what humans have meant when they have spoken of and written about "God," about divine transcendence and immanence, about God's relationship to the Earth and the cosmos as represented in various religious "models," and about the ways in which numerous theories and doctrines have influenced the manner in which humans have treated the material world and each other. Along with other feminist theologians, McFague argues that western Christianity, despite its foundational anchorage in the body ("incarnation"), has largely ignored "embodied knowing and doing," since there has existed in western thought generally a predisposition to favor mind and spirit over body. Referencing Margaret Miles' *Carnal Knowing*, McFague stresses that in Christianity the central motif has been the spiritual journey. (Think *Pilgrim's Progress*.) Christianity, she writes, "merely illustrated in its own particular way the widespread Western preference for the abstract, the universal, and the disembodied."[20]

This way of envisioning the relationship of mind or spirit to the body has had serious negative consequences in many areas of human life, including Western *man's* treatment of the material world and of women, always associated with the fecund, procreative Earth. Since the material realm was deemed inferior to the spiritual, this belief was used to justify the exploitation of the Earth, which was often perceived to be mere inert matter, totally

---

19. McFague, *The Body of God*, 1–25.

20. Ibid., 49.

devoid of spirit. (Of course, the creation myth in *Genesis* could be and often was used to justify the kind of ruthless exploitation and ravaging of the Earth that modern capitalism has epitomized.)

In insisting on the critical need to pay attention to the body, to embodiment as a fundamental state of being for humans as well as for everything else in the cosmos, McFague simultaneously reminds her readers that changing the way we think about embodiment has implications for how we live. It should influence, for example, our understanding of what justice demands of certain classes of people in relation to other classes:

> If the ecological crisis is calling for an end to narrow anthropocentrism as our moral code (what is good for us and especially "me and my tribe"), then embodiment may move us not only toward a more biocentric and cosmocentric perspective but also toward a more inclusive sense of justice for all (embodied) human beings. In an embodiment ethic, hungry, homeless, or naked human beings have priority over the spiritual needs of the well-fed, well-housed, well-clothed sisters and brothers.[21]

In a chapter on the "organic model" as a way of envisioning God, McFague quotes Ian Barbour, a Christian scholar thoroughly conversant with contemporary scientific theories, to introduce the subject:

> Cosmology joins evolutionary biology, molecular biology, and ecology in showing the interdependence of all things. We are part of an ongoing community of being; we are kin to all creatures, past and present. From astrophysics we know our indebtedness to a common legacy of physical elements. The chemical elements in your hand and brain were forged in the furnaces of the stars. The cosmos is all of one piece. It is multi-leveled; each new higher level was built on lower levels from the past. Humanity is the most advanced form of life of which we know, but it is fully a part of a wider process of space and time.[22]

Organic thinking leads to many important consequences; the chief of these may be that, in contrast to much of Christian teachings of the past, organic thinking weighs heavily against the estrangement from the Earth that many believers and others have experienced through the centuries. One of the most hopeful signs of our times, in fact, is that a great number of Earth's inhabitants, including millions in the United States, are rediscovering the

21. Ibid., 48.
22. Ibid., 27–28.

Earth as home. The organic model, McFague argues, "invites us to be at home here on earth."[23]

And it is a home that may be alive. At least that is the conviction of James Lovelock, who has proposed what he calls the Gaia theory, Gaia being the ancient Greek word for Earth. In this understanding, the Earth is "a living body in which we all participate, continually merging and emerging in rhythmic cycles."[24]

McFague notes that the Gaia theory is perfectly consonant with much Native American belief and she offers this comment from a contemporary Native American writer, Paula Gunn Allen: "The planet, our mother, Grandmother Earth, is *physical* and therefore a spiritual, mental, and emotional being."[25]

Just as I try not to be cynical or hopeless about my country's future, I try not to be naively sanguine. But it is indisputable that all over this land, there are hammers, and bells, and songs that do appear to spell out *rebirth*—the spiritual awakening our country so desperately needs. In *Adapting to the End of Oil: Toward an Earth-Centered Spirituality*, Maynard Kaufman surveys much of the literature that has emerged from the ecofeminist movement. Having taught both religious studies and environmental studies, as well as having operated a School of Homesteading located on a farm in western Michigan, Kaufman seems ideally suited to write about earth-centered spirituality. Commenting on some of the key figures in the ecofeminist circle, e.g., Charlene Spretnak and Rosemary Radford Ruether, he notes that women of this persuasion "understand that salvation means healing and healing, or health as a dynamic equilibrium, means wholeness, living as members of the earth community."[26] The contrast with the traditional Christian doctrine of salvation, the individual "saved" from sin by the mercy of a transcendent deity and thereafter destined for eternal life in heaven, could hardly be more stark.

Kaufman's discussion of the fact that we moderns live in time is significant. Preliterate peoples, archaic cultures knew nothing of history because they lived in space, not time. We, who experience our lives as existing over an extended period of time, have our Judeo-Christian heritage to thank for the concept of history, with a beginning (the Creation myth), a middle (the coming of Christ, his death and resurrection, and subsequent "sacred history"), and an end (the second coming, the establishment of God's kingdom,

23. Ibid., 31.
24. Ibid., 30.
25. Ibid.
26. Kaufman, *Adapting to the End*, 112.

the "end times," whatever). And we can thank—or curse—that heritage for our fixation on novelty, our worship of the new, and our addiction to change. And as Thomas Berry reminded us, also the anxiety that comes with living in the unpredictable, moment-to-moment, ever-changing flux of time. In the following passage, Berry elaborates on what it means for humans to live always in the shadow of a loudly ticking clock, with eyes glued to its constantly moving hands:

> The increasing attraction of an eschatological point of completion brings about a constant acceleration of change as history moves forward toward its fulfillment. Such constant change produces a shattering effect on humans, who cannot adapt to new situations with the required speed. Even if we succeed, there is in the process a draining of life's basic satisfaction, its continuity, its security. There is a loss of present meaning, because each moment of time lives under the condemnation of the next moment.
>
> We greatly need to slow down the sequence of time changes by increasing our spacial awareness [such as is found in Native American and Asian cultures]. Space is complete; time is fragmentary. Space is contemplative; time is active. Space has a present center of rest, time a future goal of attraction. Space is serenity; time is anxiety.[27]

If we consider seriously the consequences of our time-oriented personal and cultural existence as described by Thomas Berry, we might be open to the suggestion that the political awakening America seems to be experiencing would greatly benefit from a contemporaneous, undergirding spiritual awakening heavily influenced by religious myths and liturgies that honor nature and that highlight the central role of space in human experience. In this respect, many of us might learn much of value from Native Americans who, in their traditional religious practices, celebrate the land on which they live, honor various sacred sites, and understand human life in terms of the recurring seasons.

Like preliterate peoples everywhere, Native Americans did not think in terms of linear time, and because their thinking was intimately connected to their physical experience of a profound relationship with the Earth itself, their symbols and ritual practices, even the structure of their tepees, were normally circular, suggesting the ever-returning character of nature's cycles. Kaufman's belief that "these archaic ways are recessive genes in our cultural organism" which could serve at least as models for twenty-first-century Americans wishing to recover a deeper psychological and spiritual

27. Berry, *Sacred Universe*, 42.

grounding in the Earth is, I think, debatable. But it is clear that numerous Americans, raised as Christians or as Jews, as well as individuals of no religious background, who feel the need for some form of Earth-centered religious practice are taking part in rituals that celebrate the Earth's seasonal changes, such as the summer and winter solstices.

It is fairly obvious, I think, that we who live in a society such as twenty-first-century America, where even the concept of the sacred has been almost totally obliterated from our collective consciousness, will never be able to recover the oneness with the Earth and the cosmos that our ancient ancestors knew in the tiniest fibers of their being. But through imaginative reenactment of rituals, the recitation of sacred poetry, the embrace of the material world in whatever form (I have found that hugging trees and speaking to them lovingly can be a restorative exercise), it may be possible to get a glimpse of what Thomas Berry called for when he wrote about the critical necessity of establishing a "mystical communion with the Earth."

One of Kaufman's important contributions to this discussion regarding the benefits of a culture founded on a spirituality rooted in the *healing* Earth is his introduction of the concept of the demonic. Though Kaufman notes that scholars in religious studies understand that in all archaic societies the demonic existed in a dialectical relationship with the divine and thus has an ambiguous nature, he chooses to associate the demonic with the complete failure of multinational capitalism to recognize limits. (See my discussion in chapter 2 of Wendell Berry's take on the "Faustian bargain" inherent in the American way of life.) Kaufman's explication of the corrupting forces that modern capitalism has unleashed harmonizes totally with much I have written in several of these essays: "Because they embody the denial of limits most completely," he writes,

> and arrogate absolute power to themselves, I have come to think of . . . multi-national corporations as demonic structures. . . . Whereas the Faust legend portrayed the effects of demonic power on an individual level, multi-national corporations, with the protection of the United States empire in a fascist system, are demonstrating the effects of demonic power in a global system.[28]

---

28. Kaufman, *Adapting to the End*, 43.

RECOVERY OF THE CHILD'S VISION;
SECOND NAIVETÉ

For centuries, we in the west have been subject to what John Ralston Saul calls "the dictatorship of reason." That is, at least since Descartes in the seventeenth century uttered his portentous explanation for his existence—*cogito ergo sum*: "I think, therefore I am"—thinking, rationality has reigned supreme in human affairs in the western world. And our obsession with reason has come close to robbing us of a critical dimension of our being—the ability to wonder, to feel awe, to experience amazement. McFague reminds us that the root meaning of wonder is "surprise, fascination, awe, astonishment, curiosity."[29] After discussing humans' affection for animals and the capacity of animals to return that affection, McFague adds that

> a first step . . . toward a healthy ecological sensibility may well be
> a return, via a second naiveté, to the wonder we as children had
> for the world, but a naiveté now informed by knowledge of and
> a sense of responsibility for our planet and its many life forms.[30]

All those fostering and writing about the earth-centered spirituality that Kaufman discusses would surely agree. And I think they would also agree with McFague's declaration that "the goal or purpose of creation is love."[31]

One of the things I appreciate most in the writings of McFague as well as those of other ecofeminist thinkers, such as Rosemary Ruether, is a kind of "liberation" these feminists provide thoughtful males who care deeply about the health of the Earth. Not that their perspectives are all utterly revolutionary, though some certainly are, but that for an American male such as myself who came to maturity in the still quite patriarchal America of the 1950s, it has been salutary to encounter female thinkers who can write about evolution and evolutionary theory, for example, with the same ease and grace as they write about theology or poetry.

(I should quickly add that I would never wish to be identified with Lawrence Summers, who foolishly questioned women's capacities in math and science. For more than five decades I was married to a woman who began the study of architecture near her fiftieth birthday and designed award-winning passive solar houses years before solar energy achieved recognition as a major alternative to fossil fuels. In addition, I have three daughters, all

---

29. McFague, *Body of God*, 123.

30. Ibid.

31. Ibid., 157.

of whom have studied math and science; of these, one makes a living doing accounting.)

The ecofeminist thinkers discussed above bring to these issues a perspective that males, no matter how sensitive and perceptive, cannot quite manage. Raised in a society where women have had to fight for the right to equal treatment in a multiplicity of ways, they possess a sensitivity to oppression and exploitation that most white, middle-class American males cannot match. Thus when they write about powerful males ravaging the Earth as they search for minerals, oil or coal, or clear-cut an entire forest, whether or not they use the word "rape," I cannot imagine a feminist thinker not calling to mind the thousands of her sisters who have endured that absolute violation of their selfhood and dignity.

LATE NIGHT REFLECTIONS ON
NOW OR NEVER

The much-anticipated summit on global warming that took place in Paris in December 2015 brought together heads of state of more than 120 nations. Was it another instance of irreconcilable conflicts between North and South and promises to take action to reduce greenhouse emission that were never fulfilled? Absolutely not. This time something like consensus and meaningful commitments emerged from days of discussions and debate.

Mark Hertsgaard, who has been writing about this subject for years, claims that

> the summit's accomplishments deserve the adjective "historic."
> . . . By aiming to limit temperature rise to "well below" preindustrial levels and "pursue" a goal of 1.5 degrees C, the world's governments went further than ever before in aligning policy with climate science. What's more, both developed and developing nations pledged to peak greenhouse-gas emissions "as soon as possible" and to decarbonize the global economy.

A British newspaper's headline read "end of the fossil fuel era."[32]

Such utterly assured conviction that the Paris agreement spells doom for the oil, gas, and coal multinationals is, sadly, very premature. Several features of the deal are troublesome. First, nations are not *required* to reduce heat-producing gases by one pound. Reductions are voluntary and need not begin before 2020, a decision that Hertsgaard describes as "calamitous." All

---

32. Hertsgaard, "Breakthrough in Paris," 4.

that is required is that each country's officials declare "how much and how soon they *intend* to make reductions and then report them after the fact."[33]

A decision that's a critical change from the past is the declaration that temperature rise on the planet must be held to 1.5 or 2 degrees Celsius above pre-industrial era levels. But Hertsgaard emphasizes that to avoid serious overheating of the planet, "emissions must peak by 2020, not merely increase more slowly as the Paris agreement envisions."[34] And, since there is no enforcement mechanism attached to the agreement, there is absolutely no assurance that cheating will not be widespread. But self-interest now seems to have come into play for the majority of nations, north and south. And the latest scientific projections should be enough to frighten any sane official to take action: continuation of unrestrained fossil fuel consumption may result in a sea-level rise *way, way* above what most of us had once thought likely—as much as 220 feet![35] No one wants to contemplate what that will mean for the billions of Earth's poorest living along coastlines in the Global South. Even a Republican Florida governor might be forced to concede that nature has her own ways and refuses to bend to the most arrogant commands of *men*.

Despite its weaknesses, the Paris agreement does signal an encouraging new direction for the human family, largely because it demonstrates that the family can work together when its continued existence is at stake. The officials have done their job. Now it's our turn. And there are reasons for hope: the first is the divestment movement. Bill McKibben's organization 350.org, for instance, has browbeaten, cajoled, shamed, intimidated or otherwise persuaded scores of colleges and universities to withdraw their investments from the fossil-fuel enterprises. The second is the successful outcome—after months of protests, lobbying and arrests—of the campaign to scuttle the Keystone-XL pipeline.

We, the people, still have power. We seem to be learning how to use it.

33. Ibid., 5.
34. Ibid., 6.
35. Ibid.

CHAPETR 10

THE PLAGUE:
MONEY IN POLITICS

IN THIS CHAPTER I examine a crisis that no American citizen is likely to ignore, the "money-and-media election complex" analyzed by John Nichols and Robert McChesney, with superb attention to historical trends and facts and contemporary reports and data concerning the "buying" of American politicians. In the preface to *Dollarocracy: How the Money and Media Election Complex is Destroying America*, these authors quote President Jimmy Carter, who has said, "We have one of the worst election processes in the world right here in the United States of America, and it's almost entirely because of the excessive influx of money."[1]

President Carter commented on the serious damage done to our democracy by the Supreme Court's *Citizens United* decision. But some observers had noted that the system was already thoroughly corrupted, one of them offering this cryptic description: "Our democracy was already broken. *Citizens United* may have shot the body, but the body was already cold."[2]

Nichols and McChesney are masterful in summarizing the critical features of our nation's dysfunctional politics, a central one being the absolute refusal of political figures to frankly discuss the most pressing issues facing the country, and the utter failure of the major media outlets to challenge politicians and demand honest answers. What follows is a sample of the argument they put forward:

> The immediate effect of the money-and-media election complex is to encourage election campaigns, like those of 2012, that do not even begin to address the societal pathologies afflicting the people of the United States. The trillion dollars spent annually

---

1. McChesney, *Dollarocracy*, xiv.
2. Ibid., 3.

on militarism and war is off-limits to public review and debate. Likewise, the corporate control of the economy and the corporate domination of government itself get barely a nod. Stagnation, gaping income inequality, growing poverty, and collapsing infrastructure and social services—major issues all—are accorded nothing more than the market-tested drivel candidates say to get votes. The existential threats posed by climate change and nuclear weaponry are virtually off-limits as campaign-season issues; whole debates that are supposed to go to the heart of domestic and global concerns pass by without mention of them. The drug war, which has created a prison-industrial complex so vast that the United States has a greater percentage of its population imprisoned than any other nation in history, is not to be mentioned—except when obviously engaged and concerned citizens force the issue onto the ballot via the initiative process.[3]

The conclusion these authors draw from the evidence they have mustered is that "mainstream politics, following elections, seems increasingly irrelevant to addressing these grave . . . challenges."[4]

Moreover, the media, owned by the corporate interests that dole out tens of millions of dollars to influence the outcomes of elections, naturally are quite disinclined to demand answers to sensitive questions or to attempt to engage voters in free-ranging discussions and debates. Given this picture of America's "democratic" polity, it is not strange that at least half of the pubic believe that the system is "rigged" and that those taking part in even critical presidential elections are not much over half of the eligible electorate. Hence, considering how disregarded by politicians are the views of vast numbers of potential voters, it is not irrational for many of these individuals to stay at home on election day.

Nichols and McChesney analyze in great detail the money spent in the 2012 election by the presidential candidates, their party's respective campaign committees, an assortment of PACs, super-PACs, solicitors of "dark money" and wealthy individuals such as Donald Trump and Sheldon Adelson, the seventh-richest person in the United States. Counting expenditures in state and local races, right down to school boards, and the dollars spent for initiatives in many states, they arrive at the figure of $10 billion.[5]

One aspect of this whopping outlay of money by the super-rich to influence elections that I find most sinister extends beyond presidential races: contributors such as Adelson often give large sums to influence the outcome

3. Ibid., 5.
4. Ibid.
5. Ibid., 42.

of the election of a judge, for example, in a state where they were not a resident, or to support an effort to minimize the power of unions. Adelson lives in Nevada but was a major backer, for instance, of the campaign to turn Michigan into a "right-to-work" state. He is hostile toward unions and his casino is the only one in Las Vegas where the employees are not represented by one. Although the pundits noted that most of the causes and candidates Adelson supported did not prevail, he succeeded in Michigan, where the "measure that would have provided a clear constitutional protection for collective bargaining rights lost."[6] It should be noted, too, that, win or lose, money distorts democracy by artificially creating and galvanizing constituencies that would otherwise be much smaller.

Furthermore, after all election results were in, Adelson made very clear what his strategy is: to keep spending year after year, believing that in the long run his persistence and his billions will pay off. The *Wall Street Journal* noted that "Mr. Adelson's 2012 donations were double what they were in 2008, and looking ahead, he said, "he was ready to again 'double' his donations." In fact, Adelson boasted that he'd "spend that much and more."[7] With that kind of competition at the polling booth, many candidates don't size up as very threatening adversaries.

Dollarocracy is not, I think, a book for bedtime reading, not, at any rate, if one hopes for a night's sleep free of nightmarish dreams. But it *is* a book that should be required reading by any citizens who care deeply about the health of our democracy. I shall close my description of this book by citing the quoted comments of Edward Ryan, Chief Justice of the Wisconsin Supreme Court, as he addressed a graduating class from the University of Wisconsin Law School.

> There is looming up a new dark power. The accumulation of individual wealth seems to be greater than it has been since the downfall of the Roman Empire. The enterprises of the country are aggregating vast corporate combinations of unexampled capital, boldly marching, not for economic conquest only, but for political power. For the first time in our politics money is taking the field of organized power. The question will arise . . . which shall rule—wealth or man; which shall lead—money or intellect; who shall fill public stations—educated and patriotic free men, or the feudal serfs of corporate wealth?[8]

The year of this address was 1873.

6. Ibid., 60.
7. Ibid., 62.
8. Ibid., 19.

THE SECOND GILDED AGE: POOR PEOPLE
WILL DIE JUST BECAUSE THEY ARE POOR

There is no typo in the date given above. The year *was* 1873, not 1973, and the first Gilded Age was hardly under way. In 2015 we are well into the second Gilded Age, and the similarities with its predecessor are dramatic. A recent debate took place in Texas concerning the Affordable Care Act ("Obamacare") and Governor Perry's decision to reject federal funding to aid the state in expanding Medicaid to cover millions of the state's poor. According to the 2010 census, "24 percent of Texans—6.2 million," lack health insurance.[9] Two independent analysts, one a physician with a PhD at a branch of the University of Texas Medical School, the other a former employee of the Texas Comptroller's office, both concluded that Perry's decision will lead to the loss of several thousand lives. The second analyst, Billy Hamilton, estimated that were the new Medicaid coverage put in place, it would save "the lives of 5,700 adults and 2,700 children" annually.[10]

In keeping with a second Gilded Age, the author of the cover article for the October 28, 2013, issue of *Time*, Tyler Cowen, a libertarian, waded in on the health care debate. In an age of vast wealth at the disposal of a few, with many millions subsisting on meager incomes, Cowen's comments shed light on the point to which our society has "evolved." According to an article in the *Washington Spectator*, Cowen last year "argued that we need to accept that 'the wealthy will purchase more and better health care than the poor. . . . We need to accept the principle that sometimes poor people will die just because they are poor.'" To make his point absolutely clear, Cowan added that "we shouldn't screw up our health care institutions by being too determined to fight inegalitarian principles."[11]

So there we have it: some lives have more value than others both literally and figuratively—and wealth is the deciding factor. The Social Darwinism, so prominent in the intellectual and cultural milieu of the first Gilded Age, returns with a vengeance in the second. We must wait and see if Cowan is correct that "more than any other state, Texas looks like the future."[12]

As I indicate more than once in the essays collected in this book, I find it difficult to disagree with Chris Hedges that billionaires and multimillionaires like the Koch brothers, Sheldon Adelson and Donald Trump and a few hundred others have the power to completely overturn the democratic principles and mechanisms enshrined in our constitution and its amendments. Robert F. Kennedy Jr. described our situation with disturbing

9. Dubose, "Big, Cheap, Deadly," 1, 3–4.

10. Ibid., 4.

11. Ibid.

12. Ibid.

accuracy when he wrote that "America today is looking more and more like a colonial economy."[13]

Yet I am not alone in refusing to believe that all is lost. When I wrote the first draft of this essay three years ago, I was *almost* ready to concede that Chris Hedges' assessment of our national condition was correct: the power of money had virtually *destroyed our democratic polity*. Since then the publication of Nichols and *McChesney's Dollarocracy* seemed to be ultimate confirmation of that fate: money *does* finally trump democratic ideals.

Today (autumn, 2015), I am not so sure. In fact, I have to admit that, as often happens, history takes a swerve and what once seemed sure bets turn out to be guesses upended by the unpredictability of human nature or the swings of political moods.

The elections of Elizabeth Warren as senator from Massachusetts and Bill de Blasio as New York City's mayor do not, by themselves, confirm that American politics are moving beyond the neoliberal stage. There is much other evidence, however, that a new progressive era *may be on its way*. I know, I know. Such an affirmation will sound to some, after the trouncing the Democrats took in November 2014, a bit insane.

Yet, despite the overwhelming gains of the Republican Party in those elections, it may not be absolutely crazy to conjecture that American politics are inching toward a new progressive era which, given the emerging racial demographics of the country, appears to portend an end to the neoliberal hegemony of the past four decades. But before discussing signs of a political turn to the left in our politics, it may be wise to reflect for a moment on the recent turn to the right.

A number of explanations have been given for the startling Republican victories in state after state, but the following three strike me as most persuasive: First, although jobless figures had continued to drop dramatically throughout the summer and early fall of 2014, many voters reported seeing little significant change in their own economic circumstances and blamed Obama—and, by extension, Democratic politicians generally—for their suffering. Second, Obama and many of the Democratic candidates failed significantly when it came to explaining the reasons for the recession in the first place. In addition to making clear that this economic crisis was systemic, that is, caused in part by major changes in the economy from a manufacturing-based economy to one based on communication technology and finance, they shied away from a frontal attack on the robber barons of Wall Street whose reckless games with fraudulent mortgage papers brought on the housing crisis. And a great public relations opportunity was

13. McChesney, *Dollarocracy*, 7.

lost when Eric Holder did not send to prison one single officer guilty of criminal acts at Chase-Manhattan, Citibank, or Bank of America.

Since it was Wall Street donations that were indispensable to his two elections, Obama no doubt felt he ought not to bite the hand that had fed him. But putting a few Wall Street millionaires behind bars might have inspired some voters to think twice before voting for the party normally identified with exploitation of the working class. But today, as Obama's funding sources make plain, not all of the fabulously wealthy are Republicans. The third reason for the miserable showing of Democrats more or less across the board is that they lacked a coherent message. They, of course, are at a severe disadvantage since, in contrast to the Republicans who have what seems to be a fairly homogeneous constituency—mostly white, middle-aged or elderly, fairly well-off voters, buttressed by working class citizens angry about their shattered hopes of ever entering the middle class—the Democrats' constituents are all over the map. And have a great variety of agendas, demands and desires, the result being that it is difficult for the Democrats to put together a package of proposed legislation that doesn't offend some of their potential supporters.

But the Democrats once had a constituency they could count on, blue-collar Joes and Jills. And they might have won some of them back if they had launched a campaign based on principles and policies designed to appeal to men and women working in factories, mines, fast-food shops, food markets, hotels, and retail stores.

What many of the Democrats lacked was moral passion. They might have done a good deal better at the polls if they had proclaimed loudly, "It is outrageous in America for so many people to be struggling to feed their families, for there to be so many homeless people living on our streets, for there to be so many of our citizens in prison for very minor offenses, for our bridges and highways to be in a dangerous state of disrepair, for our neglect of an outdated rail system which might be transformed into one of the world's best high-speed systems, while providing millions of well-paying jobs."

The Democrats might have come out swinging for minimum wage increases. They might have proposed legislation, which in some races could have been game changing, removing the Republican-supported obstacles to union organizing. And Obama might have led them by making clear that he did not shy from waging a "class war," while reminding the nation that the Republican Party has been waging class war against workers almost from its inception, with only a brief timeout during the Teddy Roosevelt and Taft presidencies.

In short, the Democrats might have done better—although they were certain to lose in a number of races because of the unpopularity of Obama and Obamacare and the very low turnout expected in the midterms of any president's second term in office—had they been able to run as a unified party with an exciting, genuinely progressive agenda. The overwhelming question now is this: Are the results of this one election predictive of a decades-long era of reactionary Republican legislation undermining all of the sane accomplishments the Obama Administration has been able to achieve in such areas as limits on greenhouse gas emissions from coal-fired plants, the raising of miles-per-gallon standards for America's many millions of autos, health-care reform, normalization of relations with Cuba, and an important step toward humanizing the immigration system? I don't think so.

When looking at the results of the midterms, the one reason for modest optimism may be the utter irrationality of the voters. No one that I know of tells this story more convincing than does John Nichols. In the December 1/8, 2014, issue of the *Nation*, Nichols examines polling data from a number of states and concluded that in state after state, voters "chose Mitch McConnell senators and Elizabeth Warren policies."[14] He gives Alaska as an example:

> Sixty-nine percent of Alaska voters backed the boldest formal proposal for a minimum-wage increase on a state ballot—a hike of $9.75 an hour, with future increases indexed to inflation—but a substantial portion of them helped elect Republican Sam Sullivan, whose first vote as a senator will be to put McConnell in charge of blocking a federal wage increase.[15]

This pattern was repeated in Arkansas, Wisconsin, and Texas. In Wisconsin, a huge majority of voters (73 percent) supported "county advisory referendums" urging the state to accept Medicaid funds, while expanding healthcare options, yet reelected Scott Walker as governor; Walker has refused to accept federal funds. In Texas, 59 percent of the voters in the town of Denton "approved a ban on fracking on the same day that fracking-friendly Republicans won most state and local races."[16] In my home state, Massachusetts, a paid-sick-leave law proposal was approved by 59 percent of voters; but our new governor, Republican Charlie Baker, a former health-care executive, opposed the idea. What these data show conclusively is that across the

14. Nichols, "Hangover," 13.
15. Ibid.
16. Ibid.

country there are majorities in favor of progressive measures. Those same people won't elect Democrats so long as Democrats "peddle pablum."[17]

Some may find a perverse logic here: because many voters saw little hope of either party seriously addressing their concerns, having to do mostly with their economic situation, they took out their frustration and anger on the party seemingly in power, ignoring, of course, the months and months since 2010 when the Democrats were totally hamstrung by a Republican-majority House of Representatives and a strong Republican minority in the Senate determined to frustrate every effort of the Democrats to govern.

I suspect, however, that some working-class voters decided to pay back the Democrats for their enthusiastic support of trade agreements such as NAFTA that had cost them their jobs. I'm tempted sometimes, though, to give up entirely any attempt to deal logically with this conundrum and simply assert that American voters are, to borrow a phrase from a character in a Walker Percy novel, "as fickle as whores."

In all of the confusion and, for progressives, angst, is it possible to perceive a more positive side? I think it is. In a perceptive article, "A New Era for New York City," in the *Nation* (January 20, 2014), Bob Master writes about the "de Blasio moment," comparing it with that point in the civil rights movement when, as Dr. King put it, the *zeitgeist* sought out Rosa Parks.[18] Bill de Blasio's election as mayor of New York does, indeed, appear to herald just such a paradigm shift.

Bob Master discusses in some detail the back story of de Blasio's march into New York's City Hall, beginning with the campaigns of the right in the1970s and eighties to delegitimize government programs initiated by Johnson's Great Society: privatize schools and undermine efforts to unionize the working class, and promote the idea that untrammeled capitalism was the best system for every American, of whatever social class. Manufacturing, earlier the base of American riches, was shipped abroad and financial speculation, which offered inordinately grand prizes to Wall Street kingpins and bankers (as David Korten's book reminded us), became the only meaningful game in town. Wealth was supposed, we were repeatedly assured by Reagan and those who followed him, inevitably to "trickle down." It did not, of course, happen quite that way.

After the financial and housing bubbles burst in '08 and '09, Master argues, a variety of organizations and ad-hoc groups representing consumers, school parents, and other voter blocs, plus labor unions, began to see results

17. Ibid.
18. Master, "New Era," 12.

from years of opposition to the neoliberal consensus which had dominated both Republican and Democratic politics for decades.

And then, as if appearing on cue from the wings, Occupy Wall Street announced to the world what had become undeniable: the reigning economic model had been a disaster for the great majority of Americans. In a metropolis where Wall Street moguls spend millions on penthouse condos, while fast-food workers try to feed families on $8.25 an hour, it's no wonder that de Blasio's "tale of two cities" proved such a successful political slogan.

De Blasio and Warren have been joined by other progressive politicians winning public office in the recent past, and it's hard to deny that the future may look brighter for public officials in many sections of the country who have the smarts and the courage to defy the right-wing orthodoxy that has caused the nation such grief for so many years. A major reason for optimism is the rising generation of voters. Here is Master's assessment of the political significance of changing attitudes among America's young people:

> In the *Daily Beast*, Peter Beinart argued that the de Blasio campaign reflects the political crystallization of a generation of young people who have grown up in an era of dismal economic prospects and a tattered government safety net. This, Beinart predicted, will give rise to a new mass anti-corporate politics that will benefit populist politicians like de Blasio and Warren at the expense of more conventional centrists like Cory Booker and Hilary Clinton.[19]

Bill de Blasio himself speaks convincingly of a progressive movement underway in our time, one that stretches back in memory to the early twentieth century. In an interview published in the *Nation*, he commented on "a rich history—from the Progressive Era, 100 years ago, to the present—of progressive governors, progressive mayors, progressive legislators."[20]

Commenting on what is happening in New York City, de Blasio explained that his administration was attempting to accomplish progressive changes following the model of New Deal boldness and experimentation. He stressed, however, that a variety of groups and causes—unions, fast-food workers, the struggle for paid sick leave—had prepared the ground for real reform in the fight against inequality. And he called attention to the role of "a lot of advocates, nonprofits and media organizations fighting for bringing up wages and benefits."[21]

19. Ibid., 13.
20. Alterman, "Bill de Blasio," 15.
21. Ibid.

What is indisputable, I think, is that while Washington may be trapped in gridlock for the next year and probably beyond, exciting things are happening in cities and states across the country that promise a better future for millions. Increasingly, national governments seem unable to deal effectively with the problems that confront them; in response, as de Blasio observes, "Mayors all over the country, mayors all over the world [are] taking matters into their own hands."[22]

One change of attitude respecting America's chances of recovering its democratic politics that I find most striking is that of Chris Hedges. In a talk he gave in September of 2014 at the annual "Fighting Bob Festival" in Wisconsin, Hedges ripped into the Democratic Party and Barack Obama for sacrificing those who are most vulnerable, e.g., the hundreds of civilians in Gaza pummeled by Israel's ferocious bombings the previous summer; and in America—"our own poor, workers, the sick, the elderly, students, and our middle class"—to the super-wealthy and politically powerful. He described such behavior as "selling your soul to Goldman-Sachs and Exxon-Mobil."[23] And he continued, as in the past, to underscore how debauched US political life has become, with "only the façade of politics, along with elaborate, choreographed spectacles filled with skillfully manufactured emotion and devoid of real political content."[24]

Up to this point in his address, it was the same Chris Hedges I have called attention to more than once in previous essays. But then, after excoriating the feckless liberal class and the ruthless enforcers of the corporate state, he asserted his conviction that a revolution of some sort is brewing. "The tinder of revolt is piling up," he declared. "No one knows when the eruption will take place. No one knows what form it will take. But it is certain that a popular revolt is coming."[25]

Hedges then comments on the need to "discredit" the ideas used to maintain the corporate state and the elites who suck wealth from the general populace and replace them with ideas for a society where all citizens benefit from the economic structures in place. For our moment in history, this "means the articulation of a viable socialism as an alternative to corporate tyranny."[26]

By this point it should be obvious that Hedges is never afraid to be radical. Thus, after making clear his preference for the "piecemeal and

22. Ibid.
23. Hedges, "Starting a Revolution," 21.
24. Ibid.
25. Ibid., 22.
26. Ibid., 23.

incremental reforms of a functioning democracy," he is not hesitant to specify what he believes may be the only alternative to indefinite rule by corporate elites—revolt.[27]

Hedges is not yet ready to deny the possibility of a popular movement disarming ideologically "the bureaucrats, civil servants, and police—to get them, in essence, to defect."[28] Should this happen, then a nonviolent revolution would have a chance of success. But a frightening alternative waits in the shadows:

> If the state can organize effective and prolonged violence against dissent, it spawns reactive revolutionary violence, or what the state calls terrorism. And our backlash, if we on the left do not regain the militancy of the old anarchists and socialists, could be a rightwing backlash, a species of Christian fascism.[29]

Hedges concluded his address with a call for a campaign of civil disobedience for as long as it takes to "overthrow the corporate state."[30] I think he is correct. We will not regain our pilfered democratic rights unless we fight for them. But if that struggle turns violent, the availability of lethal weapons in every county of the country—one for every man, woman and child in the nation—almost guarantees substantial bloodshed. And then, I suspect, the religious right *will* take advantage of the chaos to establish by whatever means available the "Christian" society for which they have so long yearned.

Although I believe Hedges' analysis of the explosive state of American society is more or less accurate, in my opinion the revolt he predicts is not likely to happen in the very near future. It takes time for smoldering resentments and the longing for a new social order to gestate; and the remarkably vigorous recovery from the recent recession is likely to do what all past recoveries have done—reassure the majority of the population that no fundamental changes in our economic structures and practice are needed.

Nevertheless, Hedges is right: millions of Americans *do* sense the basic injustice of the current distribution of wealth in the country, as well as the inordinate power of the titans of industry; and millions are actively pursuing progressive alternatives to the destructive ways of the corporate state. It is far too early to become exuberant, however. Any number of unforeseen disasters may befall the nation.

27. Ibid.
28. Ibid.
29. Ibid.
30. Ibid.

Perhaps the critical question is this: If a majority of Americans support progressive measures such as increasing the minimum wage, providing paid sick-leave and maternity leave for all, limiting fracking for oil and natural gas, placing controls on "dirty" emissions from coal-burning power plants, and expanding access to health care, will a majority of voters rise up and really work for a presidential candidate who supports those issues. And if a candidate who does not support those issues is elected, no matter from which party, will a significant portion of the population become aroused and take to the streets? In other words, could Hedges' "revolution," without the guns and the blood, become a reality?

The astounding success of the Sanders campaign in Iowa and New Hampshire in the winter of 2016 and the wild enthusiasm of thousands of young voters for this seventy-four-year-old socialist from Vermont could be portents of a major *peaceful* revolution unfolding before our eyes. Importantly, Sanders understands the sources of the rage of working class Americans that the Donald Trump campaign has capitalize on—lost jobs, lost homes, lost hope. With his own working class background and his shunning of financial support from lobbyists and superpacs, I think it possible that some "angry white males" will see the light and become Bernie supporters. Whether or not Bernie wins the nomination and then goes on to win the election, an outcome thought totally mad just a few months ago, I believe it's clear that American politics have been permanently changed and that, with luck and a move to the left in congressional elections in November due in part to the Sanders "miracle," our nation may escape the bloody revolt Chris Hedges thinks possible.

Bernie Sanders has provided the spark. Citizens in the street will have to provide the fuel. If the November elections bring us Donald Trump—God forbid—or Ted Cruz, then a politics of mass protests will, I think, be inevitable. In periods of crisis in the past, America has been well served by a citizenry prepared to protest again and again and to go to jail when the moment seemed propitious for mass arrests. Such tactics worked during the Vietnam era; there is no reason to believe they cannot work again.

APPENDIX 1

Israel's Heartlessness: We See It in the Treatment of Palestinians

NOTE: This article was published as an op-ed piece in the July 3, 2013, issue of the Greenfield *Recorder*. Two months after it appeared, Israel launched a massive attack on the Gaza Strip, killing 2,219 Palestinians, more than half of whom were refugees from the 1948 Nakba. Among the dead were 309 children. A total of 1.3 million refugees live in Gaza, in 8 refugee camps.

AT THE FORUM ON Israel and the Palestinians held at the Congregational Church in Ashfield last month, I watched three films: *5 Broken Cameras*, *Paradise Now* and *Occupation 101*. In each of these films, the Israeli Army's treatment of the Palestinian people in the Occupied Territories was indescribably cruel.

In one episode, Israeli soldiers invaded Palestinian homes in the middle of the night and arrested boys who did not appear to be older than eleven or twelve. In another, a teenage boy, held by soldiers, was shot point-blank in the leg. Live ammunition was used to break up a crowd of unarmed Palestinians demonstrating against the taking of their land by Israeli settlers. Ancient olive trees, often the major source of income of Palestinian farmers, were uprooted by bulldozers or burned. Israeli settlers invaded Palestinian property during the night, leaving behind trailers so that in the morning they could "legally" claim the land as their own. Seriously ill or injured Palestinians on their way to hospitals were held up for hours at check points, sometimes resulting in the deaths of the patients.

A map of Palestine from 1946 shows the vast bulk of the land belonging to the Palestinians, with Jewish settlements sprinkled in the northern part of the country. A current map reveals that the Israelis now control 90 percent of the land, with the Palestinian people's share reduced to enclaves separated from each other—almost always by Jewish settlements—with travel between the enclaves tightly controlled by the Israelis.

Some years ago, Archbishop Desmond Tutu of South Africa described this maze-like system of enclaves as worse than the bantustans in which South African blacks were forced to live during the era of apartheid. In fact, repeatedly in descriptions of the conditions of life that the Palestinians must endure, the word "apartheid" was used.

In my opinion, one of the saddest aspects of this conflict is the effect such blatantly brutal treatment of one's neighbors has on the Israelis, especially the Israeli soldiers, some of whom appeared to be hardly more than adolescents. A kind of sadistic pleasure sometimes seemed to be the dominant emotional response as, for example, when a youthful soldier took a chainsaw to an olive tree, ignoring the sobbing of a Palestinian woman begging for mercy for her family. There is a price, both psychological and spiritual, to be paid for such heartlessness.

After watching these films and listening to testimony of Palestinians living in the United States, I find it hard not to conclude that Israeli policy has one of two aims: either to make life for the Palestinians so utterly intolerable that they will emigrate or to drive the Palestinians into the sea. I do not think, however, that the majority of the Palestinians will abandon their homeland—there are already seven million in the Palestinian diaspora—nor does it seem likely that Israel can ever achieve the goal of the ultra-orthodox Jews—a Jewish state occupying all of ancient Palestine. Short of a radical change in Israeli attitudes and policies, only an indefinite continuation of the present stalemate seems predictable. But humans can tolerate only so much oppression and genuine terror. In private conversations, I heard rumblings of a third intifada, likely more bloody than the previous two.

It should be clear that we are not innocent bystanders. It is our taxes, sent as "foreign aid" to Israel, that allow the Israeli Army to buy the bulldozers that demolish the homes, the tanks that rumble through Palestinian villages and the helicopters that bombard Palestinian towns and cities. As responsible citizens, we Americans ought to declare our unwillingness to continue to finance the decades-long suppression of the Palestinian people's dream of a Palestinian state with contiguous borders.

Although the Obama administration's negative vote in a recent UN General Assembly's decision to give the Palestinians "observer status" signals a continuing American refusal to relinquish its long-standing bias in favor of Israeli interests, a wiser path would be to adopt a genuine honest broker approach. In fact, it would ultimately be in Israel's best interests if American leaders could resist intimidation by the Israeli lobby and adopt a clear-sighted view of Israeli policies.

A Jewish friend has observed that because of centuries of persecution and especially the Holocaust, many Jews tend to be paranoid. Obama is no psychiatrist but, if he wishes a place in history as an outstanding president, he must summon the courage to be a hard-nosed advisor warning against the folly of any nation's leaders believing that their county can flagrantly violate the rights of fellow human beings without retribution in some form being visited upon the perpetrators.

It must now be clear that with the changes that have recently occurred in the Middle East, Israel's true security depends on lessening its isolation in an increasingly hostile neighborhood. If the United States is really Israel's steadfast friend, it will not shirk the task of warning Benjamin Netanyahu's government that American support is not infinite and that the time has come for Israel to respond with genuine seriousness to the long-ignored Palestinian cry for justice.

APPENDIX 2

Religion for the Downtrodden
and Forgotten

Further Reflections on John Spong's
"Religionless Christianity"

LIFE IN THE CONTEMPORARY, industrialized countries leaves humans exposed to the power of vast but in many respects invisible forces that cannot help but create anxiety and a debilitating feeling of impotence. One answer to this problem, the one that appears to have been efficacious for millions living in the global South, as well as for racial groups ignored or discriminated against in the wealthy countries of the North, has been *communal* action.

Sara Miles, a young American woman who had been raised as an atheist, discovered in El Salvador during the bloody civil war of the eighties the power of communal action, an aspect of Christianity that eventually led her to embrace the faith: "Watching priests, nuns, and catechists struggle for justice in Central America, I came to respect Christians more than I ever could have imagined growing up."[1]

Reading Sara Miles's *Take This Bread* reinforced a feeling I had experienced earlier, i.e., that Bishop Spong focuses too exclusively on the significance of Jesus for the *individual* who may be drawn to him and neglects almost completely the *community*, be it Latin American peasants or exploited, downtrodden and neglected African-Americans, for whom the supernatural, ever-watchful, intervening deity of orthodox Christianity has been a power that has, again and again, sustained their struggles for justice and freedom.

---

1. Miles, *Take This Bread*, 50.

Bishop Spong, I'm sure, realizes that his audience is almost exclusively white, middle- or upper-middle class, and, if not wealthy, at least free of anxiety about clothes and shoes for the children and food for the next meal. Such people can much more easily abandon faith in the "stopgap God" Bonhoeffer wrote about and that Spong declares to be a myth. Spong's dead God is *not* the God of hundreds of millions of impoverished peasants of Brazil and El Salvador and Guatemala, nor the God of growing masses of Anglicans and Roman Catholics in Africa. A dirt-poor single mother of five living in a village in Nicaragua or in one of the slums of Buenos Aires, may not pray daily to God the Father, who may seem impossibly distant, but she almost certainly prays regularly to Mary, the anguished Mother of Jesus, who is often the principal source of succor for the poor and oppressed.

In this context, the comments of Karl Marx on religion, if accurately quoted, make perfect sense:

> *Religious* distress is at the same time the expression of real dis-
> tress and the *protest* against real distress. Religion is the sigh of
> the oppressed creature, the heart of a heartless world, just as it is
> the spirit of a spiritless situation. It is the *opium* of the people.[2]

Black Baptist churches have nothing similar to the crucifixes, the paintings, the stations of the cross of Catholic churches or the icons that fill the iconostases of Orthodox churches, but even in slavery many black people had the stories: Moses leading his people out of slavery in Pharaoh's Egypt; Mary and Joseph taking the baby Jesus to Egypt to escape Herod's slaughter of the innocents; Jesus' lonely vigil on the night before the cruci-fixion and the agony of the crucifixion itself. And the reward for faith and hope—eternal life in heaven.

Any sensitive person can imagine the life-sustaining ecstasy of a black worshipper, even many decades after the end of slavery, singing, "Swing Low, Sweet Chariot / Coming for to carry me home." In Brown's Chapel, in Selma, Alabama, in March of 1965, I sensed something of the power of communal struggle as hundreds of black Christians sang, "Oh, freedom over me / And before I'll be a slave / I'll be buried in my grave / And go home to my Lord and be free."

Whatever may be the future of religion as practiced in the mainline Protestant churches and the Catholic Church of North America, people's "religion" is certainly not dying! Not only in Latin America but also in large portions of Africa an invigorated Christianity—sometimes Pentecostal, sometimes Catholic or Anglican—has developed in recent decades, normally

---

2. Marx, *Critique of Hegel's Philosophy of Right.*

closely joined with liberation movements. And liberation theology too has played a key role, especially in Latin America, in redefining Christianity as a movement for justice, equity in the distribution of resources, and dignity, in contrast to the image and too-frequent reality of the traditional church as a defender of the status quo, of the propertied class, of governments that again and again, especially in armed conflicts, have sacrificed the well-being of the masses for the interests of those with wealth and high social status.

Surely, the election of Pope Francis, whose unambiguous critique of capitalism and dramatic statements regarding the Catholic Church's preferential option for the poor have stirred the hearts of hundreds of millions worldwide, has added an incalculable dimension to what I think must be described as a "renewal" of Christianity.

APPENDIX 3

Anger and Hope

DURING THE PAST FIFTY years of my life I have lived between anger and hope—anger as I've watched the country I keep trying to love commit terrible atrocities, the Vietnam War being the greatest of these, and hope that the better angels of our nature might prevail. Though at times I have wavered, I have avoided sinking into cynicism and apathy. And once in a while I discover a thinker and a book that inspire and even thrill me. Martha Nussbaum is such a thinker and her *Political Emotions: Why Love Matters for Justice* is such a book.

Nussbaum is a philosopher who teaches at the University of Chicago Law School; she has written many books covering an extremely wide range of interests and subjects but this one should surely confirm her reputation as one of the truly outstanding public intellectuals of our day. Her idea of *teaching* political emotions strikes me as revolutionary, especially the emotions of sympathy and compassion. Of course, we already teach those emotions in our homes, our schools, our churches, synagogues and mosques. But that activity happens more or less unselfconsciously. As parents, we may say, "Don't take what's not yours," or "Don't be spiteful," or "Don't bully"— or we may simply model the virtues we consider important and leave it to schools and religious institutions to inculcate other values, such as love of country and respect for those whose ideas and values are quite different from our own.

But Nussbaum's project is different. She wants us, as a society, to study the means by which certain values, essential to the health of a democratic society, can be effectively *taught* to citizens in such a fashion as to create, in effect, a new society with a new religion, one whose major goal is to bring into being a global community focused on justice, compassion, and cooperation across racial and national boundaries.

Contrary to what I would guess would be the expectations of most readers of this book, Nussbaum opens her argument not with political theory or philosophical generalizations but with an opera—Mozart's *The Marriage of Figaro*. I cannot begin to do justice in several paragraphs to the argument in which Nussbaum summarizes the plot of the opera and the conventional interpretation of the story as two men, the Count and his servant, Figaro, engage in a contest over a woman. According to the standard interpretation, the Count, insisting on the rights of the nobleman to enjoy sexually a female servant before she is wed to someone of her social class, represents the ancient regime, while Figaro represents the new age of liberty, equality and fraternity ushered in by philosophers such as Voltaire and Rousseau. The servant Susanna is the prize for which the two men struggle, and since at the opera's end, the Count has been deceived by the plotting of his wife and Susanna and is forced to beg his wife's forgiveness, the story seems to represent the end of the medieval world of rigid class boundaries and unquestioned privileges and duties. At the opera's conclusion, according to the standard reading, Figaro has become an "apostle of a new type of citizenship, free from hierarchy."[1]

But Nussbaum thinks otherwise. In her interpretation, Mozart and his librettist, da Ponte, understand that there is little other than rank which separates the Count and Figaro; both are obsessed with status and sing about how to best the other in order to preserve his pride of "ownership." Nussbaum summarizes this fixation in these words:

> Mozart sees something that Beaumarchais [the author of the play on which the opera is based] does not see: that the ancient regime has formed men in a certain way, making them utterly preoccupied with rank, status, and shame, and that both high and low partake of this social shaping. What one does not wish to lose, the other wishes to enjoy. For neither, given their obsession, does any space open out in the world for reciprocity or, indeed, for love.[2]

Nussbaum argues that it is only the female characters—the Countess and Susanna—and Cheribino, the adolescent who has been raised among women and whose part is always sung by a woman, who are able to transcend the rigid structures and formulae of traditional society and signal a truly new, genuinely revolutionary construction of human relations—based on sympathy, compassion, a healthy portion of *joie de vivre*, and a fully

---

1. Nussbaum, *Political Emotions*, 32.
2. Ibid.

developed capacity to revel in the unpredictability and the quirkiness of human character.

Those who have seen a production of the opera will recall that the Countess and Susanna scheme to trick the Count by exchanging roles at the masked ball, thereby leading the Count, who attempts to seduce Susanna, to thus reveal to his wife his intended infidelity. So entrapped, he can only beg his wife to "excuse" him, which she immediately does.

A point that Nussbaum stresses throughout her discussion of the opera is that the women possess a key characteristic that the adult male characters lack utterly—the ability to plot mischievously and to really *enjoy* themselves in the process. Cherubino, too, at one point takes part in another plot, i.e., with Susanna's assistance, to get himself safely out of a hiding place, and Nussbaum affirms that now he, too, "has, in effect, become a woman: a coconspirator, voice of fraternity and equality, and . . . a person free from the bonds of status."[3] Caught up in the confusions of teenage romantic desire, Cherubino's passion is not for possession or status, nor is he driven by fear or shame. It is, rather, the feeling of *love* by which he is possessed.

"As Cherubino understands, this means seeking a good outside oneself, which is a scary idea. It is, nonetheless, an idea that Figaro must learn before he can be the kind of citizen Mozart . . . demands." Nussbaum is convinced that learn it he does, as revealed in a recitative expressing "both longing and pain." When he sings "Oh, Susanna, what suffering you cost me," Nussbaum believes he thus acknowledges "a good outside himself."[4] Nussbaum adds this gloss: "What's suggested here, then, is that democratic reciprocity needs love."[5]

Nussbaum explores through complex and multilayered examination of the thought of philosophers such as Rousseau, Kant, John Steward Mill, and the contemporary John Rawls the ingredients of the good society of the future that she foregrounds in this study.

She also presents in very accessible prose the results of some recent research on the development in young infants of the capacity to move beyond tyrannical demands for constant attention to something approaching reciprocity, in short, love. It is the extreme narcissism of the helpless human infant that must be tamed and converted into sympathy and fellow feeling if a society based on justice and reciprocity is ever to be achieved.

As her detailed examination of Mozart's opera suggests, it is through art that Nussbaum believes the cardinal virtues of a truly good society are

3. Ibid., 42.
4. Ibid., 43.
5. Ibid.

adumbrated—and taught. To describe how this process might unfold, Nussbaum turns to Rabindranath Tagore (1861–1941), the Indian poet, novelist, and educator. Tagore combined in his personality, his writing and his teaching a brilliant sensitivity to those aspects of human life that too often block our capacity to transcend our egoistic, self-protecting "instincts." Tagore wrote that for most humans, our world is "restricted by the limit of our sympathy and imagination. In the dim twilight of insensitiveness a large part of our world remains to us like a procession of nomadic shadows."[6] Repeatedly, Nussbaum emphasizes the ways in which an extraordinarily gifted artist like Tagore can enlarge our understanding of what's needed for the creation of a society that celebrates the variety and unpredictability of human beings. For Tagore—and for Nussbaum, of course—it is by means of the imagination that we become "intensely conscious of a life we must live which transcends the individual life and contradicts the biological meaning of the instinct of self-preservation."[7]

Tagore wrote a book entitled *The Religion of Man* in which he explicates his desire for humankind to develop a religion that transcends racial and class prejudice, as well as the prideful attitudes of an imperial power such as Great Britain. It is a religion that inculcates a deep love of nature—it is "the religion of a poet," Nussbaum writes, an artist whose favorite English poet was Wordsworth.

To give his theories great particularity, Tagore chose as an example of humans who live out in daily life the central aspects of the "religion" he champions, the Bauls of Bengal. The Bauls actually have no religion as such and eschew "images, temples, scriptures . . . ceremonials [and] declare in their songs the divinity of Man, and express for him an intense feeling of love." Nussbaum stresses the free eroticism of the Bauls whose lives "are dedicated to freedom (from both the outward compulsion of society and the inner compulsion of greed). To joy, and to love."[8]

What Nussbaum's discussion of Tagore's fascination with the Bauls makes clear is that her own vision of the good society is not so very far from this antinomian reveling in the sensuous pleasures that a truly awakened human spirit may enjoy. Critical in this way of life is "a kind of fresh joy and delight in the world, in nature, and in people, preferring love and joy to the dead lives of material acquisition that so many adults end up living."[9] Also

6. Ibid., 89.
7. Ibid.
8. Ibid., 92–93.
9. Ibid., 93.

of great importance to this vision is a refusal to espouse a fixed ideology or faith. Mozart and Tagore are, Nussbaum implies, brothers under the skin.

In its totality, Nussbaum's book is an attempt to sketch out the lineaments of a good society, one that honors basic democratic principles such as equal access to the law and equal opportunities to participate in the political, social and cultural life of the society, while striving to educate its citizens by way of poetry, music and the visual arts. What I find most fascinating in Nussbaum's discussion of those virtues that she hopes the adult citizen will exhibit is the manner in which she extrapolates from the experiences of the infant as it responds to a loving parent, i.e. the development of trust, of wonder, and freedom from a "smothering narcissism."

Explaining why the larger society needs to emulate the child, Nussbaum writes:

> The political culture needs to tap these sources of early trust and generosity, the erotic outward movement of the mind and heart toward the lovable, if decent institutions are to be stably sustained against the ongoing pressure exerted by egoism, greed, and anxious aggression.[10]

Moreover, to ensure the development of the capacity for empathy and respect for the need of others to have their own world of thought and feeling, "the resources of play and imagination" are crucial. Again and again, Nussbaum returns to the active imagination as a *sine qua non* of a healthy life for individuals and for a nation.

Nussbaum is quite aware, of course, of how likely it is that many who encounter her thought will immediately respond with the charge, "Utterly unrealistic! Humankind is too flawed for any such society as the one you've fantasized to ever exist." She deals with such objections by pointing out that good ideals acknowledge humans to be far less than perfect; that they have bodily needs as well as psychological and spiritual ones; that they are subject to all sorts of conflicting desires and drives. Ideals are thus rooted in reality. "The ideal, then, is real. At the same time, the real also contains the ideal. Real people aspire. They imagine possibilities better than the world they know, and they try to actualize them."[11]

Nussbaum thus conceives of her project as being very different from a utopian dream of a society inhabited by people who have somehow learned to be kind, generous, and loving in all their actions and relations. Rather, hers is a "dream" of how any society might strive to teach its citizens to be

---

10. Ibid., 177.
11. Ibid.

more kind, generous and loving in every aspect of their lives and in addition to experience much more fully than most of us do the wonder and joy that come from really seeing the beauty of the world with the eyes of a child. This fully awakened sensitivity is not unlike the "second naiveté" about which some ecofeminists thinkers have written.[12]

I need not stress, I hope, that the "good society" Nussbaum has created in her wonderfully fertile imagination sounds rather like the (socialist) cooperative commonwealth whose cardinal features are adumbrated by the thinkers discussed in chapter 3. I have already suggested that, while I yearn for such a society to come into being in America, I am dubious about that possibility.

Which leads to a question: Though we may feel that her "dream" stands little or no chance of complete realization, ought we to be glad for Nussbaum's vision embodied in her elaboration of a possible good society of the future? I think we should. I believe, in fact, that we ought to consider *Teaching Political Emotions* to be an extraordinary gift and wherever and whenever possible, proceed with programs that do indeed teach compassion, generosity of spirit, empathy, respect for those of different racial and religious backgrounds and love of nature and of beauty. Fortunately, there are thousands engaged in such teaching in our land today. They will not save us. No one, in fact, will save us. But they contribute greatly to making the United States once again a country we can all be proud of.

12. Ibid.

BIBLIOGRAPHY

Abrahamson, Jake. "The Science of Awe." *Sierra*, November/December 2014.

Adams, E. M. *A Society Fit for Human Beings*. Albany: State University of New York Press, 1997.

Ali, Tariq. *The Clash of Fundamentalism: Crusades, Jihads, and Modernity*. New York: Verso, 2012.

Alterman, Eric. "Bill de Blasio Is Just Getting Started." *The Nation*, January 26, 2015.

American Jewish World Service. *How Should We as Jews Respond? AJWS American Jewish World Service Short-Term Service Programs 2004 Field Handbook*.

Appy, Christian G. *American Reckoning: The Vietnam War and Our National Identity*. New York: Viking, 2015.

Arnove, Anthony. "Scenes from Iraq." *Agni* 54 (2001) 34–42.

Ashton-Warner, Sylvia. *Teacher*. New York: Simon & Schuster, 1963.

Associated Press. "From the Rich, to the Poor: Five Tycoons Who Want to Close the Wealth Gap." *Greenfield [MA] Recorder*, February 23, 2014. http://www.recorder.com/home/ 10850065-95/from-the-rich-to-the-poor.

Bacevich, Andrew J. *American Empire: The Realities and Consequences of U.S. Diplomacy*. Cambridge: Harvard University Press, 2002.

———. "Solving for X." *The Nation*, November 14, 2011.

———. *Washington Rules: America's Path to Permanent War*. New York: Metropolitan, 2010.

Badiner, Allan Hunt. *Mindfulness in the Marketplace: Compassionate Responses to Consumerism*. Berkeley: Parallax, 2002.

Bain, David Haward. *Sitting in Darkness: Americans in the Philippines*. Boston: Houghton Mifflin, 1986.

Baran, Paul A. "Crisis of Marxism? Part One." *Monthly Review*, October 1958.

———. *The Longer View: Essays toward a Critique of Political Economy*. New York: Monthly Review, 1969.

Barber, Benjamin R. "America's Knowledge Deficit." *The Nation*, November 20, 2010.

Barlow, Maude, and Wenonah Hauter. "The Great Water Crisis." *Sojourners*, November, 2013.

Barsamian, David. "The Progressive Interview: Chris Hedges." *The Progressive*, August 2011.

———. "The Progressive Interview: Noam Chomsky." *The Progressive*, October 2013.

Beauvoir, Simone de. Excerpt from *All Said and Done*. In *Women on War*, edited by Daniela Gioseffi, 111–14. New York: Feminist Free Press, 2003.

Becker, Ernest. *The Denial of Death*. New York: Free Press, 1973.

Bellah, Robert, et al. *Habits of the Heart: Individualism and Commitment in American Life*. New York: Perennial, 1985.

Berkshire, Jennifer C. "There Goes the Neighborhood School." *The Progressive*, December 2014 / January 2015.

Berman, Ari. "What's Next for the Moral Monday Movement?" *The Nation*, March 10/17, 2014.

Berry, Thomas. *The Dream of the Earth*. San Francisco: Sierra Club, 1988.

———. *The Sacred Universe: Earth, Spirituality, and Religion in the Twenty-First Century*. New York: Columbia University Press, 2009.

Berry, Wendell. "Faustian Economics: Hell Hath No Limits." *Harper's*, May 2008.

Bertell, Rosalie. *Planet Earth: The Latest Weapon of War; A Critical Study into the Military and the Environment*. London: Women's Press, 2000.

Blum, William. "The CIA, Contras, Gangs, and Crack." *Foreign Policy in Focus*, November 16, 1996. http://fpif.org/the_cia_contras_gangs_and_crack.

———. *Killing Hope: U.S. Military and CIA Interventions Since World War II*. Monroe, ME: Common Courage, 2008.

Bonhoeffer, Dietrich. *Letters and Papers from Prison*. London: Fontana, 1959.

Brentlinger, John. *The Best of What We Are: Reflections on the Nicaraguan Revolution*. Amherst: University of Massachusetts Press, 1995.

———. "Revolutionizing Spirituality: Reflections on Marxism and Religion." Unpublished essay.

Brown, Lester R. *Breaking New Ground*. New York: Norton, 2013.

———. *Eco-Economy*. New York: Norton, 2001.

———, et al. *The Great Transition: Shifting from Fossil Fuels to Solar and Wind Energy*. New York: Norton, 2015.

Brown, Norman O. *Life against Death: The Psychoanalytic Meaning of History*. Middletown, CT: Wesleyan University Press, 1959.

Bultmann, Rudolph. *Kerygma and Myth*. London: HarperCollins, 2000.

Burns, E. Bradford. *At War in Nicaragua: The Reagan Doctrine and the Politics of Nostalgia*. New York: HarperCollins, 1987.

Butler, Smedley D. "In Time of Peace: The Army." *Common Sense*, November 1935.

Camus, Albert. *Resistance, Rebellion, and Death: Essays*. New York: Knopf, 1960.

Cantor, Daniel. "A New Progressive Party." *The Nation*, July 7/14, 2014.

Carruth, Hayden. "The Intentional Alligator." *Georgia Review* 39 (1985) 243–49.

Cassidy, John. "The Return of Karl Marx." *New Yorker*, October 20 & 27, 1997.

Centers for Disease Control Vietnam Experience Study. "Postservice Mortality among Vietnam Veterans." *Journal of the American Medical Association* 257 (1987) 790–95.

Chomsky, Noam. *Deterring Democracy*. New York: Hill & Wang, 1992.

———. *Interventions*. San Francisco: City Lights, 2007.

———. "Letter." *Iraq Veterans Against the War*, December 2014, 3–4.

———. *Pirates and Emperors, Old and New: International Terrorism in the Real World*. Cambridge, MA: South End, 2002.

———. *Rethinking Camelot: JFK, the Vietnam War, and U.S. Political Culture*. Cambridge, MA: South End, 1993.

Cobb, John B., Jr. "The Anti-Intellectualism of the American University." *Soundings,* November 2, 2015.

Cockburn, Andrew. "Game On: East vs. West, Again." *Harper's,* January 2014.

Cohen, Stephen F. "Kiev's Atrocities and the Silence of the Hawks." *The Nation,* August 4/11, 2014.

Comp, Nathan J. "Blue Jeans, Big Dreams." *The Progressive,* September 2015.

Cox, Harvey. *The Seductions of the Spirit: The Uses and Misuses of People's Religion.* New York: Touchstone, 1973.

Crapo, Trish. "Reclaiming 'Awe': What Happens When You Dehumanize Language." *Greenfield Recorder,* April 5, 2014.

Cummings, e.e. "i thank You God for most this amazing." *100 Selected Poems.* New York: Grove, 1994.

Daly, Herman E. *Beyond Growth: Economics of Sustainable Development.* Boston: Beacon, 1996.

Danaher, Kevin. "The Global Paradigm Shift." *Democratic World Federalists,* February 3, 2015.

Department of State. *Country Reports on Human Rights Practices for 1986.* February 1987.

Dorrel, Frank, dir. *What I've Learned about U.S. Foreign Policy: The War against the Third World.* Film. 2005.

Dorrien, Gary. "A Case for Economic Democracy." *Tikkun,* May/June 2009.

———. *Soul in Society: The Making and Renewal of Social Christianity.* Minneapolis: Fortress, 1995.

Douglass, James W. *JFK and the Unspeakable: Why He Died and Why It Matters.* New York: Simon & Schuster, 2008.

Doyle, Kate. "The Atrocity Files: Deciphering the Archives of Guatemala's Dirty War." *Harper's,* December 2007.

Dubose, Lou. "Big, Cheap, Deadly: Rick Perry's Medicaid Policy." *Washington Spectator,* December 1, 2013.

———. "The Politics of Faith and Fusion: Moral Monday in North Carolina." *Washington Spectator,* January 1, 2014.

Dupree, Charlie. In Woodbury Forest School promotional material and confirmed in personal correspondence with the author. Circa 2005.

Eagleton, Terry. "What Is the Worth of Social Democracy?" *Harper's,* October 2010.

———. *Why Marx Was Right.* New Haven: Yale University Press, 2012.

Earth Charter Secretariat. *The Earth Charter.* San José, Costa Rica: University of Peace, June 29, 2000.

Einstein, Albert. "Why Socialism?" *Monthly Review,* May 1949. http://monthlyreview.org/2009/05/01/why-socialism.

Ellis, George F. R. "Cosmology and Religion." Chapter 10 of *When Worlds Converge: What Science and Religion Tell Us about the Story of the Universe and Our Place in It,* edited by Clifford N. Matthews et al. Peru, IL: Carus, 2002.

Ellsberg, Daniel. *Secrets: A Memoir of Vietnam and the Pentagon Papers.* New York: Penguin, 2002.

Eliot, T. S. "Four Quartets." In *The Complete Poems and Plays, 1909–1950,* 118. New York: Harcourt, Brace, 1952.

Elworthy, Scilla. *Power and Sex: A Book about Women.* Shaftesbury, UK: Element, 1996.

English, Deirdre. "Rush Limbaugh, Rick Santorum, and the Pope Walk into a Room—Your Bedroom." *Washington Spectator*, April 1, 2012.

Faulkner, William. *Light in August*. New York: Random House, 1987.

Friends Committee on National Legislation Newsletter, September 2014.

Finstuen, Andrew S. *Original Sin and Everyday Protestants: The Theology of Reinhold Niebuhr, Billy Graham, and Paul Tillich*. Chapel Hill: University of North Carolina Press, 2009.

Forché, Carolyn. "One Whole Voice." *Poetry*, February 2012.

Fromm, Erich. *The Sane Society*. New York: Holt, 1955.

———. *To Have or to Be?* New York: Bloomsbury, 1976.

Frum, David, and Richard Perle. *An End to Evil: How to Win the War on Terror*. New York: Random House, 2003.

Fulbright, J. William. *The Arrogance of Power*. New York: Random House, 1966.

Fundación DARA Internacional. *Climate Vulnerability Monitor: A Guide to the Cold Calculus of a Hot Planet*. 2nd ed. Spain: Estudios Gráficos Europeos, S.A., 2012.

Galeano, Eduardo. *Open Veins of Latin America: Five Centuries of the Pillage of a Continent*. New York: Monthly Review, 1973.

Geoghegan, Thomas. "Consider the Germans." *Harper's*, March 2010.

Gilk, Paul. *Nature's Unruly Mob: Farming and the Crisis in Rural Culture*. Eugene, OR: Wipf & Stock, 2009.

God's Mission in the World: An Ecumenical Christian Study Guide on Global Poverty and the Millennium Development Goals. Washington, DC: Episcopal Church Office of Government Relations and Evangelical Lutheran Church in America, 2006.

"The GOP: Are Party Leaders Divorcing the Tea Party?" *This Week*, December 27, 2013.

Greenblatt, Stephen. *The Swerve: How the World Became Modern*. New York: Norton, 2012.

Gross, Bertram. *Friendly Fascism: The New Face of Power in America*. Boston: South End, 1980.

Gutierrez, Gustavo. *The Power of the Poor in History*. Marynoll, NY: Orbis, 1983.

Hargarten, Jeff. "Suicide Rate for Veterans Far Exceeds That of Civilian Population." *The Center for Public Integrity*. August 30, 2013. http://www.publicintegrity.org/2013/08/30/13292/ suicide-rate-veterans-far-exceeds-civilian-population.

Harper's. "The Editors." *Harper's*, April 2013.

Hawken, Paul. Interview by Renee Lertzman. *The Sun*, April 2002.

———. *Natural Capitalism: Creating the Next Industrial Revolution*. Boston: Little, Brown, 1999.

Hedges, Chris. *American Fascists: The Christian Right & the War on America*. New York: Free Press, 2006.

———. *Death of the Liberal Class*. New York: Nation Books, 2010.

———. *Empire of Illusion: The End of Literacy and the Triumph of Spectacle*. New York: Nation, 2009.

———. "ISIS—the New Israel." *Truthdig*, December 15, 2014. http://www.truthdig.com/report/page2/isis_—_the_new_israel_20141214.

———. "Starting a Revolution." *The Progressive*, November 2014.

———. *War Is a Force That Gives Us Meaning*. New York: Public Affairs, 2002.

Heilbroner, Robert L. *Marxism: For and Against*. New York: Norton, 1980.

Helliwell, John F., et al., eds. *World Happiness Report 2013*. New York: UN Sustainable Development Solutions Network, 2013.

Helmut, Keith. "Ecological Integrity and Religious Faith." *Friends Journal*, August 2001. http://www.friendsjournal.org/2001065.

Herman, Edward S. *The Real Terrorist Network: Terrorism in Fact and Propaganda*. Boston: South End, 1982.

Hertsgaard, Mark. "Breakthrough in Paris." *The Nation*, January 4, 2016.

Hightower, Jim. *Hightower Lowdown*, May 2010.

———. *Hightower Lowdown*, September 2010.

———. *Hightower Lowdown*, November 2014.

———. "Republicans Just Sick about Climate Change." *The Progressive*, July/August 2015.

Hopkins, Gerard Manley. *The Poems of Gerard Manley Hopkins*. New York: Oxford University Press, 1967.

Horton, Scott. "Company Men: Torture, Treachery, and the CIA." *Harper's*, April 2015.

Hull, Fritz. *Earth and Spirit: The Spiritual Dimension of the Environmental Crisis*. New York: Continuum, 1993.

Institute for Policy Studies. "Wealth Inequality." http://inequality.org/wealth-inequality.

Iremonger, F. A. *William Temple, Archbishop of Canterbury: His Life and Letters*. London: Oxford University Press, 1948.

Jacobson, Louis. "Bernie Sanders Says 'Real Unemployment' Rate for African American Youth Is 51 Percent." *Politifact*, July 13, 2015. http://www.politifact.com/truth-o-meter/statements/2015/jul/13/bernie-s/bernie-sanders-says-real-unemployment-rate-african.

Johnson, Chalmers. *Blowback: The Costs and Consequences of American Empire*. New York: Holt, 2004.

———. *Nemesis: The Last Days of the American Republic*. New York: Metropolitan, 2008.

———. *The Sorrows of Empire: Militarism, Secrecy, and the End of the Republic*. New York: Metropolitan, 2004.

Jolly, David. "Deals at Climate Meeting Advance Global Effort." *New York Times*, November 24, 2013.

Judt, Tony. *Ill Fares the Land*. New York: Penguin, 2010.

Kaufman, Chuck. *Nicaragua Monitor*, March 24, 2010.

Kaufman, Frederick. "The Food Bubble." *Harper's*, July 2010.

Kaufman, Maynard. *Adapting to the End of Oil: Toward an Earth-Centered Spirituality*. Bloomington, IN: Xlibris, 2008.

Kenner, Robert, dir. *Food, Inc.* Film. Magnolia Pictures, 2008.

Kilcourse, Thomas Jefferson. *Diary of Lt. T. J. Kilcourse*. Discovered in Navy Archives, Washington, DC.

Kim, Richard. "Against the Current: New Mass Murder, Old Lesson." *The Nation*, June 23/30, 2014.

Kinsey, Mariel. *Where Is This Music Coming From? Musings of a Failed Hermit*. Ashfield, MA: Wandering Word, 2015.

Klare, Michael. *Resource Wars: The New Landscape of Global Conflict*. New York: Holt, 2002.

Klein, Naomi. "The Courage to Say No." *The Nation*, January 4, 2010.

———. *This Changes Everything: Capitalism vs. The Climate*. New York: Simon & Schuster, 2014.

Kohls, Gary G. "Teen Violence and Suicide Prevention." *Every Church a Peace Church.* Brochure.

Kolbert, Elizabeth. *The Sixth Extinction: An Unnatural History.* New York: Holt, 2014.

Kornbluh, Peter. "Crack, the Contras, and the CIA: Storm over 'Dark Alliance.'" *Columbia Journalism Review* (January/February 1997). http://nsarchive.gwu.edu/ NSAEBB/NSAEBB113/storm.htm.

Korten, David. *Agenda for a New Economy: From Phantom Wealth to Real Wealth.* 2nd ed. San Francisco: Barrett-Koehler, 2010.

Krimerman, Len. "Education-Shaped Participatory Democracy." Unpublished essay.

Kristof, Nicholas. "Lessons from the Virginia Shooting." *New York Times,* August 27, 2015.

Kunstler, James Howard. *The Long Emergency: Surviving the End of Oil, Climate Change and Other Converging Catastrophes of the Twenty-First Century.* New York: Grove, 2005.

Kwitny, Jonathan. *The Crimes of Patriots: A Tale of Dope, Dirty Money, and the CIA.* New York: Norton, 1987.

Lane, R.E. *The Loss of Happiness in Market Democracies.* New Haven: Yale University Press, 2000.

Lapham, Lewis H. "Notebook: Dar-al-Harb." *Harper's,* March 2004.

Lasch, Christopher. *The Culture of Narcissism: American Life in an Age of Diminishing Expectations.* New York: Norton, 1991.

Leibovich, Mark. *This Town: Two Parties and a Funeral—Plus, Plenty of Valet Parking!— in America's Gilded Capital.* New York: Penguin, 2013.

Lernoux, Penny. *Cry of the People: The Struggle for Human Rights in Latin America— The Catholic Church in Conflict with U.S. Policy.* New York: Penguin, 1980.

Lichtman, Richard. *The Production of Desire: The Integration of Psychoanalysis into Marxist Theory.* New York: Free Press, 1982.

Macy, Joanna. "Five Ways of Being That Can Change the World." *Center Post* (Rowe Center), spring/summer 2014.

Madison, Charles A. *Critics & Crusaders: A Century of American Protest.* New York: Holt, 1947.

Mander, Jerry. *In the Absence of the Sacred: The Failure of Technology and the Survival of the Indian Nations.* San Francisco: Sierra Club, 1992.

Manning, Richard. "Bakken Business: The Price of North Dakota's Fracking Boom." *Harper's,* March 2013.

Marx, Karl. *The Communist Manifesto.* 2nd ed. New York: Norton, 2012.

Mason, Wyatt. "You Are Not Alone Across Time: Using Sophocles to Treat PTSD." *Harper's,* October 2014.

Master, Bob. "A New Era for New York City." *The Nation,* January 20, 2014.

Mathews, Race. "The Mondragon Model: How a Basque Cooperative Defied Spain's Economic Crisis." *The Conversation,* October 18, 2012.

McCarthy, Colman. "God on Our Side." *The Progressive,* November 2001.

McChesney, Robert W., and John Nichols. *Dollarocracy: How the Money and Media Election Complex Is Destroying America.* New York: Nation, 2014.

McFague, Sallie. *The Body of God: An Ecological Theology.* Minneapolis: Fortress, 1993.

McKibben, Bill. *The End of Nature.* New York: Anchor, 1990.

Meyers, Ched. *The Biblical Vision of Sabbath Economics.* Washington, DC: Bartimaeus Cooperative Ministries, 2001.

Middlewood, Erin. "The Progressive Interview: The Spark for Occupy Wall Street." Profile of Kalle Lasn, editor of Adbusters. *The Progressive*, March 2012.

Miles, Sara. *Take This Bread: The Spiritual Memoir of a Twenty-First-Century Christian.* New York: Random House, 2007.

Nash, June. "Women In Between: Globalization and the New Enlightenment." Keynote address, Women and Globalization conference, Costa Rica, April 1, 2003.

Newton, Joshua. "Let Them Drink Coke." *New Internationalist*, April 2003.

Nichols, John. "Bernie Sanders Speaks." *The Nation*, July 20/27, 2015.

————. "A Mood of Resistance Has Opened Up." *The Nation*, November 2015.

————. "Socialist in Seattle." *The Progressive*, March 2014.

Nichols, John, et al. "The Hangover." *The Nation*, December 1/8, 2014.

Niebuhr, Reinhold. *Faith and History: A Comparison of Christian and Modern Views of History.* New York: Scribner, 1951.

————. *The Irony of American History.* New York: Scribner, 1952.

Nussbaum, Martha C. *Political Emotions: Why Love Matters for Justice.* Cambridge: Harvard University Press, 2013.

Orlowski, Jeff. *Chasing Ice.* Film. Submarine Deluxe, 2012.

Paik, Koohan. "Living at the 'Tip of the Spear.'" *The Nation*, May 3, 2010.

Parker, Laura. "Treading Water." *National Geographic*, February 2015.

Parry, Robert. "Gary Webb's Death: American Tragedy." *Truthout*, December 10, 2006.

Perez-Rivas, Manuel. "Bush Vows to Rid the World of 'Evil-Doers.'" *CNN*, September 16, 2001. http://edition.cnn.com/2001/US/09/16/gen.bush.terrorism.

Pfeiffer, Bill. "The East-West Indigenous Exchange." *Sacred Earth Network Newsletter*, spring 2003.

Pollack, A. "Estimating the Number of Suicides Among Vietnam Veterans." *Journal of Psychiatry* 147 (1990) 772–76.

Pollitt, Katha. "Subject to Debate: It's Better Over There." *The Nation*, September 20, 2010.

Pope Francis. *Laudato Si'.* Encyclical letter of the Holy Father Francis on Care for our Common Home. Rome: Libreria Editrice Vaticana, 2015.

Porter, Bernard. *Empire and Superempire: Britain, America and the World.* New Haven: Yale University Press, 2006.

Resist Newsletter, summer 2014.

Rich, Adrienne. *An Atlas of the Difficult World.* New York: Norton, 1991.

Ricoeur, Paul. *The Symbolism of Evil.* Boston: Beacon, 1969.

Robinson, John A. T. *Honest to God.* Louisville: Westminster John Knox, 1963.

Robinson, Marilynne. *When I Was a Child I Read Books.* New York: FSG, 2012.

Rocha, Zildo. *Helder, the Gift: A Life That Marked the Course of the Church in Brazil.* Cuiaba, Brazil: Editora Vozes, 2000.

Roosevelt, Theodore. *The Winning of the West.* Vols 1–4 inclusive. London: Pearl Necklace, 2014.

Rorty, Richard. *Achieving Our Country: Leftist Thought in Twentieth-Century America.* Cambridge: Harvard University Press, 1998.

————. *Contingency, Irony and Solidarity.* Cambridge: Cambridge University Press, 1989.

Ross, Carne. "Occupy Wall Street and a New Politics for a Disorderly World." *The Nation*, February 27, 2012.

Roy, Arundhati. Speaking at the World Social Forum, Porto Alegre, Brazil, January 27, 2003. In *Yes!* magazine, spring 2004.

Saavedra, Luis Angel. "Growing from the Grassroots." *New Internationalist*, May 2003.

Sandel, Michael J. *What Money Can't Buy: The Moral Limits of Markets*. New York: FSG, 2012.

Sassen, Saskia. *Expulsions: Brutality and Complexity in the Global Economy*. Cambridge: Harvard University Press, 2014.

Saul, John Ralston. *Voltaire's Bastards: The Dictatorship of Reason in the West*. New York: Vintage, 1992.

Schell, Jonathan. *The Fate of the Earth*. New York: Knopf, 1982.

"Sen. Fulbright Blasts America 'Sick Society.'" *St. Petersburg Times*, August 9, 1967.

Shalom, Stephen Rosskamm. *Imperial Alibis: Rationalizing U.S. Intervention after the Cold War*. Boston: South End, 1993.

Shanker, Thom. "Rumsfeld Rebukes U.N. and NATO on Approach to Baghdad." *New York Times*, February 9, 2003. http://www.nytimes.com/2003/02/09/international/middleeast/09RUMS.html?pagewanted=all.

Sheen, Martin. Interview by David Kupfer. *The Progressive*, July 2003.

Sheldrake, Rupert. *The Rebirth of Nature: The Greening of Science and God*. Rochester, VT: Park Street, 1991.

Shorris, Earl. *The Art of Freedom: Teaching the Humanities to the Poor*. New York: Norton, 2013.

Smith, Mychal Denzel. "The New Fight for Racial Justice." *The Nation*, September 15, 2014.

Snow, John Hall. *I Win, We Lose*. Eugene, OR: Wipf and Stock, 2016.

Sparticus Educational. "Christian Socialists." Online encyclopedia. http://spartacus-educational.com/REsocialism.htm.

Speth, James Gustave. *The Bridge at the Edge of the World: Capitalism, the Environment, and Crossing from Crisis to Sustainability*. New Haven: Yale University Press, 2009.

Spong, John. *Jesus for the Non-Religious*. New York: HarperCollins, 2008.

———. *Why Christianity Must Change or Die: A Bishop Speaks to Believers in Exile*. New York: HarperCollins, 1998.

Stephenson, Wen. "The Climate-Justice Pope." *The Nation*, September 28 / October 5, 2015.

Stich, Rodney. *Drugging America: A Trojan Horse*. Alamo, CA: Diablo Western, 1999.

Sumner, William Graham. *War, and Other Essays*. New Haven: Yale University Press, 1911.

Sunstein, Cass R. *Radicals in Robes: Why Extreme Right-Wing Courts Are Bad for America*. New York: Basic, 2005.

Thomas, Chris D. "Extinction Risk from Climate Change." *Nature*, January 8, 2004.

Tillich, Paul. *The Courage to Be*. New Haven: Yale University Press, 1952.

Truse, Nick. *Kill Anything That Moves: The Real American War in Vietnam*. New York: Picador, 2013.

Turkle, Sherry. *Alone Together: Why We Expect More from Technology and Less from Each Other*. New York: Basic Books, 2011.

Turner, Glenn. *Resist Newsletter*, summer 2014.

Turner, Trevor. "I Shop Therefore I Am." *New Internationalist*, April 2003.

UN Resources for Speakers on Global Issues. "Vital Statistics: Global Hunger." http://www.un.org/en/globalissues/briefingpapers/food/vitalstats.shtml.

US Department of Health & Human Services' National Clearinghouse on Child Abuse and Neglect Information. "Child Maltreatment 2002: Summary of Key Findings." 2013.

Van Gelder, Sarah. "The Cooperative Way." *Yes! magazine*, spring 2013.

Webb, Gary. "Dark Alliance." *San Jose Mercury News*, August 1996.

Weisbrot, Mark. "Hard Choices: Hillary Clinton Admits Role in Honduran Coup Aftermath." *Al Jazeera America*, September 29, 2014. http://america.aljazeera. com/opinions/2014/9/ hillary-clinton-honduraslatinamericaforeignpolicy.html.

Werleman, C. J. *Crucifying America: The Unholy Alliance between the Christian Right and Wall Street*. London: Dangerous Little Books, 2013.

Whitman, Walt. *Prose Works 1892*. Vol. 2. New York: New York University Press, 1964.

Williams, William Appleman. *The Tragedy of American Diplomacy*. New York: Norton, 1959.

Wordsworth, William. *Selected Poems*. New York: Penguin Classics, 2004.

World Population Balance. "Population and Energy Consumption." http://www. worldpopulationbalance.org/population_energy.

Wright, Melissa W. "The Dialectics of Still Life: Murder, Women and Maquiladoras." In *Millennial Capitalism and the Culture of Neoliberalism*, edited by Jean Comaroff and John L. Comaroff, 125–47. Durham: Duke University Press, 2001.

Index

About the Author

PRESTON M. BROWNING JR. holds a BA in history from W&L, an MA in English from the University of North Carolina at Chapel Hill, and a PhD in Religion and Literature from the University of Chicago. While a member of the English Department at the University of Illinois at Chicago for thirty years, he was a Fullbright lecturer in Yugoslavia. He is the author of *Flannery O'Connor: The Coincidence of the Holy and the Demonic in O'Connor's Fiction and Affection* and *Estrangement: A Southern Family Memoir*. He operates Wellspring House, a retreat for writers in western Massachusetts.

32380034R00189

Made in the USA
Middletown, DE
02 June 2016